RELENTLESS CHANGE:
A CASEBOOK FOR THE STUDY OF CANADIAN
BUSINESS HISTORY

Casebooks in business history are designed to instruct students in classrooms and boardrooms about the evolution of business management. The first casebook for the study of business history in a Canadian context, Joe Martin's text will help students, in both the classroom and the boardroom, understand the Canadian economy and guide them in making sound decisions and contributing to a healthy, growing economy.

Thirteen original case studies covering the mid-nineteenth to twenty-first centuries deal with different industry sectors as well as individual corporations and managers. Overviews provide context by examining major public policy decisions and key developments in the financial system that have affected business practices. Martin also presents eight original tables that trace the evolution of the sixty largest Canadian corporations between 1905 and 2005. *Relentless Change* is an invaluable resource for instructors and business students and clearly demonstrates how businesses are affected by the interaction of individual decisions, policy changes, and market trends.

JOE MARTIN is the director of the Canadian Business History program, adjunct professor of Business Strategy, and Executive in Residence at the Rotman School of Management, University of Toronto, and Chair of the Governors of the National Business Archives of Canada.

JOE MARTIN

Relentless Change:

A Casebook for the Study of Canadian Business History

UNIVERSITY OF TORONTO PRESS
Toronto Buffalo London

© University of Toronto Press 2010
Rotman/UTP Publishing
University of Toronto Press
Toronto Buffalo London
www.utppublishing.com
Printed in Canada

Reprinted 2011, 2013

ISBN 978-0-8020-9559-6

∞

Printed on acid-free, 100% post-consumer recycled paper with vegetable-based inks.

Publication cataloguing information is available from Library and Archives Canada.

University of Toronto Press acknowledges the financial assistance to its publishing program of the Canada Council for the Arts and the Ontario Arts Council.

 Canada Council   Conseil des Arts
for the Arts   du Canada

 ONTARIO ARTS COUNCIL
CONSEIL DES ARTS DE L'ONTARIO

University of Toronto Press acknowledges the financial support of the Government of Canada through the Canada Book Fund for its publishing activities.

Contents

Preface

All books begin in the mind of the author at a certain point in time. The genesis of this book took place in the early months of 2001 in Naples, Florida, in the midst of the 'dot.com' meltdown. In this pleasant setting, the author met with Rotman Professor Emeritus Jim Fleck and well-known Canadian businessman Purdy Crawford to discuss the notion of introducing a pioneering business-history course at the Rotman School of Management. With the active support of Roger Martin, Rotman's dean, the project was launched.

Others became involved. An MBA student, Amy Fisher, conducted an international market survey of business history at leading business schools. Material written by Harvard Business School (HBS)[1] Professor Thomas K. McCraw honouring the long-time, Canadian-born dean of the school, John McArthur, was reviewed. And the author sought advice from professors Nancy Koehn and Ted Tedlow of the Harvard Business School.

With this research in hand, meetings were held with prominent Canadian business people who might be prepared to contribute a total of $3 million to establish a chair in Canadian business history at the Rotman School. Lynton 'Red' Wilson, a founder of Historica, was the first to sign up and he convinced his friend Richard (Dick) Currie to support him. Others who participated were James Fleck, Anthony Fell, chairman of RBC Capital Markets, and Henry N.R. (Hal) Jackman, former lieutenant governor of Ontario and chancellor of the University of Toronto. John McArthur, former dean of the Harvard Business School, also contributed financially, and the L.R. Wilson/R.J. Currie Chair in Canadian Business History was established.

A policy board was formed consisting of the financial contributors and three academics – Dean Roger Martin, Rotman Professor Emeritus Ed Safarian, and University Professor Emeritus Michael Bliss, who contributed his significant collection of business history books to the Rotman Library/Business Information Centre.

Once all of the above was in place, original research and material to form the basis of the course, on which this book is based, had to be developed. From the beginning, it was decided that this would primarily be a case-based course[2] linked by brief overview summaries of major developments. The author's task was to drive the process, to write the overview summaries, and to build a team of case writers.

The first request was to the director of the Rotman PhD program for graduate students to assist in writing case studies. Stewart Melanson answered the call, writing four of the thirteen case studies and helping in a myriad other ways. He served as teaching assistant for the course and, after the peer-review process, played a key role in developing the arc or storyline. Stewart also recruited contract research assistant Richard Matern, who proved invaluable by co-writing a case and providing much of the background research assistance for the overview summaries, specifically the development of the tables of large corporations over time.

The search then began for other case writers. The first selected was Bob MacIntosh, the memorable CEO of the Canadian Bankers Association (CBA), who would write the case on the Bank Act of 1871. Other case writers recruited were John Turley Ewart of the *National Post* and his colleague John Geiger, then also with the *Post*, now with the *Globe and Mail*, and a noted author on the north, a necessary requirement for writing the Hudson's Bay Company case. The Inco case was co-authored by Anne Mette de Place Filippini, an LSE graduate who worked for strategic consulting firms Braxton and Monitor before joining AIC as vice-president/International Equities and is now with Burgundy Investments. The Wine case was written by David Smith, at the time an MBA student at Rotman, now project leader at the Martin Prosperity Institute. The RBC case was written by Katherine Macklem, a journalist and communications consultant.

As a result of the peer-review process, three new case studies were added to the original ten. Stewart Melanson and Katherine Macklem were again pressed into service, as was Rod McQueen, the award-winning business-history writer. The case-writing team was complemented by Mary Ann Gratton of the Scarborough campus, University of Toronto, and Allan Breznick who provided invaluable assistance as copy editors. Jennifer Grek Martin from Queen's University did the cartographic work.

In the first year, case studies were evaluated not only by the students in the course but also by a willing group of outsider reviewers. For the second year, team meetings were held with the case writers. Writers were given feedback from the students and outside reviewers and asked to modify the case studies. Then the case studies were again evaluated by the students and their comments were integrated into the third and final iteration.[3]

Reviewers included Rotman colleague Professor Michael Jalland; Lorne Larson, former CEO of Pro Gas, Calgary; Jon Martin, a managing director of Russell Reynolds; Rotman Professor Emeritus Ed Safarian; Stock Exchange Chair in Capital Markets Paul Halpern; L.R. (Red) Wilson, after whom the chair is named; as well as current and former students too numerous to mention. Assistance on historical matters was gratefully received from Professor Dimitry Anastakis of Trent University.

This book, then, has been at least five years in the making, some would contend much longer. The final inspiration for it came from students in the first two classes (fall of 2005 and 2006) of the graduate business-history course. While the students appreciated having material on the Rotman website, they also wanted it in book form. Hence the notion of publishing a textbook based on the original course material took root.

When the text was finalized, the unenviable task of pulling things together was done competently by Lilly Shneidman. The author was assisted at the end stages of the overview summaries by Adam Martin, a student at the University of Toronto Schools (UTS), who set up tables and exhibits as well as researching databases to determine aspects of the evolution of organizational structure of large Canadian corporations. Jennifer Riel, who was then a student in the original business-history course and is now associate director of the Desautels Centre for Integrative Thinking, provided invaluable assistance in reviewing both the case studies and the overviews before submission for publication.

I dedicate this book to my wife, for her tolerance, patience, and editorial assistance, as well as to my historical and managerial mentors for their inspiration. The first of these was Bill Speechley, a teacher at Gordon Bell High School in Winnipeg, who restored my interest in history. Then came my history professors at United College (now the

University of Winnipeg), Harry Crowe, Ken McNaught, Stewart Reid, and G.K. Brown; and, at the University of Manitoba, W.L. Morton and Triggvi Oleson – a distinguished group. Also deserving of special mention are two other Manitoba professors, John Warkentin in geography and H. Clare Pentland in economics. Finally, later in life, I met and was inspired by Michael Bliss of the University of Toronto and by Alfred D. Chandler, Jr of the Harvard Business School.

Upon graduation from college, I became a management consultant and spent over three decades learning about management – a wonderful experience as I worked on client issues on five continents. I also learned from colleagues, absorbing the theory of management from my predecessor as managing partner of the Canadian consulting practice of Touche Ross, A.R. (Sandy) Aird; and the practice of management from Jim Miller, managing partner of Touche Ross Canada, the best manager I ever encountered. In addition to experiential learning, I persuaded my partners to send me to the Advanced Management Program at the Harvard Business School. This was an inspiring experience and gave me the opportunity not only to study, using the case method, but also to learn about management from the likes of Robert Hayes (operations), Jim Hesketh (marketing), Warrren McFarlan (management control), and George Cabot Lodge (government-business relations). I thank them all.

NOTES

1 The Harvard Business School has been teaching business history since 1926.
2 As is noted in the Introduction to *A Concise History of Business in Canada* by Graham D. Taylor and Peter A. Baskerville, 'the case study method of instruction was particularly congenial to historical approaches.'
3 The case studies were designed for class discussion rather than to illustrate either effective or ineffective handling of a managerial situation.

Introduction

This book attempts to fill a gap in the study of Canadian business history. While popular author/historians such as Peter Newman and the late Pierre Berton have contributed volumes of valuable and highly readable material on the subject, scholarly works are rare. Two exceptions are Michael Bliss's *Northern Enterprise: Five Centuries of Canadian Business* and Graham D. Taylor and Peter A. Baskerville's *A Concise History of Business in Canada*. Both were published in the late 1980s and early 1990s, and Taylor has just published a new work, *The Rise of Canadian Business*. None of the above, however, is a casebook. Casebooks in business history are written not just as vehicles to advance the understanding of business from an historical point of view but as instruments of instruction designed to teach students about management within a particular business context. Such is the goal and scope of this book.

The study of business history through the casebook approach has its champions elsewhere, no less so than in the hallowed halls of the Harvard Business School. Seventy years ago, N.S.B. Gras and his colleague Henrietta M. Larson put it best in the introduction to their jointly authored *Casebook in American Business History*: 'The old problems arise again and again in business. We shall make little progress in profiting from past mistakes, either public or private, unless we develop a habit of learning from experience, which, in the busy-footed struggle of the present, is very difficult.'[1]

The question is, then, why is it that so little has been published on the history of Canadian business in recent years? After all, business has played a crucial role in Canada since the country's beginnings. Today, Canada has one of the most successful economies in the world and business has been a major factor in that success, giving Canadians one of the highest standards of living on the globe.

Perhaps it is assumed that Canadian business shares the same attributes as the American system. But, in fact, business in Canada has followed its own unique path. In some circumstances it has taken on a more British form of personal capitalism, and in other ways it is similar to the American pattern of managerial capitalism only on a smaller scale. In any event, it is different and offers opportunities to learn both for Canadian students and for Canadian managers.

A primary purpose of this casebook is to add a new perspective in understanding how Canada's advanced market economy has evolved. In addition, it is designed to help business students, both those in the classroom and those in the office or boardroom, make better decisions today for the future by providing insights from the past. The study of Canada's business development can teach valuable lessons. Improved decision-making processes can contribute to better outcomes and continue the progress that has made Canada the wealthy society it is today.

Better decision making arrives not just from the application of a formula or calculation. It depends upon the framing of the problems and solutions: what variables to include; which are salient; which assumptions to choose; what patterns are relevant. The goal of this book is to develop the framing abilities of those who use it and to challenge them to seek the parallels between historical situations and developments and current events and issues. The frameworks are just a starting point in the search for relevance in the past. It is hoped that they will stimulate a quest by readers for other models and theories which will illuminate business history in the future.

This book and its author owe a debt of gratitude to George D. Smith, Richard Sylla, and Robert E. Wright at the Stern School of Business, New York University, who developed a Diamond of Sustainable Growth. Their contention is that, over time and in a wide range of economies, sustainable economic growth is attained as the result of interaction among four variables. These four variables are:

- enabling political systems;
- effective financial systems;
- vibrant entrepreneurship; and
- sophisticated managerial capabilities.

The Stern Diamond Model has had a strong influence on the structure of this book and on the author's thinking.

In the pages that follow, I describe and analyse the changes in major

Canadian businesses over the past century and a half. The book (like the course on which it is based) is divided into four parts and, reflecting a deliberate decision to focus upon Canadian business as it evolved beyond the initial staples phase made famous by Harold Adam Innis of the University of Toronto and W.A. Mackintosh of Queen's University, begins in the mid-nineteenth century. The first two parts ('Laying the Foundations' and 'Wars, Depressions, and Dynamic Growth') deal with the half-centuries from roughly 1850 to 1905 and 1905 to 1955. The second two parts ('The Buoyant Years' and 'The Challenging Years') focus on the mid-twentieth century to 1980 and from 1980 to the early twenty-first century. While the book ends in 2005, it offers a glimpse into developments during the years immediately afterwards, and indeed its main purpose is to provide students with the background necessary to think about the future beyond the first decade of the twenty-first century.

Within each part there are three or four case studies (thirteen in total) illustrating different corporate events that took place during that period. In order to place the case studies in context, each part also begins with a brief overview tracing major developments affecting business during the years in question. And within each overview are four different sections, patterned on the Stern Diamond Model, in addition to an introduction and conclusion:

1. *Public Policy*. This section analyses The government's role relative to business in terms of its attitudes towards that sector. It deals specifically with major public policies including trade matters, creation of crown corporations, regulation, and levels of taxation as a percentage of GDP.
2. *Financial Systems*. This section discusses the role of financial systems in facilitating economic growth. In addition to examining the part that government plays in the creation of the financial system through legislation, e.g., the Bank Act, and the creation of crown corporations, e.g., the Bank of Canada, this section studies the role of the largest financial corporations, particularly the banks and life insurance companies.
3. *Entrepreneurs*. This section is brief. However, each part does contain a description of some of the major entrepreneurs and their contribution to economic growth.
4. *Large Corporations*. When entrepreneurs are successful, their creations sometimes become large corporations run by professional

managers. This section covers the largest of the non-financial corporations in Canada and specific developments in the various industry sectors including the increase and decrease in importance of different sectors within the Canadian economy.

At the end of each part there is an appendix listing the sixty largest corporations at a point in time. This appendix allows the reader to see the evolution of large corporations in a Canadian context. The author sincerely hopes that others will pick up on this research and make it more robust.

In conclusion, the book provides a wide range of data. The essential point to remember is that the purpose of studying business history is not to know the details of the past but to understand the future. For example, the what-if scenarios in the Canadian National Railways case study illustrate that there were options other than the one chosen, options that could have saved the Canadian taxpayer millions of dollars and provided customers with better service. The Eaton's case study illustrates how data on the 'predictable future' could have been used to ward off the challenge from Simpsons-Sears. The Royal Bank of Canada case study challenges the student to think about the options available for all of the major Canadian banks in the early twenty-first century.

A careful examination of the past will illuminate patterns and cycles. It will also give many examples of success and failure. The Spanish American philosopher George Santayana wrote: 'Those who do not remember the past are condemned to repeat it.' There is a less familiar quote from an anonymous businessman who made the observation: 'I study history so that I can make my own mistakes.' The purpose of studying the past is to prepare for the future through improved decision making based on past examples. Most people learn from their own mistakes and others' successes. This study of Canadian business history will, I hope, assist students in learning from the mistakes that others made – as well as their successes.

BIBLIOGRAPHY

Boothman, Barry E.C. 'A Theme Worthy of Epic Treatment: N.S.B. Gras and the Emergence of American Business History.' *Journal of Macro Marketing*, June 2001, 61–73.

Gras, N.S.B., and Henrietta M Larson. *Casebook in American Business History*. New York: Appleton-Century-Crofts 1939.

NOTES

1 Gras and Larson, *Casebook in American Business History*. Gras was a Canadian who became the first Isador Strauss Professor of Business History at the Harvard Business School in 1926. Boothman's article 'A Theme Worthy of Epic Treatment' is an excellent study of Gras's contribution to the field.

PART ONE

Laying the Foundations, 1850–1905

Introduction

Mid-nineteenth-century British North America was made up the United Province of Canada (Canada East and Canada West, modern-day Quebec and Ontario), Nova Scotia, New Brunswick, Prince Edward Island, Newfoundland, and Vancouver Island. The interior of the northern part of British North America contained three territories, the largest of which, Rupert's Land, was owned by the Hudson's Bay Company (HBC). The North-West Territory and New Caledonia, the southern half of present-day mainland British Columbia, made up the other two. In 1867 the British imperial Parliament passed the British North America Act creating the Dominion of Canada, with the Canadas, Nova Scotia, and New Brunswick becoming provinces of the new Dominion.

The Dominion of Canada expanded quickly, particularly in 1869 when it acquired Rupert's Land from the HBC. By the early twentieth century, Canada had become 'a great colony of the British Empire' and was well on its way to becoming a nation. In addition to growing geographically, it was growing economically as well. Canada's GDP/capita[1] more than doubled between the mid-nineteenth and the early twentieth century, making it the tenth-richest nation in the world. This record of achievement was accomplished through a blend of public policy, a sound financial system, energetic entrepreneurship, and the emergence of large non-financial corporations.

Public Policy

From the earliest days of settlement, governments have played an important role in the development of business in Canada. In the late nineteenth century, two major public-policy statements were particularly significant in this respect. The first was the British North America Act of 1867; the second was the National Policy first enunciated by Sir John A. Macdonald in 1878.

The British North America Act, passed by the imperial Parliament, was the product of conferences held in Charlottetown and Quebec City in 1864. The act not only created the Dominion of Canada but also allocated responsibility between the federal and provincial authorities, giving the federal government jurisdiction over areas such as regulation of commerce, currency, and banking. In addition, specific provisions relating to an intercolonial railway and to Rupert's Land would have far-reaching implications for business in Canada.

Macdonald's National Policy, which began as an electoral slogan to gain re-election of the Conservative Party in 1878, consisted of three interrelated parts:[2] the settlement of the west; the building of a transcontinental railway; and the adoption of a protective tariff. The third element, the protective tariff, requires elaboration. Because Canada is a trading nation, trade has always played an important role – more so than in most economies. In introducing a protective tariff, Macdonald was influenced both by the history of trade and by American policy.

Lord Elgin, the British governor general of Canada (an ardent free trader), went to Washington in 1854 to negotiate a reciprocity treaty in natural, unprocessed goods between the United States and the British North American colonies. This treaty turned out to be relatively short-lived after U.S. voters put protectionist northern Republicans into power in 1860.[3] Nonetheless, its demise did not stop the efforts of those campaigning for free trade. The first step to reduced tariffs within Canada came seven years later when the Dominion was created and the former Province of Canada agreed to reduce its tariffs to bring them closer into line with those in the Maritime provinces. In an 1878 speech to the House of Commons calling for free trade, Macdonald made it clear that he saw a protective tariff as a tool to get the Americans back to the bargaining table. He stated that a 'judicious readjustment of the Tariff ... moving (as it ought to do) in the direction of a reciprocity of tariffs with our neighbours ... will greatly tend to procure for this country, eventually, a reciprocity of trade.'[4]

The issue of reciprocal trade continued to be an important topic of debate throughout the rest of the nineteenth century. While in opposition from 1878 to 1896, the Liberal Party would from time to time campaign on eliminating the protective tariff, as in the 1891 election, when it called for 'unrestricted reciprocity' with the United States. The Conservative leader, Macdonald, responded with his famous statement 'A British subject I was born, a British subject I will die.'[5] Addressing Americans directly, he also said: 'We are perfectly willing to trade with you on equal terms. We are desirous of having a fair reciprocity treaty; but we will not consent to open our markets to you while yours remain closed to us.' Once the Liberals gained power in 1896, they too supported the tariff and in 1897 went the Conservatives one better by entering into a preferential trading relationship (a reduced tariff commonly known as an 'imperial preference') with the 'mother country.'

Although the role of government vis-à-vis business had become more active by the early twentieth century than it had been half a century earlier, it was still passive by modern standards. The prevailing attitude was best summed up as: 'The encouragement of industry, not its discouragement, is the office and duty of government.'[6]

Financial Systems

Section 91 of the British North America Act provided the federal government with powers over currency and banking as well as life insurance.[7] This was an important provision and one that contributed significantly to Canada's development of an effective financial system. Yet an examination of general textbooks on Confederation, or Christopher Moore's *1867: How the Fathers Made a Deal*, reveals little discussion of the matter. By granting the federal authority these responsibilities, Canada avoided the quarrels between centralists and decentralists that occurred in the United States from the time Alexander Hamilton introduced the First Bank of the United States in 1791 until Andrew Jackson vetoed the Second Bank of the United States in 1836. Whether the Fathers of Confederation learned lessons from the U.S. experience[8] by osmosis, or whether they were concerned by the failure of two major banks in Canada West – the Bank of Upper Canada in 1866 and the Commercial Bank in 1867 – the fact is that the passage of the Bank Act in 1871 ensured a sound currency, a necessity for any successful economy, and a nationally regulated banking system.

One of the key provisions of the Bank Act was the requirement for decennial revisions. This provided for a regular re-examination of the legislation to determine whether it was still suitable and applicable to changing times.[9] Other aspects of a sound financial system also fell into place in the late nineteenth century. In 1875 a superintendent of insurance was appointed. In the 1870s stock exchanges were incorporated in both Montreal and Toronto, and in the 1890s mining exchanges were formed in Toronto that merged into a single exchange, known as the Standard Stock and Mining Exchange. (For a listing of the thirty largest financial corporations in 1905, see Appendix 1.)

Banking

In the early years of Confederation, most major financial institutions were banks. But important life insurance companies as well as mortgage and loan and trust companies had also emerged, and these sectors were growing more quickly than the banking sector. In addition, the period from 1899 to 1905 saw the formation of Canada's first three investment banks.[10]

At Confederation, twenty-two banks were operating in Canada, the largest of which by far was the Bank of Montreal. By 1905, that number had increased to thirty-seven. The second-largest bank – the Canadian Bank of Commerce in Toronto – had been incorporated in 1867, its growth helped by its financing of the Canadian Northern Railway (CNoR). Although there were both mergers and failures, assets of all banks increased more than ninefold between Confederation and 1905[11] and the number of branches proliferated.[12]

Meanwhile, the process of consolidation was just beginning. 'In the process of consolidation, the number of banks with head offices in the Maritimes was reduced, and the concentration of financial power in Montreal and Toronto became particularly pronounced.'[13] Upstart Toronto was beginning the process of eventually supplanting Montreal as the financial centre of Canada.

Other Financial Intermediaries

While banks were the dominant financial intermediaries, their percentage share of all financial intermediary assets decreased between 1867 and 1905. At the same time, the asset share of mortgage loan companies and life insurance companies increased dramatically. The role of other financial institutions had also begun to grow.

As chartered banks were not allowed to lend money for real property purchases[14] (because the government believed the risks were too great), mortgage loan companies stepped into the void. In fact, they quickly became the second-largest financial intermediary class as their share of such assets nearly doubled during this period. The oldest and largest of the mortgage loan companies was the Canada Permanent Building and Savings Society. It and the other large mortgage loan companies were all Ontario-based.

The growth of life insurance companies was even more remarkable than that of mortgage loan companies. The early companies found the Canadian market small and by 'the 1890s Canadian life insurance salesmen traveled the world, opening new markets for their policies, importing capital to Canada where their companies could invest it profitably.'[15] By 1875, as noted above, the Canadian life insurance business was deemed sufficiently important that the government appointed a superintendent of insurance to oversee the industry. In 1899 regulations were changed to permit life insurance companies to invest in the burgeoning Canadian utility industry, a change that liberated hundreds of millions of dollars for investing in this emerging sector with its huge needs for capital. For example, three life insurance companies owned all the bonded indebtedness of the Toronto Electric Light Company,[16] which had a distribution monopoly in that city.

Legislation requiring companies to keep sufficient assets in Canada to cover their liabilities prompted some British and American firms to leave Canada, thereby creating a vacuum that both Montreal-based Sun Life and Toronto-based Confederation Life moved in to fill. (Trust companies also appeared upon the scene in the 1880s. Greater attention will be paid to the trust companies in Part Two.)

Canada was fortunate that, by the early twentieth century, it had both a legislative framework for a sound financial system and a healthy number of financial corporations in operation. Both were necessary in meeting the demands for capital that entrepreneurs and growing corporations required to carry on their activities.

Entrepreneurs

Canada has never been short of entrepreneurs since the beginning of European settlement in the seventeenth century. Among the earliest were the French fur traders Pierre-Esprit Radisson and Médard Chouart des Groseilliers, who, rejecting the policies of the government of New France,[17] went over to the English and helped establish the Hudson's Bay Company.

A century later, a handful of feisty Montreal-based Scottish entrepre-

neurs would rebel against the HBC's monopoly and create a number
of fur-trading partnerships. This included the North West Company,
which became the HBC's major rival prior to the 1821 merger of the
two companies. Scots such as Simon McTavish and William McGil-
livray were among the company's early leaders. Perhaps the first English, as distinct from Scottish, entrepreneur was John Molson, whose
beer is still sold today two and a quarter centuries after the business
was founded.

As the nineteenth century progressed, the financial system in place
made it simpler to obtain capital. While Americans such as Francis Hector Clergue of the Lake Superior Corporation played an important role,
the main entrepreneurial drive came from Canadians, either Canadian-
or British-born. Some of the best-known are Samuel Cunard and Hugh
Allan in shipping; cousins George Stephen and Donald Smith, who
were involved in the Bank of Montreal, the Canadian Pacific Railway
(CPR), and the HBC; Hart Massey and Alanson Harris in farm machinery; George Gooderham and Hiram Walker in distilling; Timothy Eaton
and Robert Simpson in retail; William Mackenzie, Henry Pellatt, Frederic Nicholls, and James Ross in railways and public utilities; and William Neilson of ice-cream fame.

Large Non-Financial Corporations

In mid-nineteenth-century Canada, agriculture played the dominant
role in the economy and was by far the largest employer. Few large
publicly traded companies existed, other than the nearly two-
century-old Hudson's Bay Company, British-owned with a Canadian
head office near Montreal. Others at the time included the Montreal Telegraph Company, the Consumers Gas Company of Toronto, the Rich-
elieu Navigation Company, and a few fledgling railway and mining
companies.

While much smaller in size than American corporations, Canadian
corporations left a bigger footprint on the Canadian economy than
did their American counterparts in the United States on the American
economy.[18] Most were Canadian-owned and located in either Montreal
or Toronto, although British investors did own such major companies
as the Grand Trunk Railway (GTR) and the HBC. American investors
(who preferred equity investment, particularly in the mining sector)
also played a role.

The largest corporation, by far, was the CPR, and Canada's big-business sector also included two other large railroads, major mining corporations, and a whole host of investor-owned electrical public utilities plus a few large manufacturing corporations. The largest of these corporations, such as the railways, had developed well beyond the owner/managed model and required sophisticated managerial capability to cope with their rapidly expanding operations. Alfred Chandler has referred to railway corporations as the pioneers in modern management because their growth marked an important turning point in business history. Railways were the first large corporate enterprises requiring the separation of ownership and management. (A list of the thirty largest non-financial corporations can be found in Appendix 2.)

Railways

In the 1850s, the principal modes of transportation within Canada were the steamboat on lakes and rivers and the stagecoach on land. By mid-century, less than 1,000 miles of railway track had been laid. The new method of travel by rail was in its infancy. Yet this was to change dramatically as the 'age of steam' ushered in a period of railway mania across Canada as it did throughout the developed world.

Like its counterparts in the United Kingdom and the United States, Canada's railroad industry began as a highly fragmented one, with hundreds of railway charters granted before the companies consolidated into a few large corporations in the 1880s. In the province of Ontario alone, some 520 acts of incorporation received approval prior to 1891. By the early twentieth century, railways were not only the dominant means of transportation; the largest of them were the biggest businesses in Canada. The stagecoach had all but disappeared, as had many steamboat companies, a prime example of the creative destructive forces of capitalism playing out on the Canadian scene. The same thing was happening elsewhere in the developed world. When the Dow Jones Index was created on the New York Stock Exchange in 1884, it consisted of eleven corporations, nine of them railroads.

Railways played a particularly important role in a country like Canada because of the vast distances involved. Between 1875 and 1905, railway capital in Canada increased more than fourfold, much of it funded by debt provided by British investors. By 1905, Canada had one transcontinental railway in operation, the CPR; another, the Grand Trunk Railway, had just been authorized to build a second railway; and the Mackenzie and Mann interests were active in starting a third – the

Canadian Northern Railway – without government authorization.[19] These railroads were the 'Big Three' of their day.[20]

Extractive Sector

In mid-nineteenth-century Canada, the extractive sector – focusing on fish, fur, forest, and farm – was made up mainly of many small, family-owned businesses (with the notable exception of the fur-trading Hudson's Bay Company). This changed radically with the advent of 'the steam revolution' and the resultant demand for coal.

While the Yukon Gold Rush[21] may have been the best-known mineral find in Canada by the late nineteenth century, coal was 'the quiet king' of the Canadian mining sector. At the time of Confederation, coal accounted for less than 10 per cent of Canada's total energy production. By 1900, however, it had surpassed wood as the nation's leading energy source, resulting in the emergence of a number of important coal-mining companies located mainly in Cape Breton and British Columbia, near the mineral source rather than the market.

But the largest and most complex Canadian extractive company in the early twentieth century (and the largest non-financial corporation in Canada after the railways) was Francis Hector Clergue's Lake Superior Corporation.[22] Clergue established his business in the Sault Ste Marie area in 1894. With capital from his native United States, he consolidated his network of companies – a hydroelectric power plant, a pulp and paper mill, an iron ore mine, a railroad, and an iron and steel works[23] – into the Lake Superior Corporation in 1902. Unfortunately, Clergue's managerial skills could not keep pace with the company's capital and maintenance requirements. He was more of an entrepreneur than a sophisticated manager, and his 'vision exceeded his managerial abilities.'[24]

By the early twentieth century, the three major companies participating in coal production as well as base-metal extraction were located in Cape Breton, the largest being Dominion Iron and Steel.[25] While the coalfields of Cape Breton were much larger than those of British Columbia, three large B.C. mining companies prospered because of their access to coal and other base metals such as copper and lead.[26] Smaller than their Cape Breton counterparts, they too became significant corporations in early-twentieth-century Canada and, like the major Cape Breton companies, obtained investment capital from the United States and Montreal as well as Toronto.

Turning from mining to forestry, for most of the nineteenth century, forestry operations were run by small owner/operators rather than large corporations. However, the situation was changing, specifically the relative decline of lumber and the increasing importance of pulp and paper as demand from the United States increased. The resulting prospects of larger-scale domestic pulp and paper manufacturing inspired William Price, of the Price family lumber barons of Quebec,[27] to rescue a failing company from receivership (with the help of British, rather than American, capital) and successfully manage the product transition through reorganization.[28]

The extractive industry thus evolved from a series of small, family-owned enterprises to a sector with major players, principally in mining. Companies ranged in size from the giant Lake Superior Corporation to the relatively small pulp and paper company owned by the Price Brothers in Quebec. In between were a half-dozen mining companies located in Cape Breton and in British Columbia close to the resource rather than the markets. In most cases, American capital was heavily involved as was capital from Montreal and Toronto. The United States was also an important export market.

Public Utilities

Mid-nineteenth-century British North America lacked both electric lighting and telephone service. In the city of Toronto, Consumers Gas, the major public utility, provided the fuel to light homes, factories, and streets. In other municipalities, local utilities provided a similar service.

By 1905, all this had changed, thanks to the development of electricity and the invention of the telephone. While electricity had been discovered in the early 1800s and was used for telegraphic and telephonic purposes, it was not until the 1870s that it could be used for power. As a result of these technological breakthroughs, enterprising businessmen mobilized large amounts of capital that permitted the creation of electrical public utilities within Canada and abroad. In the early twentieth century, investor-owned electrical public utilities represented the largest grouping among major Canadian corporations and were located not only in Quebec and Ontario but also in Winnipeg, Vancouver, and as far afield as Brazil.

Utilities could be involved in either local or long-distance generation or distribution, or they could be customers, as in the case of electric street railways.[29] They could also be part of a holding company pro-

viding more than one service. Generally speaking, they were local in
nature although they often featured interlocking directorships. (Individuals such as William Mackenzie of Toronto and James Ross of Montreal were involved in many companies.)

A major public utility and one of the largest non-financial companies in Canada was the Montreal Light, Heat and Power Company
(MLHPC). Another was the Shawinigan Water and Power Compa-
ny,[30] the largest Quebec-based generator and transmitter of electricity.
Along with two other large Quebec-based electrical utilities (the Montreal Street Railway Company and a Quebec City holding company,
the Quebec Railway Light and Power Company [QRLPC]), these four
Quebec-based electrical utilities exhibited a variety of corporate forms:
two were holding companies, another was a single-purpose entity, and
the fourth was a long-distance distributor of electricity. Given their size,
separation of ownership from management existed, but key individuals[31] played important roles.

As the nineteenth century drew to a close, most cities had small
thermal electric plants which provided street and home lighting. In
Toronto and Hamilton, plants also supplied power for the electri-
fied streetcar system. By 1902, there were 315 electric light companies
operating in Canada, 198 of which were in Ontario. But they were
mainly small enterprises; only a handful could be included among
Canada's largest non-financial companies. They included generating
companies using the power of Niagara Falls. Initially, in 1900, authority to use the Niagara River waters was given to two American corporations with Canadian names (the Canadian Niagara Power Company
and the Ontario Power Company). However, they were soon to face a
Canadian challenger: the Electrical Development Company of Ontario
(EDC).

The early electrical utility business in Toronto was very much influenced by the interplay among three individuals – William Mackenzie,
Henry Pellatt, and Frederic Nicholls. They knew finance, they knew the
new technology, and they had excellent connections not only in Toronto but also elsewhere in Canada, New York, and London.[32] In nearby
Hamilton, the Cataract Power Company provided electrical generation
and, after 1899, street railway service.[33] Outside Quebec and Ontario,
three large, investor-owned electrical utilities were located in Brazil[34]
and in western Canada.[35]

These were heady days. But investor-owned electrical utilities
reached their zenith in Canada in 1905. Going forward, utilities were

challenged first by local governments and then by provincial govern-ments.[36] While 'the encouragement of industry, not its discouragement' was the attitude of the day at the federal and provincial levels of gov-ernment, it was changing to outright hostility at the municipal level. Municipalities granted the companies operating rights and attempted to regulate them but complaints from their citizens about poor service were becoming numerous.[37]

In another sector, that of communications, it was 1880 before the Montreal-based Bell Telephone Company of Canada was established.[38] The arrival of Bell heralded the new technology of telephony, which 'unlike the telegraph before it ... would ultimately, and almost unim-aginably, connect every home and business in a continent-spanning network.'[39] For much of the twentieth century, telephony was thought of as a natural monopoly, but this was not true in the early years. By 1902, there were more than fifty companies giving Bell fierce competi-tion. But Bell had an ace in the hole: a mandate to operate nationally. By 1880, the company was doing so, except in British Columbia.

Early in the twentieth century, a number of important developments affecting Bell and the telephone industry generally would change the picture again. One was government intervention. 'At the federal lev-el ... a new consensus emerged that led the government to put Bell operations under the supervision of an independent regulatory com-mission ... the Board of Railway Commissioners.'[40] Just as the Ontario world of privately owned electrical companies was about to be disrupt-ed by government, so too was the world of privately owned telephone companies – particularly on the prairies as these companies fell under provincial government control. Subsequently, Bell focused its competi-tive efforts on the heartland of Ontario and Quebec. Led by Charles F. Sise, one of Canada's early professional managers, Bell would continue to flourish, becoming the only non-financial corporation still on the list of top thirty companies a century later.[41] By contrast, all of the investor-owned electrical utilities would be swallowed up in the public-sector maw, a different form of 'creative destruction,' with only Brookfield Properties left as a reminder of the Sao Paulo Tramway, Light and Pow-er Company, and only Power Corporation as a reminder of the early benefits of investing in electrical utilities.

Manufacturing

Manufacturing played a less significant role than agriculture in mid-nineteenth Canada, being principally concerned with meeting domestic demand for processed goods. Sawmills and grist mills met the need for wooden planks and flour. Shoemakers, tailors, breweries, and distilleries met local consumer needs. By early in the twentieth century, however, manufacturing had grown to equal agriculture for the first time in terms of percentage of GDP.[42]

The application of electricity for manufacturing purposes was a major factor in the dramatic growth of the manufacturing sector. The result was significant increases in production at plants in both Quebec and Ontario where an abundant supply of hydroelectric power was easily accessed. As the nineteenth century ended and the twentieth century began, consolidation produced a significant reduction in the number of establishments[43] in most manufacturing subsectors.[44] Even with consolidation, however, manufacturing concerns remained small relative to other sectors of the economy. The exceptions were Massey Harris and Dominion Textile, itself a product of a major consolidation in 1905.

In 1878 a new national government was elected on a platform of increased tariffs, a policy heartily supported by the Manufacturers Association of Ontario (and later the Canadian Manufacturers' Association). Canadian manufacturers had been lobbying for protection for some time because of the tariffs they faced on exports to the United States at the same time as American manufacturers enjoyed unrestricted access to the Canadian market. After the election, under the National Policy, tariffs were raised to 35 per cent on manufactured imports. It is not clear whether the National Policy's protective tariff played a role in encouraging domestic manufacturing. It is clear, however, that it played no role in getting the Americans back to the bargaining table to negotiate a reciprocal agreement between the two countries. It is also clear that the protective tariff resulted in significant American investment in Canada as American corporations set up branch plants to avoid the tariff wall. On the other hand, few Canadians copied the American example to establish American branch plants.[45]

In spite of the increase in manufacturing and consolidation in the sector, by 1905 only five manufacturing concerns counted among the thirty largest non-financial corporations. The two largest – Massey Harris and Canadian General Electric (CGE) – were Toronto-based and producer-oriented. The three smaller ones – Ogilvie Flour Mills, Montreal Cotton, and Lake of the Woods Milling – were Montreal-based with strong connections to the Bank of Montreal and the CPR,[46] and all were consumer-oriented.

The evolution from manufacturers of consumer goods to producer-oriented enterprises that sold through dealers or middlemen was also picking up. While small in comparison to the major American[47] farm-equipment manufacturers, Massey Harris was by far the biggest manufacturer in Canada and much larger than any other farm-equipment maker in the British Empire. Massey not only served the Canadian market but also exported to Europe. And, in terms of managerial evolution, the company had made the transition from family ownership to professional management early in the twentieth century.

The other four large Canadian manufacturing concerns had all been involved in consolidations and mergers, yet none approached Massey in size. And, unlike Massey, individual owners still played a management role. All five companies were Canadian-owned.

Retail

Retail in mid-nineteenth Canada was a local affair, with barter the main means of conducting transactions. While the Hudson's Bay Company was active throughout British North America, its primary business was the fur trade.[48] By the turn of the twentieth century, Canadian retail was still very much a local business, but it had grown to include well-established large retailers in Montreal (Morgan's and Ogilvy's), Toronto (Eaton's and Simpson's), Winnipeg (Hudson's Bay Company), and Vancouver (Woodward's).

That changed in 1905, when Timothy Eaton established the first national department store chain in Canada by opening a second store in Winnipeg to complement its Toronto location. By placing his first store outside Toronto in Winnipeg, Eaton was issuing a direct challenge to the Hudson's Bay Company. Yet, with hindsight, it may not have been that much of a challenge. While the Bay is considered a major retailer today, in 1905 it was mainly confined to the fur trade (a dying business) and land development (which was booming). Retail,[49] by comparison, took a back seat.

Conclusion

The latter half of the nineteenth century and the dawning years of the twentieth saw the Dominion of Canada created out of the former colonies of British North America (except Newfoundland). In those same years, the people of the new Dominion built one of the richest nations in the world.

Throughout this period, we see the creative destructive forces of capitalism at work. Old staple industries became less important, replaced by newer industries such as railways, mines, and public utilities, all with great demands for capital, alongside a fledgling manufacturing and a national retail sector. Public policy played an important and beneficial role in this process. Crucial decisions were taken at the Quebec City Conference that led to the British North America Act. The act provided the federal authority with important powers in the financial area as well as specifically requiring it to build an interprovincial railway and purchase the western lands of the HBC. Later, Macdonald's National Policy called for settlement of the west, construction of a transcontinental railway, and adoption of a protective tariff.

One of the early and important actions of the federal Parliament was to pass a Bank Act which ensured a sound currency and a stable banking system for the new Dominion, essential prerequisites of an effective financial system. Other legislation was passed regulating insurance at the federal level and mortgage and loan and trust companies at the provincial level. Financial intermediary assets grew quickly in the young country, with mortgage and loan and life insurance companies outpacing the banks. But the banks were the largest players and there were many of them, ranging in size from the giant Bank of Montreal to smaller, more local banks such as La Banque d'Hochelaga and the Union Bank of Halifax.

This financial system provided much of the capital required by the entrepreneurs of start-up companies and the managers of the emerging bigger businesses. While some entrepreneurs managed on the cash flow generated by their enterprises, many required bank or life insurance financing. Some, such as William Mackenzie, turned to both sources – to the Bank of Commerce for help with the Canadian Northern Railway and to the major life insurance companies for debt financing for his many public utility properties.

From the mid-nineteenth century to the early twentieth, dramatic changes took place. Many individual or family-owned firms disappeared. In their place were giant railway and mining corporations as well as investor-owned public utilities and an emerging manufacturing and national retail system.

Appendix 1
Top thirty financial corporations by assets, 1905

Corporation	Total Assets - $	Code
1. Bank of Montreal	153,656,568	B
2. Canadian Bank of Commerce	94,681,572	B
3. Merchants Bank of Canada	46,633,968	B
4. Dominion Bank	44,403,789	B
5. Bank of British North America	43,825,272	B
6. Imperial Bank of Canada	39,216,751	B
7. Royal Bank of Canada	36,373,576	B
8. Bank of Toronto	33,708,695	B
9. Bank of Nova Scotia	33,438,776	B
10. The Canada Life Assurance Company	30,329,365	I
11. Molson's Bank	30,161,524	B
12. The Toronto General Trusts Corporation	29,096,478	M & T
13. Bank of Hamilton	28,529,101	B
14. Union Bank of Canada	26,905,765	B
15. Bank of Ottawa	26,194,256	B
16. Canada Permanent Mortgage Corporation	25,241,115	M & T
17. Traders Bank of Canada	25,086,699	B
18. Sun Life Assurance Company of Canada	21,309,000	I
19. The Montreal City and District Savings Bank	20,246,215	B
20. Eastern Townships Bank	18,089,015	B
21. Ontario Bank	16,955,155	B
22. Standard Bank of Canada	16,619,852	B
23. Banque d'Hochelaga	15,697,107	B
24. Sovereign Bank of Canada	14,944,704	B
25. Quebec Bank	14,528,612	B
26. Banque Nationale	11,304,227	B
27. Union Bank of Halifax	11,292,160	B
28. The Huron and Erie Loan and Savings Company	11,167,270	M & T
29. Confederation Life Association	11,100,079	I
30. National Trust Company	9,420,865	M & T

CODE:
B = Banks
I= Life Insurance Companies
M & T = Mortgage and Trust Cos.

This table was compiled from data in the *Canadian Annual Financial Review,* 1906.

Appendix 2
Top thirty non-financial corporations by assets, 1905

Corporation	Total Assets - $	Code
1. Canadian Pacific Railway	319,784,846	T
2. The Canadian Northern Railway Company	57,142,394	T
3. The Lake Superior Corporation	53,916,799	E
4. Dominion Iron & Steel	38,777,952	E
5. Montreal Light, Heat and Power	27,437,732	U
6. Dominion Coal Co.	25,697,129	E
7. Niagara Falls Power Co.	25,217,204	U
8. Massey Harris	24,000,000*	M
9. The Bell Telephone Co. of Canada	15,496,303	U
10. Granby Consolidated Mining, Smelting and Power Co.	15,239,571	E
11. The Sao Paulo Tramway, Light and Power Co.	14,779,885	U
12. The Toronto Railway Co.	13,088,745	U
13. Nova Scotia Steel and Coal Co. Ltd.	13,036,064	E
14. Shawinigan Water and Power	12,259,347**(1906)	U
15. Montreal Street Railway Co.	11,827,709	U
16. The Electrical Development Co. of Ontario	11,009,811	U
17. Winnipeg Electric Railway	9,366,463	U
18. Hamilton Cataract Power	8,580,039	U
19. Canadian General Electric Co.	8,241,584	M
20. Ogilvie Flour Mills Co.	7,379,959	M
21. B.C. Electric Railway	6,904,267	U
22. Montreal Cotton Co.	6,707,921**(1904)	M
23. The Crow's Nest Pass Coal Co.	6,333,518	E
24. Quebec Railway, Light and Power Co.	5,561,529	U
25. Lake of the Woods Milling Co.	5,322,521	M
26. Consolidated Mining and Smelting Co. of Canada	4,698,888	E
27. Toronto Electric Light Co.	4,400,607	U
28. Price Bros. & Co.	4,317,500	E
29. Consumers Gas Co. of Toronto	4,223,716	U
30. Richelieu and Ontario Navigation Company	3,955,423	T
CODE: T = Transportation Cos. E = Extractive U = Utilities M = Manufacturing Cos.		

*Estimate based on research.
** No 1905 listing available.
This table was compiled from data in the *Canadian Annual Financial Review*, 1906. Niagara Falls Power retrieved from Moody's Manual of Railroad and Corporation Securities, 1906. While revenue figures would have been preferred, they were not available. There are omissions, e.g., British companies (GTR), American-controlled companies (Imperial Oil, Ontario Power Company), and private companies (Molson's).

BIBLIOGRAPHY

Ambrose, Stephen E. Nothing *Like It in the World: The Men Who Built the Trans-continental Railroad, 1863–69*. New York: Simon and Schuster 2000.

Armstrong, Christopher, and H.V. Nelles. *Monopoly's Moment, The Organization and Regulation of Canadian Utilities, 1830–1930*. Philadelphia: Temple University Press 1986.

Austin, Barbara. 'Dominion Textiles, 1905: Consolidating for Market Control.' Administrative Sciences Association of Canada (ASAC) Conference, 2000, Université du Québec à Montréal.

Bloomfield, Elizabeth, and G.T. Bloomfield. *Industrial Leaders: The Largest Manufacturing Firms of Ontario in 1871*. Guelph, Ont.: Department of Geography, University of Guelph 1989.

Macmillan, David S. *Canadian Business History, Selected Studies, 1497–1971*. Toronto: McClelland and Stewart Limited 1972.

Melvin, William. *A Commercial Gazeteer of the World*. London, 1905.

Moore, Christopher. *1867: How the Fathers Made a Deal*. Toronto: McClelland and Stewart 1997.

Porter, Michael E. 'Government Policy.' In *The Competitive Advantage of Nations*. New York: Free Press 1990. Chapter 12.

Raffan, James. *Emperor of the North, Sir George Simpson and the Remarkable Story of the Hudson's Bay Company*. Toronto: HarperCollins 2007.

Shortt, Adam. *History of Canadian Banking, 1600–1880*. Toronto: Canadian Bankers' Association 1986.

NOTES

1 GDP/capita data in Angus Maddison, *The World Economy, Historical Statistics* (OECD Development Centre 2003).

2 The National Policy bears a remarkable resemblance to three of the resolutions passed at the Republican Party convention in Chicago in 1860.

3 The Republicans abrogated the treaty in 1866, in spite not only of Canadian concerns but of American ones as well. In *The Man Who Made Us: The Life and Times of John A. Macdonald, Volume One: 1815–1867* (Toronto: Random House Canada), 376, Richard Gwynn describes a conference organized by the Detroit Chamber of Commerce to protest abrogation.

4 J.H. Stewart Reid, Kenneth McNaught, and Harry S. Crowe, eds., *A Source-Book of Canadian History: Selected Documents and Personal Papers* (Toronto: Longmans Canada 1964), 349.

5 'In 1879, even Macdonald and his key supporters, such as industrialists who stood to gain by protection, looked upon the National Policy as a second-best tactic. What they really wanted was access to American markets': Rima Berns, 'The Real Story behind Free Trade (A History of the Canadian Tariff),' unpublished paper, John Hopkins University, School for Advanced International Studies (SAIS), 1988 (49).

6 *Report of the Royal Commission on the Mineral Resources of Ontario and Measures for their Development* (1890).

7 Mortgage and loan and trust companies became the responsibility of the provincial authorities.

8 The American and Canadian banking systems are very different. The United States has thousands of banks, many of them small local ones. No American bank has a national branch banking system. Canada is much more like the rest of the world in that it has a few large banks with branches throughout the country.

9 In 1900 the Bank Act was amended to allow banks to merge without a special act of Parliament, thereby providing the legislative framework that facilitated the emergence of nationwide banks.

10 A.E. Ames, Dominion Securities, and Wood Gundy, all based in Toronto.

11 From $78.9 million in 1867 to $729,916 million in 1905.

12 Between 1889 and 1905, the number of Canadian bank branches increased 3.6 times from 402 to 1,454.

13 Jeffery Matthews, *Historical Atlas of Canada, Vol. 2* (Toronto: University of Toronto Press 1987), Plate 44, Banking and Finance.

14 This did not change until the 1960s.

15 Michael Bliss, *Northern Enterprise, Five Centuries of Canadian Business* (Toronto: McClelland and Stewart 1987), 270.

16 Armstrong and Nelles, *Monopoly's Moment*, 120–1.

17 The policies went beyond licensing based on personal relationships to heavy taxation.

18 The pattern in Canada was more like that in Australia, where large corporations also played a major role although they were in different sectors than in Canada and smaller in size.

19 The United States was also experiencing a railroad boom, but Canada's outstripped it – in the United States, there were 2.7 miles of track for every person versus 3 miles in Canada.

20 In addition to the Big Three, Canada boasted 57 other smaller companies, ranging in scope from only two miles in length to nearly 400 miles.

21 The discovery of placer gold in the Yukon in 1896 triggered the famous Klondike Gold Rush, the biggest gold rush in Canadian history. In 1893

Canada was producing less than $1 million worth of gold. Five years later, with the Klondike find, gold surpassed coal as the country's most valuable mineral. Gold topped out at $28 million in 1900, after which time it began to decline. But, after coal, gold was Canada's most valuable mineral in the early twentieth century.

22 In 1909 the Lake Superior Corporation was the thirty-eighth-largest corporation in North America as measured by assets, immediately behind Allis Chalmers and ahead of US Smelting & Refining. Alfred Chandler, *The Essential Alfred Chandler*, Thomas McGraw, ed. (Boston: Harvard Business School Press 1988), 50.

23 This survived as Algoma Steel, for many years Canada's third-largest steel producer.

24 Graham D. Taylor and Peter A. Baskerville, *A Concise History of Business in Canada* (Toronto: Oxford University Press 1994), 323.

25 Dominion Coal was also a major player. Nova Scotia Steel and Coal was the smallest and the only one financed primarily with Nova Scotia capital.

26 The Granby Consolidated Mining, the Smelting and Power Company, the Crow's Nest Pass Coal Company, and the Consolidated Mining and Smelting Company.

27 The Price family established its first business in 1817. *Financial Post Survey of Industrials* (Toronto: Financial Post Corporation Service Group, Financial Post Information Service 1933).

28 Bliss, *Northern Enterprise*, 323.

29 As Douglas McCalla notes in 'New Technologies and Their Organization,' in *The Development of Canadian Capitalism: Essays in Business History* (Peterborough, Ont. Trent University 1997): 'When generating systems first began, street railways were the principal power consumers, and thus the early electric companies tended to be closely linked to traction franchises' (142).

30 Shawinigan was established, primarily by American interests, to provide electric power to industry on the St Maurice River, north of Trois-Rivières, principally to the Canadian affiliate of Alcoa – the American aluminum giant.

31 Senator Forget, James Ross, and Herbert Holt, among others.

32 Rae Fleming, 'The Railway King of Canada: Sir William Mackenzie, 1849–1923,' PhD thesis, University of British Columbia, 1991.

33 The company is described in Viv Nelles's fascinating 'The Electric Cemetery': The Living, The Dead and the Power Question in Ontario.' Lecture delivered at McMaster University, Hamilton, Ont., 6 Feb. 2006.

34 The largest of the three was the Sao Paulo Tramway, Light and Power

Company, which morphed in later life into the Brazilian Light and Traction Company, or Brascan for short, which is now Brookfield Properties.

35 Winnipeg and Vancouver had public utilities called electric railway companies which provided electricity and public transit as well as gas.

36 In the case of the Sao Paulo Tramway, Light and Power Company, the challenge came from Brazilian government in the late 1970s.

37 As the electrical utilities moved from private to public ownership, there would clearly be a divorce between ownership and management. The dominant role played by individuals like William Mackenzie and Senator Forget would be replaced by provincial and municipal bureaucrats.

38 Bell's story is well told by Laurence B. Mussio in *Becoming Bell: The Remarkable Story of a Canadian Enterprise* (Bell Canada, 2005).

39 Ibid., 11.

40 Ibid., 22.

41 Consumers Gas Company of Toronto remained in operation but as part of Enbridge.

42 Agriculture was still a larger employer because agriculture was a less efficient sector than manufacturing.

43 The number of establishments dropped from 69,716 in 1890 to 15,197 in 1905 – Historical Statistics of Canada (Series R1-22).

44 Printing and publishing, rubber and plastic manufacture, and tobacco were the only subsectors that increased their number of establishments in this period.

45 Samuel Moore of Toronto was a notable and early exception with Moore Business Forms.

46 Taylor and Baskerville, *A Concise History*, 252.

47 International Harvester, Deere, Allis Chalmers Manufacturing, and J.L Case Threshing Machine.

48 Peter Newman contends that the Bay's first real attempt to expand beyond the fur trade dates to 1858 when, in Victoria, it tried to profit from the Fraser valley gold rush. Newman, *Merchant Princes*, 156.

49 It was not until 1910, when Smith's control was being challenged by a stockholders' group, that the company was formally divided into three departments.

CASE 1
Origins of Financial Stability in Canada: The Bank Act of 1871

ROBERT M. MACINTOSH

The stability of financial institutions, not only in Canada but in most of the developed world, is something which the business community and indeed the general public has taken for granted for more than fifty years. After the Second World War, economic reconstruction was marked by the creation of the International Monetary Fund and the World Bank. The domestic regulation of banking systems in most countries was gradually being modified and extended to cover the growing complexity of the economy, especially with the emergence of consumer credit and widespread home ownership. The enormous growth in global trade and investment also required the expansion of government oversight and international cooperation on financial governance.

Yet in the last two years, to the great consternation of almost everyone, the global financial system has come close to collapse. Extraordinary and unprecedented steps have been required by governments across the world to rescue their banks from default, and even so there have been some costly failures. There is a growing realization that financial innovation has outrun effective regulation. In the next few years there will be a concerted effort to rethink the parameters of regulation in order to re-establish public confidence in financial markets and the effective working of the market system.

Fortunately for Canadians, the Canadian banking system has been perceived as surviving the huge stress better than perhaps any other system in the world. The relative stability of the banks can be traced back to the very origins of banking law and regulation in the nineteenth century. While the world was much simpler 150 years ago, the authors of the first Bank Act in 1871 still had to understand the nature of the market economy and what was required to facilitate its growth. Trust

and confidence in the financial system had to be one of the most fundamental building blocks. This case study sets out the business problem
that the Fathers of Confederation had to deal with, and shows how they
handled it so well.

The case begins with a fictional conversation that takes place in late
1869 between Sir John A. Macdonald, the prime minister, and Sir Francis Hincks. They are discussing the unsatisfactory state of affairs in
Canadian banking. It concludes with Hincks's recommendations for
converting the banking laws of the four provinces into a contemporary national banking act. The most critical feature of the new Bank
Act had already been determined in the British North America Act of
1867 (30 Vic. Ch.3). This was the decision to allocate to the new Dominion government exclusive authority over banking, currency, interest,
and related matters. The existing bank charters in the four provinces
became valid throughout the new Dominion, but they would expire in
1871. A more comprehensive act would then replace them. This was the
issue facing Macdonald.

A closely related challenge was to ensure a national currency and
coinage. In 1869 Nova Scotia still clung to sterling instead of dollars,
and the question of having government-issued paper currency alongside (or perhaps instead of) paper notes issued by a variety of chartered banks was very much unsettled. Macdonald and Hincks both
recognized that national unity would be greatly enhanced by having
a medium of exchange which was universally accepted and trusted
throughout the Dominion.

But what was the Dominion? Macdonald was then preoccupied with
extending the Dominion from sea to sea. He had already purchased
Rupert's Land from the Hudson's Bay Company, and, under turbulent
political circumstances, Manitoba came into existence in 1870. In the
east, he was manoeuvring to bring Prince Edward Island into Confederation, and on the west coast there was the most prized addition of
all – British Columbia. For this expanding country's banking needs,
there was a branch of the Bank of British North America and also a
locally owned Bank of British Columbia. These two colonial banks had
been chartered by the British government directly and were now to
be brought under the control of the Dominion government if, as, and
when British Columbia joined Confederation. It was essential that they
too should be subject to the new banking and currency laws.

The political goal was financial stability, and the managerial challenge was to create the institutional and regulatory framework to carry
it out.

Origins of Financial Stability in Canada: The Bank Act of 1871

Note: The following conversation between Sir John A. Macdonald and Sir Francis Hincks, although based on historical events, is fictional, as is the Abbott Report contained within.

'Welcome back to Canada, Sir Francis. How long have you been away representing the Queen in the Caribbean?'

'Fourteen years, Prime Minister. But I wearied of the sedentary life. I have been following your difficulties in the dispatches I received from the Colonial Office. It's now September 1869 – two years since the first Parliament met – and I see that you have not yet been able to get a banking bill through the House. I thought I might be of service before I fade into retirement.'

'Sir Francis, your visit could not be more timely. Everyone remembers well your leadership on financial questions in the 1840s. The name Hincks commands respect from all parties in the House. We have had our differences in the past, but you would do a great service to our young country if you would help me to break the impasse among the provinces. Most of the bank charters are coming up for renewal, and we have been unable to resolve the differences between the Bank of Montreal and the rest. Another thing: since the Civil War in the States, we have been flooded with American silver coins which have no official standing. It's a huge embarrassment that the Canadian people can't do business with each other in their own national currency. And now I have a crisis. John Rose has resigned as minister of finance and departed for England.'

'I know that Mr Rose remains your friend, Sir John, but with respect you must recognize that his close ties to the Bank of Montreal, as a director of the bank, could not help but compromise his position as minister of finance. He has been constantly pressing the Bank of Montreal's views on the House committee which he chairs. Most of your Ontario supporters are very uneasy, and I understand that the Maritime bankers are now allied with the Toronto bankers in opposing Mr Rose's notion of copying the American free banking system.'

'Fortunately, Sir Francis, when we negotiated the British North America Act, we were able to persuade the four provinces that it was essential to have a national currency and a national banking system. We have watched with alarm the deterioration of the American banking system when the powers over currency and banking were allowed to fall back – until recently – into the hands of the states. My government is halfway through its first term, and the temporary banking act which we passed to continue the provincial bank charters will expire at the end of this year. What I would like you to do is to prepare a document which reviews the Dominion's financial history going back to the change of regime in 1763 and taking us up to our present impasse. I want you to explain how our financial system got us to where we are now, and how we can resolve our differences and ensure a sound national currency for the future. I am sure you share my perception that economic prosperity cannot be achieved without public confidence in our banking institutions, which is sadly lacking. Sir Francis, I want you to provide me with some proposals for a new federal Bank Act, which you can then present to the House in your capacity as our new minister of finance.'

'You do me great honour, Sir John. If your party will support a renegade Reformer, I will accept the challenge. I trust you will authorize a small augmentation of the department's staff to undertake the research and draft some proposals for your consideration. I already have in mind a young lawyer from Kingston who has worked on several bank charters. His name is Sam Abbott. I will need your support to excuse him from his duties at Queen's University, where he teaches law and political economy.'

'Sir Francis, I am more than delighted that you are willing to bring your talents and experience to this critical matter. Our first order of business will be to find you a seat in the House of Commons. As it happens, Renfrew North has become vacant, and it has the added advantage of proximity. You can move into the minister's office that is right below us here in the East Block. As to your Mr Abbott, I will leave such matters in your hands.'

The Abbott Report

To: The Right Honorable Sir Francis Hincks
Minister of Finance, Ottawa

Sir: I have the honour to present to you herewith my report on the Foundations of Banking and Currency in Canada, together with my Recommendations for a Bank Act of the Dominion of Canada.

February 13, 1870

Your obedient servant,
Samuel T. Abbott

* * *

FOUNDATIONS OF BANKING AND CURRENCY IN CANADA TOGETHER WITH PROPOSALS FOR A BANK·ACT FOR THE DOMINION OF CANADA

Banking in Early Canada: 1759–1817. Before the passing of power in Canada from France to Britain in the years 1759 to 1763, there was no financial system. There was a large supply of paper currency in circulation in Lower Canada, issued by the French government but not regarded as a safe store of value by the Canadiens. The thrifty and prudent farmers kept their savings in 'specie,' which consisted of gold and silver coins. After the fall of Quebec in 1759, the paper money became worthless, and it would be many decades before the distrust of paper money would fade away. The British military governors of Quebec from the years 1759 to 1820 held the same lack of interest in trade and finance, as did the aristocratic seigneurs who remained in Lower Canada. They too came from the landed gentry, and shared the values of the small core of impoverished landowners to whom they turned for advice. Both were contemptuous of merchants and traders, most of whom made their way to Montreal from London, New York, Boston, and Philadelphia. As a result, there was no thought of financial legislation; this meant that domestic trade and the financing of exports and imports were severely hampered until well into the nineteenth century.

By 1770, there were about 70,000 people in Lower Canada, of whom about 5,000 were English-speaking civilians. An American observer wrote: 'It is conjectured that the farmers in Canada cannot be possessed of less than one million pounds sterling in specie; they hoard up their money to portion their children; they neither let it out at interest nor expend it in the purchase of lands.'[1]

The lack of money to carry on the ordinary business of life continued to plague the economy from then till now, 1870. There was little help from Britain, where conditions were not much better. A reliable form of money – either for a means of payment or to store value, or even to help governments with their own finances – did not exist. The most commonly used currencies were a jumble of gold and silver coins. Among the gold coins, Spanish doubloons were worth almost 4 pounds sterling. Silver coins were in more useful small denominations: French crowns were worth over five English shillings, while the Spanish dol-

lar and American dollar were each worth 5 shillings, according to official decree. English and French coins were both legal tender in Lower
Canada.

But in Upper Canada, accounts were kept in 'York currency,' which
valued the dollar at 8 shillings instead of 5 shillings. How could two values exist for the pound in the same marketplace? The answer is: not very
well. Ordinary citizens were often short-changed when dealing with
merchants who had the advantage of understanding the relative value
of various coins. Clever merchants could arbitrage between Montreal,
York (York was founded in 1793 and became Toronto in 1834), New York
City, and London. But to do this required capital and patience, because
the cost of transporting gold and silver coins, the risk of theft, and the
long overseas shipping route without news all implied high risk.

The shortage of specie led to various improvisations of paper money.
In Quebec, some merchants and manufacturers issued small promissory notes called 'bon-pours.' The British army[2] began issuing its own
paper money to buy provisions, and these were put into general circulation as 'army bills.' But the lack of large-denomination money hampered foreign trade.

In 1810 the population of Montreal was 10,000, compared to 625 in
York that same year. The merchants of Montreal had great difficulty in
financing their exports of flour, potash, lumber, and fur to Britain, while
paying for imports of clothing, sugar, salt, and farm tools. A market
developed in bills of exchange, which were orders on the buyer issued
by the seller, and payable to a third party. But there was a great distance
and a time lapse of six months to two years between the transaction
and the final payment. Buyers of produce in faraway London were not
necessarily honest or capable of meeting their obligations, and the same
was true of the importers in Canada. Hence the role of a financial intermediary was to buy the bill of exchange at a discount, and this became
one of the chief functions of banks in providing credit to facilitate trade.

First Bank of the United States. These same frustrating problems in financing overseas trade applied equally in Boston and New York, through
which a growing proportion of Canada's import-export business was
directed, owing mainly to the longer shipping season. (This three-way
trade was seriously impaired during the Revolutionary War, when the
British navy blockaded American vessels.) A more formal financial
structure was needed, and in 1791 the First Bank of the United States
opened in Philadelphia.

The significance of this first national bank in the United States was that it became the forerunner to and model for the Canadian banking system. Contrary to the assertions of Prime Minister Macdonald, Scotland was not the inspiration for the Canadian system of banking, which we are now asked by him to codify in the federal act. The first attempts to define a bank charter in the Canadas were copied almost word for word and section by section from the charter of the First Bank of the United States. The author of this pioneering American act was Alexander Hamilton, first secretary of the treasury during the First Congress in Philadelphia.

Hamilton[3] was the forceful champion of the view that a sound national banking system was required as 'a major element for raising a powerful and prosperous nation.' By 1791, there were already five state-chartered banks in existence in five U.S. cities. The constitution of 1787 was silent on the critical issue as to whether banking was a federal or state matter. This became a fundamental dividing point between the American banking system and our own, as set out in the recent British North America Act. The U.S. constitution did, however, specifically assign the power to issue and regulate coinage to the federal government, and defined gold and silver as the only legal tender. The states were specifically prohibited from issuing paper money.

Aligned against Hamilton in Congress were the agrarian forces from the southern states, bankers in New York and Boston who resented the proposed location of the First Bank in Philadelphia, and a general suspicion of the elite class on the northeast seaboard. Thomas Jefferson's agrarian fantasies had been revealed by his comment that he would wish the United States 'to practice neither commerce nor navigation.'[4] Another southerner declared: 'What was it that drove our forefathers to this country? Was it not the ecclesiastical corporations and perpetual monopolies of England and Scotland?'[5]

With Washington's support, Hamilton got his way, and the First Bank of the United States was endorsed by Congress. The authorized capital was $10 million, of which $2 million was allocated to the government itself and the remaining $8 million issued to the public. It was heavily oversubscribed, and the stock rose to $300 from $25 per share. The government managed to put up its share with some highly creative accounting, and it is unclear whether the required minimum 20 per cent subscription in specie was ever achieved by the public.

As well as creating a national institution, the act incorporating the First Bank of the United States also provided a vehicle which the government could use as a safe depository for taxes and to provide loans to itself and, perhaps more important, keep the state-chartered banks in line. In this regard, the First Bank of the United States was in fact modelled on the Bank of England, founded in 1694. The Bank of England was not only a commercial bank but the chosen instrument of government and in effect a sort of central bank.

The key to exercising control over state-chartered banks was the requirement that every issuer of bank notes was required to convert its own notes – on demand – into gold or silver. The First Bank of the United States could and did accumulate the notes of banks which it considered unsound, and then presented them all at once for redemption in gold or silver. This would effectively kill any bank that had overextended itself by too much leverage of its own issue of bank notes on its reserves of gold and silver.

But there was a price to pay in the compromise legislation. The charter of the First Bank of the United States was limited to twenty years. When the charter came up for renewal in 1811, it was killed by its many enemies in Congress, partly because it had been doing its job so well. Another critical factor was that much of the public issue of stock had been acquired by British investors, and war with Britain was imminent.

During the war years from 1812 to 1814, the requirement that specie would be the only legal tender was suspended. Chaos followed. The country was flooded with paper money issued by banks of dubious credentials. In 1816 the charter of the First Bank of the United States was revived as the Second Bank of the United States, again with a twenty-year charter. But in 1836, once again, the charter was allowed to lapse by Congress for much the same reasons put forward in 1811. The United States would never again enjoy a national banking system with branches of banks across all states.[6]

The Earliest Banks in Canada. Meanwhile the merchant communities in Montreal, Halifax, and Saint John took careful note of the First Bank of the United States. By then there had been a wave of migration from New York and New England. About 30,000 immigrants from the United States who became identified in 1789 as 'United Empire Loyalists' reached the Maritimes. Another 2,000 settled in Montreal and the surrounding area, while 7,500 occupied the St Lawrence River bank from Cornwall to Kingston, and also the north shore of Lake Ontario and the Niagara area. York (modern-day Toronto) was not founded until 1793.

But the requirements of commerce made little impression on the

Colonial Office or the British Treasury. From 1793 to 1815, both the English and Scottish banking systems were very unstable. 'In 1797 the Bank of England suspended cash payments and did not resume until 1821 … It was mainly through the example of the National Bank of Scotland, started in 1824, that the transition was gradually made to the present system of a few large banks with numerous branches.'[7]

By then the Bank of Montreal was already a reality. Its articles of association had been adopted in 1817, and the bank commenced operating in 1818, even though it did not receive a provincial charter and royal assent until 1822. An earlier attempt to incorporate a Bank of Lower Canada had been made as early as 1792. Strikingly, the proposed charter of this earlier bank copied the articles of association of the First Bank of the United States, only changing the name of the bank at the top. Another attempt to establish a Bank of Quebec in 1808 also failed. The Bank of Montreal's articles were also very similar to those in the earlier aborted cases. After starting operations, the Bank of Montreal sent an officer to the New York office of the Second Bank of the United States for training.

The authorized capital of the Bank of Montreal was £250,000 or $1 million Canadian (at the official exchange rate). There was no market in the shares, because the bank was not yet chartered as a joint-stock company. However, there were serious restrictions on share ownership and on voting rights. No one could vote more than twenty shares. This was aimed at the wealthy families in New York and Boston who provided most of the capital to supplement the scarce supply in Montreal. An even more restrictive limit of ten shares was included in the articles of the Bank of New Brunswick, which was actually the first bank to receive a provincial charter in 1820. The first joint-stock bank was the Bank of Nova Scotia, incorporated in 1832. Both Maritime banks were heavily influenced by the Massachusetts banking system.

Perhaps the most critical regulation in the Bank of Montreal's articles was that the liabilities of the bank could not exceed three times its paid-in capital, and the paid-in capital had to be in specie – gold or silver. For many years, bank deposits were uncommon; the chief liability of the bank was its own bank notes, which were in effect non-interest-bearing deposits. As long as these notes were accepted by the public for general circulation, there would be no pressure on the bank to redeem them for specie. The paid-in capital thus became the reserves underlying the money supply. In fact, there was constant pressure on the Bank of Montreal, because French Canadians distrusted paper and converted the bank's notes to specie and hoarded it. This forced the bank to be prudent in its note issue. In Upper Canada the excessive issue of notes has helped lead to the recent demise in 1866 of the Bank of Upper Canada, as we shall see.

Another critical feature of the Bank of Montreal charter was that it was limited to ten years. This enabled the legislature of Lower Canada to monitor the consequences of its chartering activities. In 1831 the bank barely survived a political challenge to its charter renewal. Some bank charters have been subject to decennial review, although those in Upper Canada were granted for twenty-five years.

The Bank of Montreal's charter also forbade it from engaging in any other trade or business, and prevented the extension of credit for the purchase of real property. These two provisions, copied in other charters, have fortunately preserved the Dominion of Canada's small economy from the acquisition by the banks of our manufactures and railways, and also from the land speculation excesses which we have observed south of the border.

One feature that was absent from the Bank of Montreal's charter was the 'double liability' clause. This provision originated with the Bank of New Brunswick, which copied the Massachusetts banks. The purpose of the clause was to encourage prudent behaviour by the directors and shareholders in issuing bank notes. In the event of failure, the shareholders of the bank were required to take up an amount of stock equal to what they already owned. This has recently caused grave consternation among the shareholders of the Bank of Upper Canada. As you know, the government did not enforce this clause before our recent Confederation. The dissolution of the bank has cost our Dominion government about $1 million of its own deposits.

In the early years, the Bank of Montreal enjoyed the privilege of being the exclusive banker to the government in Quebec City. In this role it was the sole depository for government monies, the fiscal agent for the colony with the Treasury in London, and the overseer of the note issue of other banks as well as of its own notes. The Bank of Montreal patterned itself after Hamilton's First Bank of the United States, which saw itself as the chosen instrument of government financial policy. While the American bank and its successor the Second Bank went into oblivion when their charters were allowed to expire, the Bank of Montreal continued on, and today in 1870 it is still by far our largest bank.

Another feature of the Second Bank's charter was the limit of 6 per cent to be charged on advances to borrowers. This provision has also been followed in the Canadian charters, and does not seem to have been a matter of political concern. As you well know from your own experience, the Canadian railways have been able to borrow for long terms in the London bond market at 5 per cent, so a ceiling of 6 per cent on short-term loans has been somewhat academic.

The articles of association of the Bank of Montreal were silent on the power to establish branches, a power that the First Bank of the United States enjoyed. But the Bank of Montreal's directors considered that this critical privilege applied only to large urban banks. They opposed – as John Rose has asserted to this very day – branching by others. Their perception of their role was reinforced by their own personal experiences in Britain where the Bank of England stood out far above the small unincorporated 'country banks' which had no branches. Unfortunately, the British system has proven to be a poor model, and we have seen visitors from the old country come here to examine our system.

The Bank of Upper Canada. The Bank of Montreal lost no time opening branches in Kingston and York in 1818. This alarmed the merchant community in Upper Canada, partly because the Bank of Montreal was subject to the somewhat archaic French Civil Code of Lower Canada, but more generally because the merchant community's dependence on Montreal would increase. Apart from New York, Montreal was the seaport and financial centre for all trade to its west. Although at that time York had a population of only 900 souls – only half that of Kingston and a tenth that of Montreal – it was this little town of York that obtained the first Upper Canadian bank charter in 1822. The Bank of Upper Canada obtained royal assent after a bizarre political battle with Kingston, not least because nine of the bank's fifteen directors were also members of Upper Canada's Executive Council, the governing body of the colony. Its first president was William Allan,[8] who had actually been the Bank of Montreal's agent in York since 1818.

The authorized capital of the Bank of Upper Canada was £200,000, almost as much as that of the Bank of Montreal – but only £20,000 had to be paid in. Although the small York community could not raise that much, the directors and the Executive Council blinked at the deficiency. The constraint on the bank's note issue (to three times the capital paid-in with specie) was not observed, so that the note circulation exceeded the legal requirement. The Bank of Montreal gathered up the bank notes of the Bank of Upper Canada and dumped them without warning on the Bank of Upper Canada, requiring payment in specie. The Bank of

Upper Canada returned the favour, thus prolonging a 'specie war,' a contest that spread to most other banks in the Canadas.

At first, the Bank of Upper Canada made its notes redeemable at its Montreal branch office. But this only made it convenient for the Bank of Montreal to redeem its rival's notes on the spot. The Bank of Upper Canada then resorted to making its notes redeemable only at the head office in York. This forced others to face the expense and risk of transporting gold and silver hundreds of miles – a practice already highly developed south of the border. There were head offices of banks in upper Michigan – 'banking among the wildcats' – it was called. In order to escalate the battle with the Bank of Montreal, the government at York passed an act preventing out-of-province banks from operating in Upper Canada unless their notes were redeemable at York. This effectively barred the Bank of Montreal from operating in Upper Canada from 1824 until the Union of Upper and Lower Canada in 1840.

With its virtual monopoly, the Bank of Upper Canada appeared to be quite profitable for about twenty years. It enjoyed being the sole bank of deposit for the government, as well as collecting the deposits of immigrants, on both of which it paid no interest. Gradually, the legislature overcame the Executive Council's resistance to competition. Other banks appeared, such as the Commercial Bank in Kingston in 1832 and the Gore Bank[9] in Hamilton in 1835. But the Bank of Upper Canada's management caused it to become increasingly overextended in its loans to the rapidly growing business of canals and railways. In the 1850s the bank was heavily committed financially to the Grand Trunk Railway, whose president, John Ross, sat on its board. One critic observed that the bank was run by 'two old men surrounded by assorted cantankerous noodles'[10] – the directors.

As the bank slid downhill, the Bank of Montreal recaptured the role of depository to the government of the Province of Canada, and also took over the account of the Grand Trunk. In 1866 the Bank of Upper Canada failed. But it was now subject to the 'double liability' clause, which had been introduced when the two Canadas united. As you know, this became a source of serious political embarrassment to the government before Confederation, and nothing has yet been done to enforce payment by the shareholders. However, you should be made aware of the fact that our prime minister himself is indebted to the Bank of Upper Canada for $17,195.

Unfortunately for Mr Galt, the first minister of finance, the Commercial Bank of Kingston also failed soon after the demise of the Bank of

Upper Canada, mainly on account of its imprudent loans to the Great West Railway. You are aware that Mr Galt was a director of the Commercial, and there were many in Parliament who considered him compromised. So his tenure as the first minister of finance was only four months, and his successor, Mr John Rose, has now also departed.

The Gore Bank of Hamilton also failed, brought down by the bankruptcy of its large competitors and the cascading effects that these bankruptcies had on the whole mercantile community. This provided an opening for some new ventures in Upper Canada, notably the Bank of Commerce and the Toronto Bank. Keeping in mind the serious commercial situation that we have seen in Toronto because of the three bank failures, it will be important for you to consult the newcomers, especially Sir William McMaster, president of the Bank of Commerce, who is also chairman of the Senate Committee on Banking and Finance.

The Struggle among Banks for Market Share. At Confederation we had thirty-eight banks (see Table 1) and the Bank of Montreal[11] alone accounted for about 25 per cent of all the assets. Sir Francis, it is small wonder that the smaller banks have been hostile to your predecessor, Mr Rose, and to his mentor, Mr Edwin King, who is the general manager of the Bank of Montreal. For the past four years, those two persons have been attempting to impose their vision of our banking system on the authorities. They propose that we adopt the American 'free banking system' and that we accede to the transfer of the note-issuing power to the Dominion.

The concept of 'free banking' emerged in the United States after the demise of the Second Bank of the United States. The licensing of banks fell back into the hands of the states. New York and some other states decided that it was not necessary to examine individual applicants for bank charters. With 'free banking,' as it was called, anyone with enough capital could open a local bank with no branches. Many scoundrels took advantage of this populist interpretation of states' rights, and there have been numerous bank failures. A flood of fraudulent paper money appeared, some of which has drifted over the border to the Dominion. The U.S. experience makes it clear how important it is to have one national issuer of the circulating currency, both coin and paper money.

You will recall that, after the Union of Upper and Lower Canada, you yourself introduced in the legislature the 'Free Banking Act of 1850,' which allowed for the founding of local banks without branches. Several banks, such as the Zimmerman Bank in Niagara, came into

Table 1
The 'Big Six' in 1867

Share of market of twenty-four reporting banks* (approximate per cent of total assets)	
Bank of Montreal	25%
Bank of Nova Scotia	2
Bank of Commerce	1
Bank of Toronto	4
Banque Nationale	2
Royal Bank**	3
	37
Other Major Banks that Disappeared Before 1871	
Commercial Bank	12%
Gore Bank	3
Banks Not Reporting*	48%
Total	100%

* Fourteen more banks did not report. Of these, the Merchant Bank of Halifax became part of the Royal; the Bank of British Columbia and the Bank of British North America were chartered in Britain.
** The Quebec Bank became part of the Royal in 1917.
Source: Robert M. MacIntosh, Different Drummers: Banking and Politics in Canada (Toronto: Macmillan of Canada 1991).

existence. As you know, the British Treasury was much offended by this American device, and in the years of your absence in the Caribbean, this concept has been allowed to lapse. We recognize that your motives were to stabilize the market for government bonds, after the disastrous economic depression and transatlantic financial collapse of 1848, and to provide a uniform currency. By requiring banks to hold government bonds to secure their paper money issues, you would re-establish confidence in the financial system. There was very strong resistance to this proposal from all the chartered banks except the Bank of Montreal, which already held a large amount of government securities and would therefore emerge as the monopoly issuer of bank notes.

Since Confederation, John Rose has continued to press the case for the Bank of Montreal, but has met strenuous opposition from the other banks in their presentations to the House Committee. At the same time, there has been very little support for the idea of removing the power to issue notes from all the chartered banks and transferring that power to a Dominion government bank. The British Treasury has constantly pressed upon us the need to follow the British system, in which the Bank of England is the sole issuer of paper money in small denominations. But there are many in Parliament who perceive that a monopoly government bank, created solely to issue paper money, would be subject to political interference and even corruption. The bankers will, of course, passionately resist any attempt to remove their power to issue bank notes, which is their principal source of profits.

It would appear that a compromise is possible. You may wish to consider prohibiting the banks from issuing bank notes in denominations less than $4. Much of the general circulation of money in the country is for sums less than $4, and for the smaller denominations – notes of $1 and $2 – you might wish to propose the issuance of Dominion notes. In order to ensure public confidence in the Dominion notes, and to prevent some future administration from inflating the issue, it would be advisable to define them as legal tender and place an overall ceiling of $10 million on their issuance.

As for the banks' note issues, they should be required to hold a reserve of legal tender, whether it be gold or Dominion government securities, or a combination of the two. In this way we could replace the present system which limits the note issue of banks to some multiple of their paid-in capital in specie and introduce a reserve of legal tender to control the supply of money.

By these measures you would restore public confidence in the banking system, which has been seriously shaken by the failure of so many banks in Ontario.

The Rise of the Canadian Dollar. You will be gratified to realize that, with the establishment of a self-governing Dominion of Canada, you will no longer require royal assent from London. You will recall the many battles with Whitehall which you fought in the years 1851 to 1854 to keep the provincial accounts in dollars instead of sterling. The Treasury officials also insisted that the circulating currency of the colonies must be sterling. But our trading relationships with the United States had become so strong in the ordinary life of the people that they had become accustomed to the decimal currency system of the United States. All parties in the legislature applauded your resolute insistence that the Province of Canada should adopt a dollar currency as the money of account. When this was done in 1858, the banks quickly followed suit, and the Treasury Board in London gave way, not without claiming to the end that all British colonies should employ sterling.

Meanwhile, in 1854 you had also succeeded in defining the value of the Dominion dollar at 23.22 grains of gold, precisely the same as the American dollar. The British pound was 113 grains of gold, so that the pound was equal to $4.8666. For the first time there was a fixed relationship between the three currencies, which was an enormous benefit in transatlantic trade and in the conduct of daily affairs. However, the notion of a uniform currency is a matter that remains to be addressed. We still find in circulation many Spanish and French coins which are so worn that they cannot be recognized. We also have paper money issued by the banks which does not have a uniform value in all five provinces. It will be necessary for you to determine what legal tender is. It will also be necessary to establish in law a uniform paper currency for all five provinces.

In summary, Sir Francis, I have listed below what I think should be the key provisions in the new Bank Act for the Dominion of Canada. I think they will lay the necessary foundations for both a sound system of currency and a banking system that can adjust to future requirements. Here are my recommendations:

Establish a uniform federal act, replacing all provincial charters, and including the following specific features:

a) minimum capital of $500,000, of which 10 per cent to be paid up;
b) power to issue notes in denominations of $4 or more, not to exceed paid-up capital and secured by gold or Dominion notes;
c) double liability on shareholders, to be paid before realizing on the assets of a failed bank;
d) total bank liabilities not to exceed three times capital;
e) mandatory decennial revision by Parliament;
f) one vote per share;
g) prohibition against extending credit on real property; and
h) maintain 6 per cent interest ceiling.

Sequel

The recommendations in the fictional Abbott report were all part of the first Bank Act of 1871 (35 Vic. Ch.11), along with about twenty other clauses that defined the constraints on the raising of capital, the duties of directors, and the issuance of paper currency. The act remained silent on the power to have branches. But the charter of the Bank of Montreal had become the standard, and Hincks made it clear to Parliament that his intention was to encourage the banks to have multiple branches, rather than pursue the American model of single banks with no branches.

Suggested Questions

1. What were the issues faced by businesses in the 1800s in Canada as a result of operating in a multiple-currency environment? Had the banking system changed for the better by 1867? How? What were the lessons for the establishment of a sound currency?
2. What were the differences between the Bank Act proposed by John Rose and the version proposed by Sir Francis Hincks? Which of the versions would have been best for the Canadian economy? For business enterprises?
3. Why were the proposals of Sir Francis Hincks acceptable and those of John Rose not?
4. Do you think the provision for a decennial revision of the Bank Act was a wise decision, and if so, why?

Suggested Readings

Baskerville, Peter. *The Bank of Upper Canada*. Toronto: Champlain Society 1987.

Hammond, Bray. *Banks and Politics in America: From the Revolution to The Civil War*. Princeton, N.J.: Princeton University Press 1957.

Johnson, J.K. and P.B. Waite. 'Sir John A. Macdonald.' *Dictionary of Canadian Biography*, www.biographia.ca.

MacIntosh, Robert M. *Different Drummers, Banking and Politics in Canada*. Toronto: Macmillan of Canada 1991.

McDowall, Duncan. *Quick to The Frontier: Canada's Royal Bank*. Toronto: McClelland and Stewart 1993.

Powell, James. *A History of the Canadian Dollar*. Ottawa: Bank of Canada 1999.

Shortt, Adam. *History of Canadian Currency and Banking*. Toronto: Canadian Bankers' Association 1986.

'Sir Francis Hincks.' *Dictionary of Canadian Biography*, www.biographia.ca.

NOTES

1 Shortt, *History of Canadian Currency and Banking*, 31.
2 The British forces in Quebec numbered about 5,000 in 1770.
3 Alexander Hamilton was born in 1757 on the island of Nevis in the British West Indies. He moved to New York in 1774 and became one of most distinguished citizens of what was to become the United States. He was a revolutionary soldier, a founding father, a leading Federalist politician, one of the framers of the constitution, and the first secretary of the treasury. He was killed in a duel with Aaron Burr in 1804.
4 Hammond, *Banks and Politics in America*, 121.
5 Ibid., 116.
6 But, in the past two decades, the United States has been moving towards a national banking system, with many states now permitting both state-chartered and nationally chartered banks to acquire banks in other states.
7 Shortt, *History of Canadian Currency and Banking*, 11.
8 William Allan, born in Scotland in 1770, emigrated to Montreal at the age of seventeen and moved to York at twenty-six. He became the leading merchant in Upper Canada, member of the Executive Council in 1836, and president of the Bank of Upper Canada from 1822 to 1835. Allan Gardens in Toronto are on the site of his mansion.
9 The Gore Bank was named after Sir Francis Gore, lieutenant governor of Upper Canada. He astutely avoided the War of 1812–14 by taking leave of absence in England from 1811 to 1815. In his absence, Sir Isaac Brock was the provisional lieutenant governor as well as commander of the British forces in Canada. Brock was tragically killed in the war and Gore returned to York to resume his much-disliked regime.
10 Baskerville, *The Bank of Upper Canada*, cxxx.
11 For estimated market shares in 1867, see Table 1. The Bank of Montreal accounted for 25 per cent of the total assets of the ten major banks that provided statutory reports. The failure of the Commercial and Gore banks after Confederation but before the passage of the new Bank Act raised the Bank of Montreal's share to about 60 per cent of the total assets of the remaining eight major reporting banks. Two large banks, the Bank of British North America and the Bank of British Columbia, were chartered by the British government and did not report. It should be noted that all six of the present 'big six' banks listed in Table 1 existed in 1867, one with a different name. The Royal Bank was the Quebec Bank in 1867; the Merchant's Bank of Halifax, another component of the Royal, first reported its assets in 1869.

CASE 2
'Carpets, Lace & Champagne':
The Hudson's Bay Company after the
Deed of Surrender

JOHN GEIGER, with guidance from JOE MARTIN

In 1869 the Hudson's Bay Company – more formally known as the
Governor and Company of Adventurers of England Trading into Hudson Bay – consented to a deed of surrender. This deed gave up the company's trading rights and legal jurisdiction over its great empire of the
North-West.

Two centuries earlier, in 1670, King Charles II had awarded the company a royal charter as 'true Lordes and Proprietors' over the vast territory covered by Hudson Bay's tributary system. Known as Rupert's
Land, the territory was named after Prince Rupert, cousin of Charles
and the first governor of the company. This trading monopoly covered
about 3.8 million square kilometres, including more than 40 per cent
of present-day Canada, making the company the largest private landowner in history. Its claim was contested, first by France and later by
fur traders in New France. However, the eventual surrender of Rupert's
Land came about not from external forces but from forces within.

The company had been primarily engaged in the fur trade, a lucrative
enterprise which satiated the European demand for then-fashionable
beaver hats, but by the mid-nineteenth the fur trade was waning. A
growing influx of settlers both into the company's domain and into the
American west south of the 49th parallel tested its authority and – more
particularly from the standpoint of imperial and Canadian authorities –
its capacity to protect British interests in the face of U.S. expansionism.
Encroachment by U.S. commercial interests hurt the company's trading enterprise. Other incidents – such as the flight to Rupert's Land by
a Native war party following the massacre of settlers and the resulting threatened extension of U.S. lawmaking – underscored the tenuous
nature of the company's exercise of sovereignty.

Despite all of these challenges, it was the sale of controlling interest in the company to the International Financial Society in 1863 that marked the turning point. This sale transformed the HBC from a tightly held private company into to a widely held enterprise trading on the London Stock Exchange. It also changed the company's focus: the new directors were more interested in real estate speculation and economic development than the fur trade, and negotiations were opened for the sale of Rupert's Land.

The purchase of Rupert's Land would radically redraw the map of Canada. While the 1803 Louisiana Purchase from France doubled the size of the United States, adding 827,987 square miles (or 2,144,476 square kilometres) of territory, the Rupert's Land purchase increased the size of the young Dominion of Canada six times.

In July 1868 the Canadian government passed the Rupert's Land Act, enabling it to purchase Rupert's Land and the North-West (lands that drained into the Arctic and Pacific oceans) from the company. (See map of Rupert's Land.) This was a condition of Confederation and the quid pro quo that the Upper Canadians (Ontarians) had demanded in Quebec City in 1864 in response to the Maritimers' demand for an intercolonial railway.[1] The stage was set for the deed of surrender and subsequent extension of the rule of Canadian law, and the orderly settlement of lands in the North-West's 'fertile belt' – defined in the document as those lands bounded by the U.S. border in the south; the North Saskatchewan River in the north; the Rocky Mountains in the west; and finally, in the east, Lake Winnipeg, Lake of the Woods, and the waters connecting them. Royal assent was given to the surrender in 1870. This freed the company of the burden of its civil responsibilities, allowing it to concentrate on its fundamental role as a business enterprise.

No Ordinary Company

But it was no ordinary company. Under the terms of the deed of surrender, the HBC received a cash payment of £300,000, retained its posts, and received a block of land adjoining each post, for a total of 50,000 acres. What's more, the company would receive, as they were surveyed by the Dominion government, one-twentieth of the lands in the 'fertile belt.' This would eventually amount to seven million acres. Finally, the company received an inoculation against 'exceptional taxes' on its land, trade' or servants.

With the fur trade in terminal decline, the HBC had emerged as a

Map of Rupert's Land

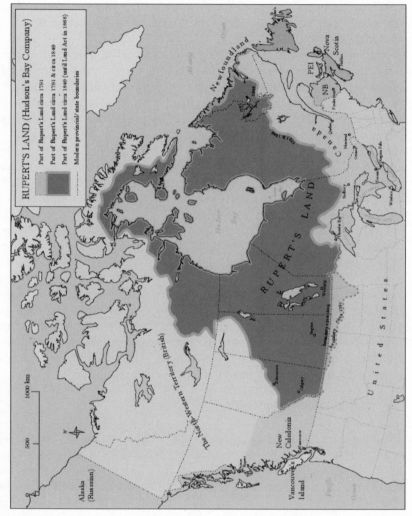

major landowner and, increasingly, a purveyor to the 'general trade.' It was better poised than any other enterprise to capitalize on the opportunities represented by the rapidly developing North-West. But, while the forces driving this transformation included major shareholders in London, the boundless opportunities presented were not immediately obvious either to the majority of the company's senior officers or to its traders in the field.

In the early days of its new incarnation, the HBC seemed much like it did in its former state. On 15 March 1871 Cyril Graham presented a report to the company's London-based governor, Sir Stafford Northcote. He was a Conservative in the British Parliament who had served as president of the Board of Trade, secretary of state for India, and chancellor of the Exchequer. An independent agent not connected with the company, he was sent from London to tour its operations as the first step in a review of its organization. Although Graham's report deals with the fur trade in depth, emphasizing its continuing dominance, it devotes only a few paragraphs to other emerging opportunities. However, those words proved portentous.

Graham informed Northcote that general business 'henceforth will claim a large part of your attention.' At the time, the base on which the HBC could build its new retail business was still small. In 1871 the population of Winnipeg numbered in the hundreds. Yet Graham predicted that, with its depots and 'a large enough staff of practiced salesmen to enable you to organize and fill a little shop anywhere at a moments notice, you could drive a flourishing and always increasing trade, and if you could only see your way to add banking you might regulate the commerce of the North West.'[2] In Donald Alexander Smith, the company had just the man to head such a diversification.

The Rise of Donald A. Smith

The towering figure of the time for the HBC was Donald Smith (who was later elevated to the peerage as Baron Strathcona and Mount Royal). Smith was a native of Scotland and veteran of the fur trade who had started in the company's service in 1838 as an apprentice clerk and worked his way up through the ranks. Smith had helped negotiate the deed of surrender, and, when opposition grew among the Métis in Red River to the proposed transfer, he was appointed special commissioner by Prime Minister Sir John A. Macdonald. The prime minister blamed the company for failing to inform residents of the Red River settlement that their interests would be unaffected by the transfer. However, in negotiations with the Métis leader, Louis Riel, Smith used his status in the HBC and the company's reputation to defuse temporarily a volatile situation. From 1871 to 1879, Smith held, in succession, the positions of company commissioner, chief commissioner, and land commissioner.

His immediate assignment was to ensure that the provisions of the 1872 Dominion Lands Act, which served to implement the terms of the deed of surrender, were applied to the company's advantage. Fortuitously, Smith was simultaneously serving in the House of Commons as the MP for Selkirk. (His political opponents in the House derisively dubbed him the 'member for the Hudson's Bay Company.') He succeeded in enhancing the company's position through various changes, including one that allowed the company to exchange its 'fertile belt' lands, which had been found to be worthless, for better land. Although he was a Conservative, Smith, apparently out of anger over Macdonald's refusal to reimburse him for expenses he claimed while negotiating with Riel, voted in November 1873 against his own party and the government, leading to the subsequent election of Alexander Mackenzie's Liberals. These circumstances strained Smith's subsequent dealings with Macdonald.

Smith was also busy developing a lucrative business partnership with his cousin, George Stephen (later Baron Mount Stephen), a self-made man who began his career at a draper establishment in Montreal. The partnership began with an informal and reciprocal arrangement: Stephen provided investment advice while Smith helped to sell to the Hudson's Bay Company the woolen goods produced by Stephen's textile mills. They formalized their dealings in myriad enterprises. These ventures included the Canada Rolling Stock Company in 1869, later the Canada Cotton Manufacturing Company, and ultimately railways. Through Stephen, Smith had his entrée into the financial community associated with the opulence of the Golden Square Mile, the upper-class district of Montreal. In its heyday, 70 per cent of the country's wealth was concentrated among its residents, the majority of whom were, like Smith and Stephen, Scots born. As his wealth grew, Smith purchased a mansion alongside his business partners and acquired a large domestic staff and an art collection that included works by Constable, Gainsborough, and Raphael. Smith became the conduit through whom Montreal financiers made investments in Manitoba. As a result of all of this, Smith's attentions were focused on his Hudson's Bay Company duties only sporadically.

Whereas some shareholders in the HBC were agitating to abandon the waning fur trade enterprise entirely, Smith was not among them. It was not that he was a hopeless nostalgic. Smith simply calculated that there would be no immediate fortune to be made as land traders. Lack of an adequate transportation system was an impediment to settlement, the North-West was almost entirely unsurveyed, and economic conditions were depressed in the 1870s. Historian John S. Galbraith judges Smith's go-slow strategy to be correct. Referring to the final decades of the nineteenth century, Galbraith writes: 'Had the Hudson's Bay Company been exclusively either a land company or a fur trading organization, its career might have been brought to a conclusion during these lean years, for neither land nor furs during this period usually brought satisfactory returns.'[3] However, continuation in the fur trade was always considered to be simply an interim measure. In November 1872 Northcote expressed the hope that 'that kind of business will continue long enough to enable us to set on a firm footing the other business of the Company.'[4]

In the view of Inspecting Chief William Joseph Christie, this was not at all certain. Indeed, it is generally agreed that 'Smith's business ventures distracted him from his management of the HBC's affairs.'[5] Feeling that Smith was neglecting the trade, Christie conveyed his concerns to the company's committee (as the board of directors was called) in London. In 1874, with Smith's concurrence, the company reorganized its operations. According to Smith, 'the growing importance and probable development of the land business rendered it desirable that a division should be made between the business of the Fur Trade and that connected with the management of the Company's Estate.'[6] Four years after it had become the greatest landowner on the continent, the Hudson's Bay Company finally created a Land Department. Smith was appointed as the company's first land commissioner, based in Montreal, and reported directly to London. His successor as chief commissioner in charge of the fur trade was James A. Grahame, an old company hand. But the division in responsibilities only further hampered initiative and Smith was soon writing London to lament Grahame's failure to seize on commercial opportunities.

Smith's immediate concern was improvement of the transportation system – historically one of the company's strengths with its cart brigades and York boats. He worked to develop steamboat service on the Red and Saskatchewan rivers and to extend railway lines into Manitoba. The HBC saw fit to invest directly in the tenuous riverboat business, which was eventually doomed by various problems, not least of which was low water levels. However, the company somehow missed out on the opportunity to invest in railways. Though he did brief the company's committee on the progress of railways, imparting information that was in its general financial interest to know, it was Smith himself who became a partner in the extremely profitable St Paul, Minneapolis and Manitoba Railway (later the Great Northern). In this he had benefited from advice from Norman Kittson, the company's agent in St Paul, who also had a stake in the enterprise. Smith's personal interests and the company's interests were so close as to be interchangeable – they even shared a lawyer.

To pursue the railroad, Smith enlisted the help of his cousin, George Stephen, a future president of both the Bank of Montreal and the CPR, and Richard B. Angus, general manager of the Bank of Montreal. These ties, to both banking and railway interests, might have been 'considered of potential advantage to the Company. There is, however, no evidence in the Company's records of any such awareness.'[7] Had Smith made the HBC aware of, and secured its involvement in, the railway business, the company might have eventually become (as Smith did) one of the central players in the syndicate that built the Canadian Pacific Railway. The company might also have become, in effect, its own heir, since 'the Canadian Pacific Railway became the true successor to the Hudson's Bay Company as the dominant business influence over half a continent.'[8] Instead, this opportunity was lost to the company. If Smith did desire greater HBC involvement, he did not pursue it with much vigour. The company did profit incidentally, such as by its ownership in a railway bridge across the Assiniboine River, although here too Smith had a piece of the action, being the largest individual investor. While a loyal company man, Smith's ultimate allegiance was manifestly to his own self-interest; he assiduously wrung personal profits from his position with the company. It is not by chance that he built the largest personal fortune in Canada.

Besides showing an interest in transportation and his varied entrepreneurial enterprises, Smith was also concerned with politics, retaining his corporate responsibilities while concurrently sitting in the Manitoba legislature and in the Canadian House of Commons. Like his efforts to enhance transportation linkages, his political involvement, which was sanctioned by Northcote, was not always a benefit to the HBC. Nevertheless, Smith was able to influence the location of government offices on company land, thereby also enhancing the value of neighbouring company-held properties. He was also able to elicit government contracts for the company to act as paymaster for the North West Mounted Police, to supply (at a commission) money for Indian treaty settlements, and to win potentially lucrative supply contracts with the police and Indian agencies. The cautious Grahame, however, demurred, letting many of these opportunities pass.

Yet Smith came under increasing scrutiny. A series of letters from London in 1878 suggested displeasure over his failure to focus adequately on company business. In 1879 Smith resigned from the HBC, confirming that 'my private affairs now require my personal care more than formerly, making it impossible for me to continue to give the Company's landed interests that close attention which their great importance demands.'[9] The company's chief factor, James Bissett, whom Smith had been using as his own lawyer, now also resigned from the company in order to establish Smith's Montreal office – housed in the Hudson's Bay Company building: 'To the Company's annoyance, in 1881 [Smith] also secured offices for himself in the Company's new building in Winnipeg. The Governor and Committee sensed that, though he was no longer on the payroll, he had no intention of letting go.'[10] They were right: he was by no means done with the Hudson's Bay Company. He was simply 'astute enough to know that to acquire power over the Company he had, in fact, to leave it.'[11]

The Rise and Fall of C.J. Brydges

The boundless potential of the first few years after the deed of surrender, however, had been squandered. Writes historian Michael Bliss: '[The company] had opportunity upon opportunity to develop profitable new business, and muffed almost all of them.'[12] Instead of dominating, even monopolizing, trade, commerce, and transportation in western Canada, the company ceded the territory to others.

Smith in particular had accomplished remarkably little for the company as land commissioner, but the appointment of C.J. Brydges as his replacement was seen as evidence that 'a change has taken place in the conduct of the Company's business which is likely to redeem all the errors once committed.'[13] Brydges was a professional manager of a new breed, an able and politically savvy administrator who had previously served as general manager of the Grand Trunk Railway. At Confederation, the Grand Trunk was the largest railway system in the world, running unbroken from Sarnia to Portland, Maine.[14] Brydges had also served as general superintendent of government railways. At the HBC, his mandate was broader than his title suggested. He was charged with land sales, but he also pushed for the development of the general trade, the process of transforming the Hudson's Bay Company's network of fur trade posts into retail shops. Belatedly, the company began chasing government supply contracts.

At the start of Brydges's term, the company was at its core still a fur-trading concern, although it dabbled in retailing to settlers, operated a few riverboats, and began to enjoy the proceeds from soaring land prices as the population of Winnipeg had jumped to 10,000 by 1880. The massive changes under way in the North-West were wrought not so much by the company's own initiative as by the Canadian Pacific Railway, which was completed in 1885. The Hudson's Bay Company had missed the opportunity to control transportation in the North-West, not to mention the chance to regulate commerce. In fact, 'having lost control over its transportation system,' it had to seek a special arrangement with the CPR to ship goods westward and furs eastward.[15]

After months of haggling, the CPR gave the company a 12.5 per cent discount on its freight, excepting flour. Donald Smith's interest in the railway company might have worked in this instance in the company's favour, although it had 'precluded the Hudson's Bay Company from using American railways to reach the Canadian West.'[16] Writes historian Michael Bliss in *Northern Enterprise*: 'The Canadian Pacific Railway was created by westerners and fur traders. But not the Hudson's Bay Company.' The honour of pounding in the 'last spike,' however, was reserved for an old company man, one of the CPR's financiers: an entrepreneur named Donald Smith.

Brydges's arrival in Winnipeg was characterized as 'a great administrative juggernaut.'[17] Smith was paid to assist in the transition, but Brydges wrote to London to report that his predecessor had failed to turn over any books or letters connected with the Land Department. He also complained about finding unpaid taxes dating back to 1872. Brydges moved swiftly to replace Smith's informal administration and sloppy bookkeeping methods with modern corporate practices. He dispatched survey crews, competed successfully for large government supply contracts, oversaw bridge construction, and arranged for hotels, sawmills, and grist mills to open on company lands, thereby encouraging settlement: 'In this country a grist mill and a store form the nucleus of a future city,' said Brydges. His administration was, however, fundamentally conservative. Brydges did not diversify. He was constrained by the definition of the company's business as established over the previous decade.

Initially, luck was with Brydges. The location of the CPR's western service yards in Winnipeg fuelled a land boom. In April 1881 Brydges reported that land sales in Winnipeg were 'something marvelous and there is evidently the maddest kind of speculation rampant.' In 1880 a 50x120 foot lot on the company's reserve averaged $295; by August 1881, the price had jumped to $1,502.[18] Brydges's response was to halt sales, calculating that 'a little judicious coyness just now … will make the attempt to buy from us more violent, and at higher prices.' In a letter to London, he wrote: 'The office now is like a fair, and the people stand in a row waiting their turn to reach the counter. It is like the crowd at the entrance to the pit of a London theatre.' The land rush was fed by an enormous influx of settlers. On one day alone – 16 April 1882 – 3,000 people arrived in Winnipeg. Soon, land lots were being offered in other settlements, with prices soaring in places as distant as Edmonton.

The HBC was in a position to offer the newcomers more than just land. It had moved, at Brydges's urging but with steady resistance from the overcautious Grahame, to replace the old fur outposts with modern retail establishments. The idea was that these stores would serve to increase the attraction of the company's land holdings. The Fort Garry shop was described as an 'old-fashioned Hudson's Bay establishment … very suitable for trading with the Indians but not for showing off the Company's goods to advantage.'[19] The shop was demolished in 1881. In its place, a new building was constructed at Winnipeg's Main and York streets. The 'departmental' store boasted steam elevators and carried everything from drygoods and groceries to liquor. A new store opened the same year in Portage la Prairie, and others followed. By 1887, the chain of department stores had reached Vancouver. The old-time Scots and half-breed traders, experienced at bartering with Indians, were gradually replaced by fresh-faced sales clerks recruited from England. Initially, the general trade was so successful that, during the 1882 boom, the Hudson's Bay Company literally could not keep goods on the shelves.

Strangely, Brydges's efforts, enthusiasm, and notably his successes agitated Smith. In 1882 Smith had sold $200,000 of his shares in the St Paul, Minneapolis and Manitoba Railway and used the money to invest in the company, becoming a major shareholder. He was, consequently, enriched by the flourishing business. Nonetheless, it is possible that Smith learned of Brydges's letters of complaint to London about his sloppy administrative practices. Another of Brydges's sins was to resist Smith's efforts to ally the HBC's activities with those of the Canadian Pacific Railway, calculating correctly that the CPR was the company's greatest competitor with respect to land sales. Indeed, Smith was also one of the principal figures involved with another of the company's competitors, the North-West Land Company. As historian Paul Nigol puts it: 'Conflict of interest was an accepted practice in the capital-deficient Canada of the nineteenth century.'[20] Brydges had no divided loyalties. He had to be concerned only with the company's interests. Such was Smith's personal hostility, however, that it led Brydges to speculate that through his own activities and attempts to improve the company, he had inadvertently thwarted 'a long pending scheme to wreck the H.B. Co. and buy it up as a wreck.'[21]

Brydges could not be touched so long as the company prospered, but when the land bubble burst – an eventuality Brydges himself had long anticipated and frequently warned his superiors about – his detractors then found their opening. Of the land purchases from the company during the boom of 1882, almost 60 per cent were defaulted. Serious allegations were soon made about purported irregularities in some of the Winnipeg land sales. These allegations originated with Smith and his partisans, including Sandford Fleming, a resident Canadian director of the company, who, like Smith, divided his loyalties between the HBC and the Canadian Pacific Railway.

The company's deputy governor, Sir John Rose, was dispatched from London to investigate the claims and the state of the company's business. Rose had served for two years in cabinet as John A. Macdonald's minister of finance before entering private banking in London. In his report, Rose expressed concern over the Hudson's Bay Company's lack of competitiveness in the general trade. He observed independent traders, operating out of tents, responding rapidly to shifting demands for goods. They telegraphed suppliers in St Paul, or even Chicago, and could fill orders in a matter of days. By contrast, the company's procedures were cumbersome. Wrote Rose: 'Many of the goods sent from England on requisitions prepared the previous year were unsuitable and a great demand existed for articles that had either not been ordered at all, or in insufficient quantities.'[22] These were precisely the sorts of deficiencies that Brydges had been fighting with Grahame to correct.

With respect to the allegations of impropriety, Rose's investigation resulted in exoneration for Brydges. Rose concluded: 'We ... trace all these reports & complaints ... to Donald Smith. He has evidently a great enmity towards [Brydges].'[23] The *Dictionary of National Biography* describes Smith as 'a good hater,' and he well earned that reputation. Nevertheless, at Smith's urging, the HBC established a subcommittee for Canada in 1884. The two members of the subcommittee appointed were none other than Smith and Fleming. All Brydges's reports and correspondence with London henceforth had to be copied to them, and key decisions were delayed while Brydges awaited their input. The system was unwieldy and worked against the company's business interests. In time, Brydges complained that Smith 'has every appearance of a desire to worry me out.' Smith's harassment of Brydges was indeed relentless. When Smith – by then the company's largest shareholder – assumed the governorship in 1889, a letter was dispatched to Brydges the same day. This correspondence informed Brydges of the company's intention to dispense with his services. Before the dismissal was formalized, however, Brydges was dead of a heart attack.

The Reluctant Retailers

At the time of the establishment of the Canadian subcommittee, an important administrative change was also made. In 1884 Joseph Wrigley was sent to Winnipeg as the HBC's first trade commissioner. His task was to shore up, as far as possible, the fur trade, but also, notably, to improve the general trade that had never received the attention it might have under James Grahame. (Grahame's resignation had been requested and received.) Like Brydges, and in contrast to Grahame, Wrigley came from outside the organization. It was immediately apparent to him that, despite its recent efforts, the company had failed to compete as a general retailer. It was not the North-West's leading retailer; its general resistance to capital spending in favour of cosmetic changes to its old posts, and its cumbersome ordering and supply procedures, had ceded business to upstart competition.

Even the company's three-year-old flagship store in Winnipeg was suffering. To begin with, its location was described as 'unfortunate, being away from the busiest part of the City' – the busiest spot being the corner of Portage Avenue and Main Street. This failing was only partly offset by the fact that the area it was situated in was Winnipeg's answer to the 'West End of London, and in the neighbourhood of the Government Officer, Lieutenant-Governor's residence, and the private houses of the best inhabitants.'[24]

The store was filled to the rafters with luxury merchandise – 'carpets, lace & champagne' – purchased during the 1882 boom. It was then unable to sell these goods when the economy faltered. Employees had failed to leave the old, less formal ways of trade behind and were only now being forced to adhere to strict new rules that forbade singing, whistling, reading newspapers, and gossiping. The workers were now also required to dust the shelves daily. Moreover, the informal manner in which credit had previously been granted was ended. Previously, credit had been given out at the discretion of clerks and not always charged to the customer's account. Even sales of wine, beer, and hard liquor were decreasing, a fact in part attributed to 'the undrinkable state in which these articles were being supplied to customers,' a result of freezing in the cellar.[25] Evidently a small problem of unregulated visits by non-employees to the wine cellar was reported, and the apparently too-generous distribution of 'samples' of liquor, cigars, and tobacco was curtailed under the new rules.

The company's retailing troubles were raised at the committee level, and Wrigley was ordered to review the entire system. He worked to streamline the company's procurement and supply systems, improve accounting procedures, and direct a limited incursion into prairie towns. But Wrigley's efforts were set back by the North-West rebellion in 1885, during which company stores were looted and buildings were burned. Unease after the uprising also seriously damaged the economy of a region already depressed. Adding to the problems were the findings of the Royal Commission on Rebellion Losses Claims, which drastically reduced the company's compensation claim. In the end, the most important achievement by Wrigley – and his last act as trade commissioner – was to oversee the company's 1891 purchase of the Calgary, Lethbridge, and Fort Macleod stores in Alberta. These stores were owned by its competitor, I.G. Baker and Sons, mercantile and grocery purveyor, headquartered in Fort Benton, Montana. The company had in this way finally acquired a large retail store in most of the leading prairie cities.

In 1891 C.C. Chipman was appointed Wrigley's successor as trade commissioner, and shortly afterwards his title was altered to commissioner when, as an economy measure, management of the Land Department was merged with that of the other business. Chipman also had the considerable advantage of enjoying Smith's support. He quickly moved to reform the company's administration and reduce the labour force. In an analysis in 1891 of the Victoria operation, for example, Chipman found a 'deplorable state of affairs.' Retail competition had been growing 'more and more keen,' thereby reducing profits. Competitors had met this reduced profit by 'increasing their turn-over by energetically pushing their business, and by reducing their expenses.' The HBC, on the other hand, had 'been showing a reduced turn-over with smaller profits and the same or greater expenses.'[26] Chipman expressed surprise to find no fewer than eight distinct administrative offices in the same building in Victoria. They were:

The Assistant Commissioner's Office
Accountant's Office
General Office
Saleshop Office
Depot Office
Depot Invoice Office
Depot Buyers' Office
Storeman's Office

Wrote Chipman: 'To put the matter in a nutshell, the Company have been keeping up several well-manned establishments under the same roof, with a scattered and disorganized staff, altogether out of proportion to that employed by other firms doing double the amount of business. With what result? A great duplication of work, unnecessary expense, and drawback to business.'[27] He suggested an immediate reorganization that would save nearly $6,000 in salaries at the Victoria operation alone. (See Exhibit 1.)

Moreover, Chipman continued Wrigley's efforts to improve the purchasing and transportation systems for the stores. He secured exclusive licences to sell brands like Hiram Walker Whiskey and Dewar's Scotch Whisky, with the result that the company boasted a competitive advantage in liquor sales. Markets were found for other items as well, including tea, carpets, off-the-rack clothing, shoes, and groceries. Still, despite Smith's support, Chipman was unable to convince the London committee of the need for greater capital investment. In 1894 he had argued that 'one of the greatest necessities of a successful Saleshop business is that it shall be conducted in a suitable and modern Building, and that it is further necessary that well assorted stocks must always be carried ... it follows that if the Company intends to successfully carry on the Saleshop trade, even more capital than is at present employed may have to be furnished ... A careful review of the past shows that when expenditure upon a building has been too limited at the outset, or when

Exhibit 1
Chipman's staff reorganization proposal

Staff at present In Westn. Dept. Office		Proposed Combined Staff	
A. Accountant,	2,190.00	A. Accountant,	2,190.00
B. Cashier,	1,080.00	B. Cashier,	1,080.00
1st Clerk,	600.00	C. Book-keeper,	960.00
F. 2nd Clerk,	480.00	D. Customs Clerk, etc	1,020.00
3rd Clerk,	420.00	E. Invoice Clerk,	840.00
G. Shorthand writer,	600.00	F. Clerk,	480.00
	5,370.00	G. Shorthand writer,	600.00
		H. Head Salesman,	1,320.00
		I. 2nd Salesman,	720.00
In Depot Office, &c.,		J. Warehouseman,	900.00
Head Clerk,	1,200.00	K. Asst. Warehouseman	600.00
Asst. Clerk,	480.00	L. Cellarman,	720.00
D. Customs Clerk,	1,020.00	M. Packer,	720.00
M. Head Packer,	720.00	N. 2nd Packer,	600.00
N. Asst. Packer,	600.00		
J. Warehouseman,	1,200.00	**TOTAL**	**$12,750.00**
K. Asst. Ware.,	600.00	**14** employees	
Asst. Ware.,	420.00		
	6,240.00		

In. Saleshop Office, etc.,	
Invoice Clerk,	900.00
I. Invoice Clerk,	720.00
C. Book-keeper,	960.00
H. Head Salesman,	1,320.00
E. 2nd Salesman,	840.00
3rd Salesman,	540.00
4th Salesman,	540.00
L. Cellarman,	720.00
	6,540.00

TOTAL	**$18,150.00**
22 employees	

Source: HBCA, A. 12/35, fo.67–80, London Inward Correspondence, Report from C.C. Chipman on the Current State of the Hudson's Bay Company, 9 Sept. 1891.

work has been done piecemeal, the ultimate cost to the Company has been increased, and in the meantime business has suffered.'[28]

Still, the committee resisted the idea of greater capital investment, since it was under pressure from shareholders who wanted to concentrate on land sales. Far from receiving support for a program of investment in the retail trade, Chipman instead faced calls to scale down or abandon the retail trade unless he could produce immediate profits. In his study of the retail trade during Chipman's tenure, Paul Nigol argues: 'The Company's conservative use of capital not only retarded the growth of the Company's saleshop business during the 1890s, it also enabled competitors to establish themselves.'[29]

Land Development versus Retail

This conservatism pervaded all of the HBC's business during Smith's tenure as governor. Despite the shareholder interest in land sales, it is an understatement to say that land sales were not aggressively pursued under his regime. Staffing was reduced in the Land Department, which cut expenses from $36,160 in 1888 to $15,610 in 1898. Whereas the CPR marketed enthusiastically to pursue sales, the HBC drastically cut its own marketing efforts. All through the final years of the nineteenth century, expenses for printing and advertising ran at one-seventh the level they had been during the 1882 boom. The CPR understood how its main business – the railway – would benefit from the settlement of western Canada. The HBC, which might have seen similar advantage to its retail operations, preferred to let its vast estates lay fallow.

Smith's strategy was 'to maintain as large a proportion of the land as possible for sale in a period of prosperity.'[30] Consequently, he did not lobby the Dominion government to speed up its surveys in the North-West, since once allocated in title these lands would have added to the company's tax burden. Smith calculated that, after CPR and crown lands were occupied by settlers, demand – and hence the value of the company's reserve lands – would grow. According to historian John S. Galbraith, these policies 'enabled the Hudson's Bay Company to reap maximum profits in the twentieth century from the tremendous increase of immigration to the Prairie Provinces and the growth of the wheat economy.' The numbers support Smith's strategy. The price of company lands declined throughout the 1890s, dipping to $4.82 per acre in 1898. The turnaround began in 1899, and by 1902 the *Economist* opined that the HBC was demonstrating 'remarkable vitality in its old age.'[31] This was reflected in the company's bottom line, and in the dividends paid, both of which began to soar. By 1913, the average price per acre had risen to $21.06 as hundreds of thousands of settlers poured into the prairie provinces.

However, the strategy that had worked for land sales did not work for the retail trade. The failure to make a large investment of capital left the HBC vulnerable to aggressive new retailers that sprung up in communities throughout the North-West. This threat became most obvious when, in July 1905, the T. Eaton Company opened a state-of-the-art retail store on Winnipeg's Portage Avenue and launched an aggressive distribution of catalogues.

The challenge from Eaton's in Winnipeg – the heart of the Bay empire – would prove a harbinger of future events. Although the HBC enjoyed a dramatic increase in short-term profits and dividends as a result of booming land sales and profits, it struggled for the next century in its new core business of retail.

Postscript

The need for a new edifice in Winnipeg had already been identified. However, even after the Eaton's store opened, the HBC's response was merely to paper over some cracks in its existing store, now two decades old. Chipman at first assured his restraint-minded masters that, while Eaton's 'undoubtedly diverted [a] considerable [amount] of the shifting trade … the general effect has not been such as to give alarm.' However, Chipman was soon advocating the construction of a new store in Winnipeg's commercial core. It was not until 1926 that a new company store opened in that city.

At the company's 1908 annual meeting, some shareholders objected to the failure to develop attractive stores that would generate more customers and sales. Smith was now referred to as Baron Strathcona after being elevated to the peerage in the British House of Lords in 1897. He was also serving as Canada's high commissioner to the Court of St James. Strathcona said at the meeting: 'The name of the Hudson's Bay Company is an advertisement of itself, and our stores do not require so many embellishments.' In fact, despite Chipman's efforts, the company's stores remained bereft of the means to compete with their aggressive young rivals.

Change had to come, and it gradually did. In 1907 Leonard Cunliffe, who had helped finance Harrods department store in London, replaced

Sandford Fleming on the committee. In 1909, Richard Burbidge, managing director of Harrods, was enlisted to travel to western Canada to report on the company's retail business. Burbidge was appalled by what he discovered. He concluded that the company was vulnerable to its competition because of its outdated merchandising and retention of old stock – which was turning over at a rate only once every twelve to forty-eight months. Burbidge's report stated that the company must 'bring its methods up-to-date to meet keen competition in Canada.' It was diplomatically worded, but, according to Peter C. Newman in his epic account of the company, *The Merchant Princes*, there was an 'unmistakable subliminal message that Lord Strathcona was running the Hudson's Bay Company into the ground.'[32] Even his biographer, in an otherwise laudatory account, concedes that Strathcona had 'allowed railways, politics, diplomacy and a myriad other interests to take his eye off the HBC ball.'[33]

A sobering assessment of Strathcona was later written by Philip Chester, who became the HBC's first general manager for Canada in 1930. Strathcona, wrote Chester, 'accentuated [the policy] of taking every possible dollar out of Canada, as he apparently believed the Deed of Surrender committed the Company to a slow, lingering death, which would come about when the acreage it had received as part of the purchase price of its monopoly had been sold.'[34]

Not everyone was prepared to close up the shop. An alliance of city of London financiers agitated for an increase in the number of outstanding company shares. At the 1910 annual meeting, four of these financiers were elected to the committee, including William Mackenzie, president of the Canadian Northern Railway, who became the committee's first ever Canadian-born member. Burbidge, too, was given a seat, and his brother Herbert was appointed to the position of saleshop commissioner. With the responsibilities of the company's senior officers again divided, C.C. Chipman became land commissioner, before 'being retired' from the service a short time later.

Strathcona had relaxed his grip. Newman writes of this new leadership: 'Almost at once they got down to the business of transforming the Hudson's Bay Company into a modern corporation.' The company's stock was split ten-for-one and its capitalization doubled through issuance of new preferred shares, raising £1 million for capital investment in its stores.[35]

Under Strathcona's leadership, Chester argued, the HBC had forfeited the opportunity to become the country's great mercantile company.

Indeed, had his strategy been prosecuted to the bitter end, the company might have forfeited its very existence with the sale of its last acre. But Strathcona succumbed before the company did. Still governor, he died in January 1914 at the age of ninety-four. He had become a major philanthropist during his final decades yet retained immense wealth at the time of his death. Lord Strathcona's estate was valued at almost $29 million after he died.

Suggested Questions

1. Diversified firms need to adjust their portfolio of business periodically. How should the HBC have changed it's portfolio? How could value have been added for shareholders?
2. The principals of the Hudson's Bay Company knew that the 200-year-old fur trade was a mature industry. The sale of its vast lands in western Canada gave the company not only cash but real estate and all kinds of opportunities, yet almost four decades elapsed before it decided on what business it wanted to be in. Why did the HBC take so long to decide to enter the retail business and miss so many opportunities along the way? Was entering the retail business a good decision?
3. Was the powerful presence of Lord Strathcona an advantage or disadvantage in terms of the long-term success of the HBC? Would such behaviour be possible today?

Suggested Readings

'Donald Alexander Smith.' *Dictionary of Canadian Biography*, www.biographi.ca.

http://www.hbc.com/hbcheritage/Our History.

Newman, Peter C. *Merchant Princes: Company of Adventurers*. Vol. 3. Toronto: Viking 1991.

Porter, Michael. 'From Competitive Advantage to Corporate Structure.' *Harvard Business Review*, 65, no. 3 (1987).

NOTES

1 Resolution 68 (of the deed of surrender, 1869) had dealt with an intercolonial railway connecting the Maritimes with central Canada. Resolution

69 read: 'The communications with the North-Western Territory [Rupert's Land], and the improvements required for the development of the trade of the Great West with the seaboard, are regarded by this conference as subjects of the highest importance to the federated provinces, and shall be prosecuted at the earliest possible period that the state of the finances will permit.'

2 Hudson's Bay Company Archives (HBCA) A. 11/100 fo. 68–91, Report to Sir Stafford Northcote from Cyril Graham, 15 March 1871.
3 John S. Galbraith, 'Land Policies of the Hudson's Bay Company, 1870–1913,' *Canadian Historical Review*, 32, no. 1 (1951): 1.
4 HBCA A.2/4, n.f., General Court Minute Books, 26 Nov. 1872.
5 Alexander Reford, 'Donald Alexander Smith,' *Dictionary of National Biography* (www.biographi.ca).
6 Alan Wilson, Introduction, in Hartwell Bowsfield, *The Letters of Charles John Brydges, 1879–1882* (Winnipeg: Hudson's Bay Record Society 1977), xxxv.
7 Ibid..
8 Michael Bliss, *Northern Enterprise: Five Centuries of Canadian Business* (Toronto: McClelland and Stewart 1987), 222.
9 Donna McDonald, *Lord Strathcona: A Biography of Donald Alexander Smith* (Toronto: Dundurn Press 2002), 253.
10 Ibid., 331.
11 Shirlee A. Smith, '"A Desire to Worry Me Out": Donald Smith's Harassment of Charles Brydges, 1879–1889,' *The Beaver*, December 1987–January 1988.
12 Michael Bliss, *Northern Enterprise: Five Centuries of Canadian Business* (Toronto: McClelland and Stewart 1987), 195.
13 W. Fraser Rae, *Newfoundland to Manitoba* (New York: G.B. Putnam's Sons 1881), 161.
14 The Union Pacific was completed two years later, making it the longest railway in the world.
15 A.A. den Otter, 'The Hudson's Bay Company's Prairie Transportation Problem,' in John E. Foster, *The Developing West* (Edmonton: University of Alberta Press 1983), 42.
16 Ibid., 43.
17 Newman, *Merchant Princes*, 86.
18 Smith, '"A Desire to Worry Me Out,"' 7.
19 Robert Oleson, 'The Past Hundred Years,' *The Beaver*, spring 1970, 19.
20 Paul C. Nigol, 'Efficiency and Economy: Commissioner C.C. Chipman and the Hudson's Bay Company, 1891–1911,' MA thesis, Department of History, University of Manitoba, 52.

21 Newman, *Merchant Princes*, 89.
22 Eleanor Jean Stardom, *A Stranger to the Fur Trade: Joseph Wrigley and the Transformation of the Hudson's Bay Company, 1884–1891* (Winnipeg: University of Winnipeg Rupert's Land Research Centre 1995), 16.
23 Shirlee A. Smith, '"A Desire to Worry Me Out,"' 8.
24 HBCA, A. 21/35, fo. 67–80, London Inward Correspondence, Letter from Thomas R. Smith on the Company's General Trade throughout the Red River, 8 July 1884.
25 Ibid.
26 HBCA, A. 12/35, fo. 67–80, London Inward Correspondence, Report from C.C. Chipman on the Current State of the Hudson's Bay Company, 9 Sept. 1891.
27 Ibid.
28 HBCA, A. 12/38, fo. 374–80, London Inward Correspondence, Memorandum of Mr. Skinner's Letter to Chipman, 12 June 1894.
29 Nigol, 'Efficiency and Economy,' 55.
30 Galbraith, 'Land Policies,' 15.
31 *The Economist*, 28 June 1902, 1014–15.
32 Newman, *Merchant Princes*, 159.
33 McDonald, *Lord Strathcona*, 470.
34 Newman, *Merchant Princes*, 159.
35 Ibid., 161.

CASE 3
Canada's First Great Manufacturing Enterprise: The Story of Massey-Harris

JOHN TURLEY EWART and STEWART MELANSON, with guidance from JOE MARTIN

In 2003 the condo market in Toronto took off. Buildings made of glass and steel sprouted in the city core, reflecting the affluent, urbane lifestyle that individuals, young couples, and empty nesters aspired to. Low interest rates and a strong economy put those lifestyles within reach for many. Downtown condos opened doors onto a new and thriving city culture that was transforming the skyline and the way people lived. Open-concept floor plans and loft-style units, offering different ways to use space, became increasingly popular. So did reclaiming buildings from Toronto's past. Those who wanted to live in Toronto's core but eschewed modern glass towers found refuge in low-rise, red and brown brick buildings that once housed the city's industrial workshops and their managers. Converting these buildings to chic condo units was demanding. Successfully re-engineering and integrating the latest home conveniences into buildings one hundred years old or older was a testament to the cutting-edge thinking and technology that drove the condo boom.

That thinking and technology saved one of the most important buildings from Toronto's manufacturing past. Completed in 1880, the Massey-Harris headquarters at 915 King Street West was in its day a measure of the change transforming the way people worked in Toronto. It stood at the heart of a much larger manufacturing enterprise. Gas was used to light the many buildings linked to the head office. A sprinkler system, likely the first in the country, protected against fire; steam elevators carried equipment and materials up and down the four floors of the main manufacturing building where tradesman, divided into specialties, made almost all the parts of the farm equipment assembled at the Massey Works. It was the first factory of its kind in Canada –

small by the standards of the large manufacturing plants that thrived in larger U.S. cities such as Chicago, but still an important step forward for Canadian business.

The factory buildings have been lost, but the command centre, the headquarters, where one of the greatest business ventures in Canada flourished, has survived as loft condominiums – once again emerging on the leading edge of change in the city, this time in housing.

Massey's Entrepreneurial Roots (1802–67)

The road to 915 King Street West began in 1802 when Daniel Massey, Sr emigrated from New York State with his wife Rebecca and their children. They settled near Cobourg, a small port town on Lake Ontario,[1] and began the arduous process of building a new life in Upper Canada, a small British colony with just 46,000 souls working its land. They brought some furniture for comfort, two oxen, farm tools, and brute strength to cut down hardwood trees, uproot stumps, and remove rocks and boulders. The Masseys, like 95 per cent of the settlers in Upper Canada, bet their futures on farming.[2] That bet paid off for their young son, Daniel Jr.

Daniel Jr Spots Opportunity

At the age of nineteen most young men in Upper Canada were living on their family's farm, learning how to work the land and hoping that, come their twenty-first birthday, they might be able to find land of their own and start on the path to independence. Not Daniel Jr. In 1817, at the age of nineteen, Daniel Jr recognized an opportunity that had not been available to his father in 1802 when the family came to Upper Canada. The population was growing quickly and the demand for virgin pine and other wood in the forests around Cobourg made clearing land a profitable venture, one made possible by the arrival of men from Ireland and Scotland looking for immediate work. Daniel Sr had been less lucky – when he cleared the land for his farm there was no market for his trees and he burned them.

Daniel Jr seized the chance this market offered and at nineteen left the family farm, rented nearby land, hired labourers – at times he employed as many as 100 men – and cleared it, selling the trees at enough profit to buy the land which he then farmed until he found a buyer. It was a process he repeated often to his own good fortune.

By 1820 Daniel Jr had made enough money to marry his childhood sweetheart, Lucinda Bradley. A year later, their first child, a daughter, was born, followed in 1823 by a son, Hart Almerrin. They had nine surviving children altogether, but of those Hart appears to have developed the closest relationship with his father; by age seven, Hart had the trust of his father and was already skilled in the handling of a team of horses.

During the 1820s, with his young family growing, Daniel Jr continued in the business of creating ready-made farms for new immigrant families. Yet he was clear-sighted enough to realize that change was coming, that the market for his trees was declining as was the number of land buyers. Once he had twelve years and 1,200 acres of cleared land behind him, Daniel Jr became full-time farmer, taking a keen interest in the labour-saving tools that the budding industrial revolution was beginning to generate – implements that he knew could bring vast change to a world that still relied on farming tools which, as he told a Cobourg paper, were 'the same as those used in the days of the Pharaohs.'[3]

One such device that promised a new age in agriculture was the American thresher, a machine that was operated by twelve men and used to separate grain from husks to help with the wheat harvest. Daniel Jr, a frequent visitor to family and friends in New York State across Lake Ontario, learned of this machine in 1830 and decided to import it to Upper Canada.[4] While a step forward, reducing the amount of labour required at harvest, this first thresher did not produce the results Daniel Jr had hoped for.

A decade later his ideas to improve the lot of farmers took shape in his small machine shop on his farm where he fabricated field implements for tilling the soil, seeding it, and harvesting crops. By this time, Daniel Jr was perfecting his skills as a machinist, fixing equipment and outfitting his neighbours with tools he made or imported. Although economic conditions deteriorated for farmers in the 1840s, Daniel's sideline of making labour-saving farm tools paid off.

The Launch of the Newcastle Foundry and Machine Manufactory Company

Crop failure, economic hardship, and famine in Europe, especially Ireland, led to an influx of impoverished immigrants to the New World in the 1840s seeking relief and a better life. In Britain, lawmakers were embroiled in a fundamental debate about that country's Corn Laws, tariffs on wheat that were designed primarily to give protection to British growers and members of the British Empire over foreign countries such as the United States and Germany. Canadian wheat producers

generally benefited from British protection against American growers until 1831, when the British government removed all tariffs on U.S.
wheat shipped using the St Lawrence. When extensive crop failures
hit Britain in 1845 and the price exacted on Britons' living standards
proved more than most were willing to bear to protect British and colonial farmers, the tide against the Corn Laws grew. In 1846 the British
government finally repealed them, leaving farmers in the Province of
Canada to compete on the merits of their wheat and its price against
Americans and the whole-wheat producing world.

Growing competition for Britain's wheat market brought hard times
to Canadian farmers and poor harvests in 1847 did not buoy prospects
for the future. Yet the economic malaise facing the Province of Canada
that year did not deter Daniel Jr from making the most important decision of his life – abandoning the farm and buying a nearby foundry
that had gone bankrupt. The purchase allowed for the launching of a
new farm-implements-making firm, one that could count on Daniel Jr's
experience along with some help from a new tariff regime imposed by
the government of Upper Canada on all imported farm machinery, a
move inspired less by protectionist ideals than by the dire need of the
government to raise revenues.[5]

Hence, in 1847, Daniel Jr bought a small foundry at Bond Head, near
Newcastle, Ontario, and sold his farm to his twenty-four-year-old son
Hart. Two years later, the foundry was moved to Newcastle and the
firm named the Newcastle Foundry and Machine Manufactory Company.[6] From there, the new company supplied the modest but expanding market for farm implements by buying manufacturing licences for
equipment designed in the United States that, if made south of the border and imported, would have faced a tariff. Daniel Jr limited capital
expense to process innovation to increase efficiencies in production,
rather than spending precious money on research.[7] He did, however,
make some modest improvements to the American-designed machinery so it would better suit Canadian conditions. This strategy proved
enough for the company to secure its footing in a market that was sure
to become more competitive in time as farmers looked for ever more
efficient ways to grow, harvest, and transport crops.

A New Generation

As the first half of the nineteenth century drew to its close, Daniel Jr had
seen great changes in the land he came to as a boy of four. The population was nearing half-a-million and farming was no longer an enter-

prise that had changed little from the days of the Pharaohs. That was made plain with the start of his company, which soon had to expand after moving to Newcastle in order to meet mounting orders for his implements. Daniel purchased another foundry nearby, employing an additional ten men. Despite the additional help, he struggled to keep up with the orders and with his workload. Demand was strong, perhaps too much so. By 1850, the strain was taking its toll on Daniel Jr, by then fifty-two years old. He called on his most trusted son, Hart, to come on board and be groomed to take over the family business.[8]

As his father's health faltered, Hart abandoned farming, just as his father had. In 1851 he moved to Newcastle with his wife and children. In 1852 the company name was changed to H.A. Massey and Company, in recognition of the new leader. Hart assumed effective management in 1854, taking full ownership in 1855, a year before his father's death.[9] Workers at the foundries had become accustomed to Daniel's leadership style. They viewed him as a hard working, hands-on manager who was pious and frowned upon all liquor. Hart Massey displayed many of his father's characteristics, such as a commitment to hard work, but he would put his own stamp on the firm's management, bringing to bear the formal education his father lacked and a new salesmanship born of his own self-confidence.[10]

Hart proved more of a risk taker too. He was constantly seeking the latest machinery to import and, in so doing, pre-empted his competitors. Like his father, Hart also oversaw improvements to tailor the imported designs to suit the needs of Canadian farmers and worked to ensure that his firm developed a reputation not only for innovation but also for excellence and quality. Massey's association with innovation was certainly advanced by the importation of machines such as the revolutionary Ketchum mower in 1851 and the Burrell reaper. In 1855 the reaper and mower were combined into a single machine called the Manny Combined Hand Rake Reaper Mower. Hart was the first to bring the invention to Canada. This reaper could cut from eight to ten acres a day, and it became extremely popular with farmers in Canada.[11]

Several significant events took place around the time of Hart Massey's ascension to the helm of his father's firm. By 1856, Cobourg was linked by rail to Montreal and Toronto via the Grand Trunk Railway. This gave the Massey firm a more reliable means to transport its wares to dealers and its own supplies to its Newcastle factory, an advantage it would need as it tried to keep at bay a new rival, the Harris Company of Brantford, Ontario, that entered the field in 1857.

The development in 1842 of Red Fife, a hardy variety of wheat suited to Canada's climate – by Scottish immigrant David Fife – and its wide use by the 1850s made farming more profitable and helped expand the market for Hart's wares. Like Hart Massey, farmers, fishermen, timber firms, and others across British North America sought ways to expand markets for their goods in the wake of Britain's repeal of the Corn Laws and the growing importance of exports to the United States. New Brunswick was the first of the colonies to launch meetings in 1849 about negotiating a trade pact with the Americans. By 1850, limited reciprocity was in effect between the United States and New Brunswick, Nova Scotia, and Prince Edward Island. Four years later, a much broader reciprocity deal included the Province of Canada.

Scarcity of Labour

These events were fortuitous for Massey, since, with agriculture now more attractive, farmers had more incentive to use capital to purchase productivity-enhancing equipment. Further, despite an influx of immigrant labour in the 1840s, the next decade saw the development of labour shortages. This lack of manpower created a need for labour-saving equipment. The labour shortages were due in part to the manpower needs of rail construction, but they were also a reflection of the vastness of the land and its small population.

In fact, the need to save on labour seemed a phenomenon peculiar to North America. In Europe, land was scarce and labour abundant, such that farmers attempted to make the most of their land. In Canada and the United States, where land was abundant and labour scarce, farmers attempted to make the most of their labour.[12] This development, in addition to the opening up of attractive markets for produce, helped spur a flurry of activity in the production of farming implements, with most of the innovation originating in the United States.

The innovation taking place in the United States led to the rapid development of new machines and patents. The rivalry between manufacturers/implement makers was intense and patent wars ensued, with rivals taking each other to court repeatedly. Fortunately for Canadian implement makers, the American firms readily licensed their inventions to them since they were more preoccupied with one another than with foreigners.

A Localized Market

Canadian implement producers also had an advantage on account of the localized nature of industry in the mid-nineteenth century. Transportation between regions was difficult in British North America and played against the forces of concentration and foreign competition in the farm-implement market which emerged after the Canadian Pacific Railway was completed in 1885.[13] With the expansion of rail linkages, the advantages enjoyed by local producers diminished as competition became both national and international.[14] Consequently, the Massey firm grew largely unimpeded by competition from the United States prior to the late nineteenth century and would likely have thrived without the added benefit generated by a 15 per cent duty imposed by the Province of Canada on manufactured foreign imports.[15]

Reciprocity Treaty of 1854

The United States wasn't deeply interested in trade with Upper Canada. It was drawn to a reciprocity trade deal – one where parties would agree on a mutual list of goods that they would trade between themselves tariff free – with British North America primarily serving as a means of winning access to new fishing rights in the waters off the shore of Britain's Maritime colonies. The deal that was eventually signed allowed for the free trade of largely primary, non-manufactured items such as fish, grain, meat, breadstuffs, timber, and minerals. Duties remained on manufactured goods, while special provisions for fishing rights and joint use of the Welland Canal were agreed to. The 15 per cent duty remained on U.S. manufactured goods imported into British North America – the Galt Tariff of 1858 was later raised to a duty of 20 per cent.

The first year of reciprocity brought a 96 per cent increase in duty-free trade items between the United States and British North America. That kind of growth was not sustainable, but, by the time the trade deal was terminated in 1866, trade to the United States had increased from 40.7 per cent of exports to 69.2 per cent.[16] Whether this increase in trade was due largely to the reciprocity deal or to more fundamental causes, such as growth in the U.S. economy and its impact on demand for goods, as well as the demand for food and materials from British North America during the U.S. Civil War, is a matter that scholars debate. For Hart Massey, the reason did not matter as much as the effect. For, whenever farming did well, his firm's prospects improved. Moreover, the Reciprocity Treaty allowed the Massey firm to import natural products, such as timber from the United States, free of duty. Timber was an important component of Hart's farm-implement business. His freedom to choose between Canadian and American sources weakened local suppliers' power and reduced his input costs. Further, coal was included in the treaty and this benefited Massey in the sale of steam-powered implements that relied on coal – if farmers could access coal more cheaply, they would be better able to afford Massey machinery.

Despite Britain's and the Province of Canada's move towards a less protectionist stance, the colonies still received significant advantages from this protectionism. British North America enjoyed lower prices for iron and steel imported from Britain, compared to the prices faced by U.S. buyers.[17] At the time, Britain had considerably better quality iron and steel as well as more efficient manufacturing processes compared to U.S. producers, placing 'British Steel' in high demand. Both reciprocity and protectionist impulses proved to be advantageous to Hart as he moved his family firm forward in a rapidly changing era.

Marketing Massey

The Civil War resulted in sustained high prices for wheat, driving more farmers into wheat growing. For Hart Massey's firm, which built implements designed for harvesting wheat, this enhanced demand presented an opportunity to grow market share and Hart seized upon it, developing innovative promotional campaigns and building sophisticated distribution channels for his equipment.

The efficiency of the Massey mower and reaper, for example, was heavily advertised along with other items in a Massey sales catalogue that Hart launched in 1862.[18] His publication contained numerous illustrations highlighting the savings and convenience generated by Massey machines. Moreover, Hart's catalogue established a direct link between manufacturer and consumer, a move that defied the usual commercial practice in which retailers acted as brokers between producers and consumers.

Hart's ability to supply and service Massey products was of equal importance. During the 1860s, Hart deemed it essential to establish distribution channels, using railways to move equipment quickly to local shops run by agents of the Massey firm who offered sales and service. Moreover, he expanded Massey's market by extending credit to his customers so they could buy an ever-increasing assortment of Massey goods using three-year instalment plans to pay for them.[19] Hart's expansion efforts were geared to the surging number of farms in Ontario, which climbed from 113,984 in 1861 to 172,258 in 1871.[20]

By 1867, Hart Massey had transformed the company from a small foundry to a large, mature, and sophisticated operation. Similarly, Alanson Harris had also been very successful in Brantford. Both the Massey and Harris firms were well ahead of their Canadian rivals, and they were about to become part of a larger political and economic experiment – the Dominion of Canada.

Canada's First Great Manufacturing Enterprise (1867–1910)

The First Dominion Day

On 1 July 1867 Cobourg was abuzz. The small harbour community on the north shore of Lake Ontario was celebrating the birth of a nation. The Province of Canada was no more. It was now split into two provinces, Ontario and Quebec, and joined with two Maritime provinces, Nova Scotia and New Brunswick. Together, they comprised a new federation some 3.5 million strong with a central government based in Ottawa.

As the Cobourg party dragged into the evening, forty-four-year-old Hart Massey was likely pondering his family business and what this new Dominion of Canada would mean for the company's future, one that was made uncertain after the United States had abrogated the 1854 reciprocity deal in 1866.[21] He had many options to consider. Should he enter the U.S. market to bypass rising tariffs on the part of the Americans? Should he try to export to Europe? Should he focus attention on domestic rivalry, and, in particular, keep his chief rival, the Harris Company, at bay?

Export (1867–90)

Hart Massey began thinking seriously about markets beyond Canada's borders when his harvesting equipment was chosen by the Toronto Industrial Exhibition to represent Canada at the 1867 International Exposition in France. Massey went on to win two gold medals at the exposition. The first was a testament to his salesmanship – a medal for his exhibit. The second was a measure of his ability as a manufacturer, for the award recognized the excellent performance of Massey's harvesters. Soon afterwards, Massey filled his first European order, selling more than twenty mowers and reapers to German customers, making

Hart Massey the first Canadian manufacturer to export Canadian-made machinery abroad.

That move abroad would not have been possible without the rise of steam-powered ships with screw propellers that cut down the time and cost involved in traversing the ocean. In fact, Massey would later find that exporting to Europe was cheaper than supplying the farms of the Canadian prairies (even after direct rail links were established): 'A factor contributing to the development of export markets prior to 1890 was the seasonality of the Canadian market, especially in the remote Canadian West, and the continued high cost of reaching that market. The latter is seen in the cheapness of ocean freight rates from Eastern Canada to England as compared with the long rail haul to Western Canada.'[22] Europe had developed a need for farm machinery in order to feed its growing urban centres more efficiently. European farm-implement makers were less experienced then Massey and had lower-quality products. All of these factors provided export opportunities for the Massey firm.

Nineteen years after the International Exposition in France, Hart attended the Indian and Colonial Exhibition in London, England, where they put the products Massey had to offer on show. The reception from the English was cold, and, except for the response of one Scottish farmer, William Ford, the whole venture may have proved a failure. Ford liked Massey's light binders and ordered six of them for the year's harvest. The Scotland trial was a great success. Ford soon ordered forty more binders and became Massey's agent in Britain. By 1888, Hart's son Walter had set up a Massey agency in Australia and sales on the European continent were going very well. In fact, Massey products were being shipped to Asia Minor, Africa, Germany, Russia, South America, Jamaica, and most British colonies.[23] However, archrival Harris soon followed Massey to Europe, and, although Massey had gained an advantage by being there first and maintained a lead, Harris was never too far behind.

Charles Takes the Helm

In 1870 Hart Massey reorganized the company, renamed it the Massey Manufacturing Company, and capitalized it with $50,000 of his own money, keeping the firm private. Hart named himself president and brought Charles Albert Massey, his twenty-two-year-old-son, on board as the vice-president and superintendent. A year later, Hart's health began to fail. He decided it was time to retire and leave the daily challenges to Charles. With their three younger children in tow, Hart and his wife Eliza moved to Cleveland, Ohio. Charles took over the reins of Massey Manufacturing.

The Move to Toronto

Charles concluded in 1878 that the demand for Massey machines had outstripped the capacity of the Newcastle plant and the workforce of the small rural town. Orders for the Canadian-designed Massey Harvester numbered 500, but Massey was able to produce only 356 Harvesters by running double shifts. Charles began talking about a new factory, and Cobourg vied to be the site, but it was Toronto that won out, with its larger pool of labour, bank head offices, and myriad railway connections.[24]

Hart returned from Cleveland to help Charles with the building of the new Toronto plant on six acres of land. Construction began in 1879 and was completed in 1880. The result was the most modern farm-implements manufacturing plant in the British Empire, located at 915 King Street West.

Domestic Rivalry and Consolidation

One of the company's concerns was the growing number of Canadian farm-implement makers who operated on minimal profit margins. By the early 1870s, a total of 252 farm-implement makers were operating in Canada. They employed 2,546 people and together generated $2.66 million in annual sales.[25]

Hart had met this challenge by pushing as far into the Canadian market as possible using an aggressive advertising campaign that started in 1862. Focusing on what he could do to win a larger share of the market that existed, he began by expanding westward from Cobourg and selling his equipment in the large and growing market around Hamilton and to the west of that city. The Massey strategy to advertise the company's products was not unique. Yet Hart compensated for this by making a big event out of the annual train delivery of new farm equipment before the harvest. The trains were decorated, a band was hired to play, and, in some instances, parades were organized to showcase the new equipment that farmers could purchase and use for the harvest.

The rival firm of Harris was also aggressive in its pricing and dis-tribution tactics. Intensified rivalry in the industry drove out many of the marginal implement makers, beginning a process of consolidation. One of those firms that could not keep up was Toronto Reaper and Mower. It opened its doors in 1877 using American capital and pro-duced machines of excellent quality that were designed and proven in the United States before being launched in Canada. This firm had par-ticular success with its mower, which by 1879 accounted for two-thirds of all mower sales in Canada, according to the firm. Massey could not afford to ignore this company.

Charles was constantly barraged with glowing reports about Toronto Reaper and Mower, which gave him even more reason to watch the company closely. His vigilance paid off in 1881 when it became evident that Toronto Reaper and Mower had expanded too quickly. It was una-ble to meet its financial obligations after launching its newest product, a light binder that cut and bound crops in small bundles, called a self-binder, reducing yet again the amount of labour for the harvest.

This was Charles's chance, and he sought advice from Hart on what to do. From these discussions, father and son decided that acquisition was the best route. In 1881 Massey Manufacturing bought the upstart competitor and could boast that the purchase had doubled its manufac-turing capacity and tied it to Van Allen and Augur, a Winnipeg imple-ment-distribution firm that would now manage their future orders on the Canadian prairies – an area that showed promise as a potential mar-ket for farm implements (see Table 1).

Above all, this acquisition bought the Massey firm the rights to make the light binders. Once Charles and Hart had developed a simplified manufacturing process, these binders gave Massey Manufacturing the technological lead again in the field of farm implements. The advantage was short-lived.

Table 1
Farm holdings in Canada and the prairies, 1871–1901

Year	Canada	Prairies
1871	367,862	–
1881	464,025	10,091
1891	542,181	31,252
1901	511,073	45,697

Source: Series M12–22 – Farm Holdings, Historical Statistics of Canada.

Alanson Harris's company was also developing a light binder and, by 1882, had perfected its manufacture. One year later, Harris's light binders were in full production, competing vigorously against the Massey alternative. Thus began the binder wars, which divided Canadian farmers between those who attested to the quality of Massey and those who favoured Harris. While the binder wars raged, political developments of import were afoot.

The Tariff

At the time the binder wars got under way, Sir John A. Macdonald was experiencing good fortune, not just politically, but economically as well. The global depression that had slowed economic growth came to an end in 1879 – the year Macdonald implemented his new tariff policy on a wide range of items. Macdonald looked upon the recovery as a testament to the effectiveness of his tariff program.

Macdonald's National Policy promised much higher tariffs, including 35 per cent on some imports, and an expanded list of products to which the tariff would apply. Roughly 10 per cent of the Massey firm's sales were generated from exports to Europe (this would later increase to 40 per cent of production exported). Tariff walls designed to protect Canadian steel and iron makers would increase the input costs for Massey, make the company less competitive in the international arena, and cut into profits.[26]

Public promises and private conversations that Charles Massey had with Conservatives during the 1878 election bought assurances that the tariff Massey paid on imported materials that he needed in order to make machines for export would be repaid by the federal government. However, the company was obliged to supply a proper accounting of its export sales and use of materials. This report would be assessed, approved, or rejected by the cabinet, thus opening the door to arbitrary political decisions.

Charles Massey had a problem. If he opposed the National Policy, he risked making enemies of Macdonald's government, which in the run-up to the 1878 vote had developed the momentum needed to form the next administration. Charles and his father decided they had to support Macdonald's party.[27] After the National Policy came in and the binder wars were in full swing, tragedy struck when Charles succumbed to typhoid in 1884. The grieving Hart Massey invited his son Walter to join the firm as secretary-treasurer. Walter and Hart would now guide the firm going forward.

Massey Lashes Out

The National Policy with its high tariffs continued to pose a challenge for the Massey firm. Over a period of several years, Hart pressed government ministers and the prime minister himself, making clear that, if tariff walls increased his input costs, Massey would be less likely to effectively compete in the export market, costing the firm both profits and jobs.[28] Finally, on 13 February 1888, Massey let loose in a Toronto *Daily Mail* interview, making it clear both that he opposed the National Policy as it pertained to his industry and, more generally, that he favoured commercial union with the United States, believing it would 'benefit' farmers 'as a whole.'

Hart Massey's litany of complaints covered two newspaper columns. He said that the National Policy 'acts against the interests of manufacturers in our line of business.' Specifically, he pointed to steel and metal parts and the inability of Canada's four rolling mills – there were two in Hamilton, one in Montreal, and another in Nova Scotia – to supply large amounts of competitively priced items for Canadian manufacturers. As a result, Hart turned to U.S. steel producers to fill the gap. The National Policy, he told the paper, would wipe out his firm's profits, force it into a loss position of $30,000, and push Massey Manufacturing out of the international market where it could not compete against American producers while paying high tariffs on input materials. Perhaps Hart Massey was lamenting the defunct Reciprocity Treaty of 1854 that had given him the best of both worlds – duties on manufactures from the United States and duty-free on inputs that he needed to make his farm equipment.

After Macdonald's death in 1891, the governing party started rethinking the National Policy. Western complaints about high tariffs on farm implements were penetrating the walls of Parliament, and for the first time in years they received favourable consideration, including from Sir George Foster, the finance minister in 1893. As a result, the tariff was reduced from 35 per cent to 20 per cent, a reduction that apparently had the support of Hart Massey.[29] As the National Policy was revised, a major merger was in the works that would transform the Massey firm.

The Merger of Massey and Harris (1891)

Both Massey and Harris had established many separate distribution networks across the country. This duplication by the two competing firms was seen as counterproductive. The competition between Massey and Harris had been particularly acute during the binder wars; however, it was only after Massey conceded technological defeat in the binder wars that he approached Harris to talk about a merger. Then, in 1891, these hitherto archrivals decided to join forces. They became Massey-Harris Company. This consolidation gave the newly merged firm many advantages, such as economies of scale in distribution by eliminating wasteful duplication.

The merger of Massey and Harris also precipitated other mergers in Canada, most notably the consolidation of the Patterson and Wisner companies, which occurred only three months after the Massey-Harris merger. This new entity posed a considerable threat to Massey-Harris since the new firm, Patterson-Wisner, though smaller, was a full-line implement maker. Massey-Harris could not make such a claim; it did not, for instance, produce seeding equipment. Responding to the threat, Massey-Harris merged with Patterson-Wisner, although it maintained the Massey-Harris name. The merger of the four firms resulted in a Canadian powerhouse that controlled almost 60 per cent of the domestic market. Consolidation and the weeding out of marginal players continued over a ten-year period, reducing the number of domestic implement makers from 221 in 1890 to 114 in 1900.[30]

The merged company continued to pursue success abroad that would protect Massey-Harris from outgrowing the domestic market, a clear possibility since Canada had so far failed to draw the number of immigrants needed to populate the unsettled prairies. The decision to focus on exports abroad as opposed to serving the western market had significant consequences for the future.

The West

The west was to become important not only because of its rapid growth but also because the farms there were on average two to three times larger than farms in Ontario or Quebec. The larger size was made possible by the new farm machinery that had become available as the Canadian west was being settled – it allowed for cultivation of larger areas and the larger areas made the machinery more efficient; hence, a better business case could be made to purchase the expensive machinery.

The Massey and Harris firms' preoccupation with export to Europe and the decision to maintain manufacturing operations solely in Ontario left the door open for American firms, such as McCormick, Milwaukee Deering, and Minneapolis Harvester, that were interested in penetrating the increasingly attractive market in Canada's west and locating their operations in the American mid-west, closer to prairie farmers. Their proximity was one factor that helped them erode Massey-Harris market share. However, if Hart Massey had entered the U.S. market before American farm-implement firms had consolidated, by building a branch plant or by acquisition of an American firm, the competitive landscape of the farm-implement industry in North America could have been altered dramatically.

Hart Massey's Final Years

In 1894 Hart Massey was seventy-one years old, and his interest in the business was waning. He did have some unfinished work to do, however. His first wish was to secure a rebate on the tariffs his firm had been paying under the National Policy for steel and parts imported from the United States that were used to make Massey equipment for export. The second was launching a U.S. Massey-Harris branch plant. This would allow the company to bypass U.S. tariff walls and enter the American market on an even playing field with U.S. competitors who were still small compared to Massey-Harris, the U.S. farm-implement industry still not having entered the consolidation phase.

The Canadian government's decision in 1894 to reduce tariffs on farm implements occurred at the same time Hart Massey achieved his first desire. He negotiated a deal with Ottawa that saw his firm receive a 99 per cent rebate on the tariff paid on U.S. materials used to make machines for export. His second desire, to open a U.S. plant, was approved in principle by his company's board in 1895, but then in 1896 Hart Massey died. Hart's death delayed U.S. expansion until 1910 and, by this time, consolidation in the American farm-implement industry was already well under way.

Conclusion

Hart Massey left a legacy of philanthropy that is still evident today in Toronto's architecture. The concert house called Massey Hall is a monument to Hart's son Charles. Several University of Toronto buildings also honour the family name, including Massey College and Hart House. Together with his father before him, and his sons, Hart created the first Canadian company to build an international brand name for itself based on manufacturing and design expertise.

Suggested Questions

1. Why did the government of Canada want a policy of tariff protection? Since the policy was designed to protect Canadian manufacturers, why did the Massey firm and family dislike it?
2. How well did Massey-Harris adapt to changing market and competitive conditions and to changing government policy? What did it do well and not so well? How so?
3. Should Massey-Harris have entered the United States earlier than it did? If so, when should it have entered and how?

Suggested Readings

Denison M. *Harvest Triumphant*. Toronto: Massey-Ferguson 1949.
Macdonald, John A. 'A British subject I was born, a British subject I will die.' In Dennis Gruending, ed., *Great Canadian Speeches*. Markham, Ont.: Fitzhenry and Whiteside 2004. 72–5.
– 'The National Policy.' In J.H. Stewart Reid, Kenneth McNaught, and Harry S. Crowe, eds., *A Source-Book of Canadian History: Selected Documents and Personal Papers*. Toronto: Longmans Canada 1964. 349–52.
Philips W.G., *The Agricultural Implement Industry in Canada: A Study of Competition*. Toronto: University of Toronto Press 1956. www.ers.usda.gov/publications/EIB3/EIB3.pdf (the rise of modern farming).

NOTES

1 Denison, *Harvest Triumphant*, 20.
2 By the 1930s, 22 per cent of the population in the United States (and similarly in Canada) worked in agriculture, a result of the advent of mechanized farming. Today, this has dropped to 1 to 2 per cent. See Carolyn

Dimitri, Anne Effland, and Neilson Conklin, 'The 20th Century Transformation of U.S. Agriculture and Farm Policy,' United States Department of Agriculture, Economic Information Bulletin Number 3, June 2005.

3 Quoted in Peter Cook, *Massey at the Brink: The Story of Canada's Greatest Multinational and Its Struggle to Survive* (Toronto: Collins 1981), 21.

4 Not until 1837 was a truly practical thresher patented. Until 1830, almost 300 labour-hours were required to work five acres with a walking plow, brush harrow, sickle, and flail and to seed it by hand; but soon the new threshers and reapers of the mid-nineteenth century would allow not just a twofold but a tenfold increase in productivity, making feasible the rise of the great urban centres of the twentieth century. See http://inventors.about.com/library/inventors/blfarm1.htm (accessed 22 March 2006).

5 The Province of Canada imposed a tariff of 7.5 per cent on almost all imports, of 10 per cent on farm machines imported from abroad, and of 15 per cent on threshers in 1847. Denison, *Harvest Triumphant*, 34.

6 www.lib.uoguelph.ca/resources/archives/agriculture/masseypages/pamphlet001.htm (accessed 10 April 2006).

7 In the United States, thirty new reaper firms had been founded by 1850, followed by a flurry of activity in inventing and patenting new farming machines. There were 62 mowing-machine and 176 grain-reaper patents filed by 1857. This was partly a result of the repeal of the British Corn Laws in 1846, opening up the British market to wheat from the United States. Further, the urbanizing of the U.S. east coast resulted in concentrated markets for farm produce and subsequent demand for implements. Canada was at this time, comparatively, a small market for both implements and farm produce.

8 Cook, *Massey at the Brink*, 23.

9 David Roberts, 'Hart Almerrin Massey,' *Dictionary of Canadian Biography*, www.biographi.ca.

10 Cook, *Massey at the Brink*, 23.

11 www.ytmag.com/articles/artint241.htm (accessed 11 April 2006).

12 Philips, *The Agricultural Implement Industry in Canada*, 5.

13 Ibid., 10.

14 G.M. Winder, 'Following America into the Second Industrial Revolution: New Rules of Competition and Ontario's Farm Machinery Industry, 1850–1930,' *Canadian Geographer*, 46, no. 4 (2002): 292–309.

15 At the time, the tariffs were received with 'indifference' by both the implement maker and the farmer. It was the Toronto Board of Trade that was concerned, owing to its worry that innovative equipment from the United States would be denied to Canadian farmers because of the tariff. This was

put to rest as it was observed that domestic implement makers were quick
to license from American firms the latest machines and produce them
economically. Philips, *The Agriculture Implement Industry in Canada*, 40–1.

16 Kenneth Norrie and Douglas Owram, *The History of the Canadian Economy*
(Toronto: Harcourt Brace 1991), 218.

17 Philips, *The Agriculture Implement Industry in Canada*, 11. For example,
McCormick (later to become International Harvester during industry consolidation in the United States at the turn of the century) sold only three
reapers in Canada in 1857. The reason is apparent when one sees the price
of $160 per reaper from the U.S. compared to $125 for a Canadian reaper.

18 This predated the introduction of catalogue retailing by Sears, Roebuck,
and Montgomery Ward in the 1870s.

19 Denison, *Harvest Triumphant*, 73.

20 Ibid., 59.

21 In 1860 the Republicans had been elected for the first time and a protective
tariff was part of their platform. This played a role in the American decision to end reciprocity with British North America.

22 Philips, *The Agriculture Implement Industry in Canada*, 46.

23 Hart Massey, interview in the Toronto *Daily Mail*, 13 Feb. 1888.

24 Denison, *Harvest Triumphant*, 69.

25 Ibid., 65–6.

26 American steel was now also competitive with British steel and of higher
quality compared to Canadian steel and, importantly, could be produced
in sufficient volume and, but for the tariff, be imported more cheaply.

27 In a letter to the House of Commons Select Committee on Depression of
Trade, dated 31 March 1876, Charles Massey succinctly stated that his family's firm did not need high tariffs to thrive. See Denison, *Harvest Triumphant*, 74. Much of the sentiment in his letter to the Select Committee was
also expressed in Hart Massey's 1888 interview in the Toronto *Daily Mail*.
Massey saw little threat from U.S. implement makers since they were still
embroiled in patent wars.

28 Cook, *Massey at the Brink*, 43. Note that exports were becoming increasingly important to Massey-Harris.

29 Ibid.

30 Philips, *The Agriculture Implement Industry in Canada*, 55.

PART TWO

Wars, Depressions, and Dynamic Growth, 1905–55

Introduction

Early in the twentieth century, Canada – with its rapidly growing population fuelled by immigration – was viewed as the 'great colony of the British Empire.' By the middle of the century, it had become a very different place, weathered by two world wars and two depressions – including the Great Depression of the 1930s which hit Canada harder than any other developed nation.[1] In spite of these cataclysmic and sobering events, however, the country made immense economic progress to become one of the richest nations in the world (as measured in terms of GDP/capita).

Over the half-century, public policy became more intrusive in areas formerly thought of as preserves of the private sector, most notably in the public utilities field. And, since governments had to cope with both wars and depressions, they required more revenue. This led, inevitably, to the 'temporary income tax,' which was used not simply to fight wars but ultimately to provide Canadians with its version of a social-safety net. Public policies also included a welcoming attitude towards foreign investment.

Canada's healthy financial system not only withstood the depressions but also played a positive role in financing war efforts. While none of the Canadian banks failed during the 1930s, the Great Depression led to the creation of the Bank of Canada – an entity that served in its early days more as a financial adviser to the federal government than as a decider of monetary policy. And it was during the Great Depression that the Toronto Stock Exchange surpassed the Montreal Stock Exchange as the major exchange in Canada.

Throughout the first half of the twentieth century, Canadian entrepreneurs continued to demonstrate vitality by creating wealth and
investing in the Canadian economy. A few ventured abroad in search
of greater fortune while others stayed within Canada – some earning
even more of their income from the United States than they did from
Canada.

The greatest transformation in Canada's economy came about through
the rise of manufacturing and more particularly the arrival of the oil-
powered internal combustion engine as the automobile replaced the
steam-powered train. By 1955, the big oil and automobile companies
were either subsidiaries of foreign, mostly American, parents or were
about to become such. Some major Canadian companies were pursuing international expansion, but most were focused on the Canadian
market or specific regions within Canada.

Public Policy

By the mid-twentieth century, attitudes about the role of government
within Canada had changed. The early-twentieth-century view that
'the encouragement of industry, not its discouragement, is the office
and duty of government' had been replaced by the concept of 'the all-
benevolent, all-powerful welfare state.'[2]

Some have argued that, because laissez-faire capitalism had failed
Canadians during the Great Depression, government intervention
provided the key to future prosperity. Well before Keynesian theory[3]
made its appearance on the Canadian political and economic stage in
the 1930s, however, governments at both provincial and municipal levels had intervened in what had been privately held, investor-owned
operations, specifically in the areas of electrical and telephone utilities.

Crown Corporations[4]

Governments have many levers at their disposal to affect business,
including the operation of enterprises either directly (like the Post
Office) or indirectly through crown corporations.[5] The theory of the
crown corporation is that it frees an enterprise from the inefficiencies of
operating within a government department by permitting it to be run
at arm's length and in a more businesslike fashion.

Early in the twentieth century, crown corporations were not common.[6] In 1906, however, a newly elected Ontario provincial govern-

ment, in alliance with municipalities, put the government into the electrical-distribution business through Ontario Hydro. Hydro, under the entrepreneurial skills of Sir Adam Beck, later expanded its mandate to include generation. This was the beginning of the movement of governments into what had been an investor-owned sector, electrical public utilities.[7]

Subsequently, the prairie provinces moved into the telephone business while others followed Ontario's lead and entered the electricity business. The next most notable move by provincial governments was into the liquor business. All provincial governments but Prince Edward Island ended Prohibition in the 1920s and then established liquor 'control' commissions as enterprises charged with the control and sale of liquor. Prior to Prohibition, the sale of liquor had been a private-sector activity.

At the federal level, the government of Canada's first major crown corporation was the Canadian National Railways (CNR), which had a slow and difficult birth between 1917 and 1923. In the mid-1930s the federal government entered the wheat-marketing business through the Canadian Wheat Board, the broadcasting business through the Canadian Broadcasting Corporation, and the airline business through the creation of Trans-Canada Airlines (TCA) as a subsidiary of the CNR.[8]

The individual most closely associated with government intervention from the late 1930s right through to the late 1950s was Clarence Decatur (C.D.) Howe, the most powerful businessman-politician of his day, possibly in all of Canadian history. When war broke out, he was made minister of munitions and supply and was responsible for Canada's huge war effort. Howe often involved prominent businessmen as dollar-a-year men to help with the war effort – men such as E.P. Taylor of Argus Corporation in Toronto, Bill (Chunky) Woodward of Woodward's department stores in Vancouver, and Gordon Scott, the managing partner of P.S. Ross and Sons, chartered accountants of Montreal. 'The activities of a host of crown corporations, the empire of the forceful C.D. Howe, maintained the production of materials needed for war supply ... or supplied services in which the national interest seemed to call for national control of development.'[9] Under Howe's leadership, the period from 1944 to 1947 became the heyday of the federal crown corporation.

Trade and Investment

Turning from crown corporations to trade, it was noted in Part One that the government introduced a protective tariff in the late 1870s as well as an imperial preference system of tariffs with the United Kingdom beginning in the late 1890s. In 1911 trade became the centrepiece of that year's federal election, popularly known as the reciprocity or free-trade election. Prime Minister Sir Wilfrid Laurier had returned triumphantly from Washington with a treaty approved by Congress and by President William Howard Taft. It was a hollow victory. The Laurier Liberals were defeated by the Borden Conservatives (with help from some powerful Toronto Liberals), thereby scuttling for years any possibility of lower tariff structures between the two countries. In a gracious concession speech to the House of Commons after his defeat, Laurier stated, 'Need I remind the House once more that when Sir John Macdonald advised the Canadian people to adopt towards the United States a policy of high tariff, it was with a view to have a commercial convention such as was negotiated last year with the American republic.'[10]

The federal government's 1926 budget brought in Canadian content requirements for domestic car production, an historic first, and at the same time introduced a lowering of the tariff which resulted in modestly lower domestic auto prices. In June 1930 the Smoot-Hawley Tariff, the highest tariff in American history, was approved by U.S. President Herbert Hoover. 'Smoot Hawley provoked retaliatory protectionist actions by nations all over the globe ... France imposed an auto tariff; so did Italy. Australia and India legislated new duties. Canada raised tariffs three times.'[11]

In fact, pre-empting Smoot-Hawley, the Liberal government in Ottawa had raised tariffs in May of that year, and when the Conservatives won the 1930 election, they increased tariffs further. 'Any item that could conceivably be made in Canada was taxed with a particular vengeance.'[12] Looking for a way out, Prime Minister R.B. Bennett hosted a conference in Ottawa in the summer of 1932 on the topic of imperial preference. While not a resounding success, the conference did result in a measure that helped Canada in both imports and exports of goods and services to the United Kingdom and its colonies.

Franklin Delano Roosevelt was elected president of the United States that same year. The new president was advised in trade matters by Secretary of State Cordell Hull, a strong supporter of international trade. In 1934, with Hull's good offices, the United States Congress passed the Trade Agreements Act, which permitted the executive to negotiate treaties for the reciprocal lowering of tariffs. The next year, a Canada-U.S. trade agreement was concluded, marking the beginning of a return to

sanity between the two North American neighbours as well as a significant shift in Canada's external relations from the United Kingdom to
the United States.

The move to freer trade internationally continued after the Second
World War with the signing of the General Agreement on Tariffs and
Trade (GATT) in 1947, signalling in general the beginning of lower tar-
iffs among nations. The first three GATT rounds 'saw the progressive
and steady reduction of tariffs on the part of all contracting parties.'[13]
Accompanying this trend towards lower tariffs was a heavy reliance in
Canada on foreign direct investment (FDI).

Government Expenditures

From the above analysis it can be seen that, by mid-century, governments at all levels within Canada were becoming more active in the
operation of what had hitherto been the preserve of the private sector
and were playing a crucial role in trade – moving from a protectionist
to a freer trade stance. In Canada as elsewhere in the world,[14] governments were spending more too. In Canada, general government expenditures grew from about 10 per cent of GDP at the beginning of the
century to over 25 per cent by mid-century.[15]

In spite of the increasingly intrusive role that governments were
playing in shaping Canada's economy, the private sector was still the
main driver of the country's extraordinary economic performance
throughout the first half of the twentieth century. Governments played
a facilitative role, albeit a more intrusive one.

Financial Systems

From a public-policy point of view, the most important initiative by far
in the first half of the twentieth century was the government's decision
to create a central bank, the Bank of Canada, during the Great Depression. In 1940 the government also introduced unemployment insurance and, after the Second World War, created the Central Mortgage
and Housing Corporation (CMHC). In 1954 the government permitted
the banks to issue home mortgage loans for the first time. Amidst all
this activism, however, the government did not follow the American
example of establishing a single national securities regulator.

At the provincial level, other interesting developments took place.
In Ontario and Alberta, the provincial governments established gov-

ernment-owned banks;[16] in Saskatchewan and Alberta, provincially owned insurance companies were established;[17] and in Quebec and Ontario, agricultural credit[18] organizations were created to supplement the private sector. But the most important initiative came from Ontario in 1914, when the government led the way in creating a system of Workmen's Compensation Insurance, with the passage of 'the first Canadian statute to accept this principle … that some level of injury is inevitable and that compensation should be provided.'[19] Within four years, four other provinces had followed suit and the remainder followed later.

Turning from public policy to the private sector, large financial corporations in Canada experienced dramatic changes throughout the first half of the twentieth century. As was learned in Part One, at the beginning of the century, banks dominated, accounting for 60 per cent of all assets, and life insurance companies and mortgage loan companies were also significant players. By the middle of the century, much was different. The banks had consolidated and were still important but accounted for just under 40 per cent of the assets of all private Canadian financial intermediaries. Life insurance companies played a more significant role since they had taken over a great deal of the real estate lending, whereas mortgage loan companies had experienced a long, slow inexorable decline into relative insignificance. At the same time, a proliferation of other financial intermediaries had emerged. These included trust companies – which had become much more important – along with acceptance companies, non-life insurance companies, and investment dealers. (See Appendix 3 for a listing of the thirty largest financial corporations in 1955.)

Banking

The period from 1905 to 1955 was one of consolidation for Canadian banks, and, while their assets grew to $13 billion, their share of all financial intermediary assets had declined. By 1955, there were five big banks: the Royal Bank of Canada, the Bank of Montreal, the Canadian Bank of Commerce, the Bank of Nova Scotia, and the newly merged Toronto Dominion Bank. In addition, there were five smaller banks, three of them French-language banks based in Quebec.

Montreal was still the main banking centre in Canada, headquarters of the two largest banks in Canada (the Royal and the Bank of Montreal). All of the banks operated with large branch networks within Canada and the biggest among them were represented in London and

New York as well as in Europe, Latin America, and the West Indies. All were involved in retail and commercial banking but not in investment banking.

Other Financial Intermediaries

The life insurance industry, which had seen excellent growth in the latter part of the nineteenth century, experienced explosive growth in the first half of the twentieth. By 1955, all life insurance companies combined owned assets of $5.6.billion, an increase of 37 times since 1905 (in contrast banks had increased 16.5 times), representing over 18 per cent of all financial assets.

Over the fifty-year period from 1905 to 1955, the competitive picture had changed dramatically. Canada Life was no longer number one. The new giant was the Montreal-based Sun Life, three times the size of its main Toronto rival, Manufacturer's Life. Trust companies, which had first appeared on the scene in the 1880s, had blossomed. Spawned by entrepreneurs, and encouraged by the government in its attempt to separate commercial banking and trust services, trust companies prospered to become an important part of the Canadian financial scene by the mid 1950s. They could also act as financial intermediaries to attract savings and invest these funds in mortgages (which banks could not do) as well as in securities and loans. The two largest were the Royal Trust and the Montreal Trust. With assets of more than $1 billion each, the Montreal-based trust companies were comparable in size to the smaller of the Big Five chartered banks.

Consumer loan companies (generally called acceptance companies) had become new and important financial intermediaries by mid-century as well. They assumed the financial risk of providing day-to-day operating capital, spanning the time gap between the production of commodities and the sale and payment for them.

Early in the twentieth century, new investment firms were started, including Max Aitken's Royal Securities, Nesbitt Thomson, Greenshields, and others. Throughout most of the period, the Montreal Stock Exchange was the major exchange in Canada, although it experienced real difficulties in the Great Depression. (Neither the Montreal nor the Toronto stock exchanges closed during the Depression years, however, as happened on some days in New York in 1933.) In 1934 the Montreal exchange was overtaken by the Toronto Stock Exchange, which had merged with the Toronto Stock and Mining Exchange to become the largest exchange in Canada and one of the largest exchanges in North America.

In addition to financing obtained through banks and public offerings, the Canadian economy was attracting huge amounts of foreign capital, particularly from the United States. American investment in Canada surpassed British investment in the 1920s and unlike British investment, which was primarily in debt, American investment was principally direct or in equities.

Entrepreneurs

The late nineteenth century was replete with names of great Canadian entrepreneurs – men such as Donald Smith (Lord Strathcona), Hart Massey, George Gooderham, Timothy Eaton, and William Mackenzie. Some of these, like Mackenzie, broadened their activities. Mackenzie started in the nineteenth century as a contractor for the CPR along with his partner Donald Mann. Early in the twentieth century, the two partners started their own railway, the Canadian Northern, as well as investing in a whole host of electrical utilities in Canada and Latin America.

As the country moved confidently into the new century, the entrepreneurial class grew accordingly. Best known of these was Sam McLaughlin, who sold his company to General Motors (GM) but remained active on the Canadian board until his death. But the name of Gordon McGregor deserves to be better known because he obtained an agreement from Ford to have sole access to the British Empire other than the United Kingdom. After raising capital from local Windsor area investors and listing on the Toronto Stock Exchange, Ford Motor Company of Canada became a global company with plants in Africa, India, Malaysia, and Australia.

Probably the greatest Canadian entrepreneur of the period was Sam Bronfman, whose Distillers Corporation acquired Seagrams in the late 1920s. Bronfman took advantage of Prohibition in the United States by selling product into that market and, when Prohibition was repealed, directly entering the market. His company became the largest Canadian corporation after General Motors, with a huge presence in the United States as well as internationally.

Garfield Weston took over his father's bakery business in the 1920s and built a major international bakery company which became the biggest in the United Kingdom. Weston, who sat in the British House of Commons during the Second World War, was not the first Canadian entrepreneur to seek his fame and fortune in the United Kingdom. The financier Max Aitken acquired control of Royal Securities, investment dealers, early in the twentieth century. He played a key role in the merger mania of the era, including the creation of Stelco. Ultimately, Aitken emigrated to the United Kingdom where he became a newspaper magnate, a confidant of Winston Churchill, and a peer of the realm, Lord Beaverbrook.

Beaverbrook's entrepreneurial genius lay in what Joseph Schumpeter referred to as the carrying out of a new organization or creating a monopoly position. His friend, Sir James Dunn, who resuscitated Algoma Steel, was another such entrepreneur, as was E.P. Taylor, the founder of Argus Corporation.

The list of Canadian entrepreneurs throughout this period is varied and extensive, including as it does retailers Henry Birks, Theodore Loblaw, and J. William Billes; publishers Joe Atkinson, John Bayne Maclean, and William Southam; manufacturers Armand Bombardier, Pat Burns, Charles Frosst, and J.M. Schneider; and those in the extractive sector like James Richardson in the grain trade, Noah Timmins in mining, and H.R. MacMillan in forestry.

Large Non-Financial Corporations[20]

By mid-century, there had been dramatic changes in this sector. Most of the investor-owned electrical public utility industry had disappeared after provincial governments, led by Ontario, took over the investor-owned operations.[21] The notable exception was Bell Telephone and its related companies, as well as BC Telephone.

Half of the investor-owned railway sector had been taken over by the government and replaced by a gigantic crown corporation, Canadian National Railways. Most of the great coal mining companies were reduced in importance because of the transition from rail (powered by steam) to automobiles (powered by oil and gasoline). At the same time, while some industry sectors were disappearing, new ones were being created. The transformative technology of the first half of the twentieth century was the development of the internal combustion engine. Big Auto, Big Oil, and, to a lesser extent, Big Steel replaced Big Rail and Big Coal as the main drivers of the economy.

Over the first fifty years of the twentieth century, Canada shifted from an economy in which agriculture was the dominant employer to one where manufacturing reigned supreme. Instead of a mere handful of large manufacturing concerns there were many by mid-century, including the two largest: General Motors of Canada (a Canadian subsidiary of an American parent); and Distillers Corporation Seagrams, a Canadian company which was a major player in the U.S. market and elsewhere.

Another impact of the arrival of Big Auto and the changing fuel requirement for the railways was the fact that the extractive sector came to be dominated by Big Oil companies rather than by Big Coal companies. Big Oil companies in Canada were, primarily, subsidiaries of American parents, whereas a half-century earlier most of the major mining companies had significant Canadian investment. In addition to the arrival of Big Auto, Big Oil, and Big Steel, new types of mineral companies were in operation producing and processing both aluminium and nickel – resources extracted by 'Canadian' companies. Finally, the number of national retail chains – both department stores and supermarkets – was growing. (See Appendix 4 for a listing of the thirty largest non-financial corporations in 1955.)

Transportation and Public Utilities

At the beginning of the twentieth century, Canada had a thriving, investor-owned transportation and public-utility sector. A half-century later, only two companies – the CPR and the Bell Telephone Company of Canada – remained among Canada's largest non-financial corporations.

By the mid-twentieth century, technological change had resulted in the emergence of a new type of transportation – by air. Much like the railroads, the fledgling airline industry in Canada gave birth to two companies: Trans-Canada Airlines, a crown corporation and subsidiary of the CNR; and the investor-owned Canadian Pacific Airlines, a subsidiary of the CPR.

In terms of public utilities, it should be remembered that, at the beginning of the twentieth century, Canada could claim a thriving, investor-owned public utility sector. In 1905 investor-owned public utilities, particularly electrical public utilities, were among the largest non-financial companies. By 1955, the investor-owned public utility sector was much reduced, leaving only one company, Bell Telephone, among the largest of the non-financial corporations.

Manufacturing

Early in the twentieth century, and throughout the industrialized world, manufacturing became the dominant sector of the economy. A tremendous degree of merger activity and consolidation occurred within manufacturing as corporations capitalized on technological advances and sought gains in efficiencies in both scale and scope. In other words, the creative destructive forces of capitalism were at work again.

Big Auto had a huge impact on the Canadian economy and particularly Ontario. The Big Three of General Motors, Ford, and Chrysler also made an indirect impact because of their demand for supplies – specifically steel. The steel industry developed very differently from the pattern in the automotive industry. Originally, companies located close to the source of raw material. Later, the centre of the industry shifted to Hamilton, Ontario, where the demand for steel was greatest. By mid-century, steel had become a vital Canadian industry and the major producers were Canadian-owned, not subsidiaries of American parents. Of the three major producers, two were among Canada's largest non-financial corporations: the Hamilton-based Steel Company of Canada (Stelco); and Algoma Steel, based in Sault Ste Marie. Although not as large as these two companies, Dofasco – also in Hamilton – was the most profitable steel manufacturer in Canada.

As important as auto and steel manufacturing had become, a strong manufacturing base still remained in indigenous industries where, historically, Canadian firms had been successful: distilling, food, and brewing. Distillers Corporation Seagram and Hiram Walker Gooderham and Worts, the two largest distillers, enjoyed combined revenues of $1.1 million – nearly as much as the two largest automotive companies, GM and Ford. Both distillers were Canadian-owned, family-controlled, and publicly traded. The Bronfmans controlled Seagrams and the Hatches controlled Hiram Walker. And both companies performed better than most Canadian firms in penetrating the U.S. market. Typical of that era, the meat-packing industry also had grown by way of mergers. In 1955 the two major Canadian meat-packing companies – Canada Packers and Burns – were both Canadian-owned, based in Toronto and Calgary respectively.

Rounding out the largest manufacturing companies in the mid-1950s were Massey Harris Ferguson, Canadian Breweries, and Canadian General Electric (CGE). Both Massey and Canadian Breweries were owned by the dominant holding company of the day, Argus Corporation. While not as dominant as it had been half a century earlier, Massey was still a major player, having acquired the Irish-based Ferguson company and changed the corporate name from Massey Harris to Massey Harris Ferguson. Canadian Breweries expanded nationally and internationally from its Ontario base, with breweries in the United States and the United Kingdom. By contrast, CGE was no longer a Canadian company but rather a subsidiary of the American giant General Electric.

From this brief survey it can be seen that the manufacturing sector experienced tremendous growth and change in the first half of the twentieth century. In place of only a handful of major manufacturing concerns in the farm-equipment, electrical-equipment, textile, and flour businesses, a whole host of companies had sprung up and thrived. By mid-century, Big Auto and its Big Steel suppliers were the major players although traditional Canadian industries and companies in the distilling, meat-packing, and brewery sectors were still playing a significant role.

Extractive Sector

Canada has always been blessed with an abundance of natural resources, which is why the extractive sector is so important to the Canadian economy. By 1955, the Canadian extractive sector was dramatically different from its condition a half-century earlier. The major reason for the change was the arrival of Big Oil, a necessary adjunct to Big Auto. New minerals (aluminium and nickel) also helped to reshape the sector, as did the development of the west coast lumber industry.

But the advent of the automobile, which in turn created a demand for gasoline, was the major impetus for fundamental change. In 1947 the discovery of oil in Leduc, Alberta, accompanied the technological advancements leading to the transformation of the province, the country, and the entire Canadian extractive sector. A mere five years later, oil production equalled coal production, and by 1955 it had grown to be three times greater than coal production. The dramatic increase in production, plus the construction of the Interprovincial Pipeline, permitted oil exports to soar to 15,000,000 barrels from zero. However, imports still accounted for the great majority of petroleum used.

By 1955, four Big Oil companies could be counted among the largest non-financial corporations in Canada where there had been none half a century earlier. Two of the four were foreign-controlled; all were based in Toronto. The biggest by far was Imperial Oil, a subsidiary of Standard Oil of New Jersey,[22] followed by British American (BA), Shell Oil of Canada, and McColl Frontenac.[23]

In addition to the four Big Oil companies, three mining companies counted among Canada's largest non-financial corporations in 1955. Of the three, only Consolidated Mining and Smelting (Cominco) had been among the largest corporations fifty years earlier. This was primarily because of technological change. International Nickel (Inco) and Aluminium Company of Canada (Alcan) were mining and creating minerals that were hardly known a half-century earlier.

In the forest-products subsector, in 1905 there had been only one company among the largest corporations – the Quebec-based Price Brothers. By mid-century, two large companies were in operation: one on the west coast (MacMillan and Bloedel, the B.C.-based lumber and wood-product company); and one in Ontario (Abitibi, a pulp and paper company).

The automotive revolution of the twentieth century transformed Canada's extractive sector. Big Oil was booming and served as the handmaiden to Big Auto. The new mining companies, International Nickel and Alcan, increased in importance because of technological change as well – developments that permitted the use of nickel and aluminium which had not been possible on any scale in the nineteenth century. Mergers and acquisitions also played a role, particularly in the cases of MacMillan and Bloedel, and also with COMINCO through its acquisition of Granby Consolidated.

By 1955, companies in the extractive sector, unlike the transportation and public-utility sectors and for the most part unlike the extractive sector of fifty years earlier, were mostly foreign-owned, usually by American parents.

Retail

In Joseph Schumpeter's *Capitalism, Socialism and Democracy*, there is a chapter titled 'The Process of Creative Destruction.' This paradoxical phrase has entered the general lexicon and is normally restated as 'the creative destructive forces of capitalism.' Schumpeter illustrates his point by referring specifically to the retail sector.[24]

Traditionally retail had been a local activity. In North America, as the nineteenth century drew to a close and the twentieth century dawned, large department store chains, some with mail-order departments, began to spring up. In the 1920s supermarket chains began to emerge as well, supplanting wholesalers and smaller single location stores. As the twentieth century advanced, certain retail organizations moved from their local base to a regional or national base, taking advantage of economies of both scale and scope.

By 1955, there were four regional or national department stores, most with their own mail-order catalogues. Eaton's and Simpson's, both Toronto-based, were the dominant players. The Winnipeg-based HBC was still a regional department store, having no operations east of the Manitoba/Ontario border. But there was a brand new player on the scene in Simpsons-Sears, a joint venture between the long-established Simpson's and the American giant Sears Roebuck.

Three food chains had also emerged: Loblaw and Dominion stores based in Ontario, and Canada Safeway stores based in western Canada. 'The construction of grocery chain stores in Canada paralleled American developments and was triggered by an inflationary spiral between 1917 and 1921 that stimulated consumer demand for low-cost suppliers.'[25] Unlike the department store chains, none of the super market chains was national in scope. Loblaw focused on Ontario plus three states in the United States, while Safeway stayed in western Canada. Dominion came closest to being a national chain, with stores in five provinces. The supermarket chains were different in ownership as well. Safeway was a subsidiary of an American parent whereas Loblaw had an American subsidiary. Dominion was not only Canadian but also a part of the penultimate Canadian holding company of the era, Argus Corporation.

Summary

Looking back at Canada's largest non-financial corporations in 1905 we find investor-owned railroads and electrical public utilities. A half-century later it is the Big Auto companies, fuelled by the Big Oil companies and supplied by the Big Steel companies, that dominate the landscape.

But that was not the whole story. Like elsewhere in the world, Canada's economy had shifted from agriculture to manufacturing. Joining Big Auto and Big Steel were major corporations in areas of historic strength in Canada – distilling, food, and brewing – all made larger and more complex as a consequence of mergers and acquisitions. Major new corporations had been born as the result of the application of the new minerals of nickel and aluminium. Finally, starting early in the twentieth century, large national department store chains had been established, followed by regional supermarket chains.

It is difficult to generalize about business, because, to paraphrase management guru Peter Drucker, there is no such thing as business, only businesses. What is clear is that the large non-financial corporations of 1955 were much larger and more complex than those of 1905.

Conclusion

Over the first half of the twentieth century, in the phrase made famous by A.R.M. Lower, Canada made the journey 'from colony to nation.' This political progress was matched by solid economic progress as GDP per capita increased 130 per cent in constant dollars in the fifty-year period, almost as great an increase as that experienced in the United States. This level of increase permitted Canada to pass both the United Kingdom and Australia in terms of GDP per capita.

While government was more intrusive than it had been a half-century earlier, the public sector at all levels was generally supportive of the private sector. The economy still flourished under a free-enterprise capitalistic system and within a business-friendly environment. As well, a sound financial system was in place, permitting the country to escape the major bank failures that the United States experienced during the Great Depression. Further reinforcement came with the establishment of a central bank, the Bank of Canada – one positive outcome of the 'Dirty Thirties.'

At the beginning of the Second World War, the government introduced Unemployment Insurance (UI). After the war the federal government created the Central Mortgage and Housing Corporation to assist people in buying their own homes and amended the Bank Act to permit the banks to make mortgage loans. At the provincial level, certain provinces started their own banks and general insurance companies, but the most important development was the creation of Workmen's Compensation Boards.

In the private sector, the banking system consolidated in the first half of the twentieth century, resulting in fewer banks. While still important, banks did not dominate the financial sector the way they had earlier (and the way they would later in the century). Life insurance companies had flourished in spite of the near failure of Sun Life during the Great Depression. And large trust and acceptance companies had become part of the Canadian financial landscape.

Entrepreneurs continued to play a major role in Canada, many in small businesses operating throughout the length and breadth of the nation. Some moved on to the larger stage – business titans like Max

Aitken, Lord Beaverbrook, Garfield Weston, the little known Gordon McGregor of Windsor, and a host of others. Probably the most success-ful entrepreneur in the 1950s was Sam Bronfman, owner of the second-largest Canadian non-financial corporation.

Large Canadian non-financial corporations were very much changed by 1955 from what they had been a half-century earlier. Not only were they much larger but among them were companies operating in new and very different industry sectors; and many more of them were foreign-owned – mainly by Americans. In 1905 the railroads had ranked at the top of Canada's largest corporations, and investor-owned electrical utilities comprised the largest grouping of companies – the majority of which were Canadian-owned. By 1955, the Big Auto and Big Oil compa-nies were Canada's major corporations. All were wholly owned subsid-iaries or about to become such and all were based in Toronto. Overall, there were more manufacturers among the largest corporations than there had been fifty years earlier, and, other than Big Auto, most were Canadian-owned and operating in traditional Canadian industries like distilling, food, and brewing. As well, a number of national department store and regional supermarket chains had emerged.

By the middle of the twentieth century, Canada was well positioned to grow economically. The outlook was positive because the country could lay claim to positive, business-friendly public policy, a sound financial system, creative entrepreneurship, and a variety of large cor-porations with both domestic and foreign ownership.

Appendix 3
Top thirty financial corporations by assets, 1955 (in $ millions)

Corporation	Total Assets - $	Code
1. Royal Bank	3,284	B
2. Bank of Montreal	2,796	B
3. Canadian Bank of Commerce	2,357	B
4. Sun Life	1,949	I
5. Royal Trust	1,448	T
6. Toronto Dominion Bank	1,279	B
7. Bank of Nova Scotia	1,193	B
8. Montreal Trust	1,171	T
9. Imperial Bank	796	B
10. Manufacturers Life	653	I
11. Banque Canadienne Nationale	645	B
12. Great West Life	556	I
13. London Life	523	I
14. Canada Life	516	I
15. National Trust	509	T
16. Mutual of Canada	489	I
17. Toronto General Trust	442	T
18. Industrial Acceptance Corporation	354	A
19. Confederation Life	341	I
20. Provincial Bank	277	B
21. Canada Trust	249	T
22. Traders Finance Corporation	248	A
23. Montreal District and City Savings Bank	221	B
24. Crown Life	220	I
25. North American Life	219	I
26. Imperial Life	218	I
27. Administration and Trust	206	T
28. General Motors Acceptance Corporation	184	A
29. General Trust	171	T
30. Crown Trust	162	T
CODE: B = Banks A = Acceptance Cos. I = Life Insurance Cos. T = Trust Cos.		

Source: *Monetary Times*, April 1957, 34–6.

Appendix 4
Top thirty non-financial corporations, 1955, by sales (in $ millions)

Corporation	Total Sales - $	Code
1. General Motors of Canada	800	M
2. Distillers Corporation Seagrams	736	M
3. Imperial Oil	701	E
4. T. Eaton Co.*	500	R
5. C.P.R.	448	T
6. International Nickel	416	E
7. Canada Packers	363	M
8. Simpson's Ltd.	350	R
9. Ford Motor Co. of Canada	346	M
10. Hiram Walker Gooderham Worts	341	M
11. Aluminum Co. of Canada	308	E
12. Massey Harris Ferguson	286	M
13. British American Oil	271	E
14. Chrysler Corp.	250	M
15. Shell Oil of Canada	250	E
16. Bell Telephone	245	U
17. Loblaw	229	R
18. Steel Company of Canada	227	M
19. Canadian Breweries	225	M
20. Dominion Stores	220	R
21. CGE	218	M
22. MacMillan & Bloedel	175	E
23. Canada Safeway	174	R
24. Hudson's Bay Co.	160	R
25. Consolidated Mining and Smelting	150 ·	E
26. Abitibi	123	E
27. Burns & Co.	122	M
28. Simpsons-Sears	120*	R
29. McColl Fronenac	115	E
30. Algoma Steel	114	M
CODE:		
T = Transportation		
E = Extractive		
U = Public Utilities		
M = Manufacturing		
R = Retail		

* Estimate.
Source: *Monetary Times,* April 1957, 34–6, Financial Post Survey of Corporate Securities, 1956.

BIBLIOGRAPHY

Anastakis D. 'From Independence to Integration: The Corporate Evolution of the Ford Motor Company of Canada, 1904–2004.' *Business History Review*, 78, no. 2 (2004): 213–53.

Anisman, Philip, 'The Proposals for a Securities Market Law for Canada: Purpose and Process.' *Osgoode Hall Law Journal*, 330, no. 19 (1981): 329–67.

Boothman, Barry. '"A More Perfect System": The Emergence of Retail Food Chains in Canada, 1919–1946.' In B.J. Branchik, ed., *Marketing History at the Centre: Proceedings of the Thirteenth Biannual Conference on Historical Analysis and Research in Marketing*. Durham, N.C.: John W. Hartman Centre, Duke University 2007. 13–23.

Creighton, Donald. *The Forked Road, Canada, 1939–1957*. Toronto: McClelland and Stewart 1976.

Dennison, Merill. *This Is Simpson's*. Toronto: Simpson's 1947.

Drucker, Peter. *Management*. New York: Harper and Row 1973.

Falkus, Malcolm. 'The New Economy.' In A.J.P. Taylor and J.M. Roberts, eds., *History of the 20th Century, No. 6*. London: New Caxton Library Service 1972.

Financial Post Survey of Corporate Securities, 1956.

Grant, James. *Money of the Mind: Borrowing and Lending in America, from the Civil War to Michael* Milken. New York: Farrar, Straus, Giroux 1992.

Hausman, William J., Peter Hertner, and Mira Wilkins. *Global Electrification: Multinational Enterprise and International Finance in the History of Light and Power, 1878–2007*. Cambridge: Cambridge University Press 2008.

Morton, W.L. *The Kingdom of Canada*. Toronto: McClelland and Stewart 1963.

Nelles, H.V. 'The Electric Cemetery: The Living, The Dead and the Power Question in Ontario.' Lecture delivered at McMaster University, Hamilton, Ont., 6 February 2006.

Safarian, A.E. *The Canadian Economy in the Great Depression*. Toronto: Carleton Library, McClelland and Stewart 1970.

Shlaes, Amity. *The Forgotten Man: A New History of the Great Depression*. New York: HarperCollins 2007.

NOTES

1 Canada's trade declined by 65 per cent; GDP/capita fell by 35 per cent; 27 per cent of the population was unemployed; and the stock market plummeted 84 per cent.

2 Morton, *The Kingdom of Canada*, 487.

3 Keynes's *General Theory*, which was published in 1936, called for government intervention in taxation and government spending and credit in
   order to address unemployment rather than leaving matters to the marketplace.
4 This section deals with the non-financial crown corporations – the financial
   ones are dealt with in the next section under 'Financial Systems.'
5 Known as State Owned Enterprises (SOEs) in many parts of the world.
6 The first was an Ontario corporation, the Temiskaming and Northern
   Ontario Railway Commission, incorporated in 1902, to help settle northern
   Ontario.
7 Nova Scotia and New Brunswick followed Ontario's example after the
   First World War, as did the federal government in northern Canada and
   Saskatchewan in the 1940s. British Columbia and Quebec began to be
   involved in the electrical business in the mid-1940s, and the Manitoba
   government, which had started in the business as early as 1920, became
   the monopoly provider in the mid-1950s. In *Global Electrification*, Hausman,
   Hertner, and Wilkins note the lead role of Ontario.
8 The provinces were relatively inactive in creating crown corporations in
   the 1930s although the Quebec government did create the Office du Credit
   Agricole.
9 Morton, *The Kingdom of Canada*, 477, 497.
10 J.H. Stewart Reid, Kenneth McNaught, and Harry S. Crowe, eds., *A Source-
   Book of Canadian History: Selected Documents and Personal Papers* (Toronto:
   Longmans Canada, 1964), 371.
11 Shlaes, *The Forgotten Man*, 99.
12 Rima Berns, 'The Real Story behind Free Trade (A History of the Canadian
   Tariff),' unpublished paper, John Hopkins University, School for Advanced
   International Studies (SAIS), 1988, 33.
13 Ibid., 37.
14 Vito Tanzi and Ludger Schuknecht, *Public Spending in the 20th Century: A Global Perspective* (Cambridge, New York: Cambridge University Press 2000), 6.
15 In 1960 government expenditures in Canada were 28.6 per cent of GDP
   versus an average of 28 per cent for most developed nations.
16 In 1921 the United Farmers of Ontario was the governing party and it
   created the Province of Ontario Savings Office. Seventeen years later, the
   Social Credit Party of Alberta was in power and it created what is now
   known as ATB (Alberta Treasury Branches).
17 In the mid-1940s both the CCF government in Saskatchewan and the Social
   Credit government in Alberta created general insurance companies.
18 The Quebec body was established in 1936 during a period of great change

in the province and was perhaps based on the French model. Ontario
followed suit in 1952 and most of the other provinces would do so in the
1960s and 1970s.

19 D.A. Smith, 'Workers' Compensation,' Canadian Encyclopedia, http://
www.thecanadianencyclopedia.com/index.cfm?PgNm=TCE&Params=A1
ARTA0008707 (accessed 15 July 2008).

20 In *The Development of Modern Business* (Houndmills, U.K., New York: Palgrave 2002), Gordon Boyce and Simon Ville note that there are a variety of
criteria for measuring change. For 1905, assets were used for both financial
and non-financial corporations because asset data was available but not
revenue for non-financial corporations. For 1955, forward revenue has
been used for non-financial corporations because it was deemed to be the
best measurement criteria, while assets were deemed to be the best measurement criteria for financial corporations.

21 Shawinigan Water and Power and BC Power were still major publicly
traded entities in mid-century, but they would not remain so for long.

22 Imperial Oil had been founded as a Canadian company to take advantage
of the oil deposits in western Ontario in 1880. However, the company had
been acquired by John D. Rockefeller's Standard Oil in 1898.

23 In the early days, the Canadian companies were not integrated producers.
The focus was on retail distribution and refining.

24 Joseph A. Schumpeter, *Capitalism, Socialism and Democracy* (New York:
Harper Torch Books 1962), 85.

25 Boothman, 'A More Perfect System.'

CASE 4

'Irrational Exuberance': The Creation of the CNR

JOE MARTIN

This is a story of 'irrational exuberance,'[1] a phrase made famous by the former chairman of the American Federal Reserve Board, Alan Greenspan. The story illustrates how irrational exuberance affected both the public and private sector, particularly Prime Minister Sir Wilfrid Laurier and corporate giant Sir William Mackenzie.

Our story begins in July 1917, when the consequences of irrational exuberance were being felt, by some for the first time. The world was at war and Canadian Prime Minister Robert Borden had returned to Canada from meetings of the Imperial War Cabinet in London, where the news was not good. Canadian casualties had been heavy that spring, particularly during the Battle of Vimy Ridge, which was captured by the Canadians but at a cost of nearly 24,000 casualties. The war had also revealed divisions within the country. English Canadians were demanding conscription of manpower for the fighting front; French Canadians bitterly opposed it.

Canada's railway situation, however, and not the war, topped Borden's agenda on 14 July,[2] when he met with Sir William Mackenzie, one of Toronto's richest and most powerful businessmen and an important political and financial supporter. A railway and utility magnate with financial stakes on three continents, Mackenzie was also a major shareholder, president, and CEO of the Canadian Northern Railway – at that time one of Canada's three transcontinental railways and one of Canada's five largest corporations.

It was the fate of the Canadian Northern, which was facing seemingly insurmountable financial difficulties, that provoked the meeting. The prime minister was not looking forward to the contretemps. The solution to what he called 'the railway mess' was not going to be well received by his friend and political supporter.

Summer 1917: 'The Railway Mess'

The recommendation of a royal commission – that traditional Canadian tool for problem solving – appointed in 1916 to study the problem was that the government take over the ailing Canadian Northern Railway. It was a solution that Borden disliked but had decided to accept. Not so Mackenzie. The railway baron argued against the decision, claiming that the commission had made serious accounting errors in its report. When it was clear that the prime minister's decision was final and that Mackenzie's plans for expansion of his beloved railway were dead, Mackenzie broke down and sobbed.[3]

Clearly unnerved to witness the distress of this corporate giant whom he admired greatly, Borden tried to comfort Mackenzie. However, the prime minister was determined to follow the advice of the majority of commission members. In any event, 'the wretched railway problems' were among many challenges Borden was facing in 1917, which for Canada, and perhaps for the entire world, was one of the most traumatic and challenging years of the twentieth century.

The all-consuming issue was the war, now entering its fourth year, a war in which 60,000 Canadians would eventually be killed. But there were other problems as well. The introduction of the Military Services Act in 1917 led to riots and demands for money as well as manpower to support the war. The minister of finance was obliged to capitulate to these demands by bringing in, for the first time, a 'temporary' income tax.[4] Consequently, pressure was mounting for a federal election, the first in six years,[5] with widespread support growing for a Union government – a coalition of Conservatives and English-speaking Liberals.

Borden and his government were grappling with many issues. Along with major internal political realignment looming at home, revolutionary sentiment abroad, led by Lenin in Russia, not to mention the war and conscription of manpower as well as wealth, the government faced other hot-button issues that needed addressing. These included: the prohibition of the sale and consumption of liquor; the granting of the electoral franchise to women; and inflationary pressures on food prices. And gnawing away amidst all these turbulent issues was 'the railway mess' – three transcontinental railways had been built for a population of just over eight million, which resulted in excessive capacity relative to demand.

The solution, Borden concluded that summer of 1917, was for the government to take over the Canadian Northern and consolidate several other railway lines, thus beginning a process which would result in the creation of the largest crown corporation in Canadian history: the Canadian National Railways, to be known by its short form the CN. To understand how Canada faced such a proliferation of railways, one must go back in time, at least twenty-one years earlier, when 'irrational exuberance' led to the construction of far too much capacity.

Sir Wilfrid Laurier's Railway Policy

In 1896 the Liberal Party, led by Wilfrid Laurier with his 'sunny ways,' was elected to form the government of Canada for the first time in over twenty years. The election marked the beginning of more than a century-long Liberal dominance of Canadian federal politics. In winning the 1896 election, the debonair Laurier became the first French Canadian prime minister in Canadian history.

Laurier has many claims to fame in Canadian history, including fifteen continuous years in office with four successive majority governments, but his railway policy is not considered one of his successes.[6] After defeating the Conservatives in 1896, Laurier simply co-opted most of the Conservative's famous National Policy: a protective tariff, which the Liberals supported until the 1911 election; the settlement of the west; and a national railway, the Canadian Pacific. However, because he shared Sir John A. Macdonald's vision of the future of Canada as a nation stretching from sea to sea, and because he had the good fortune to be prime minister during boom times, Laurier decided to go one better than Sir John A. In 1903 Laurier – who was so optimistic about the country's future that he would pronounce that the twentieth century belonged to Canada – authorized the construction of a second transcontinental railroad.

Laurier's grand scheme to encourage the building of a second transcontinental line led to both short- and long-term problems. By the 1890s, the railway network in eastern Canada was essentially complete. In western Canada, however, the period was marked by massive investments in new railway construction. In addition to the CPR, two entrepreneurs, Donald Mann and William Mackenzie, who had made their original money building parts of the CPR as contractors, were developing a new prairie network. They were also lobbying aggressively for a charter to extend their western lines into a transcontinental railway.

Meanwhile, in eastern Canada, the moribund, British-owned, Montreal-based, Grand Trunk Railway was being revitalized. In 1896 the Grand Trunk board of directors brought Charles Melville Hays up from the United States as general manager of the GTR, with a mandate to introduce 'American' methods. Hays, working with Sir Charles Rivers Wilson, president of the GTR, adopted a policy of aggressive western expansion. The consequence was that, by 1917, Canada had three major railways, not to mention a number of smaller ones competing for business. (See Exhibit 1 and 1915 Map.)

In 1903 Laurier faced pressure to force a merger of the Mackenzie and Mann railway with the GTR systems led by Hays and Wilson. Laurier refused, or was unable, to do this. Such a merger might have been a logical strategy, given the Grand Trunk's prominence in eastern Canada, and the Canadian Northern's presence across the prairies. Instead, Laurier chose the Grand Trunk to build a second transcontinental, declaring in the House of Commons that 'a railway to extend from the shores of the Atlantic Ocean to the shores of the Pacific Ocean, and to be, every inch of it, on Canadian soil, is a national as well as a commercial necessity.' (At the time, the CPR ran through Maine to Saint John, New Brunswick.) Unimpressed, Laurier's critics referred to his policy as a plan 'to carry elections rather than passengers.'

There was some justification to this criticism. The new Grand Trunk transcontinental was to achieve national status by two different methods. In the east the government of Canada was to build a line eastward from Quebec City to Moncton, and westward from Quebec City through the unsettled part of Quebec and Ontario, across the Canadian Shield, to Winnipeg. (See 1915 Map.) This government-built line was called the National Transcontinental.[7] On completion, the National Transcontinental was to be leased to the Grand Trunk Pacific (a wholly owned subsidiary of the Grand Trunk Railway) on very favourable terms. From Winnipeg, the Grand Trunk Pacific (GTP) was to build a line to Prince Rupert on the west coast.

Laurier's decision to build a second transcontinental line ultimately led to the resignation in 1903 of his minister of railways, A.G. Blair. Blair was a New Brunswick lawyer and former premier of that province who was persuaded to run federally by Laurier in the 1896 election. He was sworn in as minister of railways and canals when the Liberals were elected. Blair favoured government ownership and operation of railways, which Laurier opposed. Laurier could accept the idea of governments constructing railways but he was adamantly opposed to governments operating them.

There were longer-term consequences as well. Laurier's decision to build a new transcontinental system set off an unrealistic building

Exhibit 1
Major railway company mileage, 1904/1913

Company	1904	1913	% increase
Canadian Northern System			
Canadian Northern	2,287.50	4,760.65	
Canadian Northern, Ontario	na	503.95	
Canadian Northern, Quebec	na	742.02	
Bay of Quinte	na	105.00	
Brockville, Westport & N.W.	na	45.00	
Central Ontario	na	149.73	
Halifax and South Western	289.00	380.76	
Inverness Ry., and Coal Co.	61.00	60.91	
Irondale, Bancroft & Ottawa	na	51.00	
James Bay	4.00	na	
Under Construction	556.00	1,297.00	
Total	**2,859.50**	**6,709.02**	**134.62**
Canadian Pacific System			
Canadian Pacific	8,747.50	11,943.55	
Dom. At. & Que. Central	na	552.00	
Kingston & Pembroke	112..85	na	
Tillsonburg L.E. & Pac.	35.33	na	
Esquimalt & Nanaimo	78.00	na	
Under Construction	481.40	768.00	
Total	**8,973.68**	**12,495.64**	**39.25**
Grand Trunk System			
Grand Trunk	3,162.76	3,120.89	
Canada Atlantic	458.60	456.26	
Grand Trunk Pacific	na	1,401.97	
Central Vermont	125.20	125.20	
Under Construction	na	720.00	
Total	**3,746.56**	**5,104.32**	**37.20**
Canadian Government System			
Intercolonial	1,310.26	1,502.76	
Prince Edward Island	209.00	279.23	
Canada Eastern	136.00	na	
Total	**1,655.26**	**1,781.99**	**7.66**
All other Railways	**2,352.37**	**3,732.59**	**58.67**
Grand total	**19,587.37**	**29,823.56**	**52.26**

Source: Department of Interior, Atlases of Canada, 1906 and 1915.

Railway Map of Canada, 1915

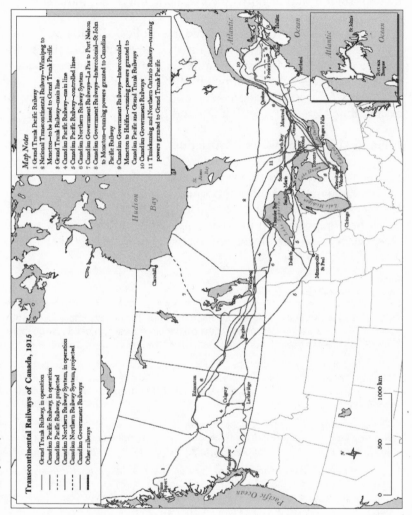

Transcontinental Railways of Canada, 1915

|||| Grand Trunk Railway, in operation
Canadian Pacific Railway, in operation
Canadian Pacific Railway, projected
Canadian Northern Railway System, in operation
Canadian Northern Railway System, projected
Canadian Government Railways
Other railways

Map Note

1 Grand Trunk Pacific Railway
2 National Transcontinental Railway—Winnipeg to Moncton—to be leased to Grand Trunk Pacific
3 Grand Trunk Railway—main line
4 Canadian Pacific Railway—main line
5 Canadian Pacific Railway—controlled lines
6 Canadian Northern Railway System
7 Canadian Government Railways—La Pas to Port Nelson
8 Canadian Government Railways—Intercolonial–St John to Moncton—running powers granted to Canadian Pacific Railway
9 Canadian Government Railways—Intercolonial—Moncton to Halifax—running powers granted to Canadian Pacific and Grand Trunk Railways
10 Canadian Government Railways
11 Timiskaming and Northern Ontario Railway—running powers granted to Grand Trunk Pacific

boom, similar to the dot.com boom of the late 1990s. This decision and other factors led to a proliferation of railways and much waste of public money in support of building more. It was a policy of 'intoxication' that invited a flood tide of railway construction and led, inevitably, to the ebb of retribution in its wake.[8]

Indeed, when Laurier announced his policy, Canada was already well served by its railways, with nearly 20,000 miles of railway trackage for a country with a population of only 5.5 million. Trackage in the United States was ten times that of Canada's, but its population was nearly fourteen times greater – and its economy was twenty times greater than Canada's. (See Table 1 and Exhibit 1.)

A Flood Tide of Railway Construction

Between 1903 and 1911 (the year that Laurier was defeated in a general election), the railway-building boom in Canada saw railway track mileage increase by 40 per cent from just over 18,000 miles to 25,400 miles, much of it superfluous. In 1911 alone, 8,000 miles of track was laid. Over the next decade, trackage doubled to more than 50,000 miles and

Table 1
The Canadian railway system in 1904

- The **Grand Trunk**, the oldest railway, headquartered in London, England, operating in eastern Canada, based in Montreal, with no extensions west but desirous to go there and with 3,750 miles of track. It had a well-established feeder system in Ontario and Quebec.

- The **Intercolonial**, provided for by an article in the British North America Act, based in Moncton, which united the Martimes with central Canada by linking Nova Scotia and New Brunswick with Quebec. It operated with 1,300 miles of track plus another 300 miles through subsidiaries.

- The **CPR**, a well-run, Montreal-based railway, with 9,000 miles of track from Saint John, N.B., to Vancouver (nearly half the trackage in Canada), operating in both east and west, with a national trunk line supported by regional feeders. Its operations were profitable.

- The **Mackenzie and Mann system** (to become the Canadian Northern System), headquartered in Toronto with strong ties to the Bank of Commerce. Its nearly 3,000 miles of track were principally on the prairies between Winnipeg and Edmonton, a part of the country experiencing dramatic growth at the time, although expansion into eastern Canada was on its wish list. Its operations were profitable.

- There were, in addition, fifty-seven other much smaller companies, ranging in size from the 382.19-mile Michigan Central in Ontario to the tiny two-mile Klondike Mines Railway in the north.

projects that had been approved before the post-war depression could not be stopped in time.

While the Grand Trunk was building its transcontinental line, Mackenzie and Mann were still holding onto their dream of making the Canadian Northern a transcontinental railway. More than a dream, it was also a practical necessity. Mackenzie and Mann's railway needed a transcontinental line in order to keep much of its western feeder traffic. An unexpected bonus for Canadian Northern, therefore, was Laurier's commitment to reciprocity with the United States in 1911 which led to the legislative authority and financial assistance for Mackenzie and Mann to build a third transcontinental line. As T.D. Regehr explains, 'the nationalistic clamour [against reciprocity] of the Opposition ... made it possible for Donald Mann to persuade the (Laurier) government that it must officially recognize and acknowledge the Canadian Northern Railway as the country's third great national highway. The bill was given royal assent on 19 May 1911 and construction was begun immediately. At the end of 1911 Mackenzie and Mann had 4,500 men at work on the Ontario mileage, and in 1912 there were 9,600.'[9]

The 1911 election marked the end of Laurier's fifteen years in power and the election of Borden's Conservative government. The new prime minister, who came into power on a platform that carefully documented the problems relating to the Grand Trunk Railway, now found his government saddled with 'the railway mess' – three transcontinental railways in a country with a population of less than 7.5 million.

For the Grand Trunk in particular, problems were exacerbated when its aggressive American-born president, Charles Melville Hays, went down with the *Titanic* in April 1912. The next year, 1913, the Grand Trunk Pacific reneged on its earlier agreement to take over the National Transcontinental (part of the Grand Trunk system). The company simply couldn't afford it. That same year, the Canadian Northern Railway – which had been expanding rapidly and burning up capital – asked the government for a $30-million handout. The government agreed to provide only half that amount and demanded an equity position in return. Canadian Northern repeatedly asked for and received huge amounts of public money. Both companies, but particularly the Canadian Northern (led by Mackenzie and Mann), had been expanding rapidly. (See Exhibit 1.)

As the war approached, however, the railways appeared to be doing well. They were earning over $250 million annually – roughly 30 per cent from passengers and 70 per cent from freight – and spending

under $200 million, leaving $50 million to service the debt and provide shareholders with a return on their investment. They were carrying more than forty million passengers and over ninety million tons
of freight using 5,000 locomotives, 5,000 passenger cars, and nearly
200,000 freight cars. This was big business all right, but it was big business that was not sustainable.

The capital structure of the industry was split among stocks (40 per
cent) and funded debt (closer to 45 cent), with the remaining 15 per
cent accounted for by government assistance mainly at the federal
level, although provincial and municipal governments contributed as
well. While the CPR capital structure was much less dependent on debt
financing than that of the GTR or the Canadian Northern, given the
level of debt financing within these two companies, there was bound
to be trouble – particularly in the London markets once war broke out.

In addition to heavy reliance on debt, the Grand Trunk and Canadian
Northern faced significant overcapacity and their costs had begun to
exceed estimates substantially. While railway construction was going
full tilt, revenue from both passengers and freight fell 5 per cent in
the recession of 1913–14, the first revenue decline in years. Canadian
Northern went back to the government again in 1914 asking for financial aid – nearly $100 million this time. The government agreed to bond
guarantees for half of that amount and the transfer of a larger block of
stock (the government now had a 40 per cent equity position in Canadian Northern).

With the outbreak of war in August of 1914, the problems – capital-
cost overruns, overcapacity, inadequate rolling stock – all became more
evident. They were exacerbated by the fact that the British government
banned the export of capital, and the London market had been the main
source of Canadian railway financing. Finally, Great Britain nationalized railways for the duration of the war, establishing a precedent for
Canada.

The Penalty Stage of Railway Development

As each year of the war passed, problems became more manifest. In
1915, although passenger traffic held up, freight traffic dropped by 14
per cent, causing gross earnings and net earnings to decline by nearly
20 per cent.

The situation was much worse for the two new transcontinentals[10]
(Grand Trunk and Canadian Northern) than for the CPR. Neither

company was able to cover operating costs let alone service its debt. In 1915, therefore, the government of Canada took over the National Transcontinental from the Grand Trunk Pacific. In spite of an expenditure of $250 million by the government to build a line from Winnipeg to Moncton, the Grand Trunk, the parent company, could not afford to operate the line, even though it was not required to pay interest on the cost of construction.

At the same time that the government was taking over operation of the National Transcontinental, Canada's minister of finance was increasingly concerned about the country's creditworthiness and ability to continue the war effort should any of the railways go bankrupt. One of Canada's most prominent businessmen, Sir Joseph Flavelle, raised the possibility of government ownership of the railways in a letter he addressed to Prime Minister Borden in 1915.[11] In light of the mother country's embrace of railway nationalization, and the dire financial circumstances faced by Canada, government ownership seemed to be an acceptable option.

The following year, 1916, the government was again required to provide financial assistance to the Canadian Northern (in which the government already had acquired a 40 per cent equity position and the railway company was now asking for $15 million) as well as to the Grand Trunk Pacific, which was asking for an additional $8 million.

The financial collapse of the two railways, Canadian Northern and Grand Trunk, would be devastating. Both companies had secured significant provincial guarantees and the Toronto-based Bank of Commerce had huge outstanding loans to Canadian Northern. A collapse would create a negative long-term impact on Canada's general creditworthiness in international financial markets, disastrous for a government that 'was already strained to the limit trying to organize and finance the increasingly ghastly war effort.'[12]

Desperately seeking a solution, Borden established a royal commission in July 1916. The chairman of the commission was A.H. Smith, president of the New York Central Railway. The other commissioners were Sir Henry Drayton from Kingston, chairman of the Board of Railway Commissioners and soon to be Canada's minister of finance, and W.M. Acworth, a British railway expert.

The three commissioners delivered a split decision in May 1917. The American chairman delivered the minority report and dissenting view. Smith recommended three main approaches: first, that the Canadian Northern take over the Grand Trunk Pacific's lines in the west and provide competition to the CPR in that part of the country; second, that in eastern Canada, the Grand Trunk do the same with the Canadian Northern's eastern lines; and, finally, that the government take over and operate the uneconomic route that ran across the Canadian Shield from Quebec to Manitoba, for both the Canadian Northern and the Grand Trunk.

There were indications that Arthur Meighen, the most powerful man in the cabinet next to the prime minister – and Borden's eventual successor – favoured the minority report. But the cabinet was of two minds on the issue, with most of its members favouring the majority report. Commissioners Drayton and Acworth opposed the acquisition of the Canadian Northern and Grand Trunk railways by either the CPR or the government. Rather, the majority report recommended that all the railways of Canada be nationalized, except for American lines and the CPR. Those to be brought into one system and nationalized included the Canadian Northern, the Grand Trunk, the Grand Trunk Pacific, the Intercolonial, and the National Transcontinental. They were all to be transferred, by act of Parliament, to a Board of Trustees, called the Dominion Railway Company. The new company would own the rail lines and the government would be responsible for the interest on the existing securities.

The new board was to be non-political, permanent, self-perpetuating, and not subject to either direct government or parliamentary control. The new Canadian National Railways would require at least $50 million to get started for both existing fixed charges and for interest on new capital. (By this point, the various railways had received over $1 billion in government assistance through loans, sale of lands, subsidies, guarantees, etc.)

Immediately after the report was presented, the president of the CPR, Sir Thomas Shaughnessy, met with the prime minister. Shaughnessy, fearing competition from a publicly owned system, proposed that the railways, including the CPR, be taken over by the government but managed by the CPR with guaranteed returns for the CPR shareholders. Cabinet rejected this proposal, partially because the idea of a railway monopoly was anathema – particularly in western Canada.

As offensive as the commission's majority recommendations were to both Shaughnessy and the CPR, not to mention to Sir William Mackenzie, Borden was resolute and worked to enact them. While Shaughnessy fumed and Mackenzie wept, Borden had other issues to deal with – life-and-death issues in proportions that no prime minister has faced, before or since. The government, which already held 40 per cent of the equity, was taking over the railway, Borden told Mackenzie in their meeting that summer. It was, he believed, the right decision.

In August 1917 the minister of finance introduced a bill to acquire the stock in Canadian Northern Railway for not more than $10 million (par value of the stock was $60 million), subject to arbitration. That same month, another bill was passed placing all government railways under the Board of Railway Commissioners. This included the Intercolonial, which had been created and owned by the government of Canada since Confederation in 1867; the National Transcontinental from Moncton to Winnipeg; and now the Canadian Northern system, operating primarily in the west and but with some lines in the east. D.B. Hanna was appointed general manager. A Scotsman with a strong railway background, Hanna had served as the third vice-president of Canadian Northern before this appointment.

In spite of strong objections from the Liberal opposition in the House of Commons to the legislation – with allegations that it was a payoff for the Bank of Commerce,[13] National Trust,[14] and Mackenzie, a well-known Conservative supporter – the bill was introduced.[15] Although the minister of finance, Thomas White, brought the legislation forward, the principal spokesperson for the legislation was Arthur Meighen, the youthful solicitor general – Ontario-born and a University of Toronto graduate with a degree in mathematics. While he was a relatively junior member, Meighen is described by his biographer thus: 'More than any other single individual he was the creator of the Canadian National Railway system.'[16] The opposition Liberals seemed to agree with that assessment, describing him, somewhat ungraciously, as 'the gramophone of Mackenzie and Mann.'

The Best Choice in Unfortunate Circumstances

If the 'railway mess' was a major issue, so too was the much postponed election in which the volatile issue of conscription loomed large. Prime Minister Borden finally went to the polls in December 1917 as the leader of a coalition Unionist party, made up of traditional Conservatives and anglo Liberals. Although other prime ministers have won larger majorities in the House of Commons, no other leader has ever scored such a commanding percentage of the popular vote: 57 per cent.

One of the new government's priorities was to acquire both the Grand Trunk Railway and its poorly performing, wholly owned sub-

sidiary, the Grand Trunk Pacific. It led to furious debate. 'The nationalization of these lines, especially the Grand Trunk itself, aroused another
furious dispute over public ownership and Meighen ... found himself
once again in the centre of controversy.'[17]

Although government-owned railways had been the norm in most
countries, this had not been the case in the United Kingdom, the United
States, or Canada prior to the war. In these three countries, while government involvement had included all manner of financial incentives
and regulations, particularly with regard to rates, it did not extend to
operating the railways. But the war changed everything. In the United Kingdom, for example, railways were immediately nationalized in
August 1914 for the duration of the war. Even in the free-enterprise
United States, the government temporarily took over the railways for a
brief period in the spring of 1918.

In Canada, Sir Wilfrid Laurier had always strongly opposed government ownership of Canadian railways, but the Intercolonial had
actually been a condition of the articles of Confederation in 1867. More
recently, in 1902, the Ontario Liberal government had created a government-owned railway, the Temiskaming and Northern Railway Company, to encourage development in the northern part of the province.
Still, the idea that government should actually own and directly operate a huge enterprise like a railway was not generally accepted in spite
of government ownership of other forms of 'public utilities.' For example, the Conservative government of Ontario had become involved as
a monopoly provider of electrical generation and distribution; and the
three prairie provinces had all created government-owned monopolies
to provide the new telephone service.

Government negotiations with the Grand Trunk began in January
1918 and dragged on for nearly two years before they were finally
resolved. The federal government was intent on obtaining Grand
Trunk's well-established feeder system in Ontario and Quebec to complement the various systems that it had been required to take over in
1917. The Grand Trunk's strategy was to persuade the government
to take the Grand Trunk Pacific off its hands, since the Grand Trunk
Pacific was seen as a major drain on its parent. Meighen and the government would have none of this. The Grand Trunk Pacific ran from
Winnipeg to Prince Rupert in British Columbia and had limited traffic
because of an absence of feeder lines that both the Canadian Pacific and
the Canadian Northern (now owned by the government) had in abundance. When the Grand Trunk's position became intractable, Arthur

Meighen applied private-sector principles to a public-sector situation and simply waited out the Grand Trunk, refusing to provide any additional financial support to the financially troubled Grand Trunk Pacific.

Amidst these protracted negotiations, the Great War finally ended. Canada had sent 640,000 men into combat, 60,000 of whom died on the battlefield, a higher fatality rate than the country would endure in the Second World War. Not that peace brought an end to railway problems, of course. The war was followed immediately by a devastating postwar recession.

Owing at least in part to the economic downturn, the Grand Trunk Railway informed the government in March 1919 that the railway could no longer operate its subsidiary line, the Grand Trunk Pacific. In response, the government appointed the minister of railways and canals, the J.D. ('Doc') Reid, as receiver (the largest receivership in Canadian history to that date by far) in charge of managing and taking over the bankrupt line. Now that the government effectively had the Grand Trunk Pacific under its control, all that remained was for it to acquire the Grand Trunk.

But 1919 saw further bitter debate in the House of Commons, not just around the bill to acquire the Grand Trunk Railway, but also around the bill to create the Canadian National Railways. The Canadian National legislation package was comprised mainly of the Canadian Northern Railway, the National Transcontinental, and the old Intercolonial. All the arguments against public ownership were trotted out. Meighen's argument in closing the debate was that public ownership was appropriate in the case of a 'monopoly.' While this claim of a monopoly was not precisely true – the newly created Canadian National would be competing with Canadian Pacific – it was true insofar that, in most of the geographic areas where they operated, the two companies would not be competing with each other.

In October 1919, after extensive negotiations between the government, led by Meighen, and the Grand Trunk, led by Alfred W. Smithers, chairman of the board, a bill to acquire the Grand Trunk was presented to the House of Commons. The two main arguments against the bill were: 1) the government should take over the Grand Trunk Pacific subsidiary but allow the Grand Trunk parent to continue operating it; and 2) if the Grand Trunk parent was close to bankruptcy, the government should let it go bankrupt rather than take over a losing proposition. Meighen responded to the two arguments in the following fashion. The new Canadian National needed the Grand Trunk lines in eastern

Canada to complete its system in a logical fashion. Although it would have good feeder lines in the west, the same was required in the more populous east. Meighen also contended that liquidation would lead inevitably to the CPR's acquisition of the Grand Trunk, and that such a situation was not tolerable.

Finally, at 3 a.m. on 5 November 1919, the Grand Trunk Acquisition Act was passed, nationalizing the Grand Trunk system. Then, with very little sleep, Meighen caught a train to Montreal later that morning to address a hostile audience at a Canadian Club luncheon. In justifying the government's decision to acquire the Grand Trunk, Meighen said: 'We now have ... the Grand Trunk system in eastern Canada. If we had not acquired that company, may I ask: Was the Canadian National Railway to be called upon to duplicate the succession of feeding systems now spread through Ontario and Quebec? Would that be a sound business investment? Would that be a proper application of capital? Is it even common sense? If not, will anyone argue or suggest that there is any possibility in the known world of making a system of railways a success which has only one gathering system in western Canada and has to support two trunk lines protruding eastwards for thousands of miles?'[18] Montreal was not impressed. Meighen was denounced as 'the father of railway nationalization,' a socialist and worse. The Montreal business community, heavily influenced by the Bank of Montreal and the CPR, not only disliked public ownership but felt that the deal had been too generous to the Canadian Northern because of its Toronto base and its links to the Bank of Commerce and the National Trust Company.

However, the act passed in the House and there was no turning back. The consolidation of the various railways into one operating system would take until 1922. In the three-year period required to complete the consolidation of the new system – a span of time that, considering the challenges involved, was relatively brief – Meighen became prime minister and served for eighteen months before he and his party were thrown from office when the Liberals were elected under William Lyon Mackenzie King, with support from the western-based, free-trade Progressive Party. The new government replaced Hanna as general manager with Sir Henry Thornton, an American-born railroader.

For the next seventy years, Canada was unique in the world, possessing two major railroads that competed with each other – one a crown corporation, CN, owned by the government, the other owned by shareholders, the CP.

What Should Arthur Meighen Have Done?

There is no doubt that the Conservatives inherited a mess in terms of the railways when they were elected to office in 1911 after fifteen years in opposition. Over one-quarter of the Conservative's 1911 'Handbook' was devoted to railway matters, particularly the party's criticisms of the Grand Trunk/Grand Trunk Pacific transcontinental railway project.

The roots of the railway mess lay in the previous government's failure to create one transcontinental line to compete with the CPR back in 1903, rather than allowing for the possibility of two. The problems relating to the Grand Trunk were compounded when, during the 1911 election, Liberal Prime Minister Sir Wilfrid Laurier authorized a third transcontinental railway, the Canadian Northern. For a country with a population at that time of less than 7.5 million, it was unsustainable. Both the Grand Trunk and the Canadian Northern had weak to nonexistent feeder systems in large parts of their territory. In addition – and in contrast to the CPR – those same two railroads were heavily reliant on debt as distinct from equity financing. The CPR was the only moneymaking railway at the time.

The minister 'for everything' who was to become prime minister, Arthur Meighen, laid out the problem this way in his speech to the Canadian Club in Montreal. 'We are at the penalty stage of railway development in this country; a price in some form has to be paid by the people of Canada. We are at the point now where an awakening of bitterness follows a night of intoxication; an ebb of retribution now follows in the wake of a flood tide of railway construction.' Not that many years later, his successor as prime minister, the Liberal William Lyon Mackenzie King, would confide in his diary: 'The whole railway business is one horrible mess – waste, waste so vast that no one can intelligently grasp the whole situation.'[19] Under the circumstances, the status quo was not an option. As Meighen went on to say in his Montreal speech: 'What confronted the present government was not a choice between something alluring on the one hand and something less alluring on the other, but a choice as to the best course that could be pursued under all the unfortunate circumstances which surrounded us – a course which would ultimately prove in the best interests of the people.'[20]

Meighen's speech brilliantly summarized the consequences of a period of irrational exuberance, but was the government's choice the right one? It was true that it had to do something, but were there options available to the government other than nationalizing the railways and creating a crown corporation, which inevitably would be subject to political as well as commercial considerations?

CN Today: The Most Efficient Carrier in North America

'The year 1923 was the first year of the consolidation of the Grand Trunk Railway and all the other units of the National Systems – the Canadian Northern, the Grand Trunk Pacific, the Canadian Transcontinental, the Inter-colonial and the other Government lines in the lower Provinces.'[21] The new railroad would be an even larger enterprise than the CPR, Canada's corporate private-sector giant. It would handle more passengers than the CPR (nearly 24 million, compared to CPR's 14.5 million) and employ more than 100,000 personnel.

From the time of its first year of consolidated operations in 1923, the CN was burdened with substantial long-term debt and was regarded as a dubious business venture. Total income before fixed charges was only $13.4 million (on gross operating revenue of $263.6 million), with total fixed charges of $66.1 million, leaving the railway with a deficit of $52.7 million. With total assets of just over $2 billion, the new company's long-term debt topped $1.9 billion.

Right from its inception, in fact, the CN was regarded as a 'white elephant,' a terrific drain on government coffers. Year after year, the company required huge subsidies to keep operating. 'The ... Canadian National Railways was ... critically viewed by financial and business interests, both as an experiment in public ownership and as a charge, in its annual deficits, on the national revenues. To have it fail, and allow its component lines to be sold, seemed to many both sound business and good national policy.'[22]

But that did not happen, and as bad as finances got in the 1920s, the situation grew considerably worse in the Great Depression of the 1930s. The company began posting even larger deficits, year after year, decade after decade. Finally, in 1992, the Conservative government under Prime Minister Brian Mulroney decided to do something about it. Mulroney appointed Paul Tellier, the clerk of the Privy Council and secretary to the cabinet, to serve as president and chief executive officer of the railway. Tellier believed strongly that the CN had to be privatized in order to be successful, and he drove the process. In November 1995, after nearly eight decades in government hands, the railway was privatized. Under Tellier's leadership, the company made significant operational improvements as well as strategic acquisitions in the United States. In 1998 CN acquired Illinois Central for $2.4 billion and three years later Wisconsin Central for $1.2 billion. More recently, CN acquired both Great Lakes Transportation for $500 million and BC Rail (including associated tax losses) for $1 billion.

When Tellier left CN in 2002 to become the CEO of Bombardier, he was succeeded at CN by Hunter Harrison, an American who was formerly with Illinois Central. A 'railroader's railroader,' Harrison has taken the company to new heights. In Harrison's brief term in office, CN has seen a dramatic increase in market capitalization. While CN is a widely held Canadian company, the largest single shareholder is the American computer magnate Bill Gates, who owns nearly 6 per cent of the company.

Within an overall Canadian context, CN is one of Canada's most important companies, employing well over 20,000 employees with assets of nearly $20 billion and revenue of over $7 billion. Now it is not only Canada's largest railway, but also the most efficient of the six major North America freight railroads with significant free cash flow.

All of this is a remarkable change from CN's chaotic beginnings as a crown corporation in 1917, through its long years as a major drain on the taxpayers of Canada, to its relatively recent privatization and current success, with glowing near-term prospects.

Suggested Questions

In addressing the railway situation, the Borden government had four major options to consider. They were:

1. To do as the government chose – create a crown corporation to own and run all major non-CPR railways while allowing the CPR to continue operating as a private-enterprise transcontinental railway;
2. To let the railways go bankrupt, leaving market forces to determine the new entity/entities to emerge;
3. To permit the CPR to take over the competing railways; and
4. To allow the Canadian Northern to operate in the west, where it had a good feeder system, and the Grand Trunk to operate in the east, with the National Transcontinental in government hands, providing joint running rights across the barren and unprofitable Canadian Shield.

Based on the facts of the case and other readings, which option would you have chosen and why?

Suggested Readings

Borden, Robert Laird. *Memoirs*. Vol. 2. Toronto: Macmillan 1938.

Glassford, Larry. 'Arthur Meighen.' *DCB*, www.biographi.ca.

http://www.cn.ca/en/company-history.htm.

Regehr, T.D. *The Canadian Northern Railway: Pioneer Road of the Northern Prairies*. Toronto: Macmillan 1976.

Stevens, G.R. *History of the Canadian National Railways*. New York: Macmillan 1973.

NOTES

1 Defined by Robert J. Shiller as 'wishful thinking on the part of investors that blinds us to the truth of our situation.' See Shiller's *Irrational Exuberance*, 2nd ed. (Princeton, N.J.: Princeton University Press 2005), xvii.

2 Borden, *Memoirs*, 2: 650.

3 Mackenzie was under tremendous stress, not only from business pressures, but also because he had come directly from his Toronto home, Benvenuto, where his wife lay dying.

4 The Income Tax War Act provided for three taxes, the Normal Tax – 4 per cent on both personal and corporate incomes – the Super Tax, and the Surtax on incomes over $6,000.

5 This is the only time in Canadian history that there was six years between elections. The normal pattern is every four years, although the maximum term is five years.

6 'Laurier had so far departed from his previous integrity that on occasion he besought Hays (president of the GTR) to alter his location surveys to serve Liberal politicians.' Stevens, *History of the Canadian National Railways*, 227.

7 The National Transcontinental built a bridge across the St Lawrence at Quebec City, which had the unique distinction of collapsing not once but twice (in 1907 and 1916) with great loss of life and money, the first time killing seventy-five men. Fortunately, 'only' ten men were killed on the second occasion.

8 Arthur Meighen's address on 5 Nov. 1919 to the Montreal Canadian Club on the topic of the Grand Trunk acquisition.

9 Regehr, *The Canadian Northern Railway*, 303, 318, and 319.

10 'The Canadian Northern was a soundly built line and served the needs of the west ... By contrast the National Transcontinental/Grand Trunk Pacific

is seen as an ill conceived, wastefully built system that ultimately dragged down the otherwise reasonably sound GTR. Hays in particular, built "castles in the air."' Graham D. Taylor and Peter A. Baskerville, *A Concise History of Business in Canada* (Don Mills, Ont.: Oxford University Press 1994), 283.

11 Donald MacKay, *The People's Railway: A History of Canadian National* (Vancouver: Douglas and McIntyre 1992), 18.

12 Michael Bliss, *Northern Enterprise: Five Centuries of Canadian Business* (Toronto: McClelland and Stewart 1987), 374.

13 Although only two-thirds the size of the Bank of Montreal, which was still Canada's major bank, the Commerce was the second-largest bank and the dominant bank in Toronto.

14 Sir Thomas White, minister of finance, had been president of the National Trust.

15 Allegations that the deal was excessively generous towards Mackenzie and Mann later proved to be unfounded. The amount awarded to them from the government takeover was barely sufficient to discharge their indebtedness to the bank. Although Mackenzie lived comfortably for the remainder of his life, the amount left to his heirs once his estate was settled and his debts were paid was relatively modest. Regehr, *The Canadian Northern Railway*, 453–4.

16 Roger Graham, *Arthur Meighen, Vol. 1, The Door of Opportunity* (Toronto: Clarke, Irwin 1960), 98.

17 Ibid., 196–7.

18 Meighen, address. See n.9.

19 MacKay, *The People's Railway*, 61.

20 Meighen, address. See n.9.

21 *Canadian Annual Review*, 1923, 342.

22 W.L. Morton, *The Kingdom of Canada* (Toronto: McClelland and Stewart 1970), 442.

CASE 5

The Role of Trade Policy in the Rise of the Canadian Automobile Industry

STEWART MELANSON, with guidance from JOE MARTIN

The automotive industry ushered in the twentieth century and represented one of its great new enterprises. The automobile fundamentally changed the way people lived, worked, and played. Cities and towns are structured differently now because of the car. And Henry Ford's assembly line introduced a revolution in the way labour worked and the level of productivity that could be achieved: mass production for mass consumption.

The Early Automotive Industry in Canada

From the time of the introduction of the motor car into Canada in the early twentieth century, the Canadian industry enjoyed tremendous growth. After the First World War, Canada was second only to the United States in vehicle production and per-capita ownership of automobiles, and it was also the third-largest market in the world in absolute terms, after the United States and Great Britain. In 1904 just over 500 automobiles were registered in Canada. At war's end, that figure had risen to over 300,000. By 1929, there were nearly 2 million.

The Canadian industry flourished because of both the National Policy, with its protective tariff that was adopted by Prime Minister Sir John A. Macdonald in the late 1870s, and the imperial preference introduced by his successor Sir Wilfrid Laurier in the late 1890s. These twin policies allowed Canada to develop a domestic auto-manufacturing industry under the protection of a tariff wall and at the same time to take advantage of preferential treatment for exports to the British Empire. However, by the 1920s, the policy of high tariffs came to be seen as having outlived its usefulness and was revised downward to spur demand for automobiles in Canada. The Great Depression saw change in tariff policy again, as protectionist policies were introduced which increased the tariff; however, when it became widely accepted that protectionism was making matters worse for the automobile industry and deepening the depression in general, the tariff was revised downward once more. Thus, it can be seen that, although automotive companies were private-sector competitors, their presence was shaped by a series of public-sector policy decisions that affected not only their establishment but also their ongoing operations in Canada.

Manufacturing and Government Policy

In 2004 Ontario, Canada's most populous province, became – for good or ill – North America's largest automobile producer.[1] In addition to vehicle production, Canada today plays a major role in the automotive supply chain.[2] Contemporary reasons have been put forward for Canada's success in the automotive industry. One is Canada's universal health-care system: 'Canada is attractive, in part, because of Medicare, which negates perhaps the largest competitive burden faced by U.S. manufacturers. GM spends roughly $1,400 a vehicle produced in the United States on health care, more than it spends on steel.'[3]

However, the automotive industry saw its beginnings six decades before Medicare, when Gordon McGregor of Walkerville, Ontario, owner of the Walkerville Wagon Works, journeyed north across the Detroit River in August 1904 to meet with Henry Ford, who had just founded the Ford Motor Company, in order to obtain licence to manufacture Ford cars in Canada. But why would Ford license to McGregor the rights to build Ford cars in the first place, if just across a river? Why not simply export them directly into Canada?

The reasons are rooted in events that took place shortly after Canadian Confederation with the emergence of a policy of high tariffs: 'The idea that the Canadian economy developed under the protective wing of the state is by now a familiar notion ... although the most persuasive accounts of the state's role focus on the resource sector and transportation improvements, the manufacturing sector offers no exception to the prevailing view. The history of Canadian manufacturing cannot be understood outside the context of the complex institutional arrangements that businessmen and legislators created to promote, protect, and regulate industrial enterprise.'[4]

The most important policy initiative was the National Policy of 1878, which, through its high tariffs, had major implications for future economic development in Canada. Although the policy of high tariffs preceded the arrival of the automobile, the tariff, set at 35 per cent, was applied to automobiles manufactured outside Canada, just as it had been to horse-drawn wagons. The tariff policy was the impetus for Ford and later Buick (which became part of General Motors), Packard, Studebaker, Chrysler, and other U.S.-based auto makers to set up production in Canada.

The Rise of the Automobile Industry in Canada

The auto industry in Canada was born in 1904 when Ford Motor Company licensed to Gordon McGregor the rights to manufacture and sell its vehicles in Canada.[5] Although the Ford Motor Company of Canada grew slowly at first, the introduction of the Model T in 1907 would see the company's fortunes take off. By 1920, Ford in Canada had become the largest automotive enterprise in the British Empire.

Gordon McGregor of Walkerville was not the only Canadian entrepreneur active in the new automotive industry. Six hundred kilometres to the northeast, in the town of Oshawa, Sam McLaughlin was also considering a new future for his business. McLaughlin, born just four years after Confederation, was co-owner of a carriage manufacturing company along with his brother, George, and his father, Robert. Robert McLaughlin had founded the company, building carriages by hand for his neighbours who admired his carpentry skill. In 1901 Sam McLaughlin and his brother went for a drive in the automobile owned by their bookkeeper. Sam was enthusiastic about this 'horseless carriage' and tried to talk his father into investing in their production. Robert said the contraptions were noisy, smelly, and dangerous. According to him, they were a 'passing fad.'

Undeterred by his father, Sam continued to test automobiles, and by 1907 he had decided that he wanted to build the Buick in Canada. Robert reluctantly agreed. Sam approached his friend Bill Durant, also a former carriage maker whom he had met ten years earlier at a professional convention. Durant had just bought the Buick Motor Company in the United States, headquartered in Flint, Michigan. Meeting in Oshawa, Durant and McLaughlin penned a three-page-long agreement that allowed Sam to build the 'McLaughlin' with Buick Motors. This concise document officially launched the birth of the McLaughlin Motor Car Company.[6] The cars had Canadian-designed bodies and American-built Buick engines.

As noted earlier, the impetus and incentive for Americans to license to Canadian operators was to overcome the Canadian tariff wall on goods manufactured in the United States. Originally set at 35 per cent, the tariff provided protection to manufacturers of carriages, bicycles, and buggies – then the main line of business for both McLaughlin and McGregor. With the advent of the automobile and the threat it posed to manufacturers of buggies and carriages, the federal government applied the 35 per cent tariff to automobiles as well. The decisions by Henry Ford and Bill Durant to license to Canadian manufacturers were made for a number of reasons. First, McGregor and McLaughlin possessed existing manufacturing plants to make horse-drawn buggies and carriages. Retooling these plants to make cars would be faster and cheaper than building a whole new plant in Canada. Further, capital was at a premium in the early days of the automotive industry. Banks saw the new industry as risky and would not lend, and growth in U.S. demand for cars absorbed what capital the U.S. auto makers had for domestic expansion. Thus, licensing was logical and expedient.

However, the 35 per cent tariff was not the whole story. Automobiles also required parts, and U.S. auto producers at the time relied heavily on outsourcing the manufacturing of their vehicle parts.[7] Government policy makers needed to take into consideration not just assembly but also parts. This required the government to do a balancing act to encourage U.S. expansion into Canada while at the same time promoting a Canadian parts industry. To achieve this balance, the tariff on parts was set at a lower rate of about 30 per cent around the turn of the century: 'Placing the tariff rates on parts on parity with the 35 per cent on completed cars would rob American manufacturers of an incentive to expand their businesses to Canada by taking away the possibility of at least beginning as assemblers.'[8] This strategy worked since it encouraged the retooling of Canadian assembly plants from producing buggies to cars by offering some cost advantages. It also encouraged domestic sourcing of parts as it gave a benefit to those who did so.

Initially, the Buick and Ford plants were largely assembly sites that put together automobiles from parts made in the United States, as were most other plants set up early on by other auto manufacturers. However, over time, parts and materials were increasingly sourced in Canada, including iron, steel, brass and bronze, jute, tubes and piping, lead, glass, lumber, and fabric.[9] Ford Motor Company of Canada would take the greatest advantage of the benefits of sourcing locally. Its fundamental strategy was mass production of a low-cost vehicle that was affordable to the masses.

To achieve this, McGregor took steps wherever possible to reduce costs as part of his company's cost-leadership approach. One step was to source parts when possible in Canada to capture the full value inherent in the tariff cost on parts. Another Ford strategy followed by McGregor was to limit the number of models offered (narrow focus) compared to other automotive manufacturers in order to achieve higher volumes for parts and materials. This resulted in volume discounts and reduced transaction costs.

Just as it had in the United States, Ford applied economies of scale in Canada in a masterful way. As a result, Ford-Canada, through low prices, made the car affordable and quickly took the lead over other manufacturers and kept it for the next two decades. GM was at first a distant second but over time it narrowed the lead. Eventually, GM was nipping at Ford's heels before it surpassed Ford in the late 1920s.[10]

It is important to note that the automobile was viewed as 'exotic' at the time and annual sales initially numbered in the hundreds. In 1906 Ford-Canada built 101 vehicles, and only 1,500 vehicles were licensed in all of Canada. Then, in 1907, the Model T was brought to market. The Model T was cheap, reliable, and standardized. Indeed, so standardized was the Model T that it came in only one colour and Ford famously said, 'Customers could have it in any colour they wanted as long as it was black.'

When all was said and done, a combination of factors – the tariff wall, scarce capital, and a situation where demand for automobiles outpaced supply – worked to Canada's advantage in the nascent automobile industry. However, these were not the only advantages.

Imperial Preference

Another important factor in the growth of the Canadian auto industry was the reinstatement of the British imperial preference in 1897 through negotiation by Prime Minister Laurier, leader of the newly elected Liberals. The imperial preference had been abolished in 1846 during an important reform of the British economy. British North America renewed its participation in the imperial preference scheme in 1897 during the period of patriotism fuelled by Queen Victoria's Golden Jubilee. Membership in the Empire and the material advantages that involved was proof for most Canadians that they participated in a power beyond the small population and new national institutions of the Dominion of Canada itself.

Canada's proximity to the United States and its membership in the Empire gave Canada a unique position. The short distance between the McGregor Wagon Works and Henry Ford's office, and the friendship between Sam McLaughlin and Bill Durant of the Buick Motor Company were, in part, incidents of felicitous geography. But Canada's history had given it another economic advantage: membership in a vast international network of colonies and dominions.

The renewal of the imperial preference under the conditions of the expanded and industrialized Empire was a golden opportunity for Canadian manufacturers. They could profit from their close relations with their American neighbours as well as exporting to other nations that were part of the British Empire – such as India, Australia, and New Zealand. Under the British preference system, these markets gave Canadian manufacturers favourable tariff treatment over U.S. manufacturers.

Imperial preference offered a special advantage to the Canadian auto industry because U.S. companies used their Canadian units to export cheaper products to imperial nations around the world. By the early 1920s, more than 80 per cent of Canadian auto exports went to imperial markets. In addition to increased economies of scale and revenue, the Canadian auto industry also reaped the benefit of a reversal of seasons: sales in southern markets such as Australia, New Zealand, and South Africa peaked at just the period when the Canadian market was in the winter slump. Export sales allowed for a smoother production and employment schedule for Canadian plants.[11]

The Ford Motor Company gave Ford in Canada the exclusive right to manufacture and sell Ford products throughout the Empire, except in the United Kingdom. Only two years after the company's inception, Ford-Canada shipped the first Canadian-built cars to Australia, part of the 25 per cent portion of its production that was designated for export: 'These exports provided Ford-Canada with greater economies of scale than would have been possible through producing solely for the domestic market and helps to explain the company's fantastic growth before 1930.'[12]

Eventually, in response to demands from colonial and Dominion governments for domestic production, Ford Motor Company of Canada opened assembly plants in places where cars could be better adapted to local markets. By the mid-1920s, Ford in Canada had wholly owned subsidiaries in Australia, India, Malaya, and South Africa. These were managed almost exclusively by Canadians and operated free of influence from Detroit.[13]

Reciprocity Revisited

In 1854 Canada had a limited free-trade agreement with the United States, referred to as reciprocity. However, the treaty was abrogated by the United States in 1866. An attempt was made to restore reciprocity with the United States in the emotionally charged Canadian federal election of 1911 that ran headlong into Canadian patriotic feelings for Great Britain and the monarchy alongside mistrust of the United States: 'In 1911, the United States Congress authorized a reciprocity agreement with Canada, which Prime Minister Laurier welcomed. In 1911, nearly 60% of Canada's imports were produced south of the border. In speech after speech, Laurier repeated that instead of paying tariff rates into the treasury, if reciprocity were enacted, consumers would see the money going into their own pockets.'[14] Reciprocity would not annul the imperial preference.[15] In theory, imperial preference and reciprocity would give Canada the best of both worlds – preferential participation in both the global British Empire and the North American economy. But Canadian industrialists were not convinced. Particularly distressing to them was Henry Ford's endorsement of free trade in principle. He told a reporter: 'Free trade brings healthy business. I can tell you that those fellows over in our Canadian unit are going to manufacture more efficiently now [under reciprocity]. They'll have to; it's going to be a better plant over here, better organization. That's another reason why it's a good thing for the manufacturer.'[16] Furthermore, Henry Ford argued that the Canadian plant in Walkerville had the size and therefore the economies of scale necessary to go head-to-head against American plants, suggesting that Canadians should not be fearful of reciprocity.

But opponents argued from a different perspective. The Conservative leader, Robert Borden, repeatedly told the voters that the reciprocity agreement marked a crucial juncture in Canada's history: 'We must decide whether the spirit of Canadianism or that of continentalism shall prevail on the northern half of this continent.'[17] Robert McLaughlin of the McLaughlin Motor Car Company wrote a letter to the editor of the *Globe* on 11 September 1911: '[Reciprocity] is anti-Canadian, and entirely opposed to the best interests of Canada's national life and welfare.' This attack on the Liberal government made the front page and ten days later the Liberals went down to crushing defeat and so did any notions of free trade.

The Sale of the McLaughlin Motor Car Company to General Motors

By the time the First World War broke out, Ford was clearly dominating the industry and had out-produced the McLaughlin Buick by over ten to one. Yet, despite the beating by Ford-Canada, Sam McLaughlin had come to the conclusion that it was time to dispose of the declining carriage business once and for all – the future was the car. Sam expected resistance, especially from his father, but was surprised at how quickly Robert acquiesced.[18] And so the McLaughlin's business soon shifted to the production of motor vehicles exclusively.[19]

With the McLaughlin family business now devoted entirely to motor vehicles, Sam McLaughlin was concerned about the renewal of the Buick contract coming up in 1923 and felt that it would not be on as good terms as those that had had been negotiated in 1907. Thinking ahead, Sam approached Durant of General Motors about selling, although he had his own way of telling the story:

> The approach to buy the McLaughlin Company had come from General Motors and the sale had taken nearly a year to complete. George, in robust health, had needed no persuading: in a lengthy memo to Sam dated July 4, 1918, George judged the proposed merger to be 'thoroughly sound' ... They had forfeited their opportunity to develop their own low-priced Canadian car, and, their 'McLaughlin' cars notwithstanding; their name was identified with Buick. Other Canadian manufacturers were going under ... and G.M.'s offer was five times the value of the McLaughlin Company.[20]

And so Sam McLaughlin, with agreement from his father and brother, sold the company to General Motors for $5 million on 14 December 1918. Sam McLaughlin remained in charge as president of the new company, called General Motors of Canada, while his brother George served as vice-president.

The Great War, Recession, and Recovery

While the growth in automotive production in Canada from 1914 to

1918 was impressive, the true impact of the First World War was more subtle. That war was not a mechanized one; vehicles were used only in a minor support capacity such as ambulances. The main impact of the Great War was full employment. With earnings high, more people could afford to buy a car. And so, in an indirect way, the war drove vehicle demand higher and, consequently, production increased greatly. (See also Exhibit 1.)

While the First World War resulted in a great expansion in Canadian industrial capacity, the end of the war saw a severe economic downturn, and it was not until the mid-1920s that this was reversed and recovery achieved. The economic peak occurred in 1917 and 1918 when the value of Canadian manufacturing reached $650 million in 1914 dollars. After the war, the value of manufacturing declined until it bottomed out in 1921 at the same level as that of 1912, approximately $475 million.[21]

By 1922, the automotive industry had consolidated, spurred by the post-First World War recession. Hundreds of companies had disappeared, either through bankruptcy or after having been bought out. However, the Canadian automobile industry saw explosive growth after 1922. (See Exhibit 1.) From 1904 until 1916, the total production of all vehicles in Canada totalled 135,000, but in 1925 alone production reached 162,000, double the production of 1918, valued at nearly $600 million. One consequence of the post-war recession and subsequent consolidation in the industry was that no independent Canadian automobile company lasted beyond the 1920s; all production came from subsidiaries of parents based in the United States.[22]

Exhibit 1
Canadian auto production, exports and domestic consumption
(years 1917–31)

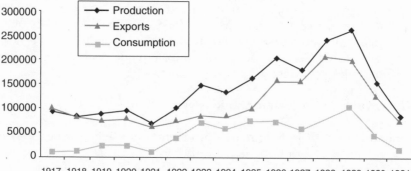

Thus, after its shaky beginnings as a field for entrepreneurs, the automobile industry became a growing, prosperous, and maturing industry through the 1920s. Ford and General Motors established hegemony as the independents disappeared. A third company emerged as a major player under the expert leadership of Walter Chrysler when he successfully turned around Maxwell Motors Company and in 1925 renamed it Chrysler Corporation. The 'Big 3' would dominate the automotive industry going forward.

Despite the disappearance of Canadian' automotive firms, Canada emerged as the second-largest producer of vehicles in the world. The next stage of the industry's growth saw the tariff reduced and the Canadian manufacturing base broadened in response to a growing outcry against higher vehicle prices in Canada compared to those enjoyed south of the border.

The Robb Budget of 1926

Although the National Policy was designed to protect domestic industry, the price difference on vehicles south of the border and those in Canada had become a source of contention. By 1926, a weakened coalition government under Prime Minister Mackenzie King[23] needed to address public concerns in order to keep the coalition alive. Thus, in the 1926 budget presented by the minister of finance, James Robb, a tariff adjustment was proposed as well as a limited abolition of the excise tax. The finance minister reported to the House of Commons: 'There is a pronounced sentiment throughout Canada that the automobile industry enjoys more protection than is needed to maintain it on a reasonably profitable basis, and in deference to that sentiment, we propose a downward readjustment of automobile, motor truck and motorcycle duties.'[24] The general tariff on non-Canadian vehicles was slashed from 35 per cent to 20 per cent for all cars valued at less than $1,200. More expensive vehicles had their tariffs reduced from 35 per cent to 27.5 per cent. The budget also abolished the excise tax of 5 per cent on the retail price of cars valued up to $1,200.

The most significant proposal in the budget was the introduction of a Canadian content scheme as a novel form of protection for, and encouragement of, the expansion of Canadian parts-making companies. The scheme allowed for a 25 per cent drawback on duties paid if 'at least fifty percent of the value of the completed vehicle was produced in the British Empire.'[25] The reference to the Empire was a consequence of Canada's participation in imperial preference, which had to be inclusive of all nations in the Empire. However, in the case of the automotive industry, this condition posed no threat to Canadian parts makers because parts and vehicle imports produced by other Empire nations were miniscule.

Dodge Bros, the Studebaker Corporation, and Chrysler all opposed the content plan vehemently because their cars did not qualify for the minimum Canadian content regulations. Ford and General Motors (eventually) had no objection to the content provision because their cars did qualify. General Motors even adopted a nationalist slogan, 'It's Better Because It's Canadian.'[26] However, Sam McLaughlin, president of General Motors of Canada, strongly opposed the legislation initially. He came out in support of the content provisions only after the government of Mackenzie King rebuffed Ford Motor Company of Canada's attempts to have minimum-content rules apply to individual models rather than to aggregate output. Unlike Ford, General Motors did not meet minimum-content regulations for all of its models although it did for total output. Still, Sam was chilly to the idea of a reduction in the tariff.

The Confrontation on the Budget

When the Robb budget was about to be tabled, Sam McLaughlin confronted King's government head-on over the intention to lower the tariff. Finance Minister Robb recalled a meeting with Sam McLaughlin in March 1926: '"Mr. McLaughlin came to me at once and declared: if you change the duty on automobiles, I will lock the doors of my plant." My reply was "That is no good and you can't bluff me. If that is your attitude, then our interview is off."'[27]

Robb was not about to be browbeaten but Sam made good on his word and, the day after the Robb budget was introduced in Parliament, the Oshawa *Daily Times* plastered across its front page on 16 April 1926: 'General Motors Closes Plant.' While the political battle created crisis, an interpersonal battle would soon resolve it. Alfred Sloan, head of the parent General Motors in the United States, disliked Sam McLaughlin. Sloan viewed McLaughlin as an old 'crony' of his predecessor, Bill Durant, whom Sloan had also disliked. Sloan saw the plant closure as an opportunity to rid himself of Sam's 'fiefdom.'[28] However, Sloan miscalculated when he publicly stated in New York: 'Due to the fact that Canadian prices will be reduced [as a result of the tariff changes in the Robb budget], it is fair to assume that consumption will be increased, with correspondingly increased profit to United States manufacturers.'[29] This statement was important in that it mentioned that demand would increase. By buying parts in Canada, and with increased demand as a result of lower vehicle prices, the Canadian operations could actually prosper under the budget provisions. Sam McLaughlin came to see the budget not as a threat but an opportunity to 'stick it to Sloan.'[30] The Oshawa plant was open that Monday, after closing for only three days.

Why Lower the Tariff?

Despite the potential economic advantages of the tariff and of Canadian content changes, the government was primarily motivated, not by economic wisdom, but by political expediency. If the Liberal government was to survive in power, it needed to satisfy voters, especially those in the rural west who resented paying higher prices for automobiles in Canada than did motorists south of the border.

Detractors of the tariff argued that, with the high cost of shipping (particularly from Europe) and the protective tariff, Canada was a captive market. The tariff, therefore, was the cause of the artificially high vehicle prices in Canada.[31] This argument, which was bolstered by the fact that the price differences between the same models south of the border and in Canada were close to the tariff rate, struck a chord with a western electorate that was seeking relief from the high costs of automobiles in the absence of any large benefit to its own region, such as a local automotive industry. In addition, Prime Minister King did not like Canadian car makers. He once described them as 'the hardest-looking lot of manufacturer's promoters I have seen, a genuinely brute force gang from Fords and other concerns.'[32]

Therefore, the auto manufacturers' objections won them only a few concessions. The government did reduce the requirement of 50 per cent Canadian content to 40 per cent until 1 April 1927. It also agreed that qualification measurements would be based on total factory output rather than individual models.

Car prices did drop: the Dominion Bureau of Statistics in 1928 reported an estimated reduction of 10 per cent from 1926 prices.[33] By then, all the Canadian auto companies qualified for the exemption. From 1925 to 1929, Canadian parts manufacturers had almost doubled their sales, and, in the same period, sales of completed automobiles in Canada doubled from 102,000 vehicles to 205,000 annually. Mackenzie King won his political gamble in 1926, satisfying the western-based Progressive

Party, whose support was crucial to his maintaining power, although Canadian consumers still paid 23 per cent to 30 per cent more than their American neighbours for their cars.[34]

Final Years of Prosperity

In 1929 production reached an all-time peak of 263,000 vehicles, more than the combined production of Britain, France, Germany, and Italy.[35] Canada exported just over 100,000 vehicles of that 263,000, almost 40 per cent of total production. However, some dark clouds appeared on the horizon. When growth in American vehicle supply exceeded the growth in demand for new vehicles, Ford saw a collapse in sales for its outmoded Model T; Henry Ford had tenaciously held on to the classic Model T, refusing to update its design to meet changing consumer tastes. But reality caught up and Ford ceased production of the Model T, withdrawing from the market temporarily in 1927 to focus on the development of its new Model A.[36]

A strange new phenomenon then occurred. When Ford stopped production, many people defied the predictions: they did not run out to buy a different car – instead they waited for the new Ford, which went on sale in early 1928 after being designed in only ninety days. This is when the concept of the car as a durable good hit home. In the 1920s, marketing efforts had been aimed at persuading purchasers to trade in their car every two to three years in order to obtain the 'latest' model. However, cars had a useful lifespan of easily twice that.

When Ford introduced its new Model A, the vehicle was a smashing success. At the first public showing of the new Model A in January 1928 in New York's Madison Square Garden, police had to hold back the eager buyers. Fifty thousand New Yorkers paid deposits on the new Ford Model A. This scene was repeated in other major cities. It was apparent that Ford had produced another winner. The next year, 1929, proved to be a banner year for the automotive industry and for the stock market. But a rude awakening was just around the corner.

Full Speed ... in Reverse: The Great Depression

The stock market crash in the autumn of 1929 signalled the end of an era. It also marked the temporary end of the era for Mackenzie King. King had made a serious mistake during the election of 1930 when, in response to Tory promises of increased protectionism and a public-works program intended to create jobs, he stated that he would not give even a five-cent piece to a Tory government to help with joblessness. Conservative leader R.B. Bennett parlayed King's callous comment into a major campaign issue and went on to win a majority government.[37] The newly elected Bennett government was to face an economic crisis of unprecedented magnitude.

When the Depression hit, disposable income dropped precipitously and discretionary purchases plummeted – consequently, consumers would hold onto their car rather than trading it in every two to three years, as they had done earlier. But, compared to the nine months that Ford owners had waited for the Ford Model A, car owners during the Depression drove their cars 'into the ground,' holding onto them for five or more years. The result was disaster for auto manufacturers in North America. 'Canadian production of vehicles tumbled steadily from 263,000 in 1929 to a low point of 61,000 in 1932 – less than a quarter of the 1929 level.'[38] (Canadian exports fared no better and plunged from 102,000 in 1929 to 13,000 in 1932.) It was as if the auto industry had stepped back twenty years in terms of production and export – with the caveat that production capacity was easily five times what it had been twenty years earlier.

After 1932, sales began to pick up as cars bought prior to the Depression began to wear out. With increasing demand, output rose to 207,000 in 1937 but dropped again the following year to 166,000; the rebound tenuous, spare production capacity was a chronic problem throughout the 1930s, compounded by protectionism.

Reversal of Tariff Policy

By 1931, it had become clear that the economic downturn was not just a temporary one – it was deepening into a crisis. The Bennett government instituted a series of measures in reaction to the Smoot-Hawley tariff, signed into law in the United States in June 1930, which increased the tariff from 27.5 per cent to 30 per cent on imported vehicles valued over $1,200 and placed a new general tariff of 40 per cent on imported vehicles valued over $2,100. Further, a 1 per cent excise tax was imposed on the duty paid on imported parts, which in 1932 was raised to 3 per cent. Another change was the complete ban of the import of used vehicles.[39]

While at first glance these changes seem modest, they had a significant impact on imports, which dropped from '23 per cent of total sales in Canada to 3.5 per cent averaged over the years 1931 to 1933.'[40] The changes also proved to be the impetus for the establishment of Packard, Studebaker, and Hudson Motors plants in Canada.

However, the result was also a widening of the price difference between Canada and the United States on vehicle prices, depressing demand for automobiles as manufacturers struggled with overcapacity. Further, the populist resentment that had prompted the 1926 Robb budget was to re-emerge: 'The resentment over the price differential [between Canada and the United States] was reinforced in the regions beyond central Canada by the fear that moves by the government to protect secondary manufacturing generally were contributing to a world-wide movement toward protection, which had the effect of reducing or eliminating international markets for the primary products which they produced.'[41] The implication here, and it is a correct one, is that the move towards increased protectionism would not help but instead would exacerbate the situation; reducing exports would drive up domestic prices, depress demand, and worsen overcapacity problems. As a result, in March 1935 the finance minister, E.N. Rhodes, directed a comprehensive inquiry into the affairs of the Canadian automotive industry by the Tariff Board. The board's report was tabled a year later, in April 1936.[42]

Although testimony presented to the board during the inquiry often expressed 'grave doubts … as to the economic wisdom of maintaining and encouraging an automobile industry in Canada,'[43] the board concluded that while the tariff burden on consumers with respect to vehicle purchases was $14 million in 1934, the benefits of having an auto industry were estimated to be several times greater, at $40 to $47 million. Thus, the Tariff Board's report concluded that 'it is good business for Canada reasonably to encourage maintenance and expansion of the Canadian automotive industry.'[44] Yet the board also found that tariffs on imported vehicles, while necessary, should be revised downward.

About-Face on the Tariff … Again: 1936 and Onward

In May 1936 the board's recommendations were implemented. These recommendations advised that general imports from the United States be transferred from the general to the intermediate tariff; the intermediate tariff would later become known as the Most Favoured Nation Tariff. The tariff on imported vehicles was reduced from 20 per cent to 17.5 per cent on vehicles under $1,200, and from 30 per cent to 25 per cent on vehicles valued at more than $1,200. (Note that a 40 per cent general tariff was applied to vehicles over $2,100.) Further, the Canadian content provisions were streamlined and simplified.[45]

The implementation of the Tariff Board's recommendations did result in casualties; Packard, Studebaker, and Hudson Motors exited the Canadian market, but they were not major players and would later disappear altogether. On the whole, the changes recommended by the Tariff Board encouraged trade and commerce between Canada and the United States, benefited consumers with lower prices, and still provided a level of protection for the Canadian automotive industry.

Conclusion

The rise of the automotive industry in Canada is a story of successful growth in which government played an important part. Government policies such as the protective tariff and imperial preference benefited entrepreneurs like McGregor and the McLaughlin family, and allowed them to start an automotive industry in Canada.

Yet, while these policies were important, they were not necessarily optimal. Many argued strongly in support of reciprocity in order that industry, including the automotive industry, might survive and even flourish under free trade. Equally, however, others argued against this form of free trade, calling it a risky adventure that threatened both Canada's identity and economic base. The reciprocity debate of 1911 touched upon social-welfare issues on the one hand and, on the other, the need to protect Canada's young industrial base for the long-term good of society. Similarly, the Robb budget raised important questions. It could be argued that the protective tariff had served its purpose and was in need of revision and so the government acted appropriately. On the other hand, some argued that the government should have acted sooner and gone even further in its policy changes by reducing the tariff further still. The matter is not straightforward.

The Depression saw a reversal of the trend towards lower duties and a move towards increased protection. Given lessons from the past, such as the experience with the drafting and implementation of the Robb budget, the wisdom of this move could be questioned. Indeed, after the effects of protectionism became apparent, the tariff was once again reduced.

The automotive industry in Canada struggled but survived the Depression, leaner, more concentrated, and still protected, albeit with a somewhat reduced tariff. Today, more than ever, parts of the automotive industry look to governments for subsidies and protection. A review of the past performance of the state's role in one industry is a useful exercise in judging the pros and cons of the ongoing relationship between government and business.

Suggested Questions

1. The reciprocity agreement failed to be ratified in Canada after the defeat of the Laurier Liberals in 1911. Strong arguments were made in support of reciprocity in order that industry might flourish under free trade. But, on the other side, arguments were advanced against this form of free trade, calling it a risky adventure that threatened both Canada's identity and its economic base. Discuss the pros and cons of the reciprocity agreement.
2. The Robb budget of 1926 had provisions that had been contemplated in earlier years but not been introduced owing to fears of the political repercussions for the minority government of Prime Minister King. How would you have advised the prime minister in the years prior to the Robb budget?
3. The 1930 Conservative Party platform called for increased tariff protection as part of the answer to the Depression and the Smoot-Hawley Tariff. With the Conservatives in power, how would you have advised the prime minister with respect to his intention to adopt more protectionist policies, especially in light of the protectionist stance of the American Congress?

Suggested Readings

Anastakis, D. 'From Independence to Integration: The Corporate Evolution of the Ford Motor Company of Canada, 1904–2004.' *Business History Review*, 78 (2004): 213–54.

Laurier, Sir Wilfrid. Speech in the House of Commons, 1911. In J.H. Stewart Reid, Kenneth McNaught, and Harry S. Crowe, eds., *A Source-Book of Canadian History: Selected Documents and Personal Papers*. Toronto: Longmans Canada 1964. 370–2.

McDiarmid O.J. 'Some Aspects of the Canadian Automobile Industry.' *Canadian Journal of Economics and Political Science*, 6 (1940): 258–74.

Reisman, Simon. 'The Canadian Automotive Industry: Performance and Proposals for Progress: Inquiry into the Automotive Industry.' October 1978. Commissioned by the Government of Canada, Ministry of Industry, Trade and Commerce.

NOTES

1 Ontario passed Michigan for the first time in auto production in 2004 by producing 2.66 million vehicles compared to Michigan's 2.58 million vehicles (as reported in the January 2005 issue of *Ward's Auto World*). Canadian output also represented 16.7 per cent of total vehicle production in North America for that year.

2 The rise of Magna International as an important global player was recognized as early as 1999 when *Forbes Magazine* named Magna the world's top auto-parts company.

3 'Ontario to Overtake Michigan as Auto Kingpin,' *Globe and Mail*, 29 Nov. 2004, A1.

4 Tom Traves, *The State and Enterprise: Canadian Manufacturers and the Federal Government 1917–1931* (Toronto: University of Toronto Press 1979), 3.

5 Perhaps because of its start in the untamed entrepreneurial days of the industry, Ford Motor Company of Canada enjoyed remarkable independence from its U.S. parent. Ford in Canada was a publicly traded company owned by more than 1,200 shareholders in both countries. Among them was Henry Ford, but the majority were Canadian. The Ford Motor Company was a private company owned by Henry Ford. Ford-Canada was dependent on the other company for engineering and design only. It was responsible for its own production, pricing, sales, and overseas subsidiaries. Anastakis, 'From Independence to Integration,' 213–14.

6 Bruce Ricketts, 'General Motors of Canada: The Axe Handle Company?' Available at http://www.mysteriesofcanada.com/Ontario/general_motors_of_canada.htm. See also http://www.newsandevents.utoronto.ca/features/mclaughlin/bio.htm (accessed 16 Aug. 2007).

7 Firms emerged in the United States to make some of the more complex and specialized parts such as the carburettor – later the 'Big Three' would backward integrate to make some of these complex parts.

8 Howard Aikman, *National Problems of Canada: The Automobile Industry* (Toronto: Macmillan 1929), 27.

9 Traves, *The State and Enterprise*, 103. The railroads benefited to the extent of over $10 million in national freight revenues from automobile products.

10 'Billy' Durant, the founder of GM, lost control of the company in 1920 and went on to a successful career on Wall Street in the 1920s. After the stock market crash of 1929, Durant ended his days managing a bowling alley back in his home town of Flint, Michigan. C.R. Geisst, *Deals of the Century: Wall Street, Mergers, and the Making of Modern America* (New York: John Wiley and Sons 2003), 62.

11 Traves, *The State and Enterprise*, 109. Note that the closed chassis that

allowed for year-round driving would not become dominant until the mid- to late 1920s, hence the winter slump.

12   Anastakis, 'From Independence to Integration,' 221.

13   Ibid. The uniquely autonomous status of Ford-Canada in the early decades of the Ford Motor Company lasted in various degrees until the 1950s.

14   'Premier Appeals to Conservatives,' *Globe*, 19 Sept. 1911, 2.

15   See, for example, the editorial in the *Globe* of 30 Jan. 1911, 'British Preference Safe,' 3.

16   Henry Ford, quoted in Traves, *The State and Enterprise*, 108.

17   Quoted in 'Reciprocity Treaty,' http://www.mta.ca/faculty/arts/canadian_studies/english/about/study_guide/debates/reciprocity.html (accessed 19 Feb. 2005).

18   Heather Robertson, *Driving Force: The McLaughlin Family and the Age of the Car* (Toronto: McClelland and Stewart 1995), 157; note also that it was in the year 1915 that General Motors replaced U.S. Rubber on the Dow Jones Industrials (DJIA) – then consisting of only twelve stocks (increased to twenty in 1916). The ascension of General Motors to the DJIA may have also influenced Sam McLaughlin, removing any doubts he may have had to drop carriages and embrace the car as the way of the future.

19   Robertson, *Driving Force*, 158.

20   Ibid., 167.

21   Kenneth Norrie and Douglas Owram, *A History of the Canadian Economy* (Toronto: Harcourt Brace Jovanovich), 427.

22   Anastakis, 'From Independence to Integration,' 226.

23   In the 1925 general election, King's governing party had won fewer seats than the opposition Conservatives and the Liberals retained power only with the support of the western-based Progressive Party.

24   Simon Reisman, 'The Canadian Automotive Industry,' 4.

25   Ibid., 5.

26   Traves, *The State and Enterprise*, 106.

27   Robertson, *Driving Force*, recounting the meeting, 230.

28   Ibid., 231.

29   Ibid.

30   Ibid., 232.

31   After the 1925 election campaign, opinion polls revealed that auto prices were a serious cause of complaint among voters. The mayor of Calgary stated that 'the whole of the West are grumbling (and have been for years) at the prices the motor car manufacturers, with the aid of high protection, have been making them pay.' Cited in Traves, *The State and Enterprise*, 105.

32   Ibid., 107, citing King's diaries.

33 Anastakis, 'From Independence to Integration,' 221.

34 Traves, *The State and Enterprise*, 112. Estimates vary.

35 Reisman, 'The Canadian Automotive Industry,' 5.

36 Henry Ford was reluctant to abandon his beloved Model T but was eventually persuaded to do so by his son Edsel. By 1926, Model T sales were down by more than a quarter-million units, and many were unsold on dealers' lots. Henry was so dedicated to the 'Tin Lizzie' that little work had been done for its replacement. As a consequence, Ford dealers had no new cars for almost nine months and had to survive on parts and service. Bill Vance, 'Reflections on Automotive History,' excerpted in *Canadian Driver*, http://www.canadiandriver.com/articles/bv/model_a.htm (accessed 14 March 2005).

37 http://www.biographi.ca/EN/ShowBioPrintable.asp?BioId=42132 (accessed 10 May 2006).

38 Tom Traves, *The State and Enterprise: Canadian Manufacturers and the Federal Government, 1917–1931* (Toronto: University of Toronto Press 1979), citing the Dominion Bureau of Statistics, Automobile Statistics for Canada, 1932.

39 McDiarmid, 'Some Aspects of the Canadian Automobile Industry,' 269–2.

40 Reisman, 'The Canadian Automotive Industry,' 7; the changes also served as an important signal that the government was taking a greater protectionist stance.

41 Ibid., 8.

42 Note that Bennett would be out of power by the time the report was presented, since he lost to King in the election of 1935 and it would be King's Liberal government that implemented the report's recommendations.

43 Reisman, 'The Canadian Automotive Industry,' 9.

44 Ibid., 9.

45 McDiarmid, 'Some Aspects of the Canadian Automobile Industry,' 273.

CASE 6
Eaton's: From the Great Depression to the Challenge from Simpsons-Sears

RICHARD MATERN and JOE MARTIN

The formation of Simpsons-Sears in 1952 was an important moment for the future of Canadian retail. A strategic and innovative partnership between the American retail giant and the number two Canadian department store chain, Simpson's, would provide Canadian consumers with a different shopping experience that would complement an unprecedented change in urban demographics and purchasing power. Eaton's, far and away the leader in Canadian retail at the time, would keep a watchful eye on the new venture. How Eaton's responded to this threat, however, was shaped by its history.

On the surface, it would appear that Eaton's did not have much to worry about in regards to energetic upstarts. In 1952 Eaton's was comfortably in the lead in department store sales, with nearly $500 million in annual sales compared with its closest competitor, Simpson's, which had less than $200 million.[1] Eaton's had over 50 retail outlets (including those of its subsidiary, Canadian Department Stores), over 180 mail-order offices, 5 factories, a life insurance company, a realty company, and other smaller subsidiaries in existence for the purpose of supporting the organization – such as a delivery company and transit insurance. Having a strong position in the upscale market, Eaton's management, including President John David Eaton, continued to focus on its downtown department stores and well-established catalogue business.

The Good Years

The T. Eaton Company Limited was founded by John David's grandfather, who had arrived in Canada from Ireland in 1854.[2] Timothy Eaton became a retail giant who transformed the nature of the retail business in Canada. When he began business in 1869 from a storefront on Yonge St in Toronto, selling primarily low-priced wares and attire, he established three fundamental policies: cash only; a one-price system that eliminated bargaining; and the guarantee of goods satisfactory or the customer's money refunded.[3] In 1884 he launched the soon to be famous Eaton's catalogue. Six years later, Eaton's opened its first factory in Toronto, and in the 1890s buying offices were opened in London and Paris. Early in the twentieth century, Eaton's went national, establishing a store in the rapidly growing city of Winnipeg, the heart of the Hudson's Bay Company's empire.

After Timothy's death in 1907, the company continued its expansion under the leadership of his son John Craig Eaton, who opened factories in Montreal, Hamilton, and Winnipeg, as well as buying offices in Europe, the United States, and Japan. Mail-order departments were also established in Saskatoon, Regina, and Moncton between 1916 and 1919.

Timothy's nephew, Robert Young (R.Y.) Eaton, took over after John Craig's death in 1922, assuming the role because John Craig's sons were considered too young and inexperienced to do so. Entrusted with the leadership position of one of the largest corporations in Canada, R.Y. took his role very seriously. Direct in manner and speech, he created waves of fear and tension through the factories and stores he visited, and preferred communication in the form of formal, detailed memos.[4] R.Y. Eaton's outlook towards the business was summarized in one comment to a store manager: 'When you own a business yourself, it is easy to be lenient, to grant largesse and to be popular with everyone. When you have been given the responsibility of running a business in trust for someone else, it is a different matter.'[5] Nevertheless, R.Y. was considered an effective manager by many and continued the company's expansion.

The bold entry of a major store into Montreal occurred in the mid-1920s, when the new Eaton's competed with the older, well-established operations of Morgan's and Ogilvy's. Montreal was followed by large-store openings in half a dozen cities in the 1920s and a second store in Toronto on College St in 1930. A chain of groceterias were started, mail-order offices were opened throughout the country, and twenty-two smaller retail outlets known as 'Canadian Department Stores' began operation in smaller Ontario centres.

Eaton's was a giant on the Canadian retail scene, garnering almost 60 per cent of department store sales in Canada, sufficient to make it the eighth-largest retailer in the world.[6] At the height of Eaton's success, it was as successful in the Canadian market, with 7 per cent of total Canadian retail sales, as Wal-Mart is today in the United States. However, like Wal-Mart, Eaton's had complex, sometimes controversial relationships with its suppliers. Manufacturers came to appreciate the steady, high-volume business that Eaton's generated, and suppliers would sell their goods to Eaton's at discounted prices. However, when the Great Depression hit in the 1930s, this arrangement placed manufacturers in an increasingly difficult position.

As GDP per capita fell, so did sales in the retail sector. Department store sales dropped 33 per cent. The first years of the Great Depression had a major negative impact on large department stores in both Canada and the United States. With reduced sales, fixed expenses put huge pressure on profit margins. To adjust for this, Eaton's and other department stores tried to accelerate turnover by reducing prices.

As the Depression deepened, Eaton's and other mass buyers began to demand lower prices than the manufacturers could accommodate. As a result, many manufacturers were forced out of business, and those that survived often paid workers subsistence wages. Additionally, independent retailers, who could not compete with the prices that department stores offered as a result of this buying power, were fearful of being forced out of business as well. The result was a chorus of complaint from both independents and manufacturers, and the government of Prime Minister R.B. Bennett took notice.

H.H. Stevens and the Price Spreads Inquiry[7]

Stepping up to the podium at the Royal York Hotel in Toronto, Minister of Trade and Commerce H.H. Stevens faced the assembly at the national convention of the Retail Shoe Merchants and Shoe Manufacturers Association on a January evening in 1934. Several hundred delegates were present, many small business owners who were contending with the worst economic crisis in Canadian history.

Stevens was a popular minister among industry leaders. Earlier in the Depression, he had complied with party discipline, questioning how many Canadians were actually affected by the economic downturn and brushing aside demands for legislation. However, Stevens and the rest of Bennett's Conservative government were feeling the pressure from Canadian voters, who were among the hardest hit in the world by the Depression.[8]

Identifying with the cause of the small businessman, angered at hearing that many young women were working in sweatshop conditions, and bombarded with the message from various sectors about the role of big business in intensifying their suffering, Stevens decided it was time to act. After making last-minute changes to his speech, he began his remarks by offering a blunt message:

> I am a Conservative in politics, in business, and in my general outlook. I believe very strongly in private property rights and individual initiative – which I consider the best method of handling the business of a nation. At the same time, I realize that greed, selfishness, and avarice cannot rear a state, and that other delinquencies, common to human nature, will creep into any system ... I challenge the businessmen of this country to face some of the evils that have developed like a canker. I warn them that, unless they are destroyed, they will destroy the system.[9]

The most controversial aspect of Stevens's speech was his critique of the department stores. Specifically, he mentioned 'the practice of mass buying of huge department and other chain store organizations, and the use of this power in the destruction of the small retailer ... and the crushing of the manufacturer who will not accept price dictation of the mass-buyer.' Stevens also described the subsistence wages that were paid to factory workers.

Stevens then called on all in the audience to denounce these practices. The crowd burst into applause, rising to their feet. Stevens felt that he had the confidence of a significant portion of the business community, and speaking publicly about this injustice provided a crucial opportunity to win back broader public support. People needed to assign blame during hard times, and rarely had the gap between the have and have-nots been more noticeable. It was difficult to feel empathy for big business.

Eaton's and the other chain stores needed to protect their public image. How to succeed in this battle became the main question, and, for R.Y. Eaton, there was no book of instructions.

Through H.H. Stevens, the government appealed to a broad constituency of small, independent businessmen. Eaton's also had a broad constituency: its customers. One method of helping its customers in hard times was keeping costs of merchandise down. Unfortunately, this action had contributed to the negative publicity in the first place.

Addressing the public through the media was another method. Confronted with Stevens's attack, R.Y responded immediately. After expressing indignation about the Stevens speech, Eaton challenged the minister to name those companies to which he had alluded. Eaton's issued a press release, in which R.Y. stated:

> So far as the T. Eaton Company itself is concerned, the practices of which
> Mr. Stevens speaks are quite contrary to the principles which Eaton's
> observes in conducting its business. If, by any chance, a buyer employed
> by the company violated these principles, the company would be the first
> to wish to know of it and to deal with it ... A considerable portion of both
> the men's and women's apparel that we sell is made in our own factories,
> and Eaton's factories could not continue to exist if the company patron-
> ized other factories using 'sweat shop' methods. The retail buyers, when
> purchasing goods in great quantities, sometimes ask manufacturers to
> quote prices on the basis of quantities, much in the same way as various
> Governmental purchasers ask for tenders on supply. This is universally
> considered to be the most equitable way of doing business.[10]

As advertisers, Eaton's and its fellow mass buyers had a good deal of leverage with media outlets like the *Globe*, and this allowed R.Y. and C.L. Burton of Simpson's to get in the first words in response to the Stevens speech. Yet, notwithstanding the cozy relationship between the media and these large department stores, Stevens received numerous letters of support from the retail sector and other industries. It was this support, along with similar developments in the United States,[11] which enabled Stevens to get reluctant agreement from the prime minister to establish a committee of the House of Commons to examine the issue more closely. It was destined to become one of the most controversial government inquiries in Canadian history.

The committee, with Stevens as chair, was established in February 1934. Fighting to defend its name as the work of the committee got under way, Eaton's turned its primary attention to the government. In preparation, R.Y. had retained the services of an economist, who pro-duced a document entitled 'The Place of the Department Store in Cana-dian Economic Life.' Providing precise statistics, the document sought to address, in detail, the main critiques of department stores in general and Eaton's in particular.

When the inquiry turned its attention to Eaton's specifically, the pri-vate company's financials were exposed to the public for the first time. The committee focused much of its attention on the salaries and wages of Eaton's staff, and emphasized the fact that many Eaton's employees were making less than minimum wage, which was then $12.50 per week.[12]

The inquiry became a royal commission, known as the Price Spreads Commission, and the intense public glare took a toll on R.Y. Eaton. A Toronto newspaper, the *Telegram*, reported that marchers in the Toronto Labour Day parade 'dipped their flags in sorrow as they passed Eaton's.' R.Y. angrily demanded a retraction. The newspaper refused, and R.Y. declared that neither he nor anyone else in the company was to communicate with the media any further.[13]

The inquiry and the reversal in consumer trends influenced changes in the business philosophy of Eaton's management. R.Y. Eaton reportedly viewed the inquiry as a warning that profits must be considered 'sinful' and felt that 'never again must there be the flimsiest excuse for an investigation.'[14] Even more than twenty years after the inquiry, the company's senior management was critical of any area where profits exceeded 1 or 2 per cent.[15]

Changing of the Guard: John David Eaton

As the Great Depression gave way to the Second World War, retail sales rebounded. The war years also saw changes at Eaton's as the Eaton family decided, in 1942, to replace cousin R.Y. Eaton with one of John Craig's sons. Of the six children of the late John Craig and Lady Eaton, John David was deemed to be the most suitable choice. Being the grandson of a retail legend would only add to the burden of leading one of Canada's largest corporations. When the presidency was offered to him, a seemingly reluctant John David replied, 'I don't expect it to be anything but difficult.'[16]

However, unlike his predecessor, economic events were on John David's side. The end of the Depression brought a 60 per cent increase in department store sales between 1939 and 1945. The return of thousands of veterans after the war and the emergence of a rapidly growing middle class presented an opportunity to regain some lost ground. John David restarted Eaton's expansion with a Vancouver store in November 1948. This was accomplished by purchasing British Columbia's largest department store chain, Spencer's. The entire Spencer's image was obliterated overnight, as Eaton's signature trademarks, right down to the uniforms of elevator operators, were put in place.[17]

Throughout his reign, John David was an elusive and reserved leader. Fortunately, despite the negative press of the Price Spreads Commission, the legend of Eaton's remained 'an integral facet of daily Canadian life ... A visit to an Eaton's store was a major happening for generations of Canadians.'[18] Yet the post-war emergence of the middle class, and its accompanying effect on population patterns, would change the nature of retailing to the detriment of department stores generally. As more people moved outside the city centre – to the suburbs – the downtown department store lost some of its allure.

Chain stores, especially food chains, almost immediately followed the move to the suburbs, which allowed people to get essential items locally. Additionally, the increase in per capita disposable income combined with the mobility enabled by the automobile increased competition from independent stores that carried more expensive, specialty items. Whether to follow this demographic shift, or to enhance one's appeal for the downtown shopper, became an important consideration for the large department stores.

A Challenger Emerges (1950–4)

The T. Eaton Company still permeated Canadian life in the 1950s. It was by far Canada's largest department store, with sixty retail outlets located in almost every province, in addition to its numerous mail-order outlets. Whether you were a Rosedale matron or a farmer from Saskatchewan, you were familiar with the Eaton's name.

However, Eaton's dominance was about to face its first real competitive challenge. In 1950 Simpson's president, Edgar Burton, and General Robert Wood, chairman of Sears Roebuck in Chicago, were introduced to one another, beginning a series of events that would lead to a new and exciting business venture in Canadian retailing.

While not seriously challenging Eaton's in sales, Simpson's was a national Canadian department store. Simpson's had retail outlets in five large Canadian cities, as well as a thriving cross-country mail-order business. Towards the end of his life, founder Robert Simpson stated, 'This store must satisfy everybody.'[19] The appointment of Charles Luther (C.L.) Burton as assistant general manager in 1912 enabled a greater push in this direction. Throughout the early part of the century, Simpson's mail-order business and overseas buying offices were expanded, and the company went public.

Similar to Eaton's, Simpson's paid great attention to enhancing the shopping experience in the downtown stores, such as the one in Toronto. This store contained lounge rooms, wide passageways surrounded by specialty shops, and the 'Arcadian Court,' which was billed as the world's largest restaurant with the space to seat over 1,300.[20]

Like John David Eaton, Edgar Burton was the quiet, unassuming son of a retailing leader. Seeking employment in the Simpson's business as an eighteen year old, a disappointed Edgar asked his father (general manager C.L. Burton) why he couldn't start work at Simpson's rather than being sent off to Chicago. His father explained that, if Edgar did well, he would be accused of being 'pushed ahead of others.'[21] Edgar grudgingly began work as a shipping clerk in Chicago, where he lived in a boarding-house room that was too small to fit even his luggage trunk. Eventually employed by Simpson's as a buyer of women's suits, Edgar Burton worked his way up to become general manager of the Toronto Simpson's store, and then became president of Simpson's in 1948, succeeding his father.

Sears in the 1930s

General Robert Wood, chairman of Sears Roebuck, was a former soldier who had fought guerillas in the Philippines and was later dispatched to the Panama Canal with the U.S. Engineering Corps as a supply officer to help supervise construction. Discussing what was thought at the time to be 'the biggest job on earth,' General Wood later stated that the distribution of labour and supplies in building the canal was similar to the mass- buying system in department stores, and that the experience had prepared him well for his future commercial endeavours.[22]

While 'the biggest job on earth' prepared Wood for the field of merchandising, his upbringing as a son of a prairie homesteader would prepare him for the American version of the Price Spreads Commission. Between 1925 and 1948, over one thousand separate bills imposing penalties on chain stores were introduced into state legislatures, many coming from the agriculturally based and economically strained American South. It was perhaps because of Wood's background that Sears was able to adapt to these challenging external forces.

The extent of legislation relating to chain stores in the United States is well illustrated by the Robinson-Patman Act of 1936. One useful explanation of the act, which is still legally enforceable, comes from Columbia University: 'The Act forbade any person or firm engaged in interstate commerce to discriminate in price to different purchasers of the same commodity when the effect would be to lessen competition or to create a monopoly. Sometimes called the Anti-Chain-Store Act, this act was directed at protecting the independent retailer from chain-store competition, but it was also strongly supported by wholesalers eager to prevent large chain stores from buying directly from the manufacturers for lower prices.'[23]

Wood was sensitive to the sentiment that saw large corporate interests cast as the villain in the late nineteenth century as agricultural unrest swept across the continent. The continuing opposition to big business in the region, specifically towards chain stores such as Sears Roebuck, was manifested in behaviour that went beyond legislation. For example, prizes were offered to children who found the greatest number of Sears catalogues to burn in the public square, while merchants paid a flat rate of a dime per catalogue brought in for destruction.[24]

Wood, however, believed that achieving broad public support and cultivating a successful business were not mutually exclusive activities. He sought to enlist public support towards a capitalist enterprise in various ways. One way was to gain the support of bankers in the smaller American towns. A traditional practice among department store chains, including Sears, was to transfer their business to a larger, central bank from smaller banks after reaching a certain minimum balance. While an efficient and standard practice, this generated hostility on the part of small-town bankers, who were influential community members. Wood suggested that the issue be re-examined. The greater expense of doing larger amounts of business with many small banks was determined to be worth the increased political and public support received.

Other methods of gaining public support included providing agricultural scholarship funds, financing community-improvement projects, and requiring store managers to take prominent social and charitable roles in their store's community. During the height of the anti-chain-store movement, Wood commissioned 'agency stores' – locally established retailers whom Sears contracted to sell merchandise. During this period, Wood also repeatedly preached the importance of corporate citizenship. His ideology was summarized in one speech: 'If our democracy is to survive, every businessman has to take his social responsibilities, his duties as a citizen more seriously, has to devote more time and thought to these responsibilities and duties.'[25]

Wood's strategy of corporate citizenship, along with his managerial skills, enabled the company to reach total sales of more than $1 billion by 1945, and by 1952 Sears was the world's largest retailer. Wood continued his expansion by entering Central and South America, but not

Canada, since it was deemed to be too small a market. However, Wood eventually came to see the potential of an entry into Canada.

Working out a Deal: The Joint Venture

After meeting Edgar Burton at a party in Chicago, Wood gave the possibility of a Canadian entry more serious consideration. Wood found that he and Burton got along well with one another, and realized that they had much in common in the ways they did business. After their meeting, Wood sent a letter to Burton asking about a potential business partnership.

Burton, while a long-time admirer of Sears, also had a strong loyalty to the company that he and his father continued to build. However, the added capital created by a partnership with Sears could enable Simpson's to extend its name into new territory. Burton agreed to the proposition on the basis that Simpson's established department stores and mail-order service would not be jeopardized.

Wood had no difficulties with these conditions, but his associates did. Sears held several meetings to work out the technicalities of the venture, and each report produced the same recommendation – don't do it. However, Wood felt that his instincts would be proven correct in the long run, and had made up his mind. During the fourth of these meetings, he pounded his fist on the table. 'Stop this. Stop it now. We're going to do it. Let's find out how to do it because we're going to do it.'[26]

It's not surprising that a deal was soon reached. The two companies formed a joint venture, Simpsons-Sears Ltd, on a 50–50 basis on 18 September 1952. Sears contributed $20 million in cash, and Simpson's contributed its mail-order business. The existing Simpson's stores would remain independent, and an agreement was reached that prevented any new Simpsons-Sears stores from opening within a twenty-five-mile radius of existing Simpson's department stores.

Sensitive to the patriotism of Canadians and to rumours that Simpsons-Sears was to be an 'import house,' the joint company issued press releases announcing that the management of the new company would be 'distinctly Canadian.' Edgar Burton was appointed president and chief executive officer. Eighty-five per cent of the goods sold in the new company were to be produced in Canada. Also cited were the benefits not only for the Canadian manufacturer but also for the Canadian consumer. Sears at the time had been doing business with more than 8,000 manufacturers who had been supplying the company for at least ten years, so its buying power would contribute greatly to the benefits of the partnership.[27]

However, things would have to be done the Sears way. The successful Sears merchandising system – one of its chief contributions to the partnership – required Simpson buyers and sales executives to be trained in the Sears method. That training, along with the import of American management executives, would ensure that the Sears system would be followed to the letter. As a new Simpsons-Sears executive told a *Financial Post* reporter: 'We've got to learn a whole new jargon, a complete new set of techniques – plenty of homework in the months ahead.'[28]

The companies that contributed to the joint venture had their own separate merchandising specialties: Sears specialized in 'hard goods' such as appliances and hardware, whereas Simpson's specialized in 'soft goods' such as clothing. These specialties complemented each other, appealing to a wider customer base than that customarily targeted by Canadian department stores.

Unlike Eaton's, Simpsons-Sears was a public company and offered a profit- sharing plan for employees. It had three classes of shares, with equal claims to dividends: 'A' shares, held by Simpson's; 'B' shares, held by Sears Roebuck; and 'C' shares, which were traded but non-voting. The separate companies of Simpson's and Sears both had had profit-sharing plans, but the new joint venture modelled its plan after that of Simpson's. The ideology behind profit sharing was consistent with General Wood's beliefs: 'The only way to make capitalism work is to make more capitalists.'[29]

Eaton's, in an attempt to appeal to Canadian nationalists, took pains to highlight that its competition was now, at least in part, American. It began to advertise itself as 'Eaton's of Canada.' The debate over 'who was more Canadian' marked the beginning of a period of tumultuous retail competition driven by changing social and economic demographics in Canadian society, and by the strategic responses of management.

Capturing the New Market: The Growth of the Suburbs

In the period after the Second World War, Sears pioneered the building of stores far out from the city centre in the newly blossoming suburbs. This innovative approach in the United States served them well in the face of demographic shifts.

The anticipation of demographic change by Sears was another result of Wood's experience in the Panama Canal. One year during the canal's construction, Wood was confined to an infirmary for a period because of illness. There was a scarcity of reading material to keep him occupied, except for a copy of the Statistical Abstract of the United States. This was this beginning of Wood's fascination with census data, which led to observations about how to meet the emerging needs of the new working- and middle-class consumer. Wood once stated: 'The trouble with most businesses is they put the cart before the horse – they look at the profits first and the customer afterwards. It should be just the reverse.'[30]

'Starting from where the customer is' was especially important when observing changing demographics in post-war society. Recognizing the massive growth of suburbia, as well as increasing car ownership, Sears correctly predicted the potential growth of consumer activity in these regions. Indeed, when a Sears store opened in one such suburb, it became a retailer's paradise, as other retailers grabbed the opportunity to locate next to the Sears store and benefit from their proximity to the heavy consumer traffic.[31]

Would the expansion strategy that Sears followed in the United States work in Canada? It was becoming obvious that shifts in urban development were occurring in Canada as well. During the period from 1941 to 1951, the percentage increase in suburban population for the entire nation was 50 per cent. In Toronto, the suburban shift during this ten-year period was most startling: while the population of the city proper grew by only 1 per cent, its suburban population increased by a staggering 82 per cent. Neighbouring Hamilton had tremendous overall growth as well, in both the city proper and its suburbs, which grew by 22 per cent and 91 per cent respectively.[32] The city of Hamilton became the focus of a well-publicized Simpsons-Sears store opening in 1954. That year also saw Simpsons-Sears stores opened in Sarnia, Burnaby, Nanaimo, Peterborough, and Moose Jaw. These store openings were followed by others in Guelph, Saint John, Port Arthur, and Ottawa in 1955.

The Simpsons-Sears location strategy was not a haphazard process: to decide whether Simpsons-Sears would fit competitively in a given place, the company analysed various factors, including city population, income characteristics, and the business volumes of other local stores. Some stores were located in downtown areas, such as those in Guelph and Moose Jaw, while others were located in suburban locations. Population-density maps were analysed to verify the direction of residential development, as were suburban road plans to anticipate traffic flow.[33]

Simpsons-Sears also had an efficient central-merchandising system to accommodate suburban centres with varying population levels: stores were classified as A, B, C, or D according to population size, and were merchandised accordingly. If items that were deemed important were missing in any stores, central-buying management was efficient in restocking those goods. The Simpsons-Sears approach to these population centres was different from the approach of Eaton's: the latter branded its outlying stores in smaller population centres as 'Canadian Department Stores.' Additionally, Eaton's store managers had more autonomy and were responsible for their own buying.

By examining statistics, Simpsons-Sears executives could safely assume the need to accommodate increasing numbers of automobiles in Canada: 37 per cent of families owned cars in 1941, 43 per cent in 1951, and 52 per cent in 1953. [34] As a result of these trends, similar to those in the United States, Simpsons-Sears believed in bringing the store to the customer, with the credo that 'Business rolls in on wheels.'[35]

Simpsons-Sears development policy required an inflexible ratio of two yards of parking space for every square yard of store area. An example of Simpson-Sears'and Eaton's differing philosophy regarding cars was evident in the city of Hamilton, where both stores had locations. Whereas Eaton's had six floors and 190,000 feet of selling space, Simpsons-Sears had 220,000 feet spread out on two floors, in addition to a seventeen-acre parking lot large enough to accommodate 1,500 cars, 'more parking space than on all of Hamilton's downtown streets.'[36]

Eaton's stores, located primarily in the downtown areas of large urban centres, had great difficulty accommodating increased automobile traffic. Eaton's management acknowledged that parking would become a potential problem in cities such as Toronto. However, Eaton's had strong evidence that it had a loyal consumer base. In the late 1940s, Eaton's had conducted a survey in order to discover the shopping patterns of Toronto housewives. While the stated purpose of the study was to find out whether sales of grocery items carried over to other parts of the store, it uncovered the fact that the majority of department store shoppers at the time were from higher-income brackets. Given Eaton's large capital investment in downtown stores, focusing on this group of apparently dependable and affluent consumers could potentially make good business sense. The company's well-established mail-order business and Canadian Department Stores could meet the needs of the non-urban customer.

Accommodating Consumer Purchasing Power: Instalment Credit[37]

The increased demand for suburban housing and greater mobility during this period was also accompanied by an increased demand for quality goods and large appliances. A consumer-driven economy was becoming increasingly evident, with a continual demand for more modern household and kitchen appliances. This demand was stimulated by increasing income: average weekly salaries, while rising slowly during the war period, gained momentum and began increasing at a steady pace from 1946.

More profound than an increase in per capita income was the increasing use of instalment credit, enabling larger segments of the population to purchase these new, modern household and kitchen appliances. Instalment credit enabled the customer to purchase large goods and pay the store back in regular amounts over a fixed period of time. While per capita income had been increasing, instalment credit enhanced the purchasing power of the majority of the population, almost transforming the standard of living single-handed.

As a result of this shift, instalment credit became an important form of purchasing power that drove the economy. It helped to fuel the post-war economy and to usher in many contemporary conveniences that had previously been beyond the means of the average citizen. For instance, when doing laundry was an all-day enterprise, the new-fangled washing machines and dryers – paid for through instalment credit in monthly payments – were heralded as modern-day miracles by many families. Other popular items that were purchased using instalment credit included stoves, refrigerators, radios, television sets, furniture, and, of course, automobiles. Yet the vastly increasing use of instalment credit was causing alarm in certain circles in the early 1950s.

Certain presidents of large Canadian banks urged caution owing to the increasing levels of debt that were being incurred by large numbers of the public. In spite of this cautionary warning, the volume of sales that instalment credit was generating was difficult to ignore. There may have been an element of risk involved in this form of buying, but the signs were evident that increasing numbers of people would be able to meet their monthly payments. Per capita disposable income doubled during the 1950s.

Revolving credit was a form of instalment credit that allowed for greater payment flexibility. Simpsons-Sears had instituted revolving credit from the outset, as it followed Wood's general philosophy that previously unattainable goods should be widely available, emphasizing a 'mass market' rather than a 'class market.' While previously in the forefront of such a movement, Eaton's in this period maintained its preference for cash payments. It was a philosophy that was an important part of Eaton's original success in the late nineteenth century, and had carried the company through the Depression. Additionally, while competing with Simpsons-Sears by offering 'no down payment' on certain items, the clientele that Eaton's now hoped to maintain would presumably not need revolving credit. Eaton's main credit arrangements consisted of a deferred payment plan, whereby monthly payments would be made but the item would not be immediately received. Also commonly used was the deposit account, which was a prestigious savings account from which customers could make purchases.

Reaching out to the Consumer: The Catalogue

Eaton's did not want to risk relinquishing its catalogue's dominant position to Simpsons-Sears. Timothy Eaton had been an innovator with the catalogue, and both Simpson's and Sears had enjoyed success relative with their own catalogue publications.

For isolated rural customers – as well as urban and suburban customers who enjoyed the convenience of telephone shopping – the department store catalogue was an essential household item. The battle between the two retail giants began with the size of their respective catalogues: the initial Simpsons-Sears catalogue released in January 1953 was the biggest that Canadians had yet seen, at 556 pages. Eaton's then countered with its biggest catalogue ever, at 676 pages, up 124 pages from its previous catalogue.[38] While the size and content of these catalogues was important, the real anticipation for consumers lay in the price competition that would inevitably ensue.

Shipping costs proved to be a key battleground when it came to providing bargains for the consumer. In the 'hard lines' such as furniture and appliances, where the competition was most intense between the two stores, Simpsons-Sears chose to cease payment of consumer shipping costs, whereas Eaton's continued to pay them. From a management perspective, excluding shipping costs seemed like a good idea because of the potential cost increases that would accompany mail order (i.e., freight and postal rates) as well as an increased flexibility in profit management.[39] The exclusion of shipping costs was also a strategy that had worked well for Sears Roebuck in the United States.

Regardless, Canadian catalogue shoppers disapproved, and Simpsons-Sears paid dearly in lost catalogue sales. Eaton's, which had always included shipping costs in the price of every item, maintained its market share in this area. For once, sticking to successful past practices was a beneficial move for Eaton's. Nevertheless, the competition remained serious, with catalogue-production divisions in each company surrounded by a tight security system.[40] Catalogues for both stores were released six times a year, and managers would rush out to get their competitor's catalogue as soon as it was distributed in order to compare pricing.

While initially hurt by their addition of delivery charges, Simpsons-Sears introduced innovations that enabled the company to recover the ground it had lost to Eaton's in the catalogue business. The establishment of catalogue-sales offices in smaller towns across the country enabled a wider distribution of goods than would have been achieved with telephones alone. Also, the advent of an automated catalogue system allowed for efficient inventory management, which enabled the operator to tell the customer immediately whether the goods were in stock or not. Previously, the customer would not have been guaranteed the item. Hence, the competition between the catalogues became not only one of price but also one of efficiency and distribution, and there Simpsons-Sears had the upper hand.

The Mid-1950s: The Department Store Scene

In the mid-1950s Eaton's maintained an impressive market share. With approximately 50 per cent of all department store sales, Eaton's was still far ahead of the competition. But there were challengers. The Hudson's Bay Company was gradually throwing off its lethargy and considering expansion eastward. And upstart Simpsons-Sears, which had been in business only since 1952, was a solid competitor in the five locations where it had stores, had already garnered around 12 per cent of the market, and was large enough to be one of Canada's largest non-financial corporations. Given the volatile nature of demographic change and increasing purchasing power facilitated by easier access to credit buying, only time would determine which retail strategy would pay off in the future. However, the changes occurring in the retail sector were apparent, and staying ahead of these changes would predict a company's long-term survival.

Suggested Questions

1. In your opinion, how did R.Y. Eaton handle the Price Spread Commission? Would you have handled the situation differently, and, if so, how?
2. How could Eaton's have used its dominant position after the war to maintain and enhance its market position?
3. As a consultant to John David Eaton, what competitive strategy would you have recommended that he take in response to Simpsons-Sears?

Suggested Readings

McQueen, Rod. *The Eatons: The Rise and Fall of Canada's Royal Family*. Toronto: Stoddart 1999.
Santink, Joy. *Timothy Eaton and the Rise of His Department Store*. Toronto: University of Toronto Press 1990.
Schumpeter, Joseph. *Capitalism, Socialism and Democracy*. New York: Torch Books 1962. Chapter 7 ('The Process of Creative Destruction').
Sears Canada. *A Legacy of Quality, Value Service, and Trust*. Sears Canada 2003.

Addendum: 'It's All about Wal-Mart in the End'

Eaton's strategy to focus on its mail-order business and urban market ultimately failed. By the late 1970s, its share of retail sales had declined rapidly after the closure of the mail-order catalogue division. In 1978 Eaton's had estimated sales of $1.5 billion[41] compared with $2.1 billion for Simpsons-Sears and $2.0 billion for the Hudson's Bay and Zellers.

Twenty years later, President George Eaton announced the company's insolvency. On 27 February 1997 Eaton's, once the entrenched leader in the Canadian retailing scene, requested protection under the Companies' Creditors Arrangements Act. In an attempt to save the company,

George Kosich, former Hudson Bay president, was appointed Eaton's new chief executive.

The new CEO oversaw a \$419-million restructuring plan. Lower-profit departments within the store were eliminated, jobs were cut, and the company went public, with the Eaton family maintaining control by holding 51 per cent of the shares. The valiant restructuring plan was to no avail and the T. Eaton Company filed for protection under the Bankruptcy and Insolvency Act on 20 August 1999.

The late 1970s were an eventful time for Simpson's as well. About to be amalgamated with the Simpsons-Sears Company, the independent Simpson's was instead scooped up by the Hudson's Bay Company in a hostile takeover.[42] Simpsons-Sears refused to top the Hudson's Bay bid since it viewed the bid as too rich (the high-bid price being a consequence of CEO Don McGiverin's strong desire to build Hudson's Bay into the largest Canadian retailer). Simpsons-Sears went on to become Sears Canada in 1984.

On 30 December 1999 Sears Canada acquired all the common shares of Eaton's, took over the remaining seven Eaton's stores, and amalgamated them under the name Sears Canada. While Sears Canada's purchase of Eaton's initially represented a promising opportunity to expand in large urban downtown cores, the task was more difficult than originally expected. The difficulties were due mainly to the fundamental differences in the organization of the companies' stores, and in particular their size. A typical Sears store had about 120,000 to 140,000 square feet of selling space, whereas a typical Eaton's store had about 800,000 square feet.[43] The organization of buying was adjusted, but the overall transition remained daunting. A drop in sales in the first quarter of 2001 and the difficulties of the transformation resulted in the sudden departure of CEO Paul Walters.

The parent company, Sears Roebuck, is now making news because of its merger with Kmart. Faced with Arkansas-based retail mammoth Wal-Mart, the two companies may see amalgamation as their only hope of survival in the present day, where economies of scale, mass-buying power, and highly sophisticated information technology offer the greatest competitive advantages.

Even with the merger of Kmart and Sears, no modern day retailer comes close to Wal-Mart's size, with the company being the first to reach sales of a quarter of a trillion dollars. Yet Wal-Mart 'only' accounts for 8 per cent of U.S. retail trade.[44] As previously mentioned, Eaton's was nearly as successful proportionately in the Canadian market in 1930, holding 7 per cent of total Canadian retail sales, as Wal-Mart is today in the U.S. market.[45]

NOTES

1 *Financial Post*, 27 Sept. 1952, 1.
2 Santink, *Timothy Eaton*.
3 Michael Bliss, *Northern Enterprise: Five Centuries of Canadian Business* (Toronto: McClelland and Stewart 1987), 209.
4 See McQueen, *The Eatons*, 49–58.
5 Mary Etta MacPherson, *Shopkeepers to a Nation* (Toronto and Montreal: McClelland and Stewart 1963), 91.
6 Eaton's statistic from Statistics Canada, *Department Stores in Canada*, 1976, 16.
7 Richard Wilbur, *H.H. Stevens* (Toronto: University of Toronto Press 1977), 108–43.
8 Canada's GDP/capita declined a precipitous 35 per cent from the peak of 1928 to the trough of 1933, compared to 30 per cent in the United States. In the United Kingdom the comparable figure was only 6.5 per cent.
9 Speech reprinted from the *Globe*, 16 Jan. 1934, 1, 14.
10 Ibid., 1.
11 Wilbur, *H.H. Stevens*, 115.
12 While it was later declared that Eaton's had complied with Ontario's Minimum Wage Act, the proper application of minimum-wage provisions was somewhat in doubt. The law required that 80 per cent of pieceworkers receive $12.50 per week. The act was then revised, however, on 3 April 1934. The word 'receive' was replaced with 'earn.' It was not clear at the time whether this revision was intended to amend or clarify the previous order. When the commission began later that year, former Eaton's factory employees testified that earning the minimum wage had become nearly impossible as clothing production grew more complicated, and that the pressure made many of them hysterical. For minimum-wage compliance, see Royal Commission on Price Spreads, *Proceedings and Evidence*, 3335; testimony on working conditions, *Price Spreads Minutes and Proceedings*, 15 Jan. 1935, 4410–15. Employees testified that working conditions were fairly good until the death of John Eaton in 1922, but that they then deteriorated sharply and continued to get worse during the Depression.
13 McQueen, *The Eatons*, 80.
14 William Stephenson, *The Store That Timothy Built* (Toronto: McClelland and Stewart 1969), 98.

15 McQueen, *The Eatons*, 117.
16 Context and quote from ibid., 93, reprinted from the Toronto *Daily Star*, 9 Dec. 1942.
17 McQueen, *The Eatons*, 99.
18 Mark Kearney and Randy Ray, *I Know the Name* (Toronto: Hounslow 2002), 80.
19 John C. Porter, *The Men Who Put the Show on the Road* (Toronto: Simpson's 1972).
20 Merrill Denison, *This Is Simpson's* (Toronto: Simspon's 1947), 11.
21 Quote and information from reprinted compilation by Toronto Star Ltd, *The Simpsons Century*, January 1972, 14.
22 *Maclean's*, 1 Nov. 1952, 29.
23 'Robinson-Patman Act,' Columbia Electronic Encyclopedia (1994), © 2000–5, on Infoplease, © 2000–6 Pearson Education, publishing as Infoplease, 24 July 2006, http://www.infoplease.com/ce6/history/A0842115.html.
24 Ibid., 15 Oct. 1952, 82.
25 The preceding examples are paraphrased from James Worthy, *Shaping an American Institution* (Chicago: University of Illinois Press), 170–96, reprinted speech on 174, from the American Retail Federation, 18 July 1939.
26 Context of deal and quote from ibid., 212.
27 *Maclean's*, 1 Feb. 1955, 11.
28 *Financial Post*, 27 Sept. 1952, 1.
29 Ibid., 18.
30 Quote from Worthy, *Shaping an American Institution*, 63; Wood's experience in infirmary at 59–63.
31 *Maclean's*, 15 Oct. 1952, 17.
32 All percentages from *Canadian Business*, November 1954, 44.
33 *Maclean's*, 1 Feb. 1955, 44.
34 *Canadian Business*, November 1954, 46.
35 *Financial Post*, 27 Sept. 1952, 17.
36 *Maclean's*, 1 Feb. 1955, 9.
37 In her doctoral thesis, Cynthia Jane Wright discusses Eaton's varying credit arrangements and how these arrangements were perceived by some of its customers. See 'The Most Prominent Rendezvous of Feminine Toronto: Eaton's College Street and the Organization of Shopping in Toronto,' PhD thesis, University of Toronto, 1993, chapter 3.
38 *Maclean's*, 1 Feb. 1955, 46.
39 James Bryant, *Department Store Disease* (Toronto: McClelland and Stewart 1977), 122.
40 *MacLean's*, 1 Feb. 1955, 47.

41 *Globe and Mail*, 2 Jan. 1979, 7.
42 Interview with Walt Pridham, retired Simpson-Sears executive, January 2005.
43 Ibid.
44 *Globe and Mail*, 18 Nov. 2004.
45 Eaton's statistic from Statistics Canada, *Department Stores in Canada*, 1976, 16.

PART THREE

The Buoyant Years, 1955–80

Introduction

'Writing about the state of Canada in 1980, three historians termed the country's recent history "a success story."'[1] On the surface, it was an amazing success story. All of the nation's post-war promise seemed to have been fulfilled.

Over the period between 1955 and 1980, Canada's GDP/capita nearly doubled.[2] Economic growth was even more spectacular than it had been in the previous half-century. Just as the economy had seen a shift from agricultural dependence early in the twentieth century to a greater reliance on the manufacturing sector as the century progressed, the period from the mid-1950s to 1980 saw the declining importance of manufacturing and the increasing importance of the service sector.[3]

There were, however, clouds on the horizon. Government attitudes towards business seemed to have shifted from neutral to negative and government was playing a greater role in the economy. The financial system appeared to be as strong as ever but rising interest rates presented challenges to business,[4] as did the changing exchange rate which was allowed to float in 1970.

Canada continued to produce highly successful entrepreneurs but many of the largest corporations were subsidiaries run by branch-plant managers, particularly in the all-important automobile and oil sectors. Finally, business in general was being challenged by dramatic changes in the price of oil.[5]

All of these events – rising interest rates and oil prices as well as a floating exchange rate, not to mention technological change – added to the challenge of managing at the micro level. These challenges were compounded by the activities of increasingly active governments at the federal and provincial levels, governments that veered from the historic norm of actively supporting and encouraging business activity to being indifferent or even hostile to the concerns of business.

Public Policy

As was noted in Part Two, a general perception in the Canada of the 1950s was that the role of government at all levels was to nudge the country towards a benevolent, all-powerful welfare state. This perception would become even more entrenched, and far-reaching, in the next quarter-century.

Apart from taking a larger share of GDP, governments also moved actively into areas formerly controlled by the private sector, as well as increasing the degree of economic regulation. This led to a growing concern within the private sector – particularly around the willingness of governments to provide 'a fair and level playing field for competition, innovation and commerce.'[6]

Crown Corporations

While Canadian governments have been active in owning and managing businesses since early in the twentieth century, particularly in public utility or 'natural monopoly' areas, in the 1955 to 1980 period, government ownership went well beyond natural monopolies.

The federal government was particularly active in acquiring businesses. In 1971 the government created the Canada Development Corporation (CDC), the purpose of which was 'to develop and maintain strong Canadian controlled and managed corporations in the private sector.' Later in the 1970s, the federal government entered both aerospace manufacturing, specifically Canadair and De Havilland, and oil businesses, with the creation of Petro Canada. By 1980, federal crown corporations such as the Canadian Wheat Board and Canadian National Railways, both with revenues of close to $4 billion, ranked among the largest corporations in Canada.

The growth of crown corporations was not restricted to the federal level of government. The provincial governments of Quebec and British Columbia followed the Ontario precedent by completing the takeover of the electrical generation and distribution systems in their provinces in the early 1960s. The provincial governments of Ontario and Alberta were also active: Alberta, through the creation of an energy company in 1973 (the Alberta Energy Corporation) as well as the purchase of an airline; and Ontario, through a direct equity investment in Suncor. There were myriad other provincial crown corporations created in a wide range of industries, particularly in the areas of housing, forestry, manufacturing, and agriculture.[7]

By 1980, revenues from provincial government enterprises had increased to over $20 billion from $150 million a quarter-century earlier, with the major enterprises involved in electrical generation and distribution. Ontario Hydro and Hydro Québec were among the largest corporations in the country. In Alberta, the government-owned telephone utility was also a major corporation.

Trade, Investment, and Regulation

By 1980, Canada had seen clear benefits from the relaxation of trade barriers. Between 1955 and 1980, Canadian exports increased 17.5 times, from $4.3 billion to $76.2 billion. The major market for Canada was more than ever the United States. While the general liberalization of trade was important to this shift, it was not as significant as the 1965 Auto Pact. As historian Michael Bliss has written: 'In the early 1960s, the nation seemed headed for an unhappy automobile future characterized by a growing trade imbalance, higher tariffs … leading to an even wider price disadvantage to Canadian motorists, taxpayer subsidies to try to encourage exports, or some combination of all of these … In 1965, the governments signed an Auto Pact removing tariffs on cars and parts, but maintaining useful market-share guarantees for Canada. Free trade instantly stimulated the desired rationalization, gave an enormous boost to parts manufacture in Canada, created tens of thousands of jobs north of the border, and reduced the final price spread for automobiles between the two countries.'[8] Owing to the Auto Pact, the Big Three shifted production to Canada, which encouraged the development of a domestic auto-parts supply business.

In addition to direct government expenditures and the operation of business through crown corporations, governments have the power to regulate the private sector. Since early in the twentieth century, governments have exercised that authority.[9] Among the better-known regulatory bodies are the National Energy Board (NEB), the Canadian Transport Commission (CTC), and the Canadian Radio-television and Telecommunications Commission (CRTC).[10]

On the other hand, while Canada had benefited from trade liberalization, concern was growing about U.S. foreign direct investment (FDI)
in the Canadian economy. This led to the establishment of the Foreign
Investment Revenue Agency (FIRA) to screen foreign investments. Nor
was this all. The 1970s featured more regulation than business was used
to in Canada. Besides the establishment of FIRA in 1973, the Conservative opposition ran for office on a platform of wage and price controls
in the general election held a year later. Following the election, the Liberal government, which had campaigned against such controls and was
returned with a majority, turned the tables and immediately introduced
them. As well as FIRA and wage and price controls, another ill-starred
regulatory initiative was the National Energy Program (NEP). The NEP
was designed to deal with oil shocks, but its approach was to punish
producers and reward consumers by keeping prices low. As a consequence, western Canada, and particularly the oil-producing province
of Alberta, became bitterly hostile towards the government of Prime
Minister Pierre Trudeau.

Government Expenditures

By 1980, government expenditures in Canada were 38.8 per cent of GDP,
up from the high 20s in 1955.[11] While the worldwide trend was towards
increased government expenditures, what was uniquely Canadian
was the enlarged role played by governments at the provincial level as
social expenditures became more important.

By 1980, the federal and provincial governments were almost equal
in their spending levels.[12] The provinces had become 'Big Spenders'[13]
primarily because of the greater expenditures required in the areas of
health, education, and social welfare, all of them provincial responsibilities. The provinces, however, did a better job of balancing their books
while the federal government ran up consistent deficits, generating a
large and growing debt. Interest charges on this debt became one of the
heaviest items of expenditure.

Financial Systems

From a public-policy perspective, financial systems were affected by
change as well. In the late 1950s, half a dozen Canadian companies had
been taken over by foreign investors and concern grew that some of the
biggest Canadian companies would soon face the same fate. In 1957 the

government moved to block this possibility by permitting mutualization of life insurance companies and thus preventing foreign takeovers.

Partially because of the need for a decennial review of the Bank Act,
the federal government appointed a Royal Commission on Banking
and Finance in 1961, chaired by Dana Porter, chief justice of the Ontario
Court of Appeal. The Porter Commission was the most wide-ranging
review of Canada's banking system since the Macmillan Commission
of the 1930s, which itself had resulted in the creation of the Bank of
Canada.

'In general, the Porter report recommended the removal of restrictions on the free flow of funds and advocated greater competition ...
It recommended a prohibition of interest rate agreements between the
banks and proposed to strengthen the office of the Inspector General of
Banks. There were scores of other recommendations, but ... the most
important one was the recommendation to remove the 6 per cent ceiling on interest rates.'[14]

The federal government and some provincial governments also
created new financial organizations to provide financing in areas
previously reserved for the private sector. In Ottawa, a Farm Credit
Corporation (FCC) was created in 1959. Five provinces then followed
Ottawa's example (Quebec had been in the business since the 1930s).
A decade later, the federal government created the Export Development Corporation (EDC), an extension of the wartime Export Credits
Insurance Corporation. Other federal government initiatives were the
creation of the Canada Deposit Insurance Corporation (CDIC) and
the Federal Business Development Bank, an extension of the wartime
Industrial Development Bank.[15] At the provincial level, the provinces of
Manitoba, British Columbia, and Quebec all followed Saskatchewan's
example and entered the auto insurance business. But the two major
initiatives were in Quebec and Alberta: the Caisse de dépôt et placement du Québec was created in 1965[16] and Alberta, in turn, created the
Heritage Savings Trust Fund.[17]

Turning to securities regulation, a number of financial scandals in
the 1960s led to the appointment of the Kimber Enquiry in Ontario.
The 1965 Kimber Report led to tighter regulatory procedures by both
the Ontario Securities Commission and the Toronto Stock Exchange.
But there was growing concern. The capital market had become one
international market and what was required was 'a system of securities
regulation that is designed with a national perspective.'[18]

In the private sector, there had been little change although the growth of banks was noticeable compared to life insurance companies. Among the largest financial institutions, the period was marked by some consolidation among the banks, the arrival of a couple of new banks, the disappearance of some of the trust companies, the arrival of a few foreign-owned life insurance companies, and the shift of head offices from Montreal to Toronto. In a much-publicized event in 1980, Sun Life announced the move of its Canadian head office from Montreal to Toronto. By then, the Royal Bank and the Bank of Montreal had also moved significant functions from Montreal to Toronto. So, while the period from 1955 to 1980 can be characterized as 'the stable past' among financial institutions in Canada, it was also the period that saw the final shift of the commercial centre of the country from Montreal to Toronto. (The thirty largest financial corporations in 1980 are listed in Appendix 5.)

Banking

By 1980, the banks were beginning to take advantage of powers they had gained from the reforms recommended by the Porter Commission. Collectively, they enjoyed enormous growth and held over $280 billion in assets, with the six largest banks accounting for 93 per cent of the total. All of the big banks had secured a significantly larger foreign exposure compared with twenty-five years earlier, and all had dramatically increased their residential mortgage business as well as their traditional commercial business.

Between 1955 and 1980, two bank mergers took place. The larger one occurred in 1961 when the Commerce and the Imperial united to create the second-largest bank in Canada, the Canadian Imperial Bank of Commerce. In 1979 the Banque Canadienne Nationale merged with the much smaller Provincial Bank to create the National Bank of Canada, making it the sixth-largest bank in the country. And two interesting newcomers appeared: the Mercantile Bank of Canada, a subsidiary of Citibank,[19] and the Bank of British Columbia, owned by the citizens of that province.[20]

Other Financial Intermediaries

While the growth of banking was particularly dynamic between 1955 and 1980, the same cannot be said for the life insurance industry. The seven largest companies grew only 6.5 times compared to Big Bank growth rates of 20 to 26 times (although the three non-mutualized companies grew faster than the norm). The same seven companies at the top in 1955 remained there in 1980, ranked in the same order, with Sun Life the largest and Confederation Life the seventh-largest. Three foreign-owned companies had risen in importance: Scottish-based Standard Life; and two US-based firms, mutually owned Metropolitan and investor-owned Prudential.

Meanwhile, a big change had taken place with respect to trust and Canadian acceptance companies. Their decline as independent entities began with the 1967 Bank Act revisions although their disappearance would not be a fait accompli for another decade or so.

During this period, the Toronto Stock Exchange consolidated its position as the dominant exchange in Canada[21] (assisted, no doubt, by the terrorist attack on the Montreal Stock Exchange in 1969) even as it was becoming less important in North American terms.

Entrepreneurs

Canada continued to spawn successful entrepreneurs in the post-war period. The most successful of these was Roy Thomson, who, like many successful Canadians before him, left for the United Kingdom to enhance his fame and fortune. Thomson was born and received his education in Toronto but began to make his fortune in northern Ontario in the newspaper and radio businesses. In the United Kingdom he invested wisely in Scottish television and purchased the *Times* of London. Later his company went into North Sea oil and travel tours. In 1964 he was made Lord Thomson of Fleet and by 1980 his company was among the largest of Canadian companies.

The other great entrepreneurial fortune made in this period was that of K.C. Irving. Unlike Thomson, however, Irving stayed at home in New Brunswick to make his fortune, although he did move to Bermuda to preserve it. Irving began his career with a Ford Motor agency and an Imperial Oil dealership. After a falling-out with Standard Oil, he borrowed money from a bank and founded his own oil company with service stations, garages, tires, and accessories, a company that was soon to acquire total domination of the New Brunswick market.[22]

Paul Desmarais is an example of an entrepreneur who focused on the opportunities provided by the break-up of the monopoly position formerly enjoyed by investor-owned electrical utilities. He acquired Power Corporation (commonly known as Power Corp) as different Canadian governments were taking over the electricity monopolies and used it as an investment vehicle to create a diversified holding company.

Thomas Bata was an entrepreneur who built his business by finding new markets, while Albert Cohen of Gendis Corporation did so by finding a new source of supply. Bata immigrated to Canada from Czechoslovakia in 1939 at the time of the Nazi invasion. In building a new company in a new land, he focused on Third World countries – overlooked by most of his competitors, who saw a problem doing business in a country where people were still going barefoot. Bata didn't see the problem; he saw an opportunity to sell shoes! Albert Cohen was from an entrepreneurial Winnipeg family. Shortly after the Second World War, he visited Japan where he made connections with Akio Morita, founder of Sony. Soon afterwards, Cohen became the first licensee in the world to import Sony products.

Other Canadian entrepreneurs made their names in retailing, particularly in Quebec (Jean Coutu, Sam Steinberg, and Antoine Turmel); in media (John Bassett and Pierre Peladeau); and on the west coast Jim Pattison established his own conglomerate, starting in the car business and expanding from there.

Large Non-Financial Corporations

By 1980 – as in 1955 – the Big Auto and Big Oil companies were still business giants, as were Canadian Pacific (CP) and Bell Canada. Other companies had grown as well – companies such as Alcan and Weston's (which had acquired Loblaw). It was also a period when non-related diversification into conglomerates became more popular. (A list of the thirty largest non-financial corporations in 1980 can be found in Appendix 6.)

Transportation and Public Utilities

By 1955, the CPR and Bell Telephone, two of Canada's oldest corporations, were still among the largest non-financial corporations in Canada. A quarter of a century later, while Canadian Pacific and Bell Canada were still among the largest corporations, they were also different. CP was once again the largest non-financial corporation in the country, but this had been accomplished by using its cash flow to diversify even further, which would lead to later problems. Bell had grown more rapidly than most of the other large corporations.[23] A regulated monopoly,

Bell grew as a result of regulated rate increases and strong performance from Northern Telecom, in which it had a 55 per cent equity stake.

In addition, there was a new player: Trans Canada Pipelines. Trans Canada was created in the mid-1950s in the maelstrom of a ferocious parliamentary debate as a modern-day CPR, a gas-transmission company with an all-Canadian route (unlike Interprovincial Pipeline – the oil pipeline).

Manufacturing

By the 1950s, the manufacturing sector had reached its zenith. Then the long slide began. By 1980, manufacturing was less important in terms of percentage of GNP than it had been a half-century earlier.[24] Not surprisingly, this macroeconomic trend was reflected at the corporate level as the number of manufacturing companies among the largest non-financial corporations declined and the growth of the major manufacturing companies trailed the growth of corporations in other sectors.

Over the period from the 1950s to the 1980s, there was evidence of 'creativity' among major corporations, most notably Moore Corporation, Northern Telecom, and the first Japanese manufacturers to hit North American shores. There was also some evidence of 'destruction' as traditional Canadian industries such as Big Steel, distilling, brewing, and food all became less important. Among North American automobile manufacturers, the picture in Canada was not clear.

Big Auto had become even more important to Canada with the signing of the Auto Pact with the United States in 1965, one of the most important events in Canadian business history. The subtitle of Dimitry Anastakis's book *Auto Pact: Creating a Borderless North American Auto Industry, 1960–1971* says it all by neatly summing up the impact of the historic agreement. 'Cars and parts,' Anastakis writes, 'continued to flow across the border unmolested by tariffs: in some years more flowed south than north, but in most years the reverse was true.' A supporting table demonstrates that Canadian auto production, which was already growing prior to the signing of the agreement, leaped from 670,000 vehicles in 1964 to over 1.8 million in 1979. At the same time, Canada's share of North American production doubled from 7 per cent to nearly 14 per cent. Whereas in 1960 Canada imported 25 per cent of all motor vehicles, a decade later it would be exporting 50 per cent of production.[25]

Those were the broad trends in the industry. But how healthy were the Big Three? Ford was doing exceptionally well, Chrysler was facing bankruptcy, and GM, the leader of the three, appeared to be holding its own. One problem they all faced, and it was particularly serious for Chrysler, was the 'Japanese invasion.' The American Big Three had been running their businesses in the same old way, manufacturing ever larger, more expensive, lower-quality cars. Across the Pacific, the Japanese identified an opportunity in North America.

The Japanese invasion did not begin in the auto sector; rather, it began in consumer products. In 1956 Sony, then known as Tokyo Telecommunications Engineering, began exporting 'its first products when a Canadian retailer decide[d] to sell their transistor radios.'[26] The Canadian retailer was Winnipeg-based Albert Cohen.[27] The next year saw the first sale of a Japanese automobile in North America by Toyota. In the 1960s and 1970s, Japanese manufacturing names became more and more common. In addition to Sony and Toyota, there was Seiko, Matshusita, Honda, Nissan, and many others selling a wide variety of consumer products ranging from cars to videotape recorders to electronic watches to portable cassette players. The Japanese invasion was the agent of creative destruction as the Japanese applied new manufacturing principles which in turn resulted in higher-quality, lower-priced products. Many traditional manufacturers in Ontario, Michigan, Ohio, and Pennsylvania were challenged by the Japanese – not only in terms of costs but also in terms of quality.[28]

At the same time that Big Auto was being challenged, Big Oil was becoming more important with four major subsidiaries of foreign parents, all based in Toronto. Collectively, Big Oil was a stronger force than it had been a quarter-century earlier as a result of the discovery in Leduc, Alberta, and the pioneering commercial development of that province's oil sands.

Beyond Big Auto and Big Oil it was obvious that not only was Big Steel less important but that industries that had once been stalwarts of the Canadian economy – distilling, brewing, meat packing – were also declining in significance. Taking their place among Canada's largest corporations were companies focused on technology such as Moore Corporation and Northern Telecom and conglomerates such as Genstar.

Extractive Sector

By 1980, Canada's extractive companies were again enjoying a commodity boom (just as they had twenty-five years earlier), having survived a post-war decline in commodity prices. And once again the oil, gas, mining, and mineral sectors were faring better than the paper and forest products sector.

Having witnessed oil prices that were once as low as $10 per barrel shoot up to $40 a barrel, the four integrated producers were still based in Toronto. However, both British American and McColl Frontenac had become Gulf Canada and Texaco Canada respectively. By 1980, there were still three large mining companies, just as there had been a quarter-century earlier. But Alcan had become the largest extractive company in Canada while Inco had not been so fortunate. Once Inco lost its monopoly position, it struggled with both geographic and product-line diversification, sometimes with unfortunate results.

On the whole, the extractive sector experienced both good and bad times in the quarter-century from 1955 to 1980 as the industry went from the post-war boom and bust in prices to a revival during the Vietnam War and the later stages of the Cold War. Out of these vicissitudes emerged a stronger energy and mining subsector but a weaker forest products sector.

Retail

By 1980, there were still seven major retailers in Canada, just as there had been in 1955, but elements of both destruction and creativity were in play. Eaton's, the number one retailer for much of the twentieth century, was no longer one of the largest corporations. Its long-time rival, Simpson's, had been sold to the venerable Hudson's Bay Company, which had finally become a more dynamic retailer under the leadership of Don McGivern. After three hundred years, the Bay had moved its head office from the United Kingdom to Canada and within Canada from Winnipeg to Toronto as the company acquired Simpson's and finally became a national retail player. Meanwhile, upstart Simpsons-Sears – a new player in the Canadian retail scene – was growing as quickly as the Bay.

Creatively speaking, the major success story of the period was Weston's/Loblaw, the supermarket chain. After the acquisition of Loblaw, Weston's became the dominant retailer in Canada, indeed one of the nation's largest non-financial corporations. Meanwhile, among the other supermarkets, Safeway was keeping up in western Canada and Dominion Stores was falling behind in central Canada. In Quebec, two new players had arrived on the scene in Provigo and family-owned Steinberg's.

Conglomerates

Conglomerates are defined as corporations 'consisting of a number of subsidiary companies or divisions in a variety of unrelated industries, usually as a result of merger or acquisition,'[29] and they have been part of Canadian business life for over a century. One of the first was the Lake Superior Corporation. At the mid-twentieth-century mark, the best-known Canadian conglomerate was E.P. Taylor's Argus Corporation, with significant investments in Canadian Breweries, Massey Ferguson, Dominion Stores, and other major Canadian corporations.[30]

Not that conglomerates are unique to Canada. Probably the best-known conglomerate in the world in the mid-twentieth century was ITT, partially because of its 250 profit centres on four continents. Conglomerates would eventually decline in favour as their results deteriorated and academics such as Michael Porter began challenging the concept behind them in widely read articles and books. In the 1960s and 1970s, however, diversification became a bit of a corporate fad.[31] In the 1970s, for example, Power Corp made a takeover bid for the venerable Argus Corporation. Power Corp, as its name implies, had begun life in the electrical business. But, as Canadian governments took over the electrical business, Power became a conglomerate and was acquired from its original owners by Paul Desmarais.[32] Policy makers in Ottawa were sufficiently concerned by this turn of events to appoint a Royal Commission on Corporate Concentration in 1975 to examine the broad issue of corporate concentration in the country.

By 1980, three major conglomerates that were large enough to rank among the largest non-financial corporations[33] led the pack in terms of revenue: International Thomson, Genstar, and Hiram Walker-Consumers' Home.[34] All three differed in various ways from each other – particularly in the degrees of diversification. For example, Thomson and Hiram Walker were essentially in three businesses, while Genstar was in twelve.

Summary

By 1980, as in 1955, Canadian industry was dominated by Big Auto, Big Oil, and, to a lesser degree, Big Steel. Likewise, Canadian Pacific and Bell Canada were still major Canadian corporations.

Manufacturing, on the other hand, was beginning its decline relative to the rest of the economy. In Big Auto, the major change was the narrowly averted bankruptcy of Chrysler and the arrival of Japanese vehicles in force. Major corporations such as Distillers Corporation Seagrams were no longer as important as they once were. The same was true of Canadian Breweries, CGE, Burns Food, and Algoma Steel. In their place were more technology-oriented companies – Moore Corporation and Northern Telecom and conglomerates such as Hiram Walker-Consumers' Home.

In terms of Big Oil, the change had been less dramatic. There were still four main companies based in Toronto, but all four of the integrated producers had become much more significant because of the Leduc discovery, which transformed Canada from being a net importer to a net exporter of oil. In the mining sector, Alcan had replaced Inco as Canada's number one mining company.

The biggest change was in retail as Eaton's and Simpson's had been replaced as Canada's major retailers by Weston's/Loblaw and the Bay.

Conclusion

The years from 1955 to 1980 were good ones for Canada. It was a period of extraordinary economic growth for the nation, a period when its economic progress was greater than that of the United States, the United Kingdom, Australia, and other developed nations. But the decade of the 1970s introduced an element of uncertainty for both entrepreneurs and corporate managers of large enterprises because of rising interest rates and oil prices and a volatile dollar. So, while the macro economy was enjoying heady growth, those operating in the micro economy had to cope with greater challenges.

At the same time, the former productive interaction between government and the private sector was becoming less positive. The government's role continued to grow in terms of share of GNP, regulatory reach, rise of new crown corporations, and performance of functions formerly undertaken by the private sector. Government's attitude had also shifted from one that was positive or at least neutral towards the private sector to one that was becoming increasingly hostile. This was true at both the federal and provincial levels. But, as provincial governments were becoming much more active and powerful, this change in tone introduced an additional cause for concern.

Nonetheless, Canada's financial system continued to function well, particularly the banks after the reforms of the Porter Commission were implemented, including the abolition of the 6 per cent interest ceiling. Life insurance companies were provided protection from foreign takeovers, and the central monetary authority, the Bank of Canada, emerged from a bitter battle between the governor and the government stronger and more independent than ever. Curiously, and in spite of increased government activism, no action was taken to create a national securities regulator.

With regard to major financial corporations, the period produced further consolidation among the big banks and, as a result, fewer players. There was also a shift of influence and power from Montreal to Toronto. Life insurance companies continued to grow but, for some of the mutualized companies, growth was lethargic rather than dynamic. When Montreal Trust disappeared as an independent company in 1980, it could not have been imagined that all of the trust companies and Canadian acceptance companies, both an important feature of the Canadian financial scene, would soon disappear as well.

Canada continued to produce entrepreneurs, some of whom moved to the United Kingdom to enlarge their fortunes, just as previous generations of Canadian entrepreneurs had done in earlier times. But Canada also benefited from hostile government environments abroad which drove entrepreneurs such as Thomas Bata, Steve Roman, and Frank Stronach to make their fortunes in Canada.

Big business got bigger but growth was uneven. CP and Bell got a lot bigger but, overall, the manufacturing sector declined. Not even Big Auto, which had the benefit of the U.S.-Canada Auto Pact, enjoyed as much growth as Bell; and Chrysler almost went bankrupt. Big Oil enjoyed another commodity boom with the discovery of oil in Leduc but had to contend with increasingly hostile governments. The retail sector experienced both creativity and destruction. Weston's/Loblaw enjoyed remarkable success, as did the venerable old Hudson's Bay Company, while Eaton's and Simpson's disappeared or were in the process of doing so. And conglomerates made their appearance among Canada's largest corporations, in line with the fads of the day.

On the whole, the period from 1955 to 1980 was one of buoyant economic growth but with danger signs on the horizon, such as escalating interest rates and oil prices, a declining dollar, and governments that were turning hostile to business. In short, it was a remarkably stable period for business, much different from the turmoil that would be experienced throughout the next quarter-century.

Appendix 5
Top thirty financial corporations by assets, 1980 (in $ millions)

Corporation	Total Assets - $	Code
1. Royal Bank	62,834	B
2. Canadian Imperial Bank of Commerce	55,428	B
3. Bank of Montreal	48,842	B
4. Bank of Nova Scotia	43,177	B
5. Toronto Dominion Bank	33,842	B
6. National Bank of Canada	16,464	B
7. Royal Trustco	8,274	T
8. Sun Life Assurance Co. of Canada	7,855	I
9. Canada Trustco Mortgage	7,605	T
10. Manufacturers Life	5,939	I
11. Canada Permanent Mortgage	5,562	T
12. Great West Life Assurance	5,089	I
13. The Mercantile Bank of Canada	4,115	B
14. London Life	3,860	I
15. Montreal City and District Savings Bank	3,599	B
16. (IAC) Industrial Acceptance Corporation	3,512	A
17. Victoria and Grey Trustco	3,479	T
18. Canada Life	3,447	I
19. Traders Group	3,394	A
20. Mutual Life Assurance Co. of Canada	3,308	I
21. Confederation Life	3,231	I
22. Standard Life Assurance	2,726	I
23. General Motors Acceptance Corporation	2,420	A
24. Metropolitan Life	2,368	I
25. Bank of British Columbia	2,338	B
26. Crown Life Insurance	2,330	I
27. National Trust	2,201	T
28. Prudential Insurance Company of America	1,851	I
29. North American Life Assurance	1,825	I
30. Central Trust	1,814	T
CODE: B = Banks A = Acceptance Cos. I = Life Insurance Cos. T = Trust Cos.		

Source: Canadian Business, July 1981.

Appendix 6
Top thirty non-financial corporations (excluding crown corporations), 1980, by sales (in $ millions)

Corporation	Total Sales - $	Code
1. Canadian Pacific	9,984	T
2. General Motors of Canada	9,451	M
3. George Weston	6,777	R
4. Ford Motor Co. of Canada	6,408	M
5. Alcan Aluminum	6,224	E
6. Imperial Oil	6,210	E
7. Bell Canada	6,037	U
8. Gulf Canada	4,030	E
9. Shell Canada	3,962	E
10. Hudson's Bay	3,814	R
11. Massey Ferguson	3,685	M
12. Inco	3,624	E
13. Texaco Canada	3,503	E
14. Trans Canada Pipeline	3,143	U
15. Simpsons Sears	2,955	R
16. Noranda Mines	2,889	E
17. Canada Packers	2,842	M
18. Canada Safeway	2,712	R
19. Dominion Stores	2,664	R
20. Provigo	2,631	R
21. International Thomson Org.	2,576	C
22. MacMillan Bloedel	2,436	E
23. Genstar	2,310	C
24. Steinberg Inc.	2,247	R
25. Stelco	2,229	M
26. Moore Corp.	2,155	M
27. Hiram Walker-Consumers' Home	2,154	C
28. Nova	2,126	E
29. Northern Telecom	2,055	M
30. Chrysler Canada	2,000	M
CODE: T = Transportation E = Extractive U = Utilities M = Manufacturing R = Retail C = Conglomerate		

Source: Canadian Business, July 1981.

BIBLIOGRAPHY

Anastaskis, Dimitry. *Autopact: Creating a Borderless North American Auto Industry, 1960–1971*. Toronto: University of Toronto Press 2005.

Black, Conrad. 'From Argus to Hollinger: An Adventure in Going Global.' The James Gillies 1991 Alumni Lecture. Toronto: Faculty of Administrative Studies, York University, 1991.

– *Conrad Black: A Life in Progress*. Toronto: Key Porter Books 1993.

Boothman, Barry E.C., and Barbara Austin. 'Another One Bites the Dust: Turnover and Failure among the Leading Canadian Firms, 1973–2003.' ASAC Conference, 2005, Toronto.

Canada. Royal Commission on Corporate Concentration. *Report of the Royal Commission on Corporate Concentration*. Ottawa: Minister of Supply and Services, Canada, 1978.

Cohen, Albert D. *The Entrepreneurs: The Story of Gendis Inc.* Toronto: McClelland and Stewart 1985.

Dawson, Laura Ritchie. 'Nationalism versus Interdependence in the Evolution of Canada's Post-War Investment Policies.' Presented at the Trade and Investment Conference, sponsored by the Centre for Trade Policy and Law at the University of Ottawa, 19 Nov. 2005, http://www.carleton.ca/ctpl/conferences/documents/Post-WarInvestmentPolicies-RitchieDawson.pdf (accessed 21 July 2008).

Fell, Antony S. *The Canadian Chartered Banks: A Dominion Securities Corporation Limited Research Report*. Toronto: Dominion Securities Corporation 1964.

Foster, Peter. 'Who's Minding the Store?' *Toronto Life*, December 2007.

Ip, Irene K. *Big Spenders: A Survey of Provincial Government Finances in Canada*. Toronto: C.D. Howe Institute 1991.

Jackman, Henry N.R., ed. *The Letters and Diaries of Henry Rutherford Jackman*. Toronto: Harmony Printing 2005.

Martin, Joe. 'The Government Squeeze.' *Journal of the Board of Trade of Metropolitan Toronto*. February 1975.

Porter, John C. *The Men Who Put the Show on the Road: Simpson's, 1872–1972*. Toronto: Simpson's 1972.

Prichard, J. Robert. *Crown Corporations in Canada: The Calculus of Instrument Choice*. Toronto: Butterworths 1983.

Province of Manitoba. *Submission of the Government of the Province of Manitoba to the Royal Commission on Banking and Finance*. 9 April 1962.

Simpson, Kieran, ed. *The Canadian Who's Who*. Toronto: University of Toronto Press 1980.

Taylor, Graham. 'Conquering Distance.' *The Beaver, Contemplating Our Century Edition*, February/March 2000.
Vining, Adam. 'Provincial Ownership of Government Enterprise in Canada.' *Annals of Public and Cooperative Economy*, 54, no. 1 (1983): 35–55.

NOTES

1 Robert Bothwell, *The Penguin History of Canada* (Toronto: Penguin Canada 2006), 403.
2 In constant dollars, comparable increases were 70.5 per cent for the United States, 79.5 per cent for Australia, and 64.3 per cent for the United Kingdom.
3 K.J. Rea, 'Growth and Structural Change since World War II,' in Rea, ed., *A Guide to Canadian Economic History* (Toronto: Canadian Scholars' Press 1991), Part VII.
4 Source: Table 176–0043, Financial Market Statistics, Wednesdays unless otherwise stated, computed annual average (per cent unless otherwise noted) (table), CANSIM (database), Using E-STAT (distributor).
5 Source: British Petroleum.
6 A description of the challenges presented by the attitudes of the federal government during this period can be found in Dawson, 'Nationalism versus Interdependence.'
7 Vining, 'Provincial Ownership of Government Enterprise in Canada.'
8 Michael Bliss, *Northern Enterprise: Five Centuries of Canadian Business* (Toronto: McClelland and Stewart 1987), 493.
9 For an excellent analysis of the early regulation of business in Canada, see Graham Taylor, 'The Regulatory Impulse,' in Taylor, *The Rise of Canadian Business* (Toronto: Oxford University Press 2008).
10 The NEB was created in 1959, the CTC in 1967, and the CRTC in 1968.
11 Vito Tanzi and Ludger Schuknecht, *Growth of General Government Expenditure, 1970–1996* (Cambridge, New York: Cambridge University Press 2000), Table 1.1.
12 Government of Canada, Fiscal Reference Tables, September 2007.
13 Irene K. Ip, *A Survey of Provincial Government Finances in Canada* (Ottawa: C.D. Howe Institute 1991).
14 Robert MacIntosh, *Different Drummers: Banking and Politics in Canada* (Toronto: Macmillan 1991), 137.
15 The various federal government crown corporations were large and important players in the financial system. The two largest, the Bank of Canada and CMHC, would rank among the ten largest financial institutions in the country, while the next three – the Export Development Corporation, the

Farm Credit Corporation, and the Federal Business Development Bank – would rank among the top twenty financial corporations.

16 By 1980, the Caisse had assets of nearly $12 billion, which made it the eighth-largest financial institution in the country, smaller than the six big banks and the Bank of Canada but bigger than CMHC or Royal Trustco.

17 The fund was created in 1976 to take some of Alberta's natural-resource wealth and invest it for future generations of Albertans. In a short four years, it had grown to over $6 billion, making it larger than all but the biggest of the long-established life insurance companies.

18 E.P. Neufeld, *The Financial System of Canada* (Toronto: Macmillan 1972), 540, 541.

19 The Mercantile Bank was originally Dutch. The purchase by Citibank was a contributing factor to the introduction of foreign-ownership controls in the 1967 Bank Act.

20 The Bank of British Columbia was the creation of the province's eccentric premier, W.A.C. Bennett. Resenting eastern domination of banking, Bennett had created the bank and given shares to the citizens of the province.

21 The dollar value of trading on the Toronto Stock Exchange enjoyed exponential growth, twenty-fourfold, in the 1960s and 1970s. Growth was particularly buoyant in the latter part of the 1970s as industrial volume increased more than sixfold while mining and oils jumped an astonishing 11.5 times: Statistics Canada, CANSIM database, Table 184 series.

22 Simpson, *The Canadian Who's Who*; and 'A private visionary,' *Maclean's*, 105, no. 52 (28 Dec. 1992): 55. Business Source Premier, EBSCO, http://search.ebscohost.com.myaccess.library.utoronto.ca/login.aspx?direct=true&db=buh&AN=9301101412&site=ehost-live (accessed 24 Aug. 2008).

23 CP grew twenty-twofold; Bell twenty-five times versus a norm of thirteen times.

24 Rea, *A Guide to Economic History*, 232.

25 Anastaskis, *Autopact*, 172 , 196, 197.

26 Neil Kagan, *National Geographic Concise History of the World: An Illustrated Time Line* (Washington, D.C.: National Geographic 2005), 361.

27 Albert D. Cohen, 'Japanese Technology Meets Canadian Salesmanship,' in *The Entrepeneurs*, chapter 16.

28 In a series of award-winning articles, Professor Robert Hayes of the Harvard Business School challenged North American manufacturers to stop marketing 'makeable' products, e.g., pet rocks, and to start making marketable products, i.e., quality products that were needed, affordable, and of high quality.

29 'Conglomerate.' The American Heritage® New Dictionary of Cultural Lit-

eracy, 3rd ed., Houghton Mifflin Company, 2005, Dictionary.com, http://
dictionary.reference.com/browse/Conglomerate (accessed 17 Aug. 2008).

30 Its interests in these companies ranged from 15.8 per cent to 23.3 per cent
and 'one or more of the members of the board are directors or officers of
these companies' (*Financial Post* card, 17 Feb. 1956).

31 The harmful effects of such a fad are examined in Case 8, dealing with
Inco's attempts at diversification as its monopoly disappeared.

32 At the time of the takeover bid, Power Corporation owned anywhere
from 38.1 per cent to 88.8 per cent of the voting stock of Canada Steam-
ship Lines, Laurentide Financial Corporation, Investors Group, Imperial
Life, and Consolidated Bathurst. Through these holdings, it controlled a
number of other corporations.

33 Argus revenue was only $6.5 million in 1980. While Power's was much
higher, it was still well below those of the three mentioned above.

34 An argument could be made that other large companies were also conglomerates, for example, Canadian Pacific. But CP described itself as a
transportation company that managed other companies through a subsidiary, Canadian Pacific Enterprises.

CASE 7
The 'Coyne Affair' at the Bank of Canada

KATHERINE MACKLEM, with guidance from JOE MARTIN

On 1 January 1955 James Elliot Coyne became the governor of the Bank of Canada. He was the bank's second governor, succeeding Graham Towers, who had run the bank from the day it was launched in 1935. A Rhodes Scholar and a lawyer by training, Coyne had been hired by Towers many years earlier, in 1938, to work in the Research Department, as an expert in agricultural matters.

Although Coyne was officially a bank employee from 1938 until his departure in 1961, his early years were marked by a number of absences from the bank. A Winnipeg native, Coyne was seconded soon after arriving in Ottawa by the deputy minister of finance, Clifford Clark, to work as a financial attaché at the Canadian embassy in Washington, D.C. Later, during the Second World War, he served in the Royal Canadian Air Force. By 1944, Coyne had returned to Ottawa and was back at the Bank of Canada as executive assistant to Governor Towers. In 1950 he was named deputy governor. And then, in late 1954, he was appointed governor of the Bank of Canada, named to the post by the Liberal government of Louis St Laurent.

By all accounts a brilliant and headstrong man, Coyne was forty-four years old when he took the top post at Canada's central bank. A long-time employee and well known to the government of the day, there was little indication at the time of his appointment that his reign as governor would erupt in what became known as 'The Coyne Affair,' nor that he would leave the post before the end of his term.

This case examines the period of history of the Bank of Canada from 1955 to 1965. It describes the state of the economy at the time, the role of the central bank, the events that led to the Coyne Affair, and, finally, how Coyne's successor, Louis Rasminsky, succeeded in re-establishing order out of the chaos.

State of the Canadian Economy

In the 1950s, Canada was emerging from the post-war, post-Depression era. Overall, the economy was stable and prosperous – the growth of GDP/capita was low until 1960, when it suddenly began to mount fairly rapidly. Using 1990 international Geary-Khamis dollars, GDP/capita was $7,291 in 1950, rising to $8,201 in 1955. By 1960, GDP/capita was at $8,753, and, at the end of the period under study, 1965, it had jumped to $10,473.[1]

The 1950s saw three cyclical expansions: from 1949 to 1953, from about 1954 to 1957, and from 1958 to early 1960. The first was driven by a boom in commodities, largely due to the Korean War. Domestic demand pressures were strong, coming from unfulfilled wartime demand for consumer goods, infrastructure expenditures, housing, and strong immigration. Inflation was high, particularly from late 1950 to late 1951, and unemployment was low.

In 1954 the country experienced a short-lived but sharp recession before entering the second period of expansion, which was driven by strong investment in the resource sector. In addition, the federal government was investing heavily in defence – in 1955, 40 per cent of the budget went to defence-related expenditures – and in some infrastructure, including the St Lawrence Seaway. And again, rapid population growth drove the housing sector, aided by government incentives. Inflation picked up once more, as did the unemployment rate.

The third expansion of the 1950s was weaker than the previous two. The Canadian dollar appreciated in value, peaking at $1.0614 on 20 August 1957, and Canadian foreign indebtedness rose. Consumer prices were largely unchanged, year over year, so inflation was low. However, unemployment rose to a post-war high of roughly 7.5 per cent.

In the 1960s, the economy remained robust. Consumer prices rose on average 2.75 per cent and the unemployment rate averaged 4.9 per cent annually.[2]

Role of the Bank of Canada

The Bank of Canada was created in 1934 and opened for business in March 1935, in the midst of the Great Depression. Its role, as set out in the preamble to the Bank of Canada Act, was 'to regulate credit and currency in the best interests of the economic life of the nation, to control and protect the external value of the national monetary unit and to mitigate by its influence fluctuations in the general level of production, trade, prices and employment, so far as may be possible within the scope of monetary action, and generally to promote the economic and financial welfare of the Dominion.'

The most important phrase in this description is 'monetary action,' which points to the primary tool at the bank's disposal, monetary policy. Today, the bank states: 'The goal of Canadian monetary policy is to contribute to rising living standards for all Canadians through low and stable inflation. Specifically, the Bank aims to keep the rate of inflation, as measured by the annual rate of increase in the consumer price index, inside a target range established jointly with the government. Since 1995, the target range has been 1 to 3 per cent.'[3] The bank manages this by setting the overnight rate target, or the interest rate at which major financial institutions borrow and lend one-day (or 'overnight') funds among themselves.

But, in its early days, the Bank of Canada did not pursue an active monetary policy. It maintained the bank rate at 2.5 per cent from its founding in 1935 until an expansionary policy was introduced in 1944 and Towers reduced the rate to 1.5 per cent. In his twenty-year tenure at the helm of the Bank, Towers changed the bank rate only twice. The second time was in 1950, when the bank raised its rate by a half a point to 2 per cent.

Coyne was the first governor of the bank to actively pursue monetary policy using the bank rate. While the circumstances of the Canadian economy were unlike those Towers had experienced, Coyne's approach to monetary policy differed dramatically from that of his predecessor. In his first eighteen months in office, he changed the bank rate six times, raising it each time. Then the pace picked up, as the bank rate became a floating rate adjusted on a weekly basis.

Monetary Policy of the Day

Governor Coyne truly introduced monetary policy to the country. Unlike his predecessor, Coyne used the bank rate regularly in his efforts to manage the money supply. In particular, Coyne was focused on keeping inflation in check, and so he maintained a tight-money policy. In an environment of prosperity, and at a time with a history of low, stable – almost static – interest rates, Coyne's actions were shocking to the nation.

As governor, Coyne saw his and the bank's objective as being to contribute both to economic growth and to the stability of consumer prices. The achievement and maintenance of price stability was not seen as an end in itself. Rather, Coyne's goal, as he put it himself in a speech in 1960, was to 'encourage overall economic growth on a sound and sustainable basis, and to facilitate economic development with a view to increasing employment opportunities and eliminating unemployment or reducing it to the lowest possible level.'[4] Coyne's main preoccupation was inflation, which he saw as much more than a danger to economic growth: 'The evils of inflation need no elaboration ... Inflation forcibly restricts consumption by exacting the greatest sacrifice from those least able to bear it. It sets up many social and economic stresses and it feeds on itself – the so-called spiral of inflation and cost.'[5]

Coyne returned to the theme of the evils of inflation in speeches that he delivered across the country. In one, in 1959, he argued: 'Inflation is particularly insidious in that it seems to some to encourage production and employment and expansion for a time, but it continually cumulates excesses, distortions, inefficiencies and injustices which in due course produce recession, loss of confidence, and contraction.'[6]

Coyne's firm and unwavering stance against inflation was contrary to a school of thought popular in his day, that of Keynesian economics. This view holds that low inflation was a small but necessary price to pay to achieve full employment. As Bank historian James Powell points out, these Keynesian economists 'maintained that in a modern economy some inflation was inevitable, given government commitment to full employment and growing trade union power, and was certainly preferable to direct controls that could otherwise become necessary. This view was given added credence by the observation in 1958 of an apparent stable, long-term relationship between inflation and employment in the United Kingdom – a so-called Phillips curve relationship – which suggested that a country could choose its desired combination of inflation and unemployment.'[7]

Coyne was also deeply concerned about both the low saving rates of Canadians and the high rate of foreign investment in Canada, two factors he considered linked. In an interview conducted in 2005 and published in the Bank of Canada publication *Bank Notes*, Coyne explains his thinking about the role of savings in the economy: 'The capitalist system requires there should be savings, and you either have to do the saving yourself or borrow from other countries who will do it for you. And I felt we were doing too much of the latter and not enough of the former, which was true.'[8]

Coyne and the Bankers

One of Coyne's early initiatives was the introduction of a minimum 15 per cent liquidity ratio for chartered bank holdings. This was the ratio of a bank's liquid assets – cash, treasury bills, and day loans – to deposits. Designed to increase the effectiveness of monetary policy in moderating a too rapid expansion of credit, the new minimum was on top of the statutory requirement of a minimum 8 per cent cash reserve. The leaders of the large Canadian banks balked at the plan. In a meeting attended by Coyne and senior bank executives, an unsigned statement describing the bankers' view of the initiative was introduced and read: the ratio was too high; it would immobilize too many assets, rendering them inaccessible in the event of need; banks would become less flexible and less responsive to the markets; and the central bank would directly control a part of the chartered banks' assets.

But, despite the protests of the bankers, Coyne prevailed. He extended the time required to achieve the minimum ratio by a few months and agreed to drop what had been his initial target of 16 per cent to 15 per cent, as gestures of appeasement. And, while the initiative was voluntary, the banks all understood that they had little choice but to comply, which they did, albeit begrudgingly. 'Even if the liquid asset ratio had achieved some purpose the gain was not enough to compensate for the damage to [the Bank of Canada's] relations with the banks,' J.D. Gibson, assistant general manager at the Bank of Nova Scotia, said at the time.[9]

The liquidity ratio was not the only Coyne initiative that rankled the bankers. In late 1956 he replaced the fixed bank rate with a floating rate, set at 25 basis points above the 91-day treasury bills established at the weekly auction. Coyne's reasons for the change were: 1) that a rate slightly higher than market rate would discourage borrowing by the banks from the central bank; and 2) that a floating rate would respond more quickly to changes in the market than would a fixed rate. Again, the bankers protested: a floating rate, they said, obscured the direction of monetary policy and the intentions of the central bank. But it was for nought. The floating rate prevailed.

Still, Coyne did not win every battle with the bankers. Also in 1956, he proposed that the banks create new savings banks from their savings departments and use their deposits to fund long-term investments, an idea that, again, was met with 'a storm of criticism'[10] on the part of the bankers. Some months later, with an election looming, the then (Liberal) finance minister, W.E. Harris, put some distance between the government and the governor when he made the following statement regarding Coyne's savings bank proposal, effectively bringing to an end all discussion of the idea: 'I wish, therefore to make it quite clear that what has happened is that the governor of the Bank has suggested for discussion certain questions and that the government does not intend to make recommendations along those lines to the House of Commons.'[11]

Federal Politics, 1950s

As mentioned above, Coyne was appointed governor of the Bank of Canada by the Liberal government of Louis St Laurent. Shortly after he took the post, the government changed. Wooed by the populist message and passionate oratory of John Diefenbaker, Canadians elected a minority Conservative government in 1957. A year later, Diefenbaker called a snap election – and he won the majority he had been seeking. Indeed, the Conservative government won the largest parliamentary majority in Canadian history, even larger as a percentage of seats than the Mulroney landslide of 1984.

Donald M. Fleming was finance minister in Diefenbaker's cabinet, for both the minority and majority governments. A fiscal conservative, Fleming was, like Coyne, an enemy of inflation. According to Powell, Fleming was a 'soulmate' of Coyne in the fight against, as Fleming put it, the 'lurking menace of inflation.'[12] Indeed, in his speech presenting the budget of 1960, Fleming left no doubt about his opinion of inflation. 'One of the most serious effects of inflation,' he said, 'is that, like any other drug, it erodes stamina and willpower.'[13] Yet, while his personal views about inflation were aligned with Coyne's, Fleming had other constraints – political constraints – to deal with.

As much as Fleming wanted a balanced budget, the government was spending heavily on defence – and, as an important minister in the cabinet, Fleming had to support his government and its decisions. In his autobiography, Fleming describes his frustration with his fellow ministers. Prime Minister Diefenbaker and Howard Green, then minister of external affairs, blamed Coyne and the Bank of Canada for the rising bank rate, going so far to suggest that Coyne should be fired. Fleming writes:

This nonsense vexed me sorely. There were times when I wearied of having to conduct elementary lessons in public finance. I went over the old familiar ground. The bank interest rate was not set arbitrarily by Mr. Coyne. The Treasury bill rate was set by a free market over which the government held no direct control. The Bank of Canada had helped to keep that rate down by buying Treasury bills. The Bank rate for the past two and a half years had been arrived at by taking the rate on three-month Treasury bills and adding one-quarter of 1 per cent to it week by week. It had thus become a kind of floating rate. The bond market, moreover, was being obliged to absorb heavy sales of government bonds by banks and the Unemployment Insurance Commission. As for Mr. Coyne, his term of office was fixed by statute and had three years to run.[14]

Today, cabinet spending policies are managed closely by the powerful Treasury Board, a committee of the Privy Council. But, in his day, Fleming was under terrific pressure from other cabinet ministers to find the money for their projects. And the pressure on Fleming had been building for some time. In both the 1957 and 1958 elections, the populist Conservatives campaigned against the tight-money policy of the Bank of Canada.

To make matters worse, in the midst of the 1958 campaign, the Bank of Canada's Annual Report rejected the notion that it was pursuing a tight-money policy. Rather, the bank called its policy one of 'sound money.' This was probably the first time in Canadian history that interest rates had become politicized – and the battle lines between Coyne and the Tories were set. When the Conservatives emerged from the vote with a landslide victory, many believed that Coyne was on his way out. For a while, at least, they were wrong.

Coyne and the Government

Just as the bank's annual report called Coyne's monetary policy a policy of 'sound money,' so did Coyne stand firm in his beliefs about the evils of inflation. And, unusual for a bank governor, in comparison both to his predecessor Graham Towers and to subsequent governors, Coyne stood out not only for his outspokenness but also for the frequency with which he spoke in public. From the fall of 1959 to the end of 1960, Coyne delivered a speech on average every couple of months. In early 1961, in the space of two and a half months, Coyne delivered four major speeches. In all his talks, he was bluntly critical of government fiscal policy, telling audiences that the government was overspending and that the Bank of Canada could not achieve economic stability on its own.

In addition, Coyne gave unsolicited advice to Finance Minister Fleming, suggesting that a more conservative fiscal house might be in order. It is little surprise, given Diefenbaker's prairie populist roots and his early antipathy to higher interest rates, that antagonism between the governor and the government would only grow. It was just a matter of time before the relationship blew up.

Coyne recalls: 'Generally speaking, we were orthodox. We felt that the government should balance its budget unless there were really good reasons to do the contrary. And as long as they balanced their budget, things were a bit easier for the central bank to run monetary policy.'[15] He maintains, however, that he was not quite so direct in his speeches. 'All I was saying in my speeches was there are things we can't do that the government can do if it chooses.'[16] But then he goes on to say that he was, in fact, criticizing the government for not acting: 'That is what got me in trouble. But I felt I had to fight a rearguard action against this surge of opinion that monetary policy could do everything and that the present monetary policy was not expansionist enough.'[17]

In his memoirs, Fleming also remembers the conflict with Coyne. He recalls that, although he did not mention Coyne by name or refer to his speeches, he nonetheless answered Coyne in his nearly two-hour presentation of the December 1960 supplementary budget. In his book, Fleming quotes directly from the speech:

> It has sometimes been asserted that the participation of foreigners in Canadian business and in our capital markets should no longer be welcome and that investment from abroad should be sharply curtailed by policies directed to this end. This is not the view of this Government. The result of blocking out foreign investors and foreign investment would be to produce a 'little Canada,' cut off from many of the contacts with the outside world that have enriched our national life. We would become comparatively isolated, and most of us would be disappointed by the effects on our economic development. In any event, it is really not open to Canada to retreat into economic isolationism … We must continue to maintain a climate hospitable to foreign investment in this country.[18]

As much as Coyne's obsession with inflation and his strict policy of higher interest rates irritated the government – indeed, interest rates in the late 1950s became a 'political hot potato,' says Powell – it seems, as Coyne himself points out, that it was his overt and very public criticism of government that was the last straw for the Diefenbaker government.

Coyne and the Economists

It was not only the government that was irked by Coyne's rigid preoccupation with inflation. Economists at universities across the country, as well, were profoundly disturbed by the governor's actions, and in the fall of 1960 twenty-nine of them signed a letter addressed to Finance Minister Fleming telling him that they had 'lost confidence in the ability of the Bank of Canada under its present management' and calling on him to 'alter the management of the Bank of Canada.'[19] (The letter is included in its entirety in Appendix A.)

Some months later, Scott Gordon, an economist at Carleton University and one of the letter's principal authors, took it upon himself to write a short book, *The Economists versus the Bank of Canada*, elaborating on the letter and its message. 'From 1955 to 1957, the Canadian economy was in an inflationary period, and businessmen and others found bank credit extremely difficult to obtain,' Gordon wrote. This was followed by a sharp recession in 1957 and 1958, but the 'Bank did not pursue an active policy of monetary ease and expansion.'[20] 'Tight money, high interest rates and a high-priced Canadian dollar are all factors that depress economic activity. They do not make economic sense.'

At the time he was writing, in January 1961, Gordon notes that the difficulties facing the Canadian economy were 'more serious than any other period since the end of the war ... Despite this state of affairs, however, we can apparently expect no help from the Bank of Canada ... [which is] unmoved by the patent facts of growing unemployment and stagnating national income.' Coyne was to blame not only for the bank's role in the poor state of the economy but also for blocking the finance minister from reducing personal income taxes, a move that would have stimulated the economy. While the book refers broadly to the Bank of Canada, it is clear that Gordon is gunning for Coyne. Gordon refers to the series of speeches that Coyne had been delivering across the country and says they portray 'a lack of general competence in economic analysis.'[21] He goes on: 'Many arguments contained [in Coyne's speeches] seem to be confused and some are clearly uninformed or fallacious.'[22]

Economist Edward Safarian, currently a professor emeritus at the Rotman School of Management, was among the twenty-nine signatories to the letter calling for new management of the Bank of Canada. He recalls that, when Coyne took over in 1955, the economy was in good shape. 'But Coyne makes a decision that there is a problem: we are importing too much capital and we're not saving enough.' To help Canadians save more, Coyne raised interest rates. 'It's an illogical argument,' Safarian says.[23] 'The saving rate is determined more by salary and income than by the interest rate. Meanwhile, raising interest rates puts pressure on the economy, which slows growth. As income growth slows, savings growth slows as well.' Coyne's tight monetary strategy had two results. First, as Safarian describes it, his actions were 'disconcerting to business people across the country, who were getting contradictory messages about what was going on.' The uncertainty was unsettling to the business climate, likely leading businessmen to act conservatively in their decision making about jobs and investments. In addition, Coyne's actions were unsettling for the general public. While the average Canadian may not have fully understood national monetary and fiscal policy, citizens certainly were well aware of the very public quarrel between the government and the governor.

The conflict was also apparent to foreigners. As early as 1957, the U.S. embassy in Ottawa noted that Coyne was not a typical central banker: 'Mr. Coyne sees fit to make subjective statements on various aspects of the economy, some of which seem to exceed the cautious pronouncements usually associated with central bankers.'[24] A couple of years later, in mid-May 1959, the embassy further suggested: 'A conflict may be developing between the Canadian Department of Finance and the Bank of Canada over monetary policy.'[25]

For Scott Gordon, the conflict between the government and the governor was, in addition to an economic mess, a full-fledged constitutional crisis. In his book, Gordon describes a key issue, one that, with the benefit of hindsight, is the most critical issue of the Coyne Affair: the relationship of the bank to the government. Since Coyne's policy to pursue a single-minded fight against inflation was widely unpopular, the government declined to take responsibility. And, when the crisis became most intense, questions were raised over whether government had power over the bank and its actions or whether the bank had become an entirely independent agency:

By denying that he has any responsibility for monetary policy or the actions of the Bank, the Minister of Finance has created a situation in which it is impossible for Parliament to discuss the Bank's policies to any purpose. The Bank has become a free-floating autocracy, a power unto itself, subject neither to Government nor to Parliament. It is an institution of immense power whose actions reach into every area of economic and financial life of the nation, but it wields this power without responsibility ... In the whole fabric of democratic government one will not find a breach that is wider or more dangerous than that presented by the existing constitutional status of the Bank of Canada.[26]

Coyne Departs

In 1961 the government decided not to renew Coyne's term in office. The final battle between the government and the governor would centre on Coyne's pension. In 1960 the bank's directors had approved changes to the bank's pension plan, including a steep increase in the governor's pension. In March 1961, first Fleming and later Diefenbaker discovered that Coyne would receive $25,000 per year, considerably more than the $13,750 that the previous governor, Towers, was receiving. It was more, too, than the pension that Diefenbaker himself was anticipating. Even though cabinet agreed that 'there was no real ground for an attack on the integrity of the governor,'[27] Diefenbaker argued that 'Mr. Coyne had been involved in the decision to raise the amount of his own pension.'[28] The prime minister reasoned that Coyne, as governor, had the right to veto board decisions, and, as he had not vetoed the decision to increase his pension, this was cause to seek Coyne's resignation. Later, in the debate in the House of Commons that followed in July, Diefenbaker claimed that the governor 'sat, knew, listened and took.'[29]

Coyne felt compelled to defend himself. A Bank of Canada press release quoted Coyne: 'This slander upon my own integrity I cannot ignore or accept ... I cannot and will not resign quietly under such circumstances.'[30] Coyne's brazenness was noted by Henry R. Jackman, the prominent financier, philanthropist, and two-time MP, in an entry in his diary made in June 1961: 'Jim Coyne ... is behaving very badly. I had felt that he had much in his favour, but his actions subsequent to Don Fleming's letter asking for his resignation put him beyond the pale of common sense.'[31] It would be a short time before the government took firm action to get Coyne out of office.

On 6 July a bill declaring the office of the governor of the Bank of Canada vacant was passed by the House of Commons; it was sent the next day to the Senate. The Liberal-dominated Senate invited Coyne to testify, an opportunity he used to present a brave and, by many accounts, brilliant defence. On 13 July 1961 the Senate defeated the bill, exonerating Coyne. That same day, Coyne resigned.

Louis Rasminsky

Louis Rasminsky, Coyne's successor, was a natural diplomat. A gentleman who dressed in formal attire, he was a 'calm and calming person who in a quiet but forceful way was a leader who inspired confidence in people,' according to economist Safarian, who, before entering the academic world, had worked under Rasminsky at the Bank of Canada. Rasminsky's calming influence was needed. He had worked closely with Fleming and was known to have a good relationship with the minister. He was considered a brilliant man, as brilliant as Coyne, but he wasn't, in the words of Simon Reisman, then a senior Finance Department official, 'a firecracker.'[32]

A month before Coyne's resignation, Rasminsky had been approached by the government to take over as governor of the bank. His reply was simply that there was only one governor and that Coyne held the office. But on 14 July, the day after Coyne resigned, Rasminsky met with Fleming, informing the finance minister that he would accept the job on condition that certain principles were accepted by the government. He had written them up on the back of an envelope – and not only did Fleming agree to them, but when the Bank of Canada Act was revised in 1967, Rasminsky's ideas were incorporated into the act. This is what Rasminsky laid out: First, 'in the ordinary course of events, the Bank has the responsibility for monetary policy,' and secondly, 'if the Government disapproves of the monetary policy being carried out … it has the right and the responsibility to direct the Bank as to the policy which the Bank is carrying out.'[33]

With this simple script, Rasminsky lay the groundwork for the bank and the government to overcome the scandal that had encompassed it for months, if not years. It became understood that, if the government expressed its disapproval of bank policy and directed it to a different policy, the governor would step down, as he would be out of step with the government.

Rasminsky also knew that, as governor, he had a fine line to tread: he could neither be dramatically out of step with the government, as was Coyne, nor appear to be at the beck and call of government, since it was essential that the bank maintain its independence. As it turned out, Rasminsky was a master at maintaining that balance. For instance, when Diefenbaker suggested that he get rid of Les Mundy, the bank's secretary and a visible supporter of Coyne's, Rasminsky told Diefenbaker that, as governor, he was responsible for the administration of the bank and that if things went wrong, the prime minister could hold him accountable.[34]

In addition, as a way of asserting his leadership, Rasminsky made public shortly after taking the post of governor a memorandum spelling out the responsibilities of the bank versus the government with respect to monetary policy and how to proceed in the case of conflict. The memorandum also included his views about monetary policy and how to mesh monetary policy with other public policies affecting the economic well-being of the nation.

Once in the governor's post, Rasminsky set to work to repair other relationships that were important to the bank. His goal was to 'again create the image and the reality of the Bank as a truly national institution removed from the hurly-burly of politics, which carries on its own business competently and is a source of objective and disinterested information and counsel to government.'[35] Displaying a wise sense of public relations, Rasminsky's memorandum was the only document he made public for many months. And, from then on, most of his public speaking was conducted through the bank's Annual Report.

Within a few months of Rasminsky's appointment to the governor's office, the Porter Commission, mandated to conduct a broad review of Canada's financial system, began its hearings. Rasminsky worked closely with bank officials on the briefs prepared for the commission. He delved once again into the touchy issue of the relationship between the bank and the government, and proposed that the Bank of Canada Act be amended to reflect the newly agreed-upon nuances to the relationship: 'While the conduct of monetary policy should remain in the hands of the central bank there is a case which the Commission should consider for amending the Statute to provide that the Government should have the power to give the Bank directives on monetary policy which are not inconsistent with other provisions of the Act. The purpose of this provision would be to strengthen the position of the central bank by making clear that Government as well as central bank is responsible for monetary policy.'[36]

Rasminsky's proposal was made official in an amendment to the Bank of Canada Act in 1967. The details were much more explicit than what he had originally jotted down on the back of the envelope. In the event that the government did not agree with bank policy, it had to direct the governor with specific terms, within a limited period of time. Additionally, it was required to make the direction public by publishing it in the *Canada Gazette*, so that, as Rasminsky wrote, 'everybody would know … If the Governor couldn't in good conscience [do that], he would have no choice but to [resign].'[37]

Rasminsky also reiterated a message that Coyne had repeated over and over – that monetary policy on its own was only one of the tools of economic regulation and 'was best used as one ingredient in a mix of government policy – that is, fiscal policy and debt management.'[38] In short, Rasminsky's message regarding the respective roles of government and the Bank of Canada was similar to Coyne's but delivered in a much more palatable, less confrontational way. Like Coyne, he was saying that the government had to do its part, too.

Conclusion

During Coyne's reign, the real issue – on top of the apparent disagreement over the bank's monetary policy – was the lack of clarity regarding the relationship between the government and the governor. As Gordon points out, the overarching problem was a constitutional one: it seemed that the government of the day had lost control over the bank and the bank was acting as an independent autocratic entity, answering to no one.

This difficult situation was exacerbated by politics. As long as Coyne's tight-money policy was unpopular, the government was loath to claim responsibility for it.

In recessionary periods, Coyne, who naturally did not have to answer to an electorate and was unsympathetic to those who did, was quick to criticize government policy. In addition, with his unwaveringly strict stance against inflation, Coyne alienated some natural allies, namely the nation's top bankers and the academics in the economics departments of universities across the country.

The situation was intensified by personality clashes. Coyne was a man with a keen intellect but who was also awkward in social settings and considered by many to be abrasive. His speeches delved into subjects that many thought went beyond the realm of the bank governor's responsibility. For instance, in a speech to the Canadian Chamber of Commerce in October 1960, Coyne called for more educational facilities, more applied research, and more development of engineering and product development in Canada, as well as less foreign ownership of Canadian industry. He concluded his speech by saying it was time 'to live within our own means and to stand on our own feet … [which would] galvanize us into such a burst of new creative and productive activity as we have never seen in this country before. I feel the time has come when only such an effort can save us, and entitle us to share in the progress of the extraordinary modern age which is now opening for the world.'[39]

At the same time, Diefenbaker displayed his own lack of political tact by focusing on Coyne's pension as the cause for dismissal. As noted by historian Desmond Morton, both men displayed poor judgment: 'Coyne's resolute insistence on tight money in the face of recession was an economic folly that earned him dismissal from the Bank of Canada in 1961. But by attacking Coyne for his retirement pension, not his principles, Dief managed the near-impossible; he made the banker a popular martyr.'[40]

Still, despite the personality clashes, and despite Coyne's contrariness and his tight- money policies, it was not the disagreement between the governor and the government over monetary and fiscal policy that put the bank in peril, that likely hindered business development in Canada, and that damaged Canada's reputation internationally. Rather, the real issue was that the players did not have an adequate mechanism to manage that disagreement. And, without it, the crisis became acute. As well, out of the crisis, both Coyne's and Rasminsky's reputations were secured. While Coyne is remembered for bringing the Bank of Canada to the brink of disaster, Rasminsky is known and honoured for the sense of calm and stability that re-emerged under his insightful leadership.

Suggested Questions

1. James Coyne took a very active role as governor of the Bank of Canada. What could have Coyne done differently in order to achieve his goals?
2. The government clashed with Governor Coyne to the point of firing him. Could the prime minister and the minister of finance have handled the situation differently, and, if so, how?
3. What was the purpose of the conditions stipulated by Louis Rasminsky for taking the job of governor? How might Rasminsky's pre-conditions and his subsequent approach to being governor have mitigated (or increased) the likelihood of a crisis between the government and the central bank going forward?

4. What is the appropriate relationship between a central bank and
    the government of a sovereign nation?

Suggested Readings

Coyne, J.E. 'Living within Our Means by Expanding Our Means to
  Live Better.' Remarks prepared for delivery to the Annual Meet-
  ing of the Canadian Chamber of Commerce in Calgary, 5 Oct. 1960.
  Bank of Canada Archives.
Fleming, Donald. *So Very Near: The Political Memoirs of the Honourable
  Donald M. Fleming, Volume Two, The Summit Years*. Toronto: McClel-
  land and Stewart 1985. Chapter 79 ('The Coyne Affair').
Gordon, Scott. *The Economists versus the Bank of Canada*. Toronto: Ryer-
  son Press 1961.
MacIntosh, Robert. *Different Drummers: Banking & Politics in Canada*.
  Toronto: Macmillan 1991. Chapter 9 ('A Hop, a Skip and a Jump').
Martin, Roger. 'The Opposable Mind: How Successful Leaders Think.'
  Harvard Business Review, June 2007.
Powell, James. 'Challenges, Confrontation and Change: The Bank of
  Canada of James Elliot Coyne.' Montreal and Kingston: McGill-
  Queen's University Press, forthcoming 2009.

Appendix A

The following is a copy of the letter sent in the fall of 1960 to Finance
Minister Fleming and signed by twenty-nine prominent economists.

  The Honourable D.M. Fleming, P.C., Q.C.
  The Minister of Finance
  Ottawa

  Dear Mr. Fleming,

  The signatories of this letter are all economists on Canadian university fac-
  ulties who are engaged independently in economic research. Economists
  have very rarely made joint representation to the Government and we do
  not profess a professional association that is authorized to speak for Canadian economists on matters of governmental policy and administration.
      This we feel is as it should be. By and large academic and research econ-
  omists should express their views on these matters as individuals – with

all the variations of emphasis and interpretation that ought to characterize independently-minded students and observers of public affairs.

Consequently, we send this joint letter to you with considerable regret that we have felt it necessary to abandon the individuality which our profession cherishes, protects and promotes.

There may come occasions in the affairs of a nation when economists must accept, albeit with regret, the responsibility of speaking with the increased power of a united voice on matters of grave public concern.

The signatories of this letter feel that such a time has come for Canada and we wish therefore to address you in this way on the matter of the management and polices of the Bank of Canada. We address you Mr. Minister as the sole shareholder of that institution who holds its shares on behalf of the Government.

We are facing serious economic difficulties in Canada both in our domestic economy and in our trade and financial relations with other nations.

The undersigned economists wish to express to you that we have lost confidence in the ability of the Bank of Canada under its present management to play its proper role in ameliorating and resolving these difficulties.

Recent public statements by the Governor of the Bank of Canada have seriously shaken our faith in the wisdom and competence of the Bank's management. As professional economists we are both puzzled and distressed by the economic reasoning contained in these public statements. This reasoning does not appear to us to approach that level of competency which is a necessary foundation for successful central bank policy. Moreover, we feel that the policies actually pursued by the Bank of Canada have not displayed sufficient concern for the difficulties and uncertainties of the financial markets or sufficient awareness of the true state of the economy in general. As economists, surely we are justified in expecting that the Bank of Canada should act as a stabilizing force in the economy and not as one whose actions tend to exacerbate our economic and financial difficulties.

We address you then, Mr. Minister, to ask that steps should be taken to alter the management of the Bank of Canada. Parliament intended the Bank to be the servant of the people, to aid and support them in difficult times and to give wise counsel and leadership. This, we are convinced, the Bank cannot do under its present management. We plead that you should appreciate the gravity of this situation and thus you should act without delay.

Yours very truly,

...

NOTES

1 OECD, *The World Economy: Historical Statistics*, Table 3: Per Capita GDP: PIB par habitant.
2 Powell, 'Challenges, Confrontation, and Change.'
3 Bank of Canada website: http://www.bankofcanada.ca/en/monetary_mod/index.html.
4 Powell, 'Challenges, Confrontation, and Change,' 5.
5 Bank of Canada, Annual Report, 1956, 11.
6 Powell, 'Challenges, Confrontation, and Change,' 16.
7 Ibid.
8 Bank of Canada, *Bank Notes: A Special Commemorative Issue*, 2005, 3.
9 Powell, 'Challenges, Confrontation, and Change,' 20.
10 Ibid., 22.
11 House of Commons, *Debates*, 26 March 1957, 2683, as cited by Powell, 'Challenges, Confrontation, and Change,' 23.
12 Fleming, 1957, quoted in ibid., 28.
13 Canada, Budget Speech delivered by the Honourable Donald M. Fleming, Minister of Finance, 31 March 1960.
14 Fleming, *So Very Near*, 68.
15 *Bank Notes*, 4.
16 Ibid., 5.
17 Ibid.
18 Fleming, *So Very Near*, 244.
19 Scott Gordon, *The Economists versus the Bank of Canada*.
20 Ibid., 13.
21 Ibid., 37.
22 Ibid.
23 Interview with Professor Edward Safarian, June 2008.
24 Bruce Muirhead, *Against the Odds: The Public Life and Times of Louis Rasminsky* (Toronto: University of Toronto Press 1999).
25 Ibid.
26 Gordon, *The Economists versus the Bank of Canada*.
27 Cabinet conclusions, Library and Archives Canada, RG 2, Vol. 6176, 1 May-12 June 1961, 1 May 1961, quoted in Powell, 'Challenges, Confrontation, and Change,' 74.
28 Powell, 'Challenges, Confrontation, and Change,' 74.
29 Ibid., 74.
30 Ibid., 75.

31 Henry N.R. Jackman, ed., *The Letters and Diary of Henry Rutherford Jackman.* Toronto: Harmony Printing 2005.
32 Muirhead, *Against the Odds*, 173.
33 Ibid., 176.
34 Ibid., 177.
35 Ibid., 179.
36 Rasminsky's statement was included in the Bank of Canada Annual Report for 1961, 3–5, as cited in Muirhead, *Against the Odds*, 186.
37 Cited in ibid., 186.
38 Cited in ibid., 188.
39 James Coyne, 'Living within Our Means.'
40 Desmond Morton, 'Strains of Affluence,' *in* Craig Brown, ed., *Brown's Illustrated History of Canada* (Toronto: Key Porter Books 2002).

CASE 8
The End of Monopoly: A New World at Inco

ANNE METTE DE PLACE FILIPPINI and JOE MARTIN

'In 2006 Inco was bought by Companhia Vale do Rio Doce, also called CVRD, a Brazilian miner of iron ore. This marked the end of Inco's history as an independent corporation. It also marked the end of hopes for the creation of a Canadian-based nickel giant.'

The 'commodities bubble,' then referred to as an extended commodities cycle, had resulted a series of merger and acquisition activity in 2005–6. For Inco, the beginning of the end was October 2005, when Inco's CEO announced that it had reached a merger agreement with its long-time Canadian rival, Falconbridge. If consummated, the merger would have created the world's largest nickel miner. The new company would also have enjoyed a more diversified revenue stream, with about half of its pro forma revenue coming from nickel and the rest from copper, aluminium, zinc, and precious metals. The combined entity would have controlled a quarter of the world's nickel production, ahead of Russian-based Norilsk. Some saw the proposed merger as a way for Inco to fend off the attentions of Xstrata, the Swiss company that had bought 20 per cent of Falconbridge a few months earlier.

Between October 2005 and October 2006, Inco's fortunes took a dramatic turn. A number of unpredicted events transpired, and these developments affected some of the biggest players in the global mining industries. A massive bidding war took place which first saw Inco attempting to acquire Falconbridge. Then, Vancouver-based Teck Cominco launched a hostile bid for Inco, which was followed by a bid by the Swiss-based Xstrata for the remainder of Falconbridge. Subsequently, Inco and Falconbridge announced a three-way tie-up deal with American copper producer Phelps Dodge. Finally, Brazilian-based Companhia do Rio Doce, which had been on the hunt for a major base-metals acquisition, made a bid for Inco alone, and Xstrata was able to acquire Falconbridge.

In one year, the dream of Canada harbouring the world's number one nickel-mining company evaporated. These changes were also indicative of a major shift in the worldwide mining industry whereby companies that used to specialize in one or two metals took on a greater range of minerals.[1]

It was an unfortunate end to Inco's long history as an independent company. Inco was once one of Canada's most important corporations and the only Canadian company ever to have been listed among the Dow 30. What opportunities were missed along the way? What missteps contributed to the end? What was inevitable and what could have been different if different decisions had been made?

The View from New York Plaza

In 1972 the headquarters of International Nickel Company of Canada were located in New York City's prestigious New York Plaza. The office enjoyed magnificent views of the Statue of Liberty, Staten Island, and the New York harbour. As a former executive describes it, 'you felt as if you could reach out and touch the Statue of Liberty, and, back then, Governors Island was still an exclusive army property.'[2]

But changes were looming at Inco's plush offices as Edward Grubb stood by the window of his office, looking down at the traffic below. Recently named president and chief executive officer, Grubb was the new man at the top of the world's largest nickel-producing company. Something had to be done to stop Inco's deteriorating performance, and Grubb had a plan.

L. Edward Grubb enjoyed a reputation as a man of action and a no-nonsense cost- cutter during his years in England. There he had served as head of International Nickel, the U.K. subsidiary of Inco, and managing director of its subsidiary, Henry Wiggin and Company. Wiggin had head offices in London and rolling mills in Hereford in western England; Grubb had restored profitability to the rolling mills organization. Before moving to England, Grubb had been with Inco in the United States, working his way up the ladder to increasingly responsible positions.

A former executive recalls that Grubb complained when he first arrived at Inco U.K. that there were more tea breaks than working hours. The executive also remarked that Grubb was not reluctant to fire employees who were not performing. The CEO cleaned house so well that, according to company lore, he regularly handed out 'DCM Badges' – short for 'Don't Come Monday.' Employees reportedly came to fear being called into Grubb's office to receive their 'badge.'

Like many others, Grubb had followed his father to Inco. William Henry Grubb had worked in the accounts department and became comptroller in the late 1920s, continuing to serve there through the difficult early 1930s. Subsequently, in 1934, Edward Grubb joined Inco fresh out of college – he was one of the company's few employees with a college degree.

Edward Grubb's personality appeared to some people to be at odds with his reputation. Although he was considered to be a 'take-charge' man of action, he actually came across as quite reserved. He was well-spoken but often appeared ill at ease in one-on-one encounters.

A Surprising Changing of the Guard

Prior to Grubb's arrival, Henry Wingate had held Inco's top position, the role of chairman and chief executive officer of International Nickel Company of Canada, since 1960. Albert Gagnebin had been serving as Wingate's second-in-command. Wingate had been expected to retire for some time, and the Inco Board of Directors met to decide the succession plan.

Everyone was expecting a smooth changing of the guard, but the board surprised everyone. The board passed over Wingate's chosen candidate and successor, Albert Gagnebin. No one had expected this. Wingate and Gagnebin had worked side by side for six years in the company's top two posts. Back in 1966, Wingate had personally chosen Gagnebin to succeed James Roycroft Gordon, the first Canadian-born president.

Instead of Gagnebin, however, the board named Edward Grubb to succeed Henry Wingate.[3] Although Gagnebin was given the title of chairman, it was Grubb who received the title of president and chief executive officer. (In the past, the chairman had served as the CEO as well.)

The board decision to appoint Grubb rather than Gagnebin sent shivers down the spines of the management ranks at New York Plaza. Wingate had always got his way with the board. But this time he hadn't. Had he made a mistake in appointing a board committee to look at the issue of succession? Had he been so sure of himself that he did not realize that the board might choose someone other than his candidate? After all, in those days the board was the CEO's creature.

Wingate had been at the helm of Inco for more than a dozen years and had had ample opportunity to reshape the board to his liking. More than half of the twenty-five directors had been appointed on Wingate's watch, including prominent chairmen from various organizations: Standard Oil, the Bank of New York, and British General Electric. Not only was it a good board, but it was also 'his' board. And Wingate had strengthened the board's Canadian contingent. He brought in the principal of Queen's University, which supplied many of Inco's engineers. Wingate also recruited the board's first French Canadian, who was the president of one of Canada's premier pulp and paper companies. Moreover, he increased the board's representation from Manitoba, where the important Thompson mine was located, from one to two.

What had happened? Why had the board selected Grubb rather than Wingate's chosen successor?

Annus Horribilis, Annus Mirabilis, Annus Horribilis

By the end of 1971, patience was running thin among board members at Inco. Just as Inco management began to feel a sense of recovery after a terrible year in 1969, it then realized that 1971 would bring bad news once again. Financial results from 1971 were dismal, revealing that sales had dropped 25 per cent and profits were more than halved. Accelerated market-share losses in the late 1960s had now been punctuated by a series of misfortunes from 1969 to 1971. On the Dow Jones, Inco's shares were changing hands at half the levels seen less than a year earlier. Inco had always been viewed as a blue-chip company, consistent with its place in the rankings as one of America's biggest and most important companies. Now it seemed to be a shadow of its former self.

These developments made it clear that major management changes were overdue.

The stomach-turning ups and downs experienced by the company since the late 1960s had shaken management to the core. How had this all come about? What had happened to Inco?

The year 1969 had been a terrible one for Inco, with poor labour relations exacerbating the country's other troubles. In spite of months of preparations, difficult contract negotiations with the United Steelworkers of America ended with an estimated 17,000 workers walking out in what was to become a four-month strike before a new agreement was signed. Henry Wingate, the company chairman, began his annual message to shareholders with these words: 'The dominant factor affecting the Company in 1969 was the … strike at our Ontario facilities. It

seriously reduced deliveries and earnings. It worked hardships on customers. It delayed construction work on our large expansion plan in
Canada. And it postponed the day when we shall be able to meet fully
our customers' demands for nickel.'

Inco's horrible year was followed by a major turnaround in 1970. In
the words of Chairman Wingate, 1970 was 'a year of solid achievement.
We operated more mines – we produced more nickel – we spent more
on capital improvements – we paid more taxes – our net sales, earnings and dividends were larger in absolute terms than at any time in
the Company's history.' Unfortunately, results collapsed unexpectedly
the following year. Nickel deliveries slumped to 382 million pounds in
1969, down from 500 million pounds in 1966. In 1970 deliveries then
recovered to 519 million pounds but then in 1971 dropped precipitously to 342 million pounds, the lowest level in ten years. (See Exhibit 1.)

Exhibit 1
Inco nickel deliveries and production, 1967–74

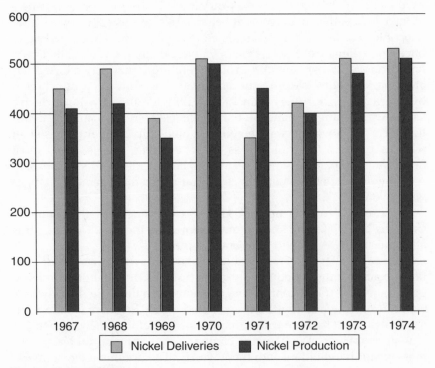

Source: Annual Reports.

Management was at a loss to explain what had happened – the company had risen from the depths to the heights, and then plunged back into the depths again! But Wingate took solace in 'a number of reassessments and hard decisions.' 'Most importantly,' he said, the company's poor performance 'has created a healthy self-questioning in many areas of our activities of the methods and assumptions which enter into the functioning of our business.'

Matters had been made worse because Inco had suffered more than its competition, accounting for 80 per cent of the industry's decline while its smaller competitors, including Falconbridge, had fared better. The nickel industry's 'supplier of last resort' paid dearly in times of excess supply, carrying huge inventory-maintenance charges. Inco's loss of its monopolistic position became increasingly evident. (See Exhibit 2.)

In 1960 there had been a dozen or so producers of refined nickel in the world. In addition to Inco and Falconbridge, there was the French firm Le Nickel, Hanna Mining in the United States, Rustenburg in South Africa, and Outokumpu in Finland. By the mid-1970s, there were nearly twice as many producers. Aside from those listed above, there were more producers in Japan, Australia, Zimbabwe, Greece, Indonesia, and Brazil, as well as Russia and Cuba.

Weak markets and large inventory charges coincided with peaking debt payments on Inco's capital expansion program. 'We were spending nearly a million dollars a day more than we brought in,' recalls an Inco executive.[4] (See Exhibits 3 and 4.)

Times Had Changed

The nickel industry was not the same, Grubb thought. He believed that a turnaround would be even tougher to achieve than the cost-cutting measures he had implemented in Hereford. He thought back wistfully to an earlier, simpler time. And he asked his secretary to pull out some old annual reports. At random he picked up the 1955 report, which included the stirring words of John Thompson, the legendary former chairman after whom Thompson, Manitoba, is named. Grubb also looked at the message of his predecessor, Henry Wingate, who was the brand-new president back in 1955 (before he was promoted to chairman in 1960) and who had just come through a level of prosperity that warranted an upbeat annual report.

The words were buoyant and revealed to Grubb the contrast between the company's past and present fortunes. Wingate's message began: 'In 1955 the Company achieved the largest production of nickel and

Exhibit 2
Inco sales as a percentage of non-communist-world nickle demand, 1950–75

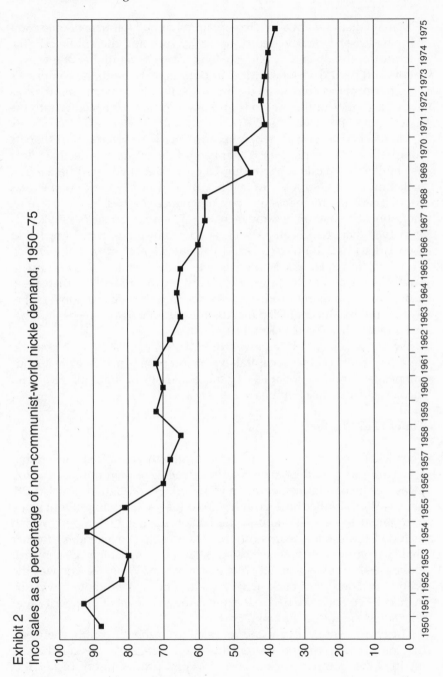

Exhibit 3
Inco capital expenditures, 1960–74

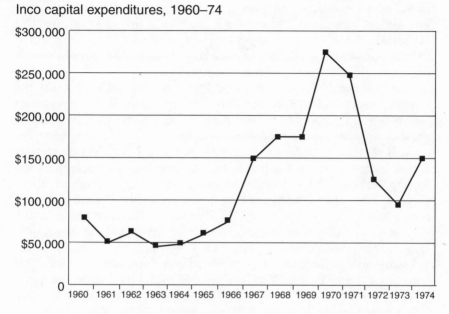

Exhibit 4
Inco inventory and long-term debt, 1968–74

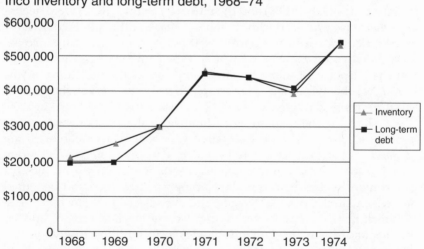

realized the highest earnings in its history. A new record was made for dividend payments to shareholders.[5] Disbursements for wages were larger than ever before.' Was there a touch of hubris in all of this? Did Wingate and Thompson recognize the external factors that contributed to their current success? Did they see how those outside developments had also sowed the seeds of future difficulties?

From the end of the Second World War until the mid-1960s (with the notable exception of 1959), nickel had enjoyed a prolonged period of above-average growth. In the two decades prior to 1965, nickel demand grew at an average 6 per cent per annum, ahead of worldwide GDP growth. A number of factors had contributed to the good times in the nickel industry. These factors included European reconstruction following the Second World War, which required high quantities of nickel; the discovery of expanded uses for nickel, including the rapid growth of the stainless steel industry;[6] the dynamic growth of the Japanese economy; the military demands of the Korean War; and the subsequent demand for strategic metals during the Cold War.

During this period, the price of nickel was determined by Inco and Inco alone. From 1929 to 1948, the price of nickel held steady at about 35 cents per pound. From mid-1948 to May 1962, the price climbed to 79 cents per pound. This was followed by more price increases: by the early 1970s, Inco's price had risen to $1.33 per pound. (See Exhibit 5.)

While there were signs of trouble earlier, the problems became clearer in the 1960s. Sales were relatively flat and earnings flatter and both the return on assets (ROA) and the return on Equity (ROE) were declining. One cause was the decline in market share. Although it would have been difficult for Inco to retain the 80 per cent market share enjoyed immediately after the war, why hadn't the company been able to sustain the 70 per cent market share it enjoyed at the beginning of the 1960s? Yet the 1960s had seen a rapid decline in market share, from about 70 per cent at the end of the 1950s to less than 50 per cent in 1969.

Why had this happened? With hindsight, the problem was easier to analyse. The tight supply situation was hardly sustainable. Strong demand and high prices were bound to encourage new competition which in turn resulted in the availability of new supply. And the U.S. government would help this development along. Inco had benefited immensely from the American government's decision to stockpile nickel, which helped smooth underlying demand cyclicality and reduced the ups and downs in demand. However, in addition to giving Inco guaranteed contracts, the U.S. government also provided subsidies to

Exhibit 5
Average annual nickel prices (refined nickel, 1950–74)

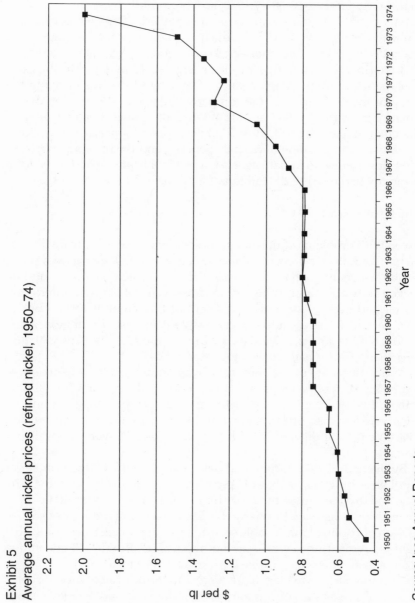

$ per lb

Year

Source: Inco Annual Reports.

Inco's competition, Falconbridge and Sherritt-Gordon. Adding to these factors was Inco's ability to control price, moving the price from $0.79 in the early 1960s to $1.38 by 1970, a 75 per cent increase.

As Grubb reflected on the past, he recalled Wingate's decision to launch a major five-year investment program. Wingate stated that 'nickel is important to economic growth. Modern technology demands and requires the type of properties it imparts to metals.'[7] In the capital-expansion program of the late 1950s, when Inco was bringing the Thompson site on stream, the company had spent $165 million over a three-year period. In 1968, as part of Wingate's plans, it had spent more than that in one year and, by 1970, it was spending nearly $300 million a year. The combination of capital spending and the build-up of inventories forced Inco to initiate debt financing in the late 1960s. By 1969, the company had nearly $200 million of long-term debt on its books.

The Grubb Era

Faced with problems of this magnitude, Edward Grubb moved quickly on his mandate to put Inco's house back in order. In less than two years, Grubb was named chairman as well as chief executive officer and he picked Edward Carter as his key man and promoted him to president. Carter had been made a vice-president of Inco in early 1971. Prior to that he had been executive vice-president of the Huntington Alloy Products Division, a subsidiary of Inco located in the United States. Grubb and Carter had worked together in England.

A drastic cost-cutting program was immediately implemented. Grubb's new regime emphasized that only profitable nickel would be mined. Planned capital expenditures were cut by $50 million and by 1973 were less than $100 million. Employment levels were reduced and overtime was eliminated. Production plans for 1972 were cut by 30 per cent.

By the end of 1972, Grubb and his team had reduced the number of employees by 4,000, or about 11 per cent of the total workforce. By 1974, Inco had dropped more than 6,000 employees from its payroll. Restructuring efforts also saw Inco write off fixed assets and reduce its U.S.$78-million portfolio of marketable securities, with proceeds going towards debt repayment. Inco's 1972 annual report noted that cash generation after investments was positive for the first time since 1965.

New methods of management were also introduced at Inco. Grubb's philosophy was one of 'no surprises.' One-year and five-year plans became mandatory under Grubb and Carter. The team also gave unprecedented autonomy to operating executives, while corporate staff was reorganized. A newly created position of financial vice-president, aimed at creating better controls, was given to Charles F. Baird, who later became CEO. Baird continued a long tradition of maintaining Inco's close ties with the United States Navy in that he had served as undersecretary of the navy in the administration of President Lyndon B. Johnson. Prior to that appointment, Baird had been a financial executive with Standard Oil (New Jersey) who had worked in London and Paris as well as New York.

The team also tried to deal with Inco's persistent problem of capital-cost overruns by creating an in-house construction-engineering department. 'Inco was better than most at underestimating costs. Capital cost overruns have brought an end to more than one CEO career at Inco,' according to a former Inco executive. In addition, Grubb and his team announced the reorganization of the sales and marketing organizations in 1972. Grubb wanted to end the status of what he called 'supplier of last resort' and take a fiercer competitive stance. Despite the loss of market dominance, Inco had continued to act as the industry association for nickel, geared simply to promote demand of nickel overall, not just Inco nickel. Inco would collect and publish general market research, organize industry conferences around the world, and freely distribute reports on its research and development efforts. No more. Under Grubb, Inco decided to stop publishing prices and detailed industry information. The company had come to realize that prices, consumption trends, and other industry data had become useful not only to its customers but also to competitors who used it to undercut Inco. Instead, Inco now provided only general guidelines, such as one indicating that 'it believed demand was likely to continue to grow at a 6% corporate annual growth rate (cagr) over a business cycle.' By the mid-1970s, management announced, 'the prices Inco charges its customers will be considered confidential information.'

Another development in 1972, which shocked the staff at New York Plaza, was Grubb's personal decision to move both home and office to Toronto. The Inco leader would soon be working out of a small office in the TD Centre,[8] thereby becoming the first CEO in Inco's history to reside in Canada. Some have suggested that Grubb's sensitivity to political issues was the main motivation behind the move. Perhaps it was an attempt to rid himself of the image of being 'just another U.S. lawyer coming to Toronto to negotiate labour relations.'

In fact, the new team did seem to be taking some steps to improve labour relations. As far back as the late 1950s, almost every time Inco renegotiated its three-year contract with the Canadian unions, there were long and costly strikes. Not only did lost production affect profitability in the negotiation years but also strikes every three years caused concern among customers. Grubb had to do something. His solution was to create a closer relationship with both the union officials and the employees at Inco's different locations. Grubb's actions in this direction received positive reviews, including from the local head of the United Steelworkers.

Diversification Efforts

Yet perhaps the most important departure from the past was Inco's diversification efforts. It started to make forays into non-nickel activities. Another vital change was its geographic expansion, aimed at helping the company to become a global producer of nickel. After the bad years, the new leadership was keen to ensure that the company could manage the swings in the business cycles. The team also saw other large companies pursuing a strategy of diversification.[9]

In 1974 Inco acquired ESB Corp, one of the world's major manufacturers of batteries. ESB management had resisted Inco's approach, and a bidding war with United Technologies saw Inco pay $234 million before the deal was done – up from its $153-million initial offer. It was a massive 100 per cent bid premium in what was to be the first hostile takeover on the New York Stock Exchange. ESB operated 100 plants in 18 countries and sold products with such well-known trade names as Ray-O-Vac. It was barely profitable, but Inco was hoping that General Motors and other car makers would use its zinc-nickel oxide battery to power its cars.

Other smaller diversification efforts saw Inco acquire Daniel Doncaster and Sons in 1975. Doncaster, a 200-year-old British corporation based in the northern city of Sheffield – the heart of the steel industry – produced high-stress metal components, including turbine blades and gear transmission systems.[10] Inco also launched a venture-capital program in 1976 with capital of $7 million. Among the most promising investments was a 24 per cent stake in Biogen, a global biotech and pharmaceutical firm known today for its successful cancer drug, Interferon. At that time, Biogen's focus was on the development of bacteria that could process ore in the ground.

For decades, Inco had sought to expand its production of nickel beyond its Canadian base. It had owned property in New Caledonia, a French island in the South Pacific, since the turn of the twentieth century. However, the French had successfully prevented Inco from mining the ore body, with the aim of protecting the French nickel producer Le Nickel. As well, talks in Guatemala had been ongoing since the 1950s. The late 1960s and early 1970s brought protracted negotiations to develop nickel projects in Indonesia, Guatemala, New Caledonia, Australia, and Minnesota.

Despite earlier investments, it was under Grubb that the main investments behind an expansion of production took place. In 1972 Inco announced its first major development outside Canada, the Indonesian Soroko project. The project was to add 30 million pounds per year in new capacity by 1976 at a cost of $135 million for the initial phase. It was being undertaken in concert with six Japanese companies, with Inco owning a 60 per cent stake. All production was going to serve the Japanese market. The project was later expanded. Concurrent with this Indonesian investment, Inco began construction in Guatemala in 1973. The Guatemalan mine had the capacity to produce 25 million pounds of nickel per year and costs were estimated to be $90 million.[11] Management significantly revised cost estimates upwards for both Indonesia and Guatemala as the projects got under way. The final price tag was $850 million for Indonesia and $230 million for Guatemala.

Inco's massive five-year investment program in Canada was completed in 1972. Under the plan, Inco spent $1 billion to modernize and expand its Canadian operations. During the 1974–7 investment phase, capital investments totalled $1.4 billion, of which 80 per cent was directed towards Inco's goal of becoming a global producer of nickel.

A Successful Break from the Past?

By the end of 1974, the Grubb regime had enjoyed three strong years of performance, with net sales more than doubling to upwards of $1.7 billion. Meanwhile net earnings had more than tripled to nearly $300 million, with the return on shareholder's equity jumping to over 20 per cent. Rebounding demand and cost-cutting efforts had restored financial health at Inco. Profitability levels were now back above the levels not seen since the 1960s.

In the 1974 annual report, Grubb and President Carter wrote proudly:

The year covered by this report was marked by a record level of sales and earnings, by your company's first diversification into a completely new line of business and by continued expansion in Canada and abroad … the company acquired ESB Incorporated, one of the world's leading battery companies, with a sound growth record and a reputation for good management … We intend to seek planned and orderly diversification … Our criteria in making acquisitions are a good earnings potential, the capacity to offset cyclical swings in earnings in the primary metals industry and a broad compatibility with our own skills and assets.

Grubb and Carter's message went on to discuss geographical diversification, stating that 'construction is well under way in Indonesia and Guatemala on facilities which will ultimately increase the Company's capacity by an additional 130 million pounds … we also have programs in various stages of development involving nickel, copper and other resources (including oil and deep sea nodules) in a number of other areas.'

In three years, from 1972 through 1974, Inco had made two bold strategic decisions: expanding its nickel production beyond Canada and diversifying into a completely new line of business, battery making. These decisions, which resulted in Inco being transformed from a mining company focused on Canadian nickel ore to a global, diversified company, was to some extend a sign of the times. The 1970s were the conglomerate-building decade in business.

The transformation carried a very large price tag. The cost of acquiring ESB Corp and the capital investments in Indonesia and Guatemala added up to $1.3 billion in total. This was well above the $1 billion that Inco had spent to modernize and expand its Canadian operations between 1968 and 1972. It was also six times Inco's annual run-rate of earnings during the 1972–4 period.

After three good years of improving performance, Grubb obtained board approval to purchase a corporate Gulfstream airplane in 1974. The Toronto media quickly got onto the story and wrote a critical article – Grubb was upset. As it happened, the criticism created by the newspaper article became a foreshadowing of more bad news to come. The year 1975 saw one of the sharpest declines in metal deliveries in the history of the nickel industry. A worldwide economic slowdown and persistent high levels of inflation hit demand. Management was taken by surprise. Inco earning's tumbled.

Three years of success and growth under Grubb and Carter had come to an abrupt end. Was 1975 a harbinger of worse to come? Inco was vulnerable, saddled with large capital commitments and a new and different business as part of its operation. Or was 1975 simply a small setback on an otherwise upward trajectory?

Suggested Questions

1. How did Inco become a monopoly? How did it protect its position? What were the major factors that led to the end of the monopoly?
2. What key strategic choices did Grubb make as CEO of Inco? What challenges was he trying to address? Assess his choices in light of Michael Porter's arguments regarding competitive advantage.
3. Given the nature of the consolidation in the industry, what lessons from history do you think are relevant? Do you think CRVD and Xstrata will be successful in developing appropriate 'corporate themes'?

Suggested Readings

Clement, Wallace. *Hardrock Mining: Industrial Relations and Technological Changes at Inco*. Toronto: McClelland and Stewart 1981.

Main, O.W. *The Canadian Nickel Industry: A Study in Market Control and Public Policy*. Toronto: University of Toronto Press 1955.

Porter, Michael. 'From Competitive Advantage to Corporate Strategy.' *Harvard Business Review*, 65, no. 3 (1987).

Schuster, Thomas. 'Merger Mania.' *Resource World Magazine*, February 2006.

Thompson, John F., and Norman Beasley. *For the Years to Come: A Story of International Nickel of Canada*. New York: G.P. Putnam 1960.

Appendix A: The Thompson-Wingate Era

American Government Stockpiling

From 1945 until the mid-1960s (with the notable exception of 1959), the nickel market had enjoyed a prolonged period of above-average growth. A major factor affecting demand was the U.S. government decision to stockpile strategic and critical materials, a decision that had its roots in the Second World War and was unprecedented in peacetime. The government stockpiling of nickel was very much a part of a strategic decision, which envisaged a hemispheric defence of which Canada was an important part. It was great for business at Inco.

The stockpiling gained tremendous impetus with the outbreak of the Korean War and the escalating tensions of the Cold War. Indeed, the American government was so concerned about the possibility of a shortage of strategic metals that the president of the Columbia Broadcasting System (CBS), the legendary William S. Paley, was appointed to investigate U.S. strategic preparedness in terms of the inventory of essential resources. The consequence for Canada was tremendous demand for strategic materials, including nickel. Between 1946 and 1955, Canadian nickel production nearly doubled – to 350,000 pounds. In 1955 non-ferrous metal exports surpassed paper exports for the first time, and paper exports were growing rapidly as well.

Nickel was in short supply, which led to a rationing of customer orders and steady price increases. (See Exhibit 5.) In the first half of the twentieth century, the increases in production consistently were greater than the price increases as Inco used lower prices to control competitive behaviour. Throughout this period, nickel prices were what Inco said they were. From 1929 until mid-1948, the price of nickel was steady at about 35 cents per pound. From mid-1948 to May 1962, the price climbed to 79 cents per pound. Then, prices really took off – by the early 1970s, the price had risen to $1.33 per pound. By 1976, Inco's list price was $2.41 per pound. Inco enjoyed a monopoly and could charge whatever price it liked.

The tight supply situation was not sustainable. Strong demand growth and high prices were bound to encourage new competition and bring more supply into the market. And the U.S. government encouraged this trend. Viewing nickel as a strategic material, the government decided to encourage production of nickel by subsidizing some of the smaller producers, such as Falconbridge, Freeport, and Sherritt-Gordon. In 1953, the American government, through the Department of Defense's Materials Procurement Agency, the stockpile supervisor, entered into an agreement with Inco under which the company was to deliver 1.3 billion pounds of nickel over the next five years. Moreover, the same agency provided Falconbridge with a loan of $6 million and a guaranteed premium price to enable Falconbridge to finance expansion.[12] Sherritt-Gordon's arrival on the scene would have been impossible under normal market conditions, but it became possible when largely underwritten by the U.S. government.[13] In Canada, meanwhile, the powerful cabinet minister C.D. Howe – who held two portfolios as minister of trade and commerce and of defence production – was also encouraging the development of resource companies.

Challenges and Opportunities in the 1950s

It was not all smooth sailing in the late 1950s, however, even for Inco. For example, with a reduction in stockpiling in 1958, 'the demand for nickel ... declined so severely in the United States, the principal market, that the Company during the first half of the year was forced to make three successive curtailments in its rate of production in Canada.'[14] This curtailment, plus a major strike in Canada, sharply reduced corporate earnings in 1958, bringing them back to the levels of a decade earlier in terms of earnings per share. (Earning per share amounted to only $2.71 in 1958, versus $2.55 in 1948.) The strike was partially the by-product of a vicious inter-union battle between the incumbent Mine Mill and Smelter Workers, a communist union, and the United Steelworkers of America, which the Steelworkers won.

The late 1950s brought opportunity as well. On 27 February 1956 a major nickel-ore discovery was confirmed as a result of drilling at Thompson, Manitoba. 'It was at a meeting in February, 1956, that the Chairman said to the directors: "Late yesterday afternoon a call came in from Manitoba to Wingate. Ralph Parker was calling, and saying: 'It looks like we've hit the jackpot.'"'[15] In December of that same year, International Nickel announced its plans for immediate development of a new nickel-mining centre in the Mystery-Moak Lakes region of northern Manitoba. In the next three years, $100 million was invested in developing the Thompson site.

The Wingate Era

On 20 April 1960 the Board of Directors met in Thompson, Manitoba, for the first time. The board was welcomed there by Manitoba Premier Duff Roblin. At that historic meeting, Henry S. Wingate was elected as chairman and chief executive officer, succeeding John Thompson.

James Richardson, vice-president of the Winnipeg-based James Richardson and Sons, and the son of a former Inco director, was elected to the board in recognition of Manitoba's new importance to Inco. Also at that meeting, J. Roy Gordon became the first Canadian president. Four new vice-presidents were also appointed. They included James C. Parlee, who was named general manager of the Manitoba Division, and Albert P. Gagnebin, appointed as vice-president of the U.S. subsidiary.

Wingate was in his mid-fifties when he became chairman. A corporate lawyer and graduate of the University of Michigan, he was tall and debonair and looked like he was born to leadership. An early positive development in his term of office was the Thompson mine. Formally dedicated in 1961, the mining and refining enterprise was brought into full operation, making Inco the second-largest producer of nickel in the world.

The first few years under Wingate's leadership were tentative. Sales declined in 1962 as the result of problems in the U.S. steel industry.[16] Wingate's 1962 report to the shareholders was one of the rare occasions where he complained of 'strong competition.' However, both profits and return on investment improved in the early years. The period 1962 to 1968 saw good growth in sales, from $452 million to close to $800 million, an increase of 73 per cent in six years. Profits were not as consistent, though; 1966 was a bad year, and the three years 1965, 1967, and 1968 were flat, showing profits in the range of $141.8 million to $143.8 million as ROI declined from a high of 19 per cent in 1964 to a low of 13.1 per cent in 1968. Part of the reason was a significant addition of debt to fund the major capital expenditures that began in 1967.

Throughout this period, Wingate was making changes in both the company's strategy and its structure. The changes were most pronounced when, in 1966, for the first time in over a decade, Wingate alone, as chairman and chief executive officer, signed the annual report. In the past, the president had signed as well.

Other changes were taking place too. The completion of the Research Laboratory at Sheridan Park in the Greater Toronto Area emphasized the company's commitment to mining and process research. Perhaps more important was the expansion of mining projects beyond Canada. In terms of mining projects, these ventures extended from Guatemala to Indonesia, to an agreement with Broken Hill PCL in Australia, to proposals for joint ventures with French interests in New Caledonia, to feasibility studies in Minnesota.

Structurally, the Board of Directors and senior management changed as Wingate built his team. Both James Parlee and Albert Gagnebin were promoted from vice-president to the new position of executive vice-president in 1964. The following year, both Parlee and Gagnebin joined the Board of Directors.

In 1966 J. Roy Gordon, the Canadian-born president who had reached retirement age, was replaced by Albert Gagnebin, but Gagnebin did not sign the annual report. As a gesture to Parlee, who had been made executive vice-president at the same time as Gagnebin, Parlee was promoted to senior vice-president. In 1967 future Chairman Edward Grubb made his first appearance in the annual reports. Grubb, assistant vice-president of the company, was promoted from managing director to chairman of Henry Wiggin, the British subsidiary.

In 1968 everyone was saddened by the death of John Fairfield Thompson, Wingate's predecessor. Thompson was an outstanding metallurgist with a PhD from Columbia. He started the research lab at Inco when he joined the company in 1906. He was a contributor to the stainless steel sink. He had served the company long and well and at the time of his death held the title of honorary chairman of the Board of Directors. The company was now truly Henry Wingate's.

In concluding the 1968 annual report, after paying tribute to Thompson, Wingate wrote: 'In 1969 we will negotiate a new contract with the United Steelworkers of America ... negotiations will commence early, on March 18, almost four months before the ... expiration date of the present contract. As we enter the negotiation period, we are prepared to do everything we soundly can to insure that there is not an interruption of employment or production, and can see no reason to expect such an interruption.'

This was the lead-up to the annus horribilis of 1969, which resulted in not only the four-month-long Steelworkers strike but also the board's decision to select Edward Grubb as chairman over Alfred Gagnebin.

NOTES

1 CVRD is the world's largest iron-ore miner and, with the acquisition of Inco, became number two in nickel.
2 Interview with Ian McDougall, former vice-chairman and CFO of Inco, 24 June 2004.
3 In Inco's 1971 annual report, Chairman Henry S. Wingate wrote: 'The Board intends to elect L. Edward Grubb as President and Chief Officer, Alfred P. Gagnebin as Chairman of the Board and Chairman of the Executive Committee ... These decisions reached and made known before the end of 1971, assure an orderly transition headed by Mr. Grubb.' However, less than two years later, L. Edward Grubb was elected chairman, J. Edwin Carter was elected president, and Alfred P. Gagnebin, Wingate's chosen

successor, retired. So much for 'the orderly transition.' A former board member declined to comment.

4 McDougall interview.

5 A level sustained for three years before being reduced in 1958 and not exceeded for seven years.

6 34 per cent of consumption in 1968, up from 22 per cent in 1954.

7 Chairman's 1970 message to shareholders.

8 However, Inco's headquarters, including its finance and legal departments, were to remain in New York City for many years.

9 For example, in 1970 Philip Morris began its diversification away from its core business by acquiring Miller's Brewing. In Canada, Imperial Tobacco followed suit, creating Imasco, whose business has diversified into retail, financial services, etc.

10 Inco's 1975 Annual Report had pictures of a supersonic Concorde jet which used nickel and titanium alloy blades forged by Doncaster and a photo-graph of Prince Charles talking with a Doncaster operator of electronic-blade inspection equipment.

11 Limited production took place in 1977; initial shipments began in 1978, with refined product reaching the marketplace in 1979.

12 R.D. Cuff and J.L. Granatstein, *American Dollars, Canadian Prosperity: Canadian-American Economic Relations, 1945–1950* (Toronto: Samuel Stevens 1978), 152–3.

13 Main, *The Canadian Nickel Industry*, 122–3.

14 International Nickel Company of Canada, Annual Report, 1958, 7.

15 Thompson and Beasley, *For the Years to Come*, 275.

16 On 11 April 1962 President John F. Kennedy held a news conference at which he told the steel industry that its price increases constituted 'a wholly unjustifiable and irresponsible defiance of the public interest.' For the print and audio record, see http://www.jfklibrary.org/jfk_press_conference_620411.html (accessed 6 Feb. 2009).

CASE 9

Canada's Black Gold: From the Leduc Discovery to the National Energy Program

STEWART MELANSON, with guidance from JOE MARTIN

The early history of oil and gas in Canada is marked by ups and downs, times of plenty and times of famine. However, if there is one truly important date for Canada's oil patch, it is 13 February 1947, the day of the great oil discovery at Leduc, Alberta, by Imperial Oil. The site of the discovery was called Imperial Leduc No. 1. So important was the find that, for the Canadian oil industry, it resulted in two calendars: 'Before Leduc and After Leduc.'[1] This find ushered in Alberta's 'golden age' of oil.

Before Leduc (1857–1946)

One of Canada's claims to fame is to being the home of the world's first successful drilled oil well. Although Titusville, Pennsylvania, claims that the Drake well drilled in 1859 represented the birth of the modern oil industry, the Drake well was drilled at least a year after the first commercial well was operating in Ontario. Just west of London, Ontario, in Enniskillen Township, the swamps and rivers were found to possess 'earth oils' – put less politely, 'black guck' that had a foul smell and killed anything it touched.[2] In 1857 Hamilton carriage maker James Williams drilled a well in the Enniskillen area that was to be the first commercial oil well drilled in the world. Later, more wells were drilled and a whole oil industry grew up around a town that came to be named Petrolia, near Sarnia in southwestern Ontario.

At the time, oil was mostly used for asphalt, lubricant, and kerosene. In Canada, demand was relatively small and therefore the oil fields of Petrolia easily met the modest domestic needs of the fledgling Dominion. As production from the Petrolia fields flowed, a group of business leaders in the oil patch banded together to create what would become and remains to this day the largest oil and gas company in Canada, Imperial Oil, incorporated on 8 September 1880. It represented an amalgamation of numerous small refiners in Petrolia and London, Ontario. However, Imperial Oil did not remain Canadian for long. The company was purchased in 1898 by John D. Rockefeller's Standard Oil Company.

At the turn of the twentieth century, Imperial Oil dominated the oil and gas sector, controlling 'virtually the entire Canadian market,'[3] including production, refining (operating the largest refinery in the country at Sarnia), and distribution. Imperial Oil also opened the nation's first commercial gas station in Vancouver in 1907 and was the first to develop a chain of gas stations with outlets nationwide. Thus, the early stages of the oil and gas sector in both the United States under Standard Oil, and in Canada through its subsidiary Imperial Oil, were monopolistic, with Standard and Imperial having approximately 90 per cent control of the market in both countries.[4] However, Standard Oil's monopoly was broken up in 1911 in the United States under anti-trust legislation. Its subsidiary in Canada would see its market share drop steadily (from 80 per cent in 1920 to 60 per cent by 1930 and then below 50 per cent by 1940) until the close of the Second World War, when the oil patch in Canada emerged as an 'overcrowded oligopoly.'[5]

While Imperial Oil had grown to dominate the Canadian market, oil production went in the opposite direction as yield began to drop. The oil fields of Petrolia had started to decline by the turn of the century and Canada had to begin importing to meet its needs. Oil was also growing in importance in the military when First Lord of the British Admiralty Winston Churchill decided to convert the British navy from coal to oil in 1912. The strategic importance of oil would rise dramatically owing to applications in military and transportation. Yet, outside Petrolia, only one other truly significant find was made prior to the Leduc strike in 1947 and that was the Turner Valley field southwest of Calgary, Alberta, dubbed 'Hell's Half Acre.'[6]

The Turner Valley field was the first commercial field in western Canada and saw three 'boom' periods: 1914–16, 1924–6, and the late 1930s. Although the Turner Valley find was significant, it was by itself insufficient to meet Canada's growing appetite for oil. In fact, with the decline of production in Petrolia, many of the more experienced oilmen left Canada to develop fields around the world.[7] While this exodus was a boon to foreign development, it meant a loss of valuable expertise in Canada that had been built up over decades in the Petrolia fields.

Fortunately, the Turner Valley field was developed by Canadian independents and this allowed for some Canadian expertise to remain in Canada. The presence of independents would turn out to be important, for they could join forces with the 'oil majors' – as the big companies are known – to prospect for more oil. This was key because the oil companies wanted to share the financial risk of exploratory drilling.

The discovery at Turner Valley prompted Imperial Oil to prospect in the Canadian west and also the Northwest Territories. The one strike Imperial made was in 1920 at Fort Norman, NWT, which proved uneconomical to develop but precipitated an important decision in Ottawa: 'Imperial's one strike ... caused immense initial excitement. *Saturday Night* magazine suggested Fort Norman had enough oil to wipe out the national debt ... believing that Canada's oil future lay in the remaining NWT, Ottawa gave little thought to the mineral rights on Alberta lands which it then controlled. In 1930 the lands and the rights were given to the province [of Alberta].'[8]

Ottawa's belief in the future of oil in the Northwest Territories and its poor prognosis for Alberta seemed to be justified since exploration – primarily by Imperial Oil and sometimes by Shell – continued to come up dry, except for Turner Valley. By 1946, no significant finds had been forthcoming and Canada's need for oil was growing ever greater: 'Canada experienced a new era of industrial development after World War II, partly filling the void left by the collapse of Germany and Japan. Advancing from fifth to third rank among the trading nations of the world, Canada demanded greater quantities of oil year by year to energize factories and propel a nation on wheels. Yet the nation virtually was without oil, supplying less than 10 per cent of its petroleum requirements from domestic sources in 1946.'[9]

The Maritimes relied on oil from Venezuela. Quebec, the largest Canadian market at the time, met its needs through a combination of American and Venezuelan oil. Ontario, Manitoba, and British Columbia relied almost solely on oil imported from the United States. While Alberta and Saskatchewan were self-sufficient in oil production, they were just barely so and total Canadian production was only 20,000 barrels per day from a multitude of small fields.[10] At the end of the Second World War, Canada was a lightweight in oil and gas on the global scene with dim prospects. But all this would change in a relatively short span of ten years, beginning with the spectacular find on 13 February 1947 by Imperial Oil – Imperial Leduc No. 1 south of Edmonton.

After Leduc (Part I): The Beginning of Alberta's Golden Age of Oil (1947–56)

After 133 consecutive dry holes, Imperial Oil struck it rich at Leduc. But Leduc was more than a lucky find – it was also the result of patient efforts by Imperial Oil. The other major oil companies, including Shell, had all but given up on Alberta.[11] The Leduc field was estimated to possess 200 million barrels of oil, which represented a huge find by Canadian standards – much larger than the Turner Valley field. Yet Leduc was soon to be dwarfed by even larger finds.

The discovery at Leduc triggered great interest among the other oil majors, and soon, in addition to Imperial Oil and Shell, other companies entered the fray. Now Texaco, Gulf, British Petroleum, McColl-Frontenac, and Petrofina were also seeking a piece of the action. New discoveries came fast and furious, including the 1948 Redwater find northeast of Edmonton. Reserves there were estimated at 750 million barrels of oil. But both Leduc and Redwater would be dwarfed by the huge discoveries southwest of Edmonton in the early 1950s, such as the Pembina field, pegged at over 'one billion barrels by primary production and millions more [barrels] by secondary recovery.'[12] This transformed Alberta into a world-class oil and gas player, with Imperial Oil maintaining the largest piece of the action; Imperial accounted for 35 per cent to 40 per cent of total Canadian production during the period from 1947 to 1956.

Along with the entry of new oil and gas players came a flurry of new investment. This included significant development of infrastructure to distribute and refine what was produced. By 1954, more than $2 billion in capital had flowed into the western Canadian oil patch, with most of the capital provided by big U.S. oil companies. In the years between 1947 and 1956, the capital employed in Canada's oil and gas sector had increased tenfold over the amount during the entire period from the Turner Valley discovery in 1914 up to Leduc in 1947.[13] Capital amounting to $2 billion was a very large sum for the times, especially given Canada's small population.

This nine-year period was all the more remarkable in that it propelled Alberta to second place behind Texas in world oil and gas development activity.[14] So promising were development prospects in the Wild Rose province after Leduc that Imperial Oil sold its stake in its South American subsidiary, International Petroleum, in 1948. The company did this 'in order to supply large sums of additional funds to continue aggressive oil finding efforts in Western Canada ... to provide adequate refining facilities and to provide economical transportation for crude oil and products to their markets.'[15] The sale was extraordinary given that, prior to Leduc, production at the International Petroleum subsidiary was well over ten times Canadian production and, further, was increasing while Canadian production was decreasing. (See Table 1 below.)

Canadian oil production increased elevenfold, such a tremendous increase that Canada moved from being a place of negligible output to sixth in the world's rankings of oil-producing nations. By 1956, this country was meeting 60 per cent of its own oil needs, in spite of the doubling of domestic consumption from 1946 to 1956[16] (see also Table 1). In addition to this growth in production, foreign direct investment in Canada's oil patch went into building a refining and distribution infrastructure that would be at the time the largest oil and gas pipeline system in the world and today is still one of the largest.

Oil and Gas Distribution and Economic Geography

Oil and gas distribution in Canada has been criticized for being oriented in a north-south rather than east-west direction, giving the impression that Canadian oil and gas suppliers favour supplying the United States over domestic requirements. In the Canadian Maritimes, oil is imported from foreign sources while Alberta oil and gas is exported to the United States. On the surface, this might not appear to be logical; why import the same commodity you are also exporting to a foreign market? While this has given some fodder for conspiracy theories,[17] the reality is more mundane.

Alberta is a long way from the Maritime market and building a pipeline to supply markets in eastern Canada would be very expensive. At the time of Leduc and subsequent discoveries, it was much cheaper

Table 1
Oil production/consumption in thousands of barrels per day (mb/d), 1946 and 1954

Year	Imperial Oil Production (mb/d)	Canadian Production (mb/d)	Canadian Consumption (mb/d)
1946	6,034	20,000	210,000
1954	96,533	260,900	435,000

Source: Current Information Card, Imperial Oil Ltd, Financial Post Corporation Service, 1946–55.

and more expeditious to build a north-south pipeline system to supply markets that were in relatively close geographic proximity. Alberta
oil and gas production exceeded the needs of the closest markets in
Canada's west, for example, to British Columbia via Trans Mountain
Pipeline, and the surplus was exported to U.S. markets in the Midwest.
However, Interprovincial Pipelines did construct an oil pipeline to Sarnia, Ontario, in the early 1950s to Imperial Oil's refinery.[18] In fact, the
cheapest route for Imperial Oil's pipeline to the Sarnia refinery took
it south of Lake Superior and into the United States. The location of
this route raised little protest in Canada and was another example of
the distribution system for Alberta oil and gas being a rationalization
of the needs of both Canada and the United States: 'The closeness of
the Canada-US economic relationship was built on proximity, similar business cultures, consumer preferences, linkages between related
industries and an interdependence between US capital and technology
and Canadian resources and markets … a market integration that was
logical by economic terms.'[19] The oil majors developed the distribution
system based on economic geography. Supplying Alberta oil and gas
to markets in eastern Canada would have resulted in Canadians in the
Maritimes paying much higher energy costs;[20] thus, politically, it was a
non-starter since it was cheaper for Atlantic Canada to import.

The market integration of the oil and gas sector made economic sense,
just as economic rationalization in the automotive industry spurred the
1965 Auto Pact, which optimized automobile production in Canada
and the United States to serve Canadian and American markets as an
integrated whole.[21] However, the high level of FDI eventually resulted
in rising 'political and social resistance,'[22] discussed below.

A Partnership of Big Oil, Independents, and Government

The meteoric rise of the Canadian oil and gas sector would not have
been possible without the combination of a massive mobilization of
capital and expertise by the large U.S. oil majors and the activities of
smaller players, including many Canadian such as Pacific Petroleums
and Home Oil. Even the Canadian Hudson's Bay Company, a retailer
that continued to own mineral rights on its extensive land holdings, got
into the fray after Leduc. It held a 25 per cent interest in Hudson's Bay
Oil and Gas Company (HBOG), with 75 per cent control by U.S.-based
Continental Oil (which later became Conoco Inc.). In fact, through the
1950s, HBOG grew much faster than HBC's retail operations, building

on the post-Leduc oil bonanza. In addition to HBC, many firms whose main line of business were outside the oil and gas sector made forays into this burgeoning field to get a piece of the action. These included Dome Mines through a new subsidiary created in 1950, Dome Explora- tion – which became Dome Petroleum in 1958 – backed by Ivy League university endowment funds. By 1954, more than 1,200 firms were doing business and investing in the Alberta oil patch. The players, big and small, some old hat in the oil and gas sector and some new to the industry, were all 'hoping for a big strike.'[23]

When it came to exploration and development, the independents and the majors maintained what was at times an uneasy relationship, but they needed each other. The majors needed the independents to prospect their vast lease holdings and thereby diversify their own risks; drilling wells was expensive and the majors were quite happy to let entrepreneurial 'wildcatters' be the ones to run the risks of drilling a string of dry wells. But, when a wildcatter struck oil, both the majors and the wildcatters earned a big payout, making it worthwhile for many with an entrepreneurial spirit to take those risks.[24]

Further, the smaller independents needed the majors for another rea- son – to hold the large leases of crown land for prospecting. The majors could afford the leasing costs paid to the provincial government for large tracts and could hold the land for long periods of time to allow for thorough prospecting.[25] Thus, the majors benefited by diversifying risk and by more efficient prospecting of leased crown lands. This in turn benefited the independents, who would be rewarded for discoveries on leased land without themselves bearing the burden of the high costs of leasing and holding land for prospecting. The provincial government benefited not only from the leasing fees but also from the royalties for any production that came of finds developed on leased land.

Overall, the Canadian and Alberta provincial governments were relatively passive towards foreign direct investment in the oil and gas sector. They allowed nearly unfettered development of the Canadian oil and gas sector by foreign multinational oil companies.[26] In fact, in some cases, government regulation was welcomed, although not nec- essarily at the outset. In the 1930s, the Alberta provincial government, now in control of mineral rights within the boundaries of the province and concerned with the rapid exploitation of the Turner Valley field, enacted legislation to conserve oil and gas reserves so as to husband resources for future needs. At first, the majors were less than enthu- siastic about the measures. After Leduc, however, they embraced the legislation since it came to be seen as a method to prevent a glut of production and a price collapse in the burgeoning Alberta oil patch.[27]

After Leduc (Part II): The FDI Debate and the Era of Pragmatism (1956–70)

The foundations for the FDI debate were laid in 1956 when C.D. Howe and the Liberal government pushed for an all-Canadian gas pipeline to be built by Trans Canada Pipelines. The idea appealed to nationalistic sentiment but was chronically short of investor and purchaser confidence in such a venture's viability. Trans Canada Pipeline debates took place in the House of Commons. Allegations that Liberal cabinet ministers were engaging in insider trading in Trans Canada shares led to a scandal and resignations from the cabinet. This weakened the Liberals and set the stage for the rise of the Conservative Party. However, on assuming power in 1957, the Conservatives inherited the nationalistic sentiments that remained following the Trans Canada Pipeline debates.[28]

Studies and Reports

In the late 1950s and through the 1960s, economic nationalism was on the rise, focusing in particular on level of FDI and foreign control of Canadian industries, with approximately 75 per cent of FDI originating in the United States.[29] This prompted the federal government to initiate studies and inquiries in order to make it plain that the government was listening and responding to the concerns of Canadians. But high levels of FDI were actually precipitated by government policies dating back to Confederation. The protective tariff of the National Policy (1879) was a reaction to the U.S. abrogation of the Reciprocity Treaty and the high tariffs adopted by the United States. The National Policy ushered in an era of high tariffs in an unsuccessful attempt to get the Americans back to the bargaining table. However, change in policy direction can have unintended consequences:

> Geography and history have made it inevitable that the economic structures of Canada and the United States should become closely intertwined. The common North American setting and atmosphere which makes, or has made, so similar many of their political and economic problems, the

large interchange of population, and the to some extent complementary nature of their resources have conspired to produce a growth of interdependence which public policy … [has] been powerless seriously to impede. Indeed, the very attempts on Canada's part to preserve an independent economy, through tariffs, through Imperial preference, through appeals to local patriotism, have not infrequently promoted the 'American penetration' which they were designed to repel … By 1973 Canada had the highest incidence of foreign ownership of any major industrial country and the United States accounted for over 80 percent of the total.[30]

The National Policy promoted foreign direct investment in industries that in turn led to high levels of foreign ownership. While it is true that foreign ownership of the Canadian oil and gas sector was very high, 'access to the resources themselves remained largely in Canadian control through licensing arrangements for timber, minerals, oil and gas, etc. located on crown land.'[31] It was also recognized that foreign expertise was needed in the oil and gas sector to develop Leduc given the 'failure of the early Turner Valley field to generate a sizable number of viable independent firms.'[32] U.S. oil majors invested significant funds and took great risk in prospecting Canada for oil and gas while facing the possibility that they might have little to show for the expense. Once significant discoveries were made, U.S. majors poured capital (as well as expertise) into Canada to develop the resources and to build a refining and distribution infrastructure that produced jobs and supplied government coffers with royalties and licence fees. Together, entrepreneurs, 'Big Oil,' and an enabling government created a whole new industry in Canada centred around oil and gas where relatively little had existed before.

One persistent argument against FDI was that Canada would be largely a branch- plant economy and exporter of raw materials and importer of finished goods. One assertion is that, with respect to oil and gas, 'the successful penetration of international capital into the western Canadian oil play following the Leduc discovery of 1947 [had] implications … the failure of the oil industry to affect a transformation in the Alberta economy away from a dependence upon primary production.'[33] This statement implies that Alberta produces and exports the crude out of the country for refining and other value-added processes in the energy value chain. However, the major U.S. oil companies did invest in refining, distribution, and marketing in Alberta and Canada as a whole. Canada refines more product than it consumes and is an exporter of refined petroleum products to the United States, suggesting that concerns regarding Canada being confined to the role of exporter of raw materials are not well founded, at least in oil and gas.[34]

Still, public concern over high levels of FDI required some government response, even if only a symbolic one. Starting with the 1957 Royal Commission on Canada's Economic Prospects, commonly known as the Gordon Commission after its chairman, Walter Gordon, a series of studies and reports was undertaken to examine the effects of high levels of FDI on the Canadian economy. However, the Gordon Commission's 1957 Economic Report, and the Watkins Report that followed in 1967, both under Liberal administrations, contained more bark then bite. Even when recommendations from the reports led to tangible legislation, such as 1963 legislation resulting in punitive tax treatment for Canadian editions of American magazines, the United States was quick to respond with counter-legislation to punish Canada's 'heavy-handed approach to economic independence.'[35] The result was always the same: a hasty retreat and return to a pragmatic approach to bilateral trade and investment relations between the United States and Canada such that Canada continued to be a desirable destination for FDI.

Oil and Gas Legislation

In 1958 the Borden Commission's Energy Report,[36] which had a stated purpose to study the effectiveness and gaps in Canadian energy policy, recommended that Ottawa create a body that would advise the federal government on energy policy and regulate the interprovincial transport and marketing of energy resources. The body created was called the National Energy Board and was established in 1959. In 1961, upon the recommendation of the NEB, Ottawa created the National Oil Policy (NOP). The purpose of this policy was to protect the Canadian energy industry from imports of cheap foreign oil. The NOP allowed for higher oil prices in the western provinces and Ontario (to promote greater exploration and development of energy resources) while the eastern provinces were to continue to rely on imports. Even though the oil patch was dominated by large foreign companies, the NEB and the NOP did not pose any significant barriers to operations in Canada by the oil majors. In fact, the policy of higher prices (a few cents a barrel above the world price) and protection against foreign imports to promote exploration and development was beneficial to Alberta producers.

Canadian oil production, particularly in Alberta, enjoyed large surpluses with respect to local domestic consumption needs. Therefore, by 1970, western Canada shipped almost one million barrels of oil a day southward to the United States while eastern Canada relied on nearly the same volume of oil in the form of cheap imports. Despite the slightly elevated price, the NOP did not give incentives for further exploration. With low oil prices, the Canadian independents began to disappear, bought out by the larger oil majors. In 1962 the last significant integrated Canadian independent oil firm, Canadian Oil Companies, was bought by Shell and the distinctive White Rose logo disappeared. The logo was considered a national symbol and its disappearance fuelled increased debate on the FDI issue.[37]

Despite increased nationalist public sentiment for greater control of the Canadian oil patch, the oil majors increased their grip on the industry. By 1970, the Canadian oil and gas industry was dominated by foreign majors, including Imperial Oil, Gulf, Shell, Texaco, Petrofina, Mobil, and Conoco. Dome Petroleum was the exception, since it was majority-owned by Canadian shareholders (Dome had become the largest natural gas producer in Canada). However, the massive activity in the oil patch did serve to build a large reservoir of Canadian talent and oil expertise from which to draw in future, even if, for the time being, these employees worked mostly for the foreign majors.

The government 'two-track' approach was as follows: first, establish royal commissions and issue reports in order to appease the public nationalist's concerns; second, maintain a pragmatic stance in responding to the reports' recommendations to allow Canada to remain a desirable destination for FDI. This twin approach prevailed throughout the administrations of prime ministers John Diefenbaker and Lester Pearson; at the same time, Canada enjoyed significant economic expansion. This pragmatic approach would not survive the oil shocks of the 1970s and Prime Minister Pierre Trudeau's administration. The FDI debate was to enter a new interventionist phase.[38]

After Leduc (Part III): The Oil Shocks and the Interventionist Phase (1970–80)

During the Trudeau era[39] and within the context of the oil shocks, policy was to change radically. Public distrust of foreign ownership in Canada had hardened and Kari Levitt's treatise on the perils of FDI, *Silent Surrender: The Multinational Corporation in Canada* (1970), provided ideological direction for Canadian nationalists. The Trudeau regime responded with a set of policy changes that represented an interventionist approach to develop a greater and more independent Canadian presence in the energy sector that had until then been dominated by foreign multinationals.[40]

However, interventionist policies at the federal level, and Canada's overlapping responsibilities for resource management between levels of government, were a source of tension and conflict between provincial and federal levels of government. For the next ten years, the provinces (primarily Alberta) and Ottawa clashed repeatedly on jurisdiction over energy resources and energy policy. Key disputes arose over revenue sharing; whether domestic prices should be on par with global prices for oil and gas; and federal intrusion into the industry through, in 1975, the creation of a crown corporation – Petro-Canada. The establishment of Petro-Canada marked the federal government's foray into the energy sector as a major oil and gas player. However, the greatest tension came with the announcement of the National Energy Program in 1980.

After the publication of Levitt's influential book, the 1972 election resulted in a Liberal minority government in Ottawa that was dependent on the New Democratic Party (NDP) to maintain power. The balance in the House of Commons was as follows: Liberals, 109; Progressive Conservatives, 107; NDP, 31; Social Credit, 15; and independents, 2. Meanwhile, a Marxist splinter group of the NDP, the Waffle movement, attempted to push the NDP further left and supported and fuelled nationalist sentiment in Canada. Trudeau, dependent on NDP support and cognizant of hardening public opinion on FDI in Canada, acted upon the recent Wahn Report and particularly the more interventionist Gray report.[41]

From 1972 until 1976, numerous policy initiatives were implemented. One included utilizing the Canada Development Corporation (formed 1971) as an instrument to buy back 'Canada' from multinationals through investment in industries heavily dominated by foreign investment such as mining, chemical, and oil and gas. In 1974 the Foreign Investment Review Agency was created to review new foreign investment in Canada for possible 'deleterious effect.' As an absurd example of intervention, Alberta's government under Peter Lougheed moved to increase royalty rates, and, at the same time, Ottawa declared provincial royalties no longer eligible as a deduction for federal tax purposes, 'creating certain situations in which the marginal tax rates surpassed 100 per cent.'[42]

The creation of Petro-Canada in 1975 was one of the most significant interventions by Ottawa. Players in the oil and gas sector resented this government intrusion. They saw no solid reason for Ottawa's interference other than ideology or politics. In their view, Canadian independents were already emerging and the private sector had done a good job developing supply and infrastructure that was at the time more than adequate to meet domestic requirements in the most economical way. Many companies also resented the fact that the government was not only competing with the private sector but also gave many advantages to Petro-Canada for exploration and development on federal lands such as rights to offshore exploration, for which Ottawa would cover up to 80 per cent of the costs. In fact, such intervention would seem to be ill-advised given the instability of the Middle East. Because Canada was a stable country in close proximity to U.S. markets, oil and gas companies felt that this was all the more reason to promote exploration and development of domestic sources; intervention could put a chill on foreign investment at a time when it was most needed.[43] However, during the interventionist period, environmental factors also played a major role – among these factors were the politically induced oil shocks of the 1970s.

The Oil Shocks and Government Response

In 1973 the Yom Kippur War broke out between Israel, Jordan, Egypt, and Syria. While Israel emerged victorious from the conflict, Arab countries protested against the Western world's support for Israel by imposing an oil embargo on the West. The resulting supply shock saw oil prices more than triple in the face of oil shortages. The same price shocks were felt in natural gas as well.

In 1973 Trans Canada Pipelines' natural gas contracts came up for renewal and the negotiation went to arbitration;[44] the decision handed down resulted in a 400 per cent increase (14 cents to 60 cents per million cubic feet [MCF]). More contract renewals came up in 1974, and arbitration led to a decision to price natural gas at approximately $1.15 per MCF, doubling what was already a quadrupling of price in the prior year. However, the latest price increase did not go in effect owing to the intervention of the federal government, which was concerned that the rapid price increases would upset voters. Although the government acted to cap domestic prices on natural gas, it also set an export price of $4.95 per MCF.[45] The great price disparity between gas that was exported versus gas sold domestically required further government intervention. A formula was provided to even out revenues for export and domestic sales, in order to prevent export of all of the province's gas. Still, the export price was not appreciated in the United States, given that U.S. majors had poured the capital into the Alberta oil and gas patch to make production surpluses for export a reality.

Also, the NEB was revising 'tests' for export volumes which required there to be a surplus for foreseeable Canadian future needs. However, the federal NDP pressed for restriction of exports unless 100 years of future production to meet Canadian needs could be guaranteed. If this had been implemented, exploration would have stopped since the requirements were so extreme that firms exploring for and developing gas (investments/projects/ventures) for export (the domestic market's current requirements were already well met) would be blocked for the foreseeable future.

Fortunately, a more reasonable future supply cushion was required by the NEB and this did spur pipeline development for export. This development in turn opened up more production through exploration along the pipeline route; with a pipeline in the vicinity, the economics of gas finds were greatly improved since distribution capability was close at hand and in place. Such exploration and development led to plenty of production surplus and the NEB for the most part approved all exports. Note also that the potential for export markets opened up capacity to allow more players in; with this came, as always happens, more competition, development, and exploration. Thus, because of the NEB's decision to set a reasonable cushion to protect national interests, market forces were not unduly constrained and the balance played out well, to the satisfaction of industry and government.

One of the reasons that Canadian oil and gas exports garnered so much attention was growing concern over peak production and dwindling reserves: 'After an auspicious two decades following the Second World War, the supply outlook for oil and gas has deteriorated continuously since the mid-1960s, and the rate of decline has been accelerated by large exports to the United States.'[46]

Production Increases Slow and Then Peak in Canada and the United States

By 1970, conventional oil exploration and development had slowed. The sense in the industry was that in Canada the 'easy finds had all been made.'[47] Although Imperial Oil, the largest integrated oil major operating in Canada, did continue to increase production, the rate of growth slowed and then peaked in 1974. For Canada as a whole, oil reserves peaked by 1970, suggesting that new finds did not even replace what was produced (see Table 2). As oil production in Canada was dropping off, so too did production in the United States. Our southern neighbour reached a maximum daily oil-production output in 1971 of approximately 10.5 million barrels per day.

Declining oil reserves, large volumes of exports to the United States, and the dominance of U.S.-based majors in the Canadian oil and gas industry together intensified the FDI debate. In addition to oil and gas

Table 2
Imperial Oil: Oil production and oil and gas reserves: 1956–78

Year	Oil Production (mb/d)	Proved Oil Reserves (cubic metres)	Marketable Natural Gas Reserves (thousand cubic metres Mcf.)
1956	105,000	452,793,000	486,298,000
1957	97,000	456,779,000	513,730,000
1958	77,000	503,094,000	577,230,000
1959	84,000	555,728,000	659,908,000
1960	79,000	584,577,000	760,530,000
1961	97,000	663,222,000	832,147,000
1962	108,000	712,028,000	879,512,000
1963	109,000	1,035,919,000	929,523,000
1964	114,000	1,248,270,000	1,284,000,000
1965	115,000	1,398,000,000	1,315,000,000
1966	127,000	1,557,000,000	1,395,000,000
1967	141,000	1,627,000,000	1,447,000,000
1968	150,000	1,661,000,000	1,544,000,000
1969	154,000	1,665,000,000	1,638,000,000
1970	170,000	1,623,000,000	1,717,000,000
1971	183,000	1,584,000,000	1,764,000,000
1972	262,000	1,524,000,000	1,722,000,000
1973	279,000	1,431,000,000	1,729,000,000
1974	337,000	1,330,000,000	1,831,000,000
1975	265,000	1,244,000,000	2,028,000,000
1976	236,000	1,180,000,000	2,165,000,000
1977	230,000	1,120,000,000	2,231,000,000
1978	231,000	1,090,000,000	2,322,000,000

Source: Canadian Association of Petroleum Producers (CAPP) Statistical Handbook; www.capp.ca/GetDoc.aspx?DocID=146286; and Current Information Card, Imperial Oil Ltd, Financial Post Corporation Service, 1972–81.

outflows, the debate also targeted capital outflows from multinationals repatriating profits. The concern was that outflows of the profits of multinationals harmed Canada's economy and worsened the balance of payments.[48] However, capital outflows should be expected, given the large investments made in Canada's oil and gas sector. In fact, the Nixon administration in the United States was concerned that not enough profits were being repatriated by its multinationals. In 1971 it formed the Domestic International Sales Corporation to provide incentives to multinationals to 're-nationalize production and to export from home plants not foreign affiliates.'[49]

Further, the 1965 Auto Pact had come under scrutiny in the United States and the government seriously considered its repeal in order to appease American voters who were discontented over capital outflows. By 1970, Canada had reversed its trade deficit, largely thanks to the Auto Pact.[50] By now, '32 percent of Canada's exports to the United States were in the automotive sector compared to 5 percent prior to the agreement.'[51] Although the FDI debate intensified regulatory uncertainty, the rapid increases in oil and gas prices led to a renewed interest in the Alberta oil sands and resulted in consideration of further FDI on a massive scale. For example, Imperial Oil laid out plans in 1977 to invest $6 billion in development of oil sands production at Cold Lake, Alberta. Further, another $6 billion was expected to be provided by Imperial's partners as a joint venture. This represented a huge sum at the time, but, while Imperial was working through the complex process of putting in place such a massive investment, new legislation dramatically changed the playing field.

The National Energy Program[52]

On 28 October 1980, under the newly re-elected Trudeau government, the National Energy Program was introduced by Marc Lalonde, then minister of finance. The program was a response to rapidly rising oil prices and was imposed on the provinces by the federal government after two years of fruitless negotiations over pricing and revenue sharing between Alberta and the federal government.

The NEP was controversial for several reasons. First, Canada's constitution splits responsibility for natural resources between the provincial and federal levels of government (section 109 of the Constitution Act, 1867). Owing to overlapping jurisdiction, policy on resources had historically been determined by negotiation and bargaining between the two levels of government. Yet the NEP was implemented without consultation with industry or the provinces and furthermore was viewed as an unprecedented level of intrusion into provincial jurisdiction over resource policy. Secondly, the NEP reversed Alberta's hard-won concessions from Ottawa to let oil and gas prices trend towards parity between Canadian domestic energy prices and global market prices. The domestic market would be buffered from rising world oil prices through price controls on domestic production and government subsidies of energy imports.

The NEP was also different because it represented a first in implementing, in addition to a supply-side policy, a demand-side policy, by promoting energy conservation through grants to switch to alternative-energy sources. However, measures in the NEP to keep domestic energy prices artificially below global market rates had the opposite effect on conservation. Lower energy prices promoted greater energy consumption than would have been the case if energy prices had been allowed to reach parity with world prices, supporting the view that the NEP was ill-conceived. The NEP also introduced measures to promote greater Canadian control and ownership of the domestic energy sector, which was largely controlled by U.S.-based multinationals. These measures included a special tax to fund acquisitions by the crown corporation Petro-Canada as well as favouring Canadian firms in the allocation of exploration grants.

The legacy of the NEP was increased resentment and distrust between Ottawa and the western provinces. The latter saw the NEP as a high-handed intrusion into provincial prerogatives over their resources and as a revenue grab to benefit central and eastern Canada at their expense. An industry insider said in an interview that the NEP put foreign direct investment in the Canadian oil and gas sector into a 'deep freeze.' Imperial Oil's Cold Lake project would be one of many casualties: 'In 1977 [Imperial Oil] proposed, subject to approvals, construction of a plant at Cold Lake [Alberta] for the extraction of 22,000 m^3 of synthetic crude oil daily from bitumen deposits. Capital costs of the project estimated at $12 billion and equity participation in about 50% of the project would be offered to interested companies. The project was suspended July 8, 1981, pending resolution of energy issues by the federal and provincial governments.'[53]

Many oil companies left the province of Alberta in response to the NEP, aggravating unemployment. Even the independents whom the NEP was supposed to help received little benefit from it when they saw that 'the tax numbers added up to disaster.'[54] Alberta's premier, Peter Lougheed, retaliated with countermeasures including reducing oil production and holding up approvals for oil sands development projects; Lougheed was admired by Albertans for his resolute leadership in opposing the NEP.

The National Energy Policy was dismantled after the Conservatives were elected in 1984. Nevertheless, when Brian Mulroney became prime minister, the NEP remained a painful memory for many Albertans. Lingering resentment of the loathed policy embodied western alienation with Ottawa and played a significant role in reshaping Canadian politics. Opposition to the NEP and disenchantment with central Canada led to the rise of western separatist movements and incited citizens to support the growth of such new political groups as the Reform Party, which in turn morphed first into the Canadian Alliance and later the Conservative Party.

Conclusion

In the early stages of discovery and exploitation of Canada's oil and gas resources, domestic firms were largely the key players, but, over time, foreign firms increasingly took on the role of exploration and development, as well as the risks and significant costs of doing so. With Leduc and the other major oil reserve discoveries that followed, massive FDI flowed into Canada to exploit the finds. Further, the foreign oil majors developed massive refining and distribution networks to carry the oil to market. During the FDI debates of the 1960s, which led to the implementation of investment controls in the 1970s, it was frequently argued that foreign control of Canada's resources is undesirable given repatriation of profits out of Canada and the distribution network favouring U.S. markets. However, with the history of oil and gas exploration and exploitation in Canada better understood, the issue of FDI becomes more nuanced.

The story of oil in Canada illustrates the importance of government policy in shaping the development of industry within national borders as well as promoting (or impeding) trade and foreign direct investment. The case raises important questions about the role of market forces in guiding the development of natural resources and their distribution, about policies around foreign direct investment, and about the wisdom of dividing resource rights between the federal and provincial levels of government.

Suggested Questions

1. This case examines foreign direct investment in Canada with specific attention to the oil and gas sector. Given the strategic importance of energy, what are the key benefits of FDI and what are the key concerns?
2. The oil majors, governments, and Canadian independents worked together to develop Alberta's oil and gas sector following the Leduc find from 1947 to 1970. What was done well and what could have been done better? You may also consider the history prior to Leduc (1947) in your discussion and identify underlying causes and issues, both good and not so good.
3. As CEO of Imperial Oil, what issues would you have with government policy in the 1970s and why? Which policies worked and, among those that did not, what were the alternatives?

Suggested Readings

Chastko, Paul. *Developing Alberta's Oil Sands: From Karl Clark to Kyoto*. Calgary: University of Calgary Press 2004.
Dawson, Laura Ritchie. 'Nationalism versus Interdependence in the Evolution of Canada's Post-War Investment Policies.' Paper presented at the Centre for Trade Policy and Law Investment Conference, University of Ottawa, November 2004.
Gould, Ed. *Oil: The History of Canada's Oil & Gas Industry*. Victoria: Hancock House Publishing 1976.
Knight, Oliver. 'Oil – Canada's New Wealth. *Business History Review*, 30, no. 3 (1956): 297–328.

NOTES

1 Gould, *Oil*, 99.
2 Michael Bliss, *Northern Enterprise: Five Centuries of Canadian Business* (Toronto: McClelland and Stewart 1987), 243.
3 Graham D. Taylor and Peter A. Baskerville, *A Concise History of Business in Canada* (Toronto: Oxford University Press 1994), 331.
4 H.M.K. (Hugh) Grant, 'The Petroleum Industry and Canadian Economic Development: An Economic History, 1900–1961,' PhD thesis, University of Toronto 1986.

5 Ibid., 1 (abstract).
6 For a colourful account of western Canada's first commercial oil field, see David Finch, *Hell's Half Acre: Early Days in the Great Alberta Oil Patch* (Surrey, B.C.: Heritage House Publishing 2005).
7 Gould, *Oil*.
8 Bliss, *Northern Enterprise*, 518. The original provinces at the time of Confederation retained the rights to natural resources. It took many years before the newer provinces received the same rights, which caused resentment.
9 Knight, 'Oil,' 297.
10 Ibid.
11 Bliss, *Northern Enterprise*.
12 Knight, 'Oil,' 305.
13 Ibid.
14 Ibid. $2 billion in 1950 is equivalent to approximately $20 billion in 2008 dollars; www.bank-banque-canada.ca/en/rates/inflation_calc.html. Given Canada's population then, it would be similar, by today's standards, to $60 billion being poured into Alberta, which is on par with the massive capital outlays for oil sands development.
15 Current Information Card, Imperial Oil, 22 Sept. 1948, Financial Post Corporation Service.
16 Dawson, 'Nationalism Versus Interdependence.'
17 For an example, see Peter Cizek, 'Scouring Scum and Tar from the Bottom of the Pit,' *Canadian Dimension*, July/August 2006.
18 Bliss, *Northern Enterprise*.
19 Dawson, 'Nationalism versus Independence,' 4.
20 Knight, 'Oil.'
21 Dimitry Anastakis, *The Auto Pact: Creating a Borderless North American Auto Industry, 1969–1971* (Toronto: University of Toronto Press 2005).
22 Dawson, 'Nationalism versus Independence,' 5.
23 Bliss, *Northern Enterprise*, 525.
24 Ibid., 525, and Knight, 'Oil.'
25 Based on observations of an industry insider passed on to the author during an in-depth interview. Also noted in the interview was that the independents would play an increasingly important role in creating an independent Canadian oil and gas industry as they built up both capital and expertise.
26 Dawson, 'Nationalism versus Independence.' This was also corroborated in an interview with a retired executive who has more than forty years experience in the oil and gas sector in Canada. He pointed out that, relative to today, the level of regulation at that time was far less burdensome.

27 Bliss, *Northern Enterprise*. Also, Current Information Cards, Imperial Oil, Financial Post Corporation Service, 1946–1955, commented that production capacity exceeded production throughout the period.

28 Bliss, *Northern Enterprise*.

29 Dawson, 'Nationalism versus Independence.'

30 Ibid., 4.

31 Ibid., 6.

32 Grant, 'The Petroleum Industry,' 1.

33 Ibid., 1–2.

34 See Canadian Petroleum Products Institute website, refining: www.cppi.ca/Refining_Marketing_Distribution.html. It can also be said that the Canadian automotive industry prospered under the 1965 Auto Pact, being a net exporter of completed vehicles. Even after the pact's demise, the automotive industry in Canada has fared well compared to the United States despite the fact that, since the 1930s, all automotive firms in Canada have been subsidiaries of foreign automotive manufacturers.

35 Dawson, 'Nationalism versus Independence,' 10.

36 Henry Borden was president of the company that became Brascan.

37 Bliss, *Northern Enterprise*.

38 Dawson, 'Nationalism versus Independence.'

39 Pierre Elliott Trudeau was prime minister from April 1968 to June 1979 and from March 1980 to June 1984.

40 Dawson, 'Nationalism versus Independence.'

41 Ibid. and Bliss, *Northern Enterprise*.

42 Bliss, *Northern Enterprise*, 535; the oil and gas players in Alberta were upset by Lougheed's policy of increasing royalty rates but approved of his stance in pressuring Ottawa to move domestic prices towards parity with world prices.

43 Based on interview notes with an industry insider and drawn also from Bliss, *Northern Enterprise*, and Dawson, 'Nationalism and Independence.'

44 Negotiation, followed by arbitration, occurred between Gulf and Trans Canada to set a single industry price with all other suppliers accepting the result.

45 This was the culmination of a decade-long NEB revision to the export price of natural gas, as described in G.C. Watkins and L. Waverman, 'Canadian Natural Gas Export Pricing Behaviour,' *Canadian Public Policy*, 11, special issue 1 (1985): 415–26.

46 Bruce Willson, *The Energy Squeeze: Canadian Policies for Survival* (Toronto: Canadian Institute for Economic Policy 1980), 91.

47 Bliss, *Northern Enterprise*, 531.

48 Grant, 'The Petroleum Industry,' and Willson, *The Energy Squeeze*.

49 Dawson, 'Nationalism versus Independence,' 13.

50 Anastakis, *The Auto Pact*.

51 Dawson, 'Nationalism versus Independence,' 13; note that the Canadian automotive sector is dominated by foreign firms.

52 Sources for this section include, Bliss, *Northern Enterprise*; Dawson, 'Nationalism versus Independence'; and the following websites: http:// www.abheritage.ca/abpolitics/events/issues_nep.html; http://www. thecanadianencyclopedia.com/index.cfm?PgNm=TCE&Params=A1AR TA0005618; http://www.thecanadianencyclopedia.com/index.cfm?PgNm =TCE&Params=A1ARTA0002613 (all accessed 25 June 2008).

53 Current Information Card, Imperial Oil, Financial Post Corporation Service, 1981, 4. Emphasis added.

54 Bliss, *Northern Enterprise*, 542. The major tax problem was the Petroleum and Gas Royalty Tax (PGRT).

PART FOUR

The Challenging Years, 1980–2005

Introduction

Canada had many positive things going for it in 2005: a strong dollar, an historically low unemployment rate, a government surplus with a declining debt, and a current account surplus, not to mention the huge potential of the Alberta oil sands as the price of oil rose.

But getting to that high point had not been easy. The bright promise forecast in 1980 had not been realized. Over the period from 1980 to 2005, Canada's economic performance matched neither the growth of other Western industrialized nations nor its own historical pace.[1] The healthy growth rate of the late 1970s had given way to the recession of the early 1980s, the worst economic period in Canadian history since the Great Depression. Not only had GDP/capita dropped 4.2 per cent between 1981 and 1982, another recession hit hard in the early 1990s, to be followed by a further slowdown at the beginning of the twenty-first century.[2]

The reality of slower economic growth in both the public and private sectors produced a variety of responses. The federal government's 'Leap of Faith' into the Canada-U.S. Free Trade Agreement (FTA) in 1988 was the most dramatic. Another was 'the little bang' of 1987 – legislation that permitted chartered banks to enter the trust, investment banking, mutual fund, and insurance businesses. (The term 'little bang' was used to distinguish the new policy from the 'big bang' felt in London when the United Kingdom deregulated its financial markets.) Still, times were tough. In the quarter-century from 1980 to 2005, business managers had to cope with volatility in interest rates and oil prices and the fluctuating Canadian dollar,[3] all factors presenting significant challenges for the private sector.

In addition, the impact felt by technological change was greater than ever before as the personal computer arrived on the scene in the early 1980s, followed by the World Wide Web in the early 1990s. The good news from a Canadian perspective was the development of the ubiquitous BlackBerry, which came to market at century's end, a product of Waterloo-based Research in Motion (RIM).

The other good news was that the change of millennium did not produce the technological crash that some had predicted. But the bad news was the terrorist attack on New York's World Trade Center on 11 September 2001, which resulted in significant restrictions to the free flow of goods and services across the Canada-U.S. border as a result of increased 'security' measures.

Public Policy

In the 1980s the 'prevailing intellectual consensus concerning the role of government in the economy'[4] began to change. That change, involving a diminishment in the role of the state, was not as dramatic in Canada as it was in the United Kingdom or the United States, but it was evident that Canadians were also revisiting some long-held attitudes. In fact, government expenditures as a percentage of GDP topped out in 1992 and declined modestly thereafter. By 2005, they were at the lowest level as a percentage of GDP in thirty years. In addition, a measure of privatization had taken place – mostly at the federal level – along with some attempts at deregulation.

Crown Corporations

While much of the world committed itself to privatizing state-owned enterprises in the 1980s, Canada did not follow suit. This is not to say there were no privatizations in Canada, just that there were not many and most were at the federal rather than the provincial level. The largest and best known of these privatizations were Air Canada, Canadian National Railway, and Petro-Canada.

Though there was less activity at the provincial level, both Manitoba and Alberta privatized the government-owned telephone companies and Alberta privatized the liquor stores. In Ontario, the government started to privatize Ontario Hydro, then stopped. But it did sell Highway 407, making it the 'largest privatization in Canadian history.'[5]

There was also a dramatic change in the amount of revenue generated by both federal and provincial crown corporations over the twenty-five-year period. With respect to federal crown corporations, it was a relatively modest revenue growth; but there was dramatic growth in the revenue of provincial crown corporations, primarily because they were involved in the liquor and gambling businesses. The largest non-financial crown corporation in 2005 was Hydro Québec, with revenues of nearly $11 billion. The other large provincial crown corporations were involved in electrical generation and distribution, liquor sales, and lotteries or gaming.

Trade, Investment, and Regulation

The history of free trade flows throughout this text. In Part One, the protective tariff and the National Policy were discussed. In Part Two, attention was paid to the defeat of reciprocity in the 1911 general election. And in Part Three, the focus was on the increase in trade as the result of global trade liberalization through GATT.

The early 1980s saw Canada experience its worst setback economically since the Great Depression. Partially because of the severe economic setback, Prime Minister Pierre Trudeau appointed a Royal Commission on the Economic Union and Development Prospects for Canada. A former senior cabinet minister, Donald Macdonald, chaired the commission and in his report noted that 'the recession of 1981–82 ... left scars not just on those who lost their jobs, homes, farms, or businesses, but on the Canadian psyche as a whole.'[6] Macdonald called upon the government of Canada to undertake a 'leap of faith' and enter into a free-trade agreement with the United States. Part of the report's reasoning was based on concerns that an increasingly protectionist United States, using non-tariff barriers (NTBs) and countervailing duties, could do irreparable harm to the Canadian economy.

Macdonald's report was accepted by the Mulroney government.[7] The pact was signed in October 1987 but an election was required in Canada before the agreement could take effect. The 1988 election was the first free-trade election in seventy-seven years, and, for the first time, the free traders won. With the Mulroney government back in power, the FTA came into effect on 1 January 1989. While the government party in power changed in 1993, the agreement was not ripped up (as had been threatened by anti-free traders within the new governing party, the Liberals) but rather was embraced. Trade between the two countries boomed and Canada clearly benefited. In 1994 the government accepted the broader North American Free Trade Agreement (NAFTA), which covered Mexico as well.

On the world scene, general progress was also made in liberalizing trade. In 1995 GATT was changed to the World Trade Organization (WTO). As the twentieth century drew to a close, there were high hopes that the WTO, with its stronger mandate, heralded an even brighter future for increases in world trade. By 2005, however, the Doha round, begun in 2001 with the intention of addressing agricultural and other issues, appeared to be failing as the result of contention both in the streets and in the corridors of power, both corporate and political.

In the area of regulation, the Foreign Investment Review Agency was replaced by Investment Canada in the 1980s. For Canada's business community, the rhetoric of deregulation was a welcome change, not to mention the policies that followed – like the deregulation of 'the trucking and airline industries ... and liberalized regulation of financial institutions.'[8] The business community believed, as academic research has shown, that 'deregulation in Canada has resulted in a more focused and likely more robust regulatory role by government.'[9]

The abolition of FIRA and the National Energy Program, plus the evolution of the economy, changed foreign investment both inside and outside Canada. As recently as 1987, FDI in Canada exceeded the amount that Canadians invested abroad by more than 40 per cent. But a decade later there was a swing the other way; in 1997 Canadians began investing more abroad than foreigners were investing in Canada. By 2000, the amount invested abroad exceeded FDI by 20 per cent,[10] in spite of the fact that Canada's dollar was at an historic low. As a consequence, 'the issue of U.S. foreign control has become largely redundant in Canadian public policy.'[11]

Government Expenditures

By 2005, total general government outlays as a percentage of GDP had declined modestly to 39.3 per cent in Canada, while the average for the G7 countries had risen to 40.8 per cent.[12] The range was from a low of 36.6 per cent in the United States to a high of 48.3 per cent in Italy.

At the provincial level, however, governments were spending 47 per cent of all tax dollars while the federal authority's share was down to 37 per cent. A primary reason for the gap was that provincial governments bore responsibility for the rapidly increasing expenditure areas of health, education, and social welfare. Another contributing factor was that interest charges paid for in federal dollars peaked in 1990 and had been falling gradually since then.

Financial System

The period from 1980 to 2005 was marked by dramatic change in the financial system. The process of change began with the regular Bank Act revisions in 1980. 'The 1980 Bank Act, which allowed the entry of foreign banks into Canada, recognized the impossibility of maintaining the protected Canadian market.'[13]

In late 1986 and early 1987, change was even more dramatic when Canada experienced its own 'little bang' in terms of financial deregulation. Simultaneously, the Ontario government decided that investment dealers could be acquired by other financial institutions and the federal government announced that banks and other financial institutions could engage in a full range of financial intermediary activities. What had been four separate 'pillars' – commercial banking, investment banking, trust business, and life insurance – could now be integrated.[14] At the same time, an important organizational change occurred. The federal government created the Office of the Superintendent of Financial Institutions (OSFI), which integrated the offices of the superintendent of insurance and the inspector general of banks.

In the late 1980s, a consensus emerged on the monetary front that the key to controlling inflation lay in the control of the money supply, that is, with the Bank of Canada. Formal inflation targets of 2 per cent were adopted by the bank in the early 1990s when John Crow was governor, following the example of New Zealand. This action significantly decreased the rate of inflation and the prime rate.

In the 1990s there was also a public-policy change concerning life insurance companies. Insurance companies were seeking to move away from mutualization, a business model popular in the 1950s, because of the large costs associated with the industry's technological requirements. Under the policy change, the industry was allowed to demutualize, which a number of major players subsequently did.

In terms of organization, the federal government had not privatized the large financial crown corporations as it had privatized the non-financial ones. The same five large financial crown corporations were still in existence: the Canada Mortgage and Housing Corporation, the Bank of Canada, the Export Development Corporation, the Farm Credit Corporation, and the Business Development Bank of Canada (formerly the Federal Business Development Bank). All five were among the largest financial institutions in the land.[15]

The largest of these five by far in 2005 was CMHC, with assets of over $100 billion. CMHC had grown much more rapidly than most corporations in the public or private sector because of the introduction of lower eligibility requirements for mortgages. As a consequence of this growth, the corporation became twice the size of the Bank of Canada.

By far the largest provincial crown corporation involved in finance was the Caisse de dépôt et placement du Québec. The Caisse experienced phenomenal growth, with assets approaching $200 billion by 2005, making it much larger than CMHC. In 2005 the Caisse's mission was officially modified to achieving optimal return on capital while at the same time contributing to Quebec's economic development.

The only other provincial financial crown corporations among Canada's largest financial institutions were both in Alberta: the Alberta Heritage Savings Trust Fund and the Alberta Treasury Branches. The latter was an Alberta government bank,[16] a product of the 1930s that had surpassed the Trust Fund in size.

In summary, the government played a major role in shaping public policy governing the financial system and financial crown corporations. If the period from 1955 to 1980 can be characterized as 'the stable past,' the period from 1980 to 2005 is best described as 'the turbulent present.'

One thing that did not change in the 1980–2005 period was the number of securities regulators operating within Canada. In spite of pleas by leading lawyers and academics, the federal government's Wise Persons Panel, and former Imasco CEO Purdy Crawford, who led an Ontario panel examining the issue, implementation of a single national securities regulator appeared not only to be a dream but an impossible dream at that. (For details on all of the large financial corporations, turn to Appendix 7.)

Banking

With regard to private-sector operations, the landscape in 2005 was much different from what it had been a quarter-century earlier.

The period between 1980 and 2005 was one of highs and lows for Canadian banks. For some time, Canadian banks had been known for their stability. Indeed, there were critics who contended that Canadian banks over-emphasized security. That was not the case in the early 1980s.

'Following the Mexican default in 1982, the situation worsened and by year-end approximately forty nations were in arrears on their interest payments and a year later twenty-seven nations, including Mexico, Brazil, Venezuela and Argentina, were in negotiations to restructure their loans. This was a global banking crisis of major proportions and many major banks, including the big Canadian banks, spent the better part of a decade restructuring this debt and gradually writing it off. During this crisis the index of Canadian bank shares fell by 42%.'[17]

The debt crisis in less developed countries marked a particularly bad time for Canadian banks. In an article in *Fortune* magazine, Rollie Frazee, CEO of the Royal Bank, was interviewed as the representative Canadian banker. He told *Fortune* that 1983 was the worst year of his life, influenced no doubt by the loan-loss provisions the bank had to make.[18] But international problem loans were not the only cause for concern. The failure of two small western banks, the Northland and the Canadian Commercial Bank, in 1985 raised concerns about the stability of Canadian financial markets. While the failures were at small, regional institutions, they were the first since 1923.[19]

Nonetheless, partially as a consequence of the 'little bang' of the late 1980s, Canadian banks enjoyed tremendous growth over this period and by 2005 held nearly $2 billion in assets, with the Big Six controlling nearly 95 per cent of the total. The Royal Bank continued its remarkable record of dominance in Canada while four of the other big banks performed in very different ways: the laggards of 1980, TD and Nova Scotia, became leaders; and the leaders of 1980, BMO and the Commerce, became laggards. Coming in just under these five were six other banks holding assets of at least $5 billion. The largest was the Banque Canadienne National/National Bank – one of Canada's oldest banks and sometimes included among the Big Six of Canadian banking. Three of the remaining five large banks were foreign: UK-based HSBC, the fifth-largest bank in the world; Netherlands-based ING; and U.S.-based Citibank. Rounding out this group was the Laurentian Bank of Canada and the Canadian Western Bank, a proudly western Canadian regional bank.

Beyond these large banks were the smaller domestic banks, foreign bank subsidiaries, and foreign bank branches. The relatively recent increase in the number of banks in Canada was the result of changes in 2001 relating to both ownership and capital requirements. The ownership amendments followed the loosening of ownership rules dating back to 1980.

Other Financial Intermediaries

In terms of large financial intermediaries, life and health insurers rank just below the banks.[20] The life industry saw tremendous growth and consolidation within this period, partially because of the demutualization that took place in the late 1990s. Starting in 1999, Manulife, Clarica (formerly Mutual Life), and Canada Life became public companies with a combined market capitalization of $14.4 billion. Sun Life and La Vie Industrielle soon followed suit and the total market cap of the five demutualized companies amounted to $24 billion. Manulife emerged as the largest of the Canadian companies, surpassing Sun Life by a wide margin.

Perhaps the biggest change in the insurance industry was the emergence of Montreal-based Power Financial, controlled by the Desmarais family. The company made a number of insurance acquisitions, including Great West Life Assurance, London Life, and Canada Life. (In addition to these two major insurance properties, Power owns Investor's Group and Mackenzie Financial, two of Canada's major mutual fund companies.)

For other financial intermediaries, the period from 1980 to 2005 was also a time of dramatic change. Trust companies disappeared, as did the large Canadian-owned non-automotive acceptance companies. Taking their place among the largest financial institutions in the country were credit unions/caisses populaire (the biggest of which, and by a considerable margin, was le Mouvement des caisses Desjardins), diversified holding companies, venture capital funds, and mutual fund companies.

Over the past quarter-century, three diversified financial holding companies, all family or individually controlled (Power Corporation, Fairfax Financial Holdings, and E-L Financial Corp), have emerged as among the largest financial institutions in Canada. And, in recent years, venture capital funds have become more important as financial intermediaries in the Canadian financial markets.

Entrepreneurs

The closer one is to the present, the more difficult it is to be objective. For some, the stereotypical entrepreneurs of the period may have been Lord Conrad Black, who ended up facing trial in Chicago; Jack Gallagher of ill-fated Dome Petroleum; or Robert Campeau of real estate fame who made and then lost millions of other people's money.

This is an unfair picture. Canadian entrepreneurs have made outstanding contributions in terms of employment as well as personal wealth and, frequently, magnanimous philanthropic gestures. The one that first comes to mind is Frank Stronach, who created Magna, the auto-parts supplier, second only to General Motors of Canada among Canadian manufacturers in 2005. No fewer than four other entrepreneurs or entrepreneurial families created corporations that, by 2005, ranked among the largest in Canada. In order of size, they were: Gerry Schwartz, whose vehicle is Onex Corporation; the Sobey brothers, whose Empire Company controls Sobey Stores; Alain Bouchard, who created Alimentation Couche Tard, a convenience-store chain that does more business in the United States than in Canada; and Murray Edwards, the Saskatchewan native who was one of the driving forces behind Canadian Natural Resources.

Close behind these corporations in size is Rogers Communications, which was founded by Ted Rogers – surely the epitome of the totally focused entrepreneur as described by Schumpeter. And close behind Rogers are several other large corporations created or led by Canadian entrepreneurs such as the Florenceville, New Brunswick-based McCain brothers who founded a company with a substantial global reach. On the prairies, three entrepreneurs founded major Canadian corporations: Izzy Asper created Can West, the media company; in Calgary, Ron Southern founded Atco, the pre-fabricated builder; and J.R. Shaw founded Shaw Communications, which started in cable TV and branched into other media.

Probably the best-known Canadian product with a market well beyond Canada is the BlackBerry, manufactured by Research in Motion and created by entrepreneurs Mike Lazaridis and Jim Balsillie. Because of the innovative nature of the product, theirs is the kind of entrepreneurship that would have excited Schumpeter. Similarly, he would have been intrigued by the success of Isadore Sharp in building a chain of luxury hotels.[21]

Finally, there is Jeffrey Skoll, the first employee and first president of eBay. Like earlier Canadian entrepreneurs such as lords Beaverbrook and Thomson – both of whom left Canada for the United Kingdom to make their fortune – Skoll left too – but he went to the United States to make his.

Large Non-Financial Corporations

In 2005 Big Auto and Big Oil continued to dominate although in both sectors there were significant changes. The major supplier to Big Auto was no longer Big Steel but Big Auto Parts. And, with the exception of Weston's, retailing was totally changed.

The period from 1980 to 2005 also saw an increase in large family-owned businesses, the increasing importance of non-American corporations in the automotive sector, a major shift westward in head offices in the extractive sector, and a shift eastward in retailing head offices. In terms of foreign ownership, much seemed to be the same. But the period did bring even more technological change, still related to the computer but more to software than to hardware. If IBM was the symbolic company of the previous quarter-century, Microsoft was the symbol of the most recent quarter-century.

What follows is a description of what has happened in the major industry sectors in the past quarter-century with occasional hints about the future. (See Appendix 8 for a listing of the thirty major non-financial corporations in 2005.)

Extractive Sector

By 2005, the extractive sector had become much more important than at any time in Canada's history. The energy sector represented close to one-quarter of the S&P/TSX market capitalization. As in 1980 and before that in 1955, the oil, gas, and minerals[22] industries were enjoying a boom in commodity prices.

For most of the twentieth century, when people thought of energy, they thought of Big Oil and the four largest companies in Canada: Imperial, Shell, Gulf, and Texaco, all with head offices in Toronto. By 2005, it was significantly different. Gulf and Texaco were gone, and there was a third integrated producer in Canadian-owned Petro-Canada. In addition, there were five Canadian independents and two other corporations, a refiner and a pipeline company. Along with this greater diversity came a much higher degree of Canadian ownership. In geographic terms, all but Ultramar had their head offices in Calgary. None was in Toronto.

The price of oil, which made the oil sands economically more viable, played a significant role in the increased importance of the energy companies. It was expected that the long-term demands for oil from the new Asian giants and the instability of many of the conventional oil-producing countries would contribute to maintaining a higher price. And, while Imperial Oil and Shell had seen more decision making shifted to Houston, Canadian companies expanded from their Alberta base to become more North American – even global – as several enterprises launched operations and made investments in the North Sea, Africa, Europe, and South America.

On the surface, the mining industry had changed little over the years. By 2005, there were three mining companies among Canada's largest non-financial corporations, just as there had been twenty-five and fifty years earlier. But, though Alcan was still on the list (at least for a little while longer), Inco and Noranda were not. A process of consolidation was taking place, with companies that formerly mined one or two minerals – gold, nickel, copper, and/or coal – becoming more diversified as they sought economies of scope. Major international giants were becoming bigger – companies like BHP Billiton, Rio Tinto, and Anglo-American.

This was to have a significant impact on Canadian mining in that Alcan, Inco, and Falconbridge would be acquired by foreign firms. In a very short period of time, in fact, mining would become somewhat like the automobile industry: foreign-owned with foreign markets but with the raw resources and workers based in Canada.

By 2005, there was no longer a pulp and paper company among Canada's largest corporations. Generally speaking, the industry had a gloomy outlook in the early twenty-first century for a variety of reasons, including increased costs and the increased value of the Canadian dollar. The forest-products sector appeared to be continuing its long-term downward spiral.

Manufacturing

The first half of the twentieth century had been marked by the rise of manufacturing, particularly Big Auto. By contrast, the second half of the twentieth century and the early part of the twenty-first were marked by a decline in the relative importance of the manufacturing sector in general and of the major corporations within the sector, including Big Auto. With the worldwide trend to lower-cost production accelerated by globalization, this relative decline is predicted to continue in Canada and the rest of the developed world.

By 2005, the dominant manufacturers were still the automotive companies, as they had been for most of the last eighty-five years. All were subsidiaries but what was different was that they were now the big four, not three, and, of the four, two were non-American: Chrysler had become Daimler Chrysler and Honda Canada had emerged as one of

the major players. As in previous years, one of Canada's largest manufacturers was a supplier to the auto industry, but it was supplying
auto parts, not steel. Enter Magna International, an auto-parts supplier
– nowhere on the list of Canada's major corporations a quarter-century
earlier but which by 2005 had become one of the great Canadian success stories of the last half of the twentieth century. The year 2005 also
saw the Big Three's market share dip below 50 per cent for the first
time, a result of the major trend in the automotive industry for forty
years: the rise of the Japanese automotive manufacturers – Toyota,[23]
Honda,[24] Nissan, and Mazda.[25]

Historically, the major supplier to the automotive sector in Canada
had been the steel industry, but, by 2005, steel had been eclipsed by
auto-parts suppliers. In fact, the three largest Canadian steel companies
were smaller relative to the rest of the industry and were either foreign-
owned or about to become so.

Other major manufacturers were in the high-technology end of manufacturing – companies like Bombardier, Onex Corp, and Nortel Networks, all three among the thirty largest non-financial corporations in
2005 and all three Canadian-owned.[26] The rest – with the exception of
RIM – were either Canadian subsidiaries of American parents like IBM
Canada or in the process of being acquired. Bombardier and Onex were
new to the list in 2005, while Nortel had been one of Canada's largest
corporations for over a quarter of a century.

What is ahead for Canadian manufacturers? To survive in the future,
they must have the economies of scale provided by the whole North
American market, not simply the Canadian market. In an increasingly
globalized world, the North American market can only be a first step,
albeit an important, necessary first step. Canadian manufacturers must
also have the necessary marketing plans and distribution networks to
move their products to market. And finally they must have the managerial competence to manage a large global enterprise. This is a tall
order but a necessary precondition for Canada to have a manufacturing
sector in another twenty-five years.

Retail

The quarter-century from 1980 to 2005 saw dramatic change among the
large Canadian retailers. The sector was transformed from one dominated by traditional department store and supermarket chains based in
Ontario and the west and predominantly Canadian-owned to one con-

sisting of a mix of food and convenience chains with ownership spread among Toronto, Nova Scotia, and Quebec within Canada – to Arkansas in the United States.

No longer was a traditional department store listed among the largest Canadian retailers. This is not to say that large department stores disappeared. The Hudson's Bay Company and Sears Canada (formerly Simpsons-Sears) were still in business. But iconic names of Canadian retail – Eaton's and Simpson's – were long gone. Taking their place were American-owned specialty stores like Costco and Home Depot (in competition with Canadian Tire) as well as Wal-Mart.

The largest retailer by a wide margin was still Weston's/Loblaw but it presented the only evidence of continuity. The second-largest retailer in Canada in 2005 was very much a new arrival, an innovator and a challenger to Weston's: Wal-Mart Canada. Taking the place of the Bay, Simpsons-Sears, Canada Safeway, Dominion Stores, Provigo, and Steinbergs among the largest Canadian companies was Stellarton, Nova Scotia-based Empire Company (owner of Sobeys), Jean Coutu Group of Longueil, Quebec, and Alimentation Couche Tard, also of Quebec.

Transportation and Public Utilities

A major change affecting large corporations in Canada in the past 100 years has been the decrease in relative importance of the transportation and the investor-owned public utility sector. By 2005, BCE (Bell Canada Enterprises) stood out as the only company consistently included among the largest Canadian non-financial corporations over the past century. In the twenty-five-year period between 1980 and 2005, Bell acquired and divested itself of many enterprises, including (in a move that involved a $7.5-billion write-down in 2002) the overseas long-distance carrier Teleglobe Inc., which it had earlier acquired from the government of Canada. Because of greater deregulation and the emergence of wireless, Bell faced greater competition and in 2005 it was in the process of shifting from being a conglomerate back to its roots as a phone company. It was generally conceded that BCE would face significant challenges in the near future.

Canadian Pacific, a Canadian icon for decades, is no longer among the country's thirty largest non-financial corporations. How did this come to pass? The explanation is straightforward. CP was Canada's largest corporation as recently as 1980 but it was no longer a railway company. Instead, it had developed into a conglomerate, even though it still claimed transportation as its main business. In 2001 the decision was made to break up Canadian Pacific into its component parts so that, by 2005, CP was not only smaller than the privatized Canadian National Railways but was also the smallest of the six major North American railways.

Looking to the future, challenges loom for Canadian companies operating telephone companies, railways, or electrical generation and distribution companies. Currently, Canada's 'telcoms' are protected from acquisition but how long this will last in a globalizing world is a subject for conjecture. The railways are now North American enterprises and their future success or failure will depend on how well they perform in North America, not just in Canada. Turning to electricity, the question to be posed is this: Does it make sense to have the electrical systems owned by provincial and municipal governments rather than by private investors?

Publishing Industries

Thomson Corp and Quebecor Inc. were classified as publishers by the *Financial Post* in 2005. But both companies were a far cry from historic 'mom and pop' publishing operations. Indeed, both firms posted revenues of over $10 billion that year.

In 1980 International Thomson Organization was Canada's largest conglomerate, but, by the early twenty-first century, it had moved from newspaper publishing to providing specialized electronic information. Although both Thomson and Quebecor have been principally in the publishing business, with similar top lines and asset size, there is no comparison either in their profitability or in their market capitalization. In 2005 the Thomson Corporation's market cap was more than 5.5 times greater than Quebecor's.

Summary

As the twentieth century passed into history, the pace of change within the non-financial sector accelerated. Unlike twenty-five years earlier, Big Oil was more in the ascendancy than Big Auto (because the price of oil was soaring) and Big Steel had been replaced by Big Auto Parts. Companies changed too. Imperial Oil and Shell were still there but with head offices in Calgary, not Toronto, while Gulf and Texaco were gone; and a host of Calgary-based energy companies had emerged. Rather than an industry made up, primarily, of subsidiaries, the energy sector now featured a number of Canadian-owned companies.

Big Auto was substantially different too. GM, Ford, and Chrysler were all arguably weaker than they had been in decades while the Japanese companies had emerged as major competitors. Big Auto's major supplier in 2005 was Magna, an automotive-parts company that had not even been in existence a quarter-century earlier.

Manufacturing generally had declined in importance. Massey Ferguson, Canada Packers, Stelco, and Moore Corporation had all been sold, mostly to American purchasers. In their place were Bombardier and Onex Corporation as well as Nortel.

In the retail sector, the last quarter of a century had seen the steady decline of general department stores. Weston's/Loblaw was the only retailer still large enough to rank among Canada's largest corporations. Dominance by the Bay, Simpsons-Sears, and the supermarket chains had been replaced by Wal-Mart, Nova Scotia-based Empire, and Quebec-based Jean Coutu and Alimentation Couche Tard (both of which recorded the majority of their sales in the United States).

The largest of the mining companies were either foreign-owned or about to be foreign-owned. Former conglomerate Thomson was now an electronic publisher. The CPR was still around but no longer one of Canada's largest corporations. Only Bell, now known as BCE, was still a major company and a symbol of corporate continuity from the nineteenth century.

Conclusion

The years 1980–2005 were marked by public-policy attempts to improve Canada's economic performance. Over this period, Canada entered into free-trade agreements, the federal government got its fiscal house in order, and the governments of Canada and Ontario facilitated the 'little bang' which permitted the chartered banks to become much larger financial-service corporations offering investment banking, trust services, mutual funds, and insurance. In addition, the Bank of Canada set a target for inflation, and life insurance companies were permitted to demutualize. But a national securities regulator was not yet in the cards.

In spite of all of these changes, the Canadian economy did not perform as well as it had in the past nor as well as a number of other major industrial nations. Canada's performance was particularly hard hit by two severe recessions in the early 1980s and early 1990s and by a slower economy at the beginning of the twenty-first century. Contributing to the challenges faced by managers were volatile interest rates and oil prices and a fluctuating Canadian dollar.

For most of this narrative we learn that, as corporations grew larger, professional managers assumed a greater importance. Also, as one looks at how corporations evolved in the period from 1980 to 2005, we see a revival of the entrepreneurial role among some of Canada's largest corporations. While this is most evident among non-financial corporations, particularly in the retail sector, it can be seen among financial corporations as well – specifically among the diversified holding companies.

Looking to the future, there is clear evidence that the nation must do better economically if Canadians are going to continue to enjoy the kind of lifestyle they have become accustomed to. This will require a positive interaction among government, the financial system, entrepreneurs, and big business. Too often, the question posed is: What will government do? The real question that needs to be posed is: What will government, the financial system, entrepreneurs, and big business do together?

It is hoped that government will continue the policy shift that has been evident at least for the past two decades and remain supportive of the private sector. The financial system is solid, with regular reviews of the Bank Act and sound monetary policies at the Bank of Canada. However, legislation may be required to open up the Canadian financial system to foreign banks if Canadian banks are to enjoy that privilege outside Canada.

In the non-financial sector, Canadian subsidiaries of the automobile companies will continue to be managed by their parent companies, although the parents may no longer be American. In the extractive sector, the key issue is whether or not the large but widely held Canadian enterprises will be able to grow and expand from their Canadian base to become global players, or whether they will be taken over by foreign investors. In the retail sector, there will be increasing forays by international retailers.

One thing is clear: the 'threat' of foreign takeover is no longer restricted to takeovers by American companies. Nor are opportunities for Canadian businesses to acquire foreign firms any longer restricted to the United States. The imperative is that all Canadian corporations must have an international strategy in order to avoid becoming victims of the 'creative destructive' powers of capitalism. 'Whether it is an offensive strategy or a defensive strategy, whether ... in the manufacturing or in the service sector, they require that strategy now. The reason for this is simple, the simplest reason of all – the survival of the enterprise.'[27]

Appendix 7
Top thirty financial corporations by assets, 2005 (in $ millions)
(not included are wholly owned subsidiaries of corporations already on the list)

Corporation	Total Assets - $	Code
1. Royal Bank	469,521	B
2. Toronto Dominion Bank	365,210	B
3. Bank of Nova Scotia	314,025	B
4. Bank of Montreal	297,532	B
5. Canadian Imperial Bank of Commerce	280,370	B
6. Manulife Financial Corp.	181,810	I
7. Mouvement des Caisses Dejardins	118,068	CU
8. Power Corporation	112,999	D
9. Sun Life Financial	110,866	I
10. National Bank of Canada	107,598	B
11. Great West Life Co.*	102,161	I
12. HSBC Bank of Canada	49,210	B
13. Fairfax Financial Holdings	32,059	D
14. ING Bank of Canada	21,024	B
15. General Motors Acceptance Corporation	20,542	A
16. Laurentian Bank of Canada	16,507	B
17. Caisse Centrale Desjardins	15,757	CU
18. Ford Credit Canada	14,248	A
19. Citibank Canada	12,919	B
20. Industrial Alliance Insurance & Financial Services	11,973	I
21. Dejardins Financial Security Life Assurance Co.	11,921	I
22. Vancouver City Savings Credit Union	11,756	CU
23. ING Canada Inc.	9,926	I
24. Coast Capital Savings Credit Union	8,200	CU
25. Daimler Chrysler Canada Finance Inc.	7,637	A
26. Aviva Canada Inc.	7,256	I
27. E-L Financial Corp. Ltd.	6,955	D
28. Fonds des Solidarite des travailleurs du Quebec	6,508	VC
29. Canadian Western Bank	5,705	B
30. Northbridge Financial Corp.**	5,163	I
CODE: B = Banks I = Insurance Cos. CU = Credit Unions D = Diversified Financials (Holding Cos.) A = Acceptance Cos. VC = Venture Capital Funds		

* 75% held by Power Financial Corp.
** 59% held by Fairfax Financial holdings.
Source: Financial Post FP500, June 2006.

Appendix 8
Top thirty non-financial corporations, 2005, by revenue (in $ millions)

Corporation	Total Revenue - $	Code
1. General Motors of Canada	34,991	M
2. George Weston	31,363	R
3. Imperial Oil	27,797	E
4. Magna International	27,624	M
5. Alcan Inc.	24,607	E
6. Daimler Chrysler Canada	20,819	M
7. BCE	19,105	U
8. Bombardier	17,759	M
9. Petro Canada	17,585	E
10. Encana Corp.	14,276	E
11. Onex Corp.	16,559	M
12. Shell Canada	14,171	E
13. Ford Motor Company of Canada	13,809	M
14. Wal-Mart Canada	13,500	R
15. Honda Canada	13,000	M
16. Nortel Networks	12,786	M
17. Empire Co.	12,435	R
18. Jean Coutu Group (PJC)	12,118	R
19. The Thomson Corp.	10,539	P
20. Husky Energy	10,245	E
21. Alimentation Couche-Tard	10,216	R
22. Quebecor Inc.	10,208	P
23. Novelis	10,089	E
24. Suncor Energy	9,957	E
25. Falconbridge Ltd.	9,867	E
26. ACE Aviation Holdings	9,830	T
27. Ultramar Ltd.	9,543	E
28. Canadian Natural Resources Ltd.	8,741	E
29. Enbridge Ltd.	8,453	E
30. Telus Corp.	8,143	U
CODE: T = Transportation E = Extractive U = Utilities M = Manufacturing R = Retail P = Publishing		

Source: Financial Post FP500, June 2006.

BIBLIOGRAPHY

Boothman, Barry E.C., and Barbara Austin. 'Another One Bites the Dust: Turnover and Failure among the Leading Canadian Firms, 1973–2003.' ASAC Conference, 2005.

Chandler, Alfred D., Jr, and James Cortada. *A Nation Transformed: How Information Has Shaped the United States from Colonial Times to the Present*. Oxford and New York: Oxford University Press 2000.

Cohen, Andrew. *While Canada Slept: How We Lost Our Place in the World*. Toronto: McClelland and Stewart 2003.

Collins, Jim. *Good to Great: Why Some Companies Make the Leap ... and Others Don't*. New York: HarperCollins 2001.

Crispo, John. *Rebel without a Pause: Memoirs of a Canadian Maverick*. Toronto: Warwick Publishing 2002.

Darroch, James L. *Canadian Banks and Global Competitiveness*. Montreal and Kingston: McGill-Queen's University Press 1994.

– 'Global Competitiveness and Public Policy: The Case of Canadian Multinational Banks.' *Business History, Special Issue on Canadian Multinationals and International Finance*, ed. Gregory P. Marchildon and Duncan McDowall, vol. 34, no. 3 (1992): 153–76.

Doern, G. Bruce, Margaret M. Hill, Michael J. Prince, and Richard J. Schulz. *Changing the Rules: Canadian Regulatory Regimes and Institutions*. Toronto: University of Toronto Press 1999.

Eden, Lorraine, and Maureen Appel Molot. 'Canadian National Policies: Reflections on 125 Years.' *Canadian Public Policy*, 19, no. 3 (1993): 232–51.

Financial Post FP 500.

Foster, Peter. *Towers of Debt: The Rise and Fall of the Reichmanns: The Olympia & York Story*. Toronto: Key Porter Books 1993.

Friedman, Thomas L. *The World Is Flat: A Brief History of the Twenty-First Century*. New York: Farrar, Straus and Giroux 2005.

Glick, Leslie Alan. *Multilateral Trade Negotiations: World Trade after the Tokyo Round*. Totawa, N.J.: Rowman and Allanheld 1984.

Gotlieb, Allan. *The Washington Diaries, 1981–1989*. Toronto: McClelland and Stewart 2006.

Mandel-Campbell, Andrea. *Why Mexicans Don't Drink Molson*. Vancouver and Toronto: Douglas and McIntyre 2007.

Martin, Joe. 'Going International.' *Business Quarterly*, 57, no. 4 (1993): 72–7.

Martin, Roger. *The Opposable Mind: How Successful Leaders Win through Integrative Thinking*. Boston, Mass.: Harvard Business School Press 2007.

McQueen, Rod. *Leap of Faith: The Macdonald Report.* Toronto: Cowan and Company with assistance from Woods Gordon, Clarkson Gordon, 1985.

Meyer, Sir Christopher. *DC Confidential: The Controversial Memoirs of Britain's Ambassador to the U.S. at the time of 9/11 and the Iraq War.* London: Weidenfeld and Nicholson 2005.

Mulroney, Brian. *Memoirs, 1939–1993.* Toronto: McClelland and Stewart 2007.

Newman, Peter. *The Secret Mulroney Tapes: Unguarded Confessions of a Prime Minister.* Toronto: Vintage Canada 2006.

Rugman, Alan M. 'Continental Integration and Foreign Ownership of Canadian Industry: A Retrospective Analysis.' Draft Paper for the A.E. Safarian Conference at the Rotman School of Toronto, revised, March 2004.

Schulich School of Business. *Success: Canadian Leaders Prepare for the Next Century.* Toronto: Key Porter Books 1996.

Van Hasselt, Caroline. *High Wire Act: Ted Rogers and the Empire That Debt Built.* Mississauga, Ont.: J. Wiley 2007.

NOTES

1 Canada's economic performance between 1980 and 2005 as measured in GDP per capita was not as good as that of Australia, the United States, or a resurgent United Kingdom. Organization for Economic Co-operation and Development, *OECD Factbook* (Paris: OECD Publications 2008).

2 In the same period, the TSE 300 experienced two severe bear markets – from November 1980 to July 1982 and from September 2000 to September 2001.

3 Oil declined from over $90 per barrel (2007 dollars) to below $20 before rising rapidly in the early twenty-first century. Interest rates declined from a high of nearly 20 per cent in the early 1980s to below 5 per cent in the early twenty-first century. The dollar was trading in the mid-80s in 1980 and declined further to less than 70 cents US in 1986. It rose to over 90 cents in the early 1990s before declining to a low of less than 62 cents in 2002. It closed at 86 cents on 31 Dec. 2005.

4 Letter from Michael Walker, executive director of the Fraser Institute, 11 May 2006.

5 Guy Giorno, 'Revisiting Ontario's Common Sense Revolution,' *National Post*, 26 June 2007.

6 McQueen, *Leap of Faith*, 2.

7 For a Washington insider's view of the FTA negotiations, Ambassador Allan Gotlieb's *Washington Diaries* is must reading.

8 Eden and Appel Molot, 'Canadian National Policies,' 43.
9 Doern, Hill, Prince, and Schulz, *Changing the Rules*, 394.
10 In terms of operating revenue, 31.1 per cent of the Canadian economy was foreign-controlled compared to 37.6 per cent thirty years earlier.
11 Rugman, 'Continental Integration.'
12 Table 55, G7 General Government Total Outlays, Fiscal Reference Tables, September 2007. Department of Finance, Canada's New Government.
13 Darroch, 'Global Competitiveness and Public Policy,' 165.
14 Banks are allowed to sell life insurance but not from their branches.
15 This examination has not extended to federal and provincial pension plans. These plans are now large, e.g., the CPP Investment Board has assets of $90 billion, nearly as large as CMHC.
16 Early in the twenty-first century, the Ontario government privatized the Ontario Savings Bank.
17 Excerpts from the David Dodge Lecture, Humber College, by Anthony S. Fell, 15 April 2008.
18 Bank provisions were required not only for the debt of less-developed countries but also for companies such as Dome Petroleum, Massey-Ferguson, and the highly cyclical real estate business.
19 Darroch, *Canadian Banks and Global Competitiveness*, 166. In 1986 Alberta's GDP dropped nearly 25 per cent. See Irene K. Ip, *Big Spenders* (Toronto: C.D. Howe Institute 1991), Figure A1, 219.
20 Department of Finance, Fact Sheet on the Canadian Financial Services Sector, June 2005, lists mutual fund companies as the second-largest group after the banks. But that is because the agency counts assets under management (AUM).
21 See Roger Martin, *The Opposable Mind*, chapter 2 ('No Stomach for Second-Best').
22 In 2005 metals and mining, excluding gold and steel, represented anywhere from 5.5 per cent to 6.5 per cent of the TSE.
23 Toyota was not in the top thirty because it operated two separate companies in Canada – Toyota Canada and Toyota Manufacturing Canada. This division can be traced back to 1950, when the 'banks demanded that Toyota accept a reconstruction plan as a precondition of aid. Noting Toyota's history of excessive production without consideration of demand, the banks ordered it to create a separate sales company.' Thomas K. McCraw, *Creating Modern Capitalism* (Cambridge, Mass.: Harvard University Press 1997), 416.
24 Honda opened its first Canadian manufacturing centre in 1986 at Alliston, Ont. Honda Canada represented nearly 15 per cent of Honda's global sales in 2005.

25 In 2005 in U.S. dollars, Toyota Motor had a market cap of $175 billion; Honda, $54.6 billion; Daimler, $56.4 billion; Ford, $15.2 million; and GM, $11.5 billion, less than troubled Nortel Networks' $12.6 billion.
26 Financial Post Annual Survey.
27 Joe Martin, 'Going International.'

CASE 10
The Free Trade Agreement and the Canadian Wine Industry

DAVID SMITH, with guidance from JOE MARTIN

On 20 November 1987, at the end of a busy day, Donald Ziraldo, the passionate and entrepreneurial head of Inniskillin Wines – one of Canada's best-known producers of premium wines – thinks about the future of his business in light of potentially massive changes. Prime Minister Brian Mulroney had recently committed the nation to a free- trade agreement with its most important trading partner, the United States. Free-trade negotiations between Canada and the United States began in May 1986 and by October 1987 an agreement was reached; however, the details for each industry were still to be worked out.

As Ziraldo loads his briefcase and turns towards the door, he hesitantly places his hand on the light switch and wonders whether the impact of the FTA will have negative and far-reaching consequences – not just for his company but for the entire Canadian wine industry. Just last night he heard scathing comments from a member of Canada's intellectual community, the novelist Mordecai Richler, who weighed in on the matter: 'If a free trade deal meant that the dubious wines of Niagara would be displaced by the far more palatable stuff distilled in California, I would not be displeased. There is only so much I'm prepared to drink for my country.'[1]

Meanwhile, Donald Triggs, head of Fisons PLCs global horticultural business, thinks about his early days as an executive for Labatt Brewery's wine business. Triggs gives some thought as to what his next move will be in light of the impending trade deal. He wonders whether free trade will provide an opportunity to build a lucrative business. He picks up the phone and places a call to his old friend Allan Jackson.

The following year, on 21 November 1988, Canadians went to the polls in what was arguably one of the two most important elections in Canadian history, and the first election held on the subject of free trade in seventy-seven years. Prime Minister Mulroney defeated the sceptics and was re-elected on a free-trade platform. Shortly thereafter, in December 1988, the free-trade bill was approved by the Canadian Parliament and came into effect on 1 January 1989.

How would Ziraldo's company fare in a free-trade environment when even the staunchest supporters of free trade conceded that the Canadian wine industry could not possibly survive? How would it compete, and what activities would enable the industry to prosper? Would the deal truly mean 'lights out' for Inniskillin and the Canadian wine industry? And what would be the result of the phone call from Donald Triggs to his old friend Allan Jackson?

The Second Generation of Pioneers

By the 1960s, despite the decline in the number of Canadian wineries, a distinctly entrepreneurial spirit had gained momentum in the burgeoning North American wine industry. In 1966 Californian vintner Robert Mondavi rejected his family's long-standing traditions and followed his own instincts. His goal was to upgrade the American consumer's wine-drinking experience. He spent time and capital improving wine technology, replacing inferior vines with better fruit, and moving strategically towards the promotion of wineries as a tourist destination, thereby laying the groundwork for wine-related agro-tourism in North America.[2] Australia would soon follow suit.

This rebellious attitude made its way north to the Niagara region, where Donald Ziraldo and Karl Kaiser developed what was to become the Inniskillin Winery. Ziraldo was an entrepreneur who ran a family nursery business in Niagara-on-the-Lake, Ontario. Kaiser was an amateur winemaker from Austria who emigrated to Canada in 1969. The birth of Inniskillin arose after Ziraldo first tasted wines crafted by Kaiser, who had used vines purchased from Ziraldo's own nursery. After one sip, Ziraldo realized that he had met a master winemaker, and this encounter marked what was to be the beginning of a very fruitful relationship.

But it wasn't that easy to give this business legs. In 1972 Ziraldo and Kaiser were actually turned down in their first attempt to obtain a government licence to open their winery. However, a couple years later, in 1974, Ziraldo and Kaiser received a manufacturing permit that allowed them to produce a maximum of 10,000 gallons of wine.

Ultimately, the tenacity of the Inniskillin duo led them to the door of General George Kitching, chairman of the Liquor Control Board of Ontario (LCBO), who, considering the massive consolidation that had occurred in the industry, wanted to increase competition within the Canadian wine market[3] (and, perhaps, to reduce the growing power of existing suppliers for his LCBO outlets). In 1975 Kitching granted the first new licence since 1929, thereby approving Ziraldo and Kaiser's shared vision for 'a premium estate winery producing varietal wines from grapes grown in the Niagara Peninsula.'[4]

Initially, Kaiser ended up making only 3,500 gallons of a blended wine called Vin Nouveau. The LCBO also allowed him three 500-litre barrels in which he fermented a small yield of a single variety called Maréchal Foch. One of Inniskillin's biggest competitors at the time, controlled by Labatt Breweries, featured a printed ad in the local newspaper promoting another wine named Maréchal Foch, but a valuable procurement connection at the LCBO managed to place the Inniskillin product at the LCBO's rare wine store in Toronto's market district. This enabled Inniskillin Maréchal Foch to position itself among consumers with a more discerning palate, and became a gateway to instant success.

Renowned wine critic Tony Aspler recalls the event hosted by the *Globe and Mail* in 1975 that compared a notable French wine to Kaiser's Inniskillin Maréchal Foch in a blind taste test. Kaiser's wine won hands down, an event that became a defining moment for the Canadian wine business. Ziraldo recalls: 'The six tasters had to do a retasting, because they thought it was impossible for a Canadian wine to beat out a named-village wine from Beaujolais.'[5]

In 1978 Inniskillin purchased the Brae Burn Estate in Niagara, which was believed to have been designed by famous architect Frank Lloyd Wright. The grounds included a barn built in the 1920s which Ziraldo and Kaiser converted into a barrel storage and retail facility, and a cornfield they transformed into forty acres of vinifera grapevines. At the time, many Germans had begun to settle in the area and make their own wine with European varietals. This practice confirmed Ziraldo's theories about the future of 'wine growing' within this unique microclimate. And so began the vintner-led move upmarket and the end of the practice of using old vines of the labrusca variety. Labrusca, the wild hybrid grape first cultivated so long ago by Johann Schiller, had become a staple of Ontario's wines, but its quality was increasingly being called into question. The inferior grapes had to go, argued Ziraldo and Kaiser, or else the consumers would.

This decision truly marked a turning point in the Canadian wine industry, as cited by the Grape Growers of Ontario: 'More growers began responding to the changing market, changing consumer tastes toward more premium wines, and the maturation of the industry. While public opinion suggested that vinifera grapes could not be grown in Ontario, several prescient growers thought otherwise. They proved the naysayers wrong. The subsequent growth of cottage wineries[6] has reflected the boom in our grape and wine industry. Today, there are more than 90 wineries in Ontario producing about 80 per cent of total Canadian wine volume.'[7]

The Vital Shift in Grape Varieties

The craft of winemaking consists of four major components: 1) inputs; 2) climate; 3) soil; and 4) artisanship. There are only certain varieties of raw inputs, namely grapes, that will make a satisfying and potable wine, and in Canada very few regions exist where the vines will yield worthy fruit. Fortunately, there are two unique micro-climates: the first is within the interior of British Columbia, including the Okanagan valley, and the second is the Niagara region of Ontario. In addition, small quantities of wine are crafted in Quebec, Nova Scotia, Prince Edward Island, New Brunswick, and Newfoundland, with the latter two provinces known for their fruit-borne wines. However, a number of factors, including soil, drainage, climate, and vegetation, all create volatility in the growing environment. Successful navigation through these potential obstacles enables vintners to produce unique vintages that distinguish good years from bad years. Those that experience 'good years' will be able to prove it in the quality of the wines they release at that time. However, the confluence of factors needed to produce high-quality wines does not occur every year.

As such, viticulture, the process of breeding and researching grape varieties, has been an important part of the adaptation process for grape growers in Canada. The challenges of a harsh climate led to experiments to find a grape that would meet consumer needs. It was clear that something had to happen to the grapes. Consumer tastes were evolving and the grapes commonly used in Canadian wines were not meeting expectations. In Aspler's words, 'perhaps the most significant vintage in the history of Canadian wine was 1988. That year, the Wine Content Act in Ontario banned the use of labrusca grapes in table wines.'[8]

Although the vitis labrusca was naturally adapted to the harsh Canadian climate, this grape limited wine growers in terms of the variety of uses. It could not produce what consumers were beginning to demand: delicate, dry wines that were 'cellarable' (having the potential to be stored and aged in a wine cellar). As a grape better suited for jam and juice than fine wine, labrusca varieties were considered subordinate, and they were the butt of a thousand jokes for the 'foxy' flavour and aroma given off by the wine they produced.

B.C. wine expert Julianna Hayes remarks on the tough transition for vintners and grape growers alike: 'When Free Trade entered the picture in the '80s, the rules of the game changed. Growers now faced a brutally competitive market and hybrids [grapes] were not going to cut it. The government offered to sponsor experimental vineyard plots to determine which varieties of the vinifera grapes would ripen properly and survive B.C.'s frosty winters. The knowledge gained from these experiments gave wine makers the head start they needed to produce quality wines without years of costly trial and error.'[9] But this change would come at a premium. In order to convert a hectare of labrusca grapes into vinifera, it would cost approximately $17,000 – no small amount for a farmer or a winery, considering that these varieties, although popular, were significantly more fragile and sensitive to climate challenges.

So, in an effort to help with the transition to a post-FTA marketplace, the provinces of Ontario and British Columbia set up a $100-million Grape and Wine Adjustment program, in cooperation with the federal government. This initiative was designed to finance the changes associated with the market shift and to provide subsidy assistance for twelve years, allowing farmers to acclimatize themselves to the new market conditions and pricing structure. In addition, the province of Ontario contributed another $45 million in forgivable loans.

All of this activity forced the vintners to reduce their yields in order to achieve the target quality, which, in turn, affected the supply of grapes as they waited for their crops to mature over the next three to five years. Wines produced in Ontario were affected by the shortage and the Wine Content Act was relaxed to allow a minimum of 30 per cent Ontario-grown product, down from the previous minimum of 70 per cent.[10]

Grapes from the Niagara region accounted for 95 per cent of the Ontario crop but contributed only 20 per cent of the supply that local vintners needed to make their wine. In British Columbia, the Okanagan valley similarly accounted for 95 per cent of the province's crop but supplied only 6 per cent of the local wineries' needs. Thus, the wineries from both provinces were forced to buy their inputs on the international market from their trading partners, adding volatility to their pricing structure. Most of the foreign wine came from California and was blended with local lots according to the above percentages to augment the insufficient local yields. This shift was a massive undertaking for Ontario wineries that required imports of 2.5 million litres of wine in 1987, rising to 6.4 million litres in 1990.

But the pendulum swung back as a result of insufficient consumer demand, with both streams of grape production causing a surplus. The federal and provincial governments stepped in to buy up the overage at a cost of $11.5 million, and the vintners would then convert the grapes to juice for sale to other markets. According to the Grape Growers of Ontario, as part of the provincial Grape Acreage Reduction Program, the objective was to remove industry surplus and make room for grapes that could be used for the higher-quality wines towards which consumers were gravitating: 'Between 1989 and 1991, growers removed 8,000 acres of labrusca and hybrid vines and, over time, replaced them with Vitis vinifera vines, traditional European varieties.'[11] These grapes would produce a lower yield but deliver a higher quality based upon better fruit, including such well-known varieties as Cabernet Franc, Chardonnay, Gamay Noir, Riesling, Cabernet Sauvignon, Gewürztraminer, Merlot, Pinot Blanc, Pinot Gris, Sauvignon Blanc, and Pinot Noir.[12]

Consumers' tastes were improving, but the ease of making a profit from a commodity product was not. Winemakers needed to take differentiation measures to find better margins.

From Pop to Pinot Noir

Looming on the horizon was a shift in consumer preferences for wine. In the 1970s and early 1980s, Ontario wines were not appealing, whether they came from a screw-top bottle, a four-litre box, or, the wine container viewed with such chagrin by connoisseurs, the tetra-pak carton. Nor were B.C. wines insulated from scathing comments like those made by Mordecai Richler in 1987. In 2001 an article in *Maclean's* magazine described the burgeoning B.C. winery, Mission Hill, this way: 'Twenty years ago, B.C. wine needed a stepladder just to hit the heights of mediocrity. The industry was protected by a cozy arrangement: the vineyards, full of lowbrow hybrid and labrusca grapes, were guaranteed sales to the wineries, whose screw-top plonk was granted a preferential rate at provincial liquor stores.'[13] It would seem that the production paradigm remained: those who anticipate an output of better quality than the inputs are certainly headed for trouble.

That said, the majority of Canadian consumers did not know the difference either way. For decades, Canadians did not drink much fine wine, or even inferior wine for that matter. The average consumption per capita[14] was around six to seven litres per year, with Americans consuming slightly more. Compared to the French and Italians, who drank between fifty-five and sixty litres per year, Canada's market for wine was immature. In the 1970s, as North Americans began to travel more often to Europe, they began to taste fine wines from France and Italy.[15] They would soon bring these taste experiences and expectations home.

In 1973 eight million bottles of a sweet, pinkish carbonated 'wine' beverage called Baby Duck were sold in Canada.[16] This lucrative beverage was produced by the esteemed Peller family through its Niagara-based Andrés winery and eased the transition from soft drinks to alcohol for many new drinkers. Although it was the bane of many a connoisseur's tastes, Baby Duck was often the first wine sipped by young Canadian adults who had reached drinking age, as well as the first 'wine' tried by non-wine drinkers looking to expand their horizons.

In the 1980s, building on the success of Baby Duck, some wine companies, in an effort to build demand and reverse the trend of waning wine consumption, made forays into the promotion and sale of wine coolers, a blended cocktail of wine and fruit juices intended to attract the beer-drinking market. However, the high advertising costs associated with selling this unwitting ugly duckling ended up diluting revenues. Ironically, while this strategy ultimately failed to draw beer drinkers, the novelty of wine coolers instead attracted wine consumers and cannibalized the very market the industry was trying to augment.[17]

Underscoring this period of heightened consumer awareness was a growing appreciation for wine: 'For the American wine industry, November 17, 1991, was the Fourth of July and Bastille Day rolled into one. That was the date on which CBS's *60 Minutes* first aired a news feature program called "The French Paradox."'[18] In this episode, CBS broadcast the results of an inquiry revealing a perceived paradox concerning the reason why people in France tend to suffer a relatively low incidence of coronary heart disease despite a diet rich in saturated fats. One mitigating theory put forward during the program was the consumption level of red wine in France.

The premise explored in the broadcast was that drinking red wine could have significant health benefits and reduce the risk of heart disease. This was not new information for the medical community: 'In 1974, 17 years before the *60 Minutes* broadcast, a study of more than 5,000 men and women in Framingham, Massachusetts, found that people who consumed moderate amounts of alcohol demonstrated a significant reduction in the risk of coronary heart disease (CHD).'[19] All the same, wine's health benefits came as a revelation to the public.

Consumers began to take a new interest in wine. This awareness was generated by changes in the industry, European tourism, revelation of the 'French Paradox,' and the move towards the use of better grapes paired with better production technology. Those changes, in addition to the economic factors of 'rising incomes of the middle class and a new appreciation for European cuisine,'[20] resulted in a significant shift in consumer preferences.

A major contributing factor to the success of this shift was the dedication of trade groups like the Canadian Vintners, the Grape Growers of Ontario, and a new appellation-control process called the Vintners Quality Alliance (VQA) led by Inniskillin's Donald Ziraldo. These trade groups motivated the industry to migrate from the labrusca blends towards premium, varietally based wines made from vitis vinifera grapes and produced in smaller batches. Just as the growers found that better vines yielded less fruit but concentrated the flavour, consumers began to reveal that if they were going to drink wine, they might drink less but would demand a better quality. Fortunately for the industry, premium wines tended to have higher margins.

A Vintner's View of Exports and Imports

French economist Frederic Bastiat once said, 'If goods can't cross borders armies will.' Many international conflicts have originated because of misaligned economic motives, and structures have been put in place to regulate the flow of goods to ensure a form of market reciprocity. There are, however, limitations to these structures, and the international wine trade is not excluded from this debate.

In their book *Thinking Strategically*, Avinash Dixit and Barry Nalebuff[21] discuss some of the implications of international trade on the structure designed to negotiate trade relations, the Geneva-based General Agreement on Tariffs and Trade.[22] Complicated quotas and import restrictions set up by the GATT became more of a hassle than an effective tool for market survival. Therefore, cooperation and internal innovation became the keys to success. In the context of trade negotiations, countries 'should have confidence that defection will be punished and cooperation rewarded. This is a major problem for the European countries looking to enforce the General Agreement on Tariffs and Trade. When one country complains that another has cheated on the trade agreement, GATT initiates an administrative process that drags on for months or years. The facts of the case have little bearing on the judgment, which usually depends more on the dictates of international politics and diplomacy. Such enforcement procedures are unlikely to be effective.'[23]

In light of this, the impact of Canada's small supply of grapes and wine on the global market is miniscule, with the exception being 'icewine,' which caused a stir in Asia. The European Union (EU) does not recognize the VQA guidelines as equivalent to its appellation-control systems in France and Italy. Britain does, but its purchases of Canadian wine are insignificant. Canada imports the vast majority, nearly 78 per cent,[24] of its wine from Europe, but there is a conflict in reciprocity, since Canada is barred from exporting to the EU, which refuses to buy Canadian wine. The imbalance does not end there, since the EU provides massive subsidies for its own grape growers. In 1985 the EU enacted a program called the European Community Common Agricultural Policy, designed to provide over $1 billion in funds to European producers. Not surprisingly, this program outraged the EU's trading partners.

With a view to the future, Canadian vintners needed to ask tough questions that would affect their destinies as artisans and business owners. Where were the other markets, given the fact that Canada does not have the domestic market to support the quantity of wine made here? In light of European attitudes and Canada's geographic location, was it time for Canadian wine makers to explore opportunities south of the border?

Wine and the Free Trade Agreement

The FTA election of 1988 was – and to some extent still is – laced with controversy. However, where the FTA concerns wine, consumer demand has been the key determinant thus far. (See Appendix A for highlights of the wine section of the FTA.)

According to one U.S. source,[25] Canada in 1989 was the biggest export market for U.S. wines, primarily those from California. However, American wines constituted only 5 per cent of Canada's imports.

This percentage was expected to rise to 25 per cent if all of the entry barriers were removed by the FTA. The important point to note is that Californians sell 70 per cent of their wine within the United States,[26] so they are not desperate for new markets.

Within Canada there is a much smaller internal market for wine consumers. Accordingly, Canadian producers of premium wines need to find export markets for their products, whereas California vintners do not. This is a key difference in Canada's approach to the sale of wine, and a barrier to the growth of the Canadian wine industry. Following the early discussions on free trade and the eventual implementation of the FTA, the volume of U.S. wine exported to Canada leapt from 433,000 litres in 1986 to 2.4 million litres in 1990. The value of these imports increased by a multiple of four[27] as Canadians found a taste for the premium wines of California. Americans have attributed this phenomenal growth to the dismantling of trade barriers and tariffs, as well to a general increase in Canadian incomes.

Conversely, in 1992, Canada exported only 117,348 litres of wine to the United States, worth U.S.$260,000.[28] Canada's total export output could have been equal to the amount of inventory shrinkage or spillage that some large U.S. wineries contend with in any given year.

The Dynamics of Regulation

Milton Friedman famously said that 'anything that government can do, private enterprise can do for half the cost,' and he may well be correct, but the fact remains that regulation and price control of liquor are a reality in Canada. Initially, the regulation of liquor, primarily a provincial function, was aimed at fulfilling the social mission of controlling drunkenness and poverty after the repeal of Prohibition. Over time, regulation evolved into a monopolistic force for massive revenue generation from mark-ups and taxes collected by provincial governments.

In the United States, eighteen 'control states' directly regulate the sale of alcohol, whereas the remaining thirty-two issue licences to private sellers. The latter are called 'licensure' states and 'conditions can be placed on these licenses, which help the states more indirectly control the sale of alcohol.'[29] A different pattern of distribution options and systems exists in Canada. Most provinces have a provincial monopoly, although there are some variations. In Quebec, the Société des alcools du Québec (SAQ) operates with 400 provincial outlets, but alcohol is also sold in many other locations, including grocery and convenience stores, with mark-ups controlled by the SAQ. The province of Alberta has a policy that allows more than 600 private businesses to sell liquor at their own prices, but Alberta gains provincial revenue by being the exclusive distributor of alcohol and spirits to the various locations. In the absence of a provincial sales tax, government income is derived from the mark-ups. British Columbia has a system similar to that of Ontario, with 200 provincially run stores and more than 200 other distribution points that are private businesses licensed by the province. Private sellers purchase wine directly from the wineries but are limited in the price variance compared to levels set in the provincial outlets.

The most significant among the provincial systems is the Liquor Control Board of Ontario, the largest aggregate purchaser of wine and alcohol in the world. With more than 600 retail stores and over 100 winery-owned stores licensed by the province, the board is one of Canada's 100 largest corporations. Before the FTA was passed, the LCBO also licensed wineries to operate shops on site at the wineries to sell their home-grown products. (See Appendix B for revenue and tax details on a typical bottle of wine.) The limitation was that only those products produced on site could be sold there, and these wineries were not permitted to stock any products from wholly owned subsidiaries. Although these winery licences were placed under moratorium as part of the FTA, a finite number of existing licences could still be bought and sold.

Grape Supply, Pricing, and Sales

The FTA also flattened the competitive structure which the provinces had previously set up to favour local wineries. Preferential protection ended. Consequently, over a ten-year period from 1989 to 1998, distributors were forced to raise the mark-up added to the wholesale price of wine from 1 per cent to 60 per cent, to equal that of the imports. Half of the increase came in the first two years, which hit wineries hard, but it satisfied trading partners who disliked the 'unfair' treatment. This change forced Canadian wineries to compete beyond the price advantage they had previously enjoyed and to deliver real features and benefits. It was becoming clear that consumers wanted improvements in the quality of Canadian wines. Vintners were being called upon to address the perception that imports were more refined and sophisticated than similar Canadian products; Canadian wineries had their work cut out for them.

Wanting to protect the grape growers of its province by insulating itself from the outside, the Ontario government passed the Wine Content Act, limiting the use of non-Ontario based grapes and juices to 15 per cent. However, a little more than ten years later, in 1986, fearing the impending negotiations around free trade, the Ontario government attempted to stave off competition from abroad. It did this by subsidizing local wines through the Niagara Accord. This program imposed a mandatory 66 per cent mark-up on foreign wines, giving Ontario wines a temporary edge over the competition, but this advantage was short-lived and was rejected as an item for cost reduction in the FTA agreement. The mark-up was eventually removed altogether when the GATT came into the picture shortly thereafter.

The mark-up on domestic wines had a massive effect on the revenues of Canadian wineries and is best described by *Wine Spectator* magazine's Bruce Sanderson: 'In Canada, the sale and distribution of wine is controlled by provincial government monopolies. Consequently, wineries realize greater revenues through direct sales. For example, according to the British Columbia Wine Institute, a trade organization, a B.C. wine selling for $12.95 (Canadian) at the winery generates $5.98 profit. Sold by the British Columbia Liquor Distribution Branch, whose mark-up is $5.80, that profit dwindles to 18 cents.'[30] According to the annual reports from the LCBO, in 1988, 29 per cent of wine sales, or $161 million, came from Ontario wines, 0.2 per cent from wine produced by other Canadian provinces, and 8.6 per cent from winery store sales, but a whopping 62 per cent or $345 million came from imported wines. In 1990 this increased to $385 million or 65 per cent of sales, while Ontario's wine sales dropped to 25 per cent or $149 million.[31]

The profit impact of foreign goods had left an indelible impression on the minds of Canadian vintners, and something needed to be done to change the public perception of their wines as well as Canada's track record of such exports. Who better to engage this challenge than one of the industry's pioneers?

Icy Innovations

With the same innovative spirit that catalyzed the granting of Inniskillin's licence in 1975, Ziraldo and Kaiser set out to bring another golden idea to the fore. Ziraldo was leading the charge in the early 1980s for the VQA label. Both he and others knew that a quality-control process of labelling Ontario wine by its designated viticultural area, grape origin, and contents would boost consumers' perceptions of Ontario wine standards. A VQA system would parallel the standards and consumer recognition enjoyed in France and Italy. In these countries, wine standards follow a set of rules known as the AOC (Appellation d'Origine Contrôllée) in France and the DOC (Denominazione d'Origine Controlata) in Italy.

Meanwhile, Kaiser occupied himself with developing a unique product that had its roots in his Austrian homeland. Kaiser considered the challenging climate he faced in Canada and determined that the Niagara region's unique micro-climate had elements he could harness for a new product. In 1983 he began experimenting with naturally frozen grapes, harvesting them during the winter's long nights. The process of freezing and thawing of the grapes dehydrates the fruit and concentrates the sugars, acids, and extracts in the berries, thereby intensifying the flavours and adding complexity to the wine made from it.[32]

After trying a number of modern technologies to extract this new elixir, Kaiser reverted to using traditional presses once used by European families to make their own wines since these devices had the right compression power and were easily disassembled for storage. The unfortunate part of this process was that the concentrated harvest would produce only 5 per cent of the traditional yield. Another troubling limitation was that only a very limited number of grape varieties like Vidal could be used to provide both the acidity and Brix, or sweetness level, required for a premium product. Inniskillin's first vintage of this 'icewine' was released in 1984, an entire year behind schedule, because the prior year's crop was pillaged by thousands of local birds that discovered the sweet reserve in the grapes the night before picking was to begin!

In a recent interview, Ziraldo recalls how, back in 1989, the FTA was 'scaring us to death.'[33] However, the Inniskillin duo persevered in the face of this adverse market reality. And it was with the innovation of icewine that Inniskillin truly made its mark on a global scale. In 1991 Ziraldo and Kaiser's 1989 Vidal Icewine was awarded the Grand Prix d'Honneur, the top honour at the world's most prestigious wine expo in Bordeaux, France. This was revolutionary and groundbreaking news for European, U.S., and even Canadian wine consumers. Given its Canadian origins, the wine produced in this finicky winter process had yielded remarkable attention. Historically, the production of icewine had been forbidden in the European Union, which had lived under very strict rules for wine production for many years. Now Canadians were developing and marketing this coveted – albeit expensive – product, which could range in price from $50 to $80 per half-bottle.

This sweet little wine, packed in a bottle originally designed for olive oil, took the world by storm. Sales and demand for icewine spanned the globe, with much of the business stemming from Japan. At the time, Inniskillin's only export was its icewine, and the company hoped that it would become a flagship for Canada's other varieties and a beachhead for other markets. But Ziraldo and Kaiser knew that repeating their success with icewine might prove difficult with other products, and they wondered how many Italians would want to buy a bottle of Canadian red over their own beloved Chianti.

Competition by the Barrel

By the late 1980s, the wine industry in Canada featured a wide range of competitors ranging from large domestic players, medium domestic players, and boutique markets like farms and the cottage wine industry to international players, including companies based in the United States. All knew how to compete in a tough market. Wine companies even saw competition from those who made their own wine at home in an effort to continue their ethnic traditions and avoid the high taxes on purchasing alcohol. Some estimate that this home-grown industry produced more than twenty-five million litres per year. (See Table 1.)

In the past, wine companies had always competed on price, quality, brand recognition, and distribution. After the FTA, however, the insular world in which Canadian wineries had grown up changed drastically forever, and, arguably, for the better.

As Tony Aspler remarked on the innovation driven by the cottage wine industry in those years: 'There's a category of small wineries that are driving quality across the country. And we're seeing greater use of grape varieties beyond the ubiquitous Chardonnay and Cabernet Sauvignon.'[34] Faced with several local competitors in an array of sizes, some vintners thought it would make sense to increase scale to venture into new markets or at least to stave off the increased competition both within and outside Canada. The innovators knew that the Canadian wine industry had to continue down the path of evolution in order to survive against formidable global competitors.

A Few Sips of the Vincor Story

Among the Canadian wine industry's competitive forces are those wine

Table 1
Wine company market shares in Canada (%)
(figures include wine, coolers, and cider but not sales from winery-owned stores)

	1991	1992	1993
Major Domestic Producers			
Vincor	22.5	23.4	22.0
Andrés	9.5	9.4	8.8
Mission Hill	2.2	3.7	3.9
Cellier du Monde	3.0	3.5	3.8
Intermediate Domestic Producers			
Calona	3.2	3.2	3.0
Geloso	1.3	1.2	1.6
London	0.9	0.9	0.9
Major Estate Wineries			
Pelee Island	0.3	0.4	0.5
Colio	0.2	0.3	0.3
Kittling Ridge	0	0	0
Major Import Suppliers			
B&G (France)/Seagrams	3.5	5.7	5.4
Gallo (U.S.)	2.1	2.5	2.9
Pait (France)	2.8	2.6	2.4
Kressman (France)	1.9	1.9	1.8
Roux/Tarride (France)	0.8	1.0	1.1

Source: Vincor Files. Table 1 was adapted from page 7 of 'Vincor International Inc.' written by Darren Roberts under Prof J.N. Fry (1996). Version (A) 2003-03-01.

companies that span the entire nation and offer an array of brands at various prices. One such company had humble origins dating back to 1874, when the Niagara Falls Wine Company came into existence. That same company became the T.G. Bright and Company in 1911. Over the years, the company gained momentum following a consolidation strategy, but the biggest moves were still to come.

Wine maven Donald Triggs had at one time served as a senior executive at John Labatt and was responsible for its Ridout wine business in Canada and the United States. In 1989 Triggs led a bold effort that would result in great change within the industry. It involved his friend, Allan Jackson, a scientist who had joined Labatt and quickly become responsible for national quality control of production in Labatt's B.C.

and Ontario holdings. Arguably, Jackson's biggest contribution to the venture was to 'initiate a wine research program in association with the National Research Council, to improve the quality of Canadian table wines.'[35]

The period of uncertainty prior to the FTA, combined with other industry factors, caused Labatt to divest itself of its wine interests. Conversely, the same circumstances that repelled Labatt from the wine business attracted Triggs and Jackson. In 1989 the duo performed a leveraged buyout of the Labatt's Ridout business, renaming it Cartier Wines.[36] Reflecting back to 1989, Triggs saw the future shaping up this way: 'The wine industry braced for a flood of cheap imports due to the [FTA]. You had two choices as a Canadian wine producer,' recalls Triggs. 'Go to higher price points if you wanted to stay small. Or get bigger fast if you were in the popular-priced segment.'

Cartier Wines, the vehicle that Jackson and Triggs created out of Labatt's Ridout wine business, initially pursued both avenues, but its partners knew that growth and scale were important to their plans. In 1992 Cartier bought Ziraldo and Kaiser's Niagara-based Inniskillin Wineries, then known for its premium offerings and pioneering icewines. Later, in 1993, 'they teamed up with industrialist Gerry Schwartz and the Ontario Teachers Pension Plan to take over T.G. Bright & Co., a maker of popular-priced wines ... and doubled annual sales to $125 million.'[37] This newly formed entity was dubbed Vincor International. With the new structure in place, a network of 160 licensed retail stores were consolidated under the Wine Rack brand. Under the changed economy, Triggs and Jackson needed to design a strategy that would address the growing market and shifts in consumer preferences.

Half Full or Half Empty?

Canadian wineries were no strangers to adversity, and their executives were constantly tested with new challenges. For the more entrepreneurially oriented, these challenges became opportunities.

The Grape Growers of Ontario note that 'in 1993, the Wine Content Act was changed to allow a minimum of 10% Ontario-grown product and up to 90% imported product. A severe crop failure in Ontario, due to bad weather, reduced the availability of grapes. This change was only to take effect for one year.'[38] With the recent crop volatility, and with their boutique winery as part of a much larger entity, how would Ziraldo and Kaiser continue to be advocates for both the industry and their own innovative and entrepreneurial brand? Would their artisan products be replaced by commodities?

With a much bigger and a changed economic environment, the newly created Vincor needed to build a long-term strategy that would address the shifts in consumer preferences and emerging markets. Based on the zeal and energy that both Triggs and Ziraldo have demonstrated in the past, would they continue to see opportunities in adversity?

Suggested Questions

1. It was generally predicted, by Mordecai Richler and others, that the Canada-U.S. Free Trade Agreement would have dire consequences for the Canadian wine industry. However, the opposite turned out to be true. Why?
2. If you were Donald Ziraldo and Karl Kaiser in 1993, what would you do with Inniskillin Wines, now part of a larger company?
3. If you were Donald Triggs, CEO of the newly formed Vincor, what would your next move be? What would your three- to five-year plan look like?

Suggested Readings

Drucker, Peter. 'What Makes an Effective Executive.' *Harvard Business Review*, 82, 6 (2004).

Gruending Dennis. 'John Turner and Brian Mulroney , 25 October 1988.' In *Great Canadian Speeches*. Toronto: Fitzhenry and Whiteside 2004. 230–3.

Hart, Michael. 'Full Circle: The New Reciprocity.' In *A Trading Nation: Canadian Trade Policy from Colonialism to Globalization*. Vancouver: UBC Press 2002. 367–98. http://winesofontario.org/PDFs/Medi-aKit.pdf.

Appendix A:
Trade Policy for Wine: Canada-United States Free Trade Agreement

Chapter Eight: Wine and Distilled Spirits

Chapter Eight of the FTA provides for the reduction of barriers to trade in wine and distilled spirits which arise from measures related to their internal sale and distribution. It constitutes a partial derogation from

the national-treatment provisions of Chapter Five. The specific measures covered concern listing, pricing, distribution practices, blending
requirements, and the standards and labelling requirements affecting
distinctive products. The objective of the chapter is to provide over
time equal treatment for Canadian and U.S. wine and distilled products
in each other's market. Canadians will, as a result, enjoy greater access
to a wide variety of California wines at competitive prices. The brewing
industry is not covered by this chapter (but see Chapter Twelve).

The chapter specifies that measures concerning listing for sale of
wine and distilled spirits are to be transparent, treat Canadian and U.S.
products in the same way, and be based on normal commercial considerations. Any distiller or wine producer applying for a listing is to be
informed promptly of listing decisions and given the reasons for any
refusal and the right to appeal such a decision. Estate wineries in British Columbia that existed on 4 October 1987 and that produce less than
30,000 gallons annually may be automatically listed in that province.

On pricing, the chapter allows a provincial liquor board or any other
public body distributing wine and distilled spirits to charge the additional cost of selling the imported product. Differential charges on wine
that exceed this amount are to be reduced over a seven-year period
from 1989 through 1995. The method for calculating this differential
is specified. Differential charges on distilled spirits that exceed this
amount are to be eliminated immediately when the agreement comes
into force. All other discriminatory pricing measures are to be eliminated immediately.

On distribution, measures can be maintained that allow wineries or
distilleries to limit sales on their premises to wines and spirits produced
on those premises. Similarly, Ontario and British Columbia are not prevented from allowing private wine outlets existing on 4 October 1987
to favour their own wine. The Quebec provision relating to in-province
bottling of wine for sale in grocery stores is grandfathered.

Canada has agreed to eliminate any measure requiring that distilled
spirits imported in bulk from the United States be blended with Canadian spirits.

The chapter provides for mutual recognition of Canadian whisky
and U.S. bourbon as distinct products. This means that the United
States will not allow the sale of any product as Canadian whisky unless
it has been manufactured in Canada in accordance with Canadian laws.
Canada will not permit the sale of any product as bourbon unless it has
been manufactured in the United States in accordance with U.S. laws.

Appendix B: Revenue Distribution in Ontario

Where Your Money Goes

Revenue Distriubtion:
LCBO versus WRS Outlets for 750ml bottle of table wine

Source: Grape Growers of Ontario, www.grapegrowersofontario.com/the growers/ongrapewine_industry/wine_facts, 2005.

NOTES

1 'The Journal,' CBC Television, 19 Nov. 1987.
2 Michael Silverstein and Neil Fiske, *Trading Up* (Toronto: Portfolio Hardcover 2003), 183–7.
3 Eugene Luczkiw, *The Niagara Cottage Wine Industry Study*, http://www.entreplexity.ca/research/pdf/niagara_cottage_wine.pdf , 1994, 5 (this website and the ones below were accessed 14–18 July 2005).
4 Inniskillin: http://www.inniskillin.com/en/winery/history.asp?location= winery&secondLocation=history.
5 Tony Aspler, http://tonyaspler.com/pub/articleview.asp?id=353&s=5.
6 The Alberta Gaming and Liquor Commission defines a cottage winery as a

'facility that manufactures wine for sale through the AGLC and for sales to the general public at the orchard/winery (farm gate) site.'

7 Grape Growers of Ontario website: www.grapegrowersofontario.com.

8 Ibid.

9 B.C. Wines website, http://www.bcwine.com/aboutbcwines.html.

10 Grape Growers of Ontario website.

11 Ibid.

12 Ontario Ministry of Agriculture Food and Rural Affairs, http://www.omafra.gov.on.ca/english/crops/facts/graperec.htm.

13 Ken MacQueen, *Maclean's*, 114, no. 35 (27 Aug. 2001): 36.

14 Based on total population; per capita consumption would be higher if based on drinking-age population. Conversion: litres times .26418 equals gallons.

15 Canada's Cultural Gateway: http://www.culture.ca/perspective-pointde-vue-e.jsp?data=200411/tcp01200112004e.html.

16 CBC Archives, http://archives.cbc.ca/400d.asp?id=1-69-1041-5824.

17 John Spears, 'Andres Hopes to Boost Image for Struggling Canadian Wines,' Toronto *Star*, 20 Nov. 1986, E1.

18 Peter Kupfer, 'Revisiting the French Paradox,' *Wine Enthusiast*, http://winemag.wineenthusiast.com/issues/feb03/frenchparadox.htm.

19 Ibid.

20 Silverstein and Fiske, *Trading Up*, 183.

21 Avinash Dixit and Barry Nalebuff, *Thinking Strategically* (New York: W.W. Norton 1993), 105.

22 Now the World Trade Organization.

23 Dixit and Nalebuff, *Thinking Strategically*, 105.

24 Dale Heien and Eric Sims, 'The Impact of the Canada-United States Free Trade Agreement on US Wine Exports,' *American Journal of Agriculture Economics*, 82 (February 2000): 173–82.

25 Carl T. Hall, 'Wine Curbs Draw Fire,' San Francisco *Chronicle*, 9 May 1989, C1.

26 Simon Tuck and Campbell Clark, 'Wine Industry Fears It Will Get the Lumber,' *Globe and Mail*, 25 Aug. 2005, B1.

27 Heien and Sims, 173–82.

28 Ibid.

29 The Marin Institute, http://www.marininstitute.org/alcohol_policy/state_alcohol_control.htm.

30 Bruce Sanderson, 'Canada's Revival: Impressive New Chardonnays, Rieslings and Ice Wines Reflect a Transformation in the Vineyards,' *Wine Spectator*, 31 Oct. 1999, 3.

31 See Appendix B for recent data on revenue distributions for Ontario wine.
32 Inniskillin website.
33 Interview with Donald Ziraldo, GrapeRadio, Show #39, 1 Aug. 2005.
34 Tony Aspler's Archives, http://www.tonyaspler.com/pub/articleview. asp?id=15&s=5.
35 Jackson-Triggs, http://www.jacksontriggswinery.com/en/aboutUs/our-Proprietors/index.html.
36 Ibid.
37 Michael Ryval, 'Glass Half Full,' *Globe and Mail*, 28 Sept. 2001, B45.
38 Grape Growers of Ontario website.

CASE 11
The Collapse of Confederation Life

ROD MCQUEEN, with guidance from JOE MARTIN

When regulators seized Confederation Life Insurance on 11 August 1994, the company had $19 billion in assets, was the fourth-largest insurance company in Canada, and ranked among the top thirty in North America. Previously, a widely held view about bankruptcies among major financial services firms was captured by the phrase, 'too big to fail.' In this case, 'too big to fail' came to mean that nobody believed bankruptcy was possible until it suddenly became inevitable.

Initially, the total loss to policyholders, bondholders, and creditors looked as if it could amount to as much as $2.6 billion, making 'Confed' the largest loss in the history of financial firms. The next biggest failures were Barings at US$1.3 billion, Banco Ambrosiano at US$1.4 billion, and Franklin National at US$1.8 billion. Thrown into disarray were 300,000 policyholders and annuitants in Canada as well as another 450,000 individuals worldwide, half of them in the United States.

There was also the worry that Canada's 127 life insurance companies, which employed 96,700 people and did business in twenty countries, might suffer collateral damage to their corporate credibility. Of particular concern was their business in the United States: Americans held $730 billion in life insurance issued by Canadian companies.

The failure of Confederation Life, so implausible just a few years before, was the result of changes in regulations, ill-conceived expansion strategies, and exceedingly poor risk management.

The Founding Fathers

Confederation Life was founded in 1871 by John Kay Macdonald, a Scottish immigrant who realized that, of the twenty-four life insurance companies then operating in Canada, only one was Canadian. That sole Canadian company, Canada Life, conducted more business in Canada than any of the rest. Clearly, a market existed for another homegrown participant.

Confed's first offices were two rented rooms in the Masonic Hall on Toronto Street. Growth came so quickly that in 1899 the company acquired an entire block bounded by Yonge, Richmond, Victoria, and Queen streets, where it built a seven-storey Romanesque headquarters building complete with spires.

From 1902 to 1914, Confed opened offices in Great Britain, the West Indies, and Central America. During the 1920s, expansion continued to the United States, Hong Kong, and Singapore. The company launched innovative products and was the first life insurance company in Canada to issue policies without requiring medical exams. The Great Depression and the Second World War slowed the rate of growth, but by 1953 Confed had written one million policies. Moreover, it had run out of room in the downtown office so the company moved its headquarters north to a new building at 321 Bloor Street East.

Three generations of the Macdonald family dominated the company. Charles Strange Macdonald, son of the founder, served as president from 1930 to 1944. J.K. Macdonald, grandson of the founder, joined Confed in 1926, rose to the position of president and held that post from 1947 to 1969, and then remained as chairman.[1]

In the early 1950s, several small Canadian insurance companies were bought by foreigners. When larger Canadian firms such as Sun Life and Manufacturers Life became the target of U.S. interests, the government of Canada passed legislation in 1957 permitting mutualization (i.e., the acquisition of the company from shareholders by the policyholders) of any life insurance company. In 1958 five of the largest – Sun Life, Manulife, Canada Life, Equitable, and Confed – approved mutualization in a move that kept U.S. buyers at bay. They bought back their stock from shareholders in a process that took up to ten years.

The Modern Era Arrives

In 1969 J.K. Macdonald, who had run Confed since 1947, turned sixty-five. He was replaced by J. Craig Davidson. (Three generations of Macdonalds had been in charge for fifty-one of Confed's first ninety-eight years.) Davidson suffered from poor health. Rather than replace him with the most likely internal candidate, Pat Burns, who had joined

Confed in 1946 right out of high school, the board hired an outsider, Jack Rhind, who at the age of fifty-fix had just retired as president of National Life.

With 2,500 employees and $1.7 billion in assets, Confed was four times the size of National, but Macdonald and other members of the board believed that Rhind was a better fit for the role because he had more social graces than the rough-hewn Burns, who always made a point of refusing to stand up along with everyone else whenever J.K. Macdonald entered a room.

Rhind, who came up the investment side of the business rather than the actuarial side that spawned most life insurance leaders, found Confed a lackadaisical place. He would dress down officers whom he judged were performing poorly, sometimes in front of their peers. But, for all his effort and experience, Rhind made no major changes and became frustrated by what he saw as Confed's culture of contentment. At one point, when Rhind learned that a competitor had bought a trust company that Confed was also trying to acquire, he complained, 'I'm going to be the only kid on the block without an electric train. Get me an electric train.'[2]

As Rhind began looking forward to his second retirement, he told the board in 1979 that Pat Burns should be his successor. This time, the board concurred. Burns was named chief operating officer as well as a director in 1980. Still annoyed that he had been passed over the first time around, Burns vowed he would show the world what a mistake had been made.

It was Rhind who served at the helm of the company during the recession in the early 1980s, so Burns missed learning any lessons from that downturn. Although Canada's economic performance was the worst since the Second World War, it was a yeasty time for the insurance sector. Outsiders were brought in (Bob Bandeen from CN to run Crown Life, Earl Orser from Eaton's to head London Life) as the sector geared up to offer one-stop shopping to clients who, as it turned out, had no interest in getting a guaranteed investment certificate, buying insurance, and investing in mutual funds all from the same agent at the same firm.

Pat Burns Takes the Reins

Although he was not named CEO until 1985, Burns worked behind the scenes during the intervening years to build a new management team that was more to his liking. Among his five new vice-presidents was Bill Douglas, in charge of corporate development. Douglas had followed Burns up the corporate ladder and was everything Burns was not: a cerebral university graduate who was given to outbursts of creative thinking on corporate strategy. It turned out that, separately, neither was enough; together they were too much.

At a 1985 company retreat, Burns challenged management to shed its passivity and become more entrepreneurial. Confed was no longer going to be just an insurance company, he said, it must develop into a well-rounded financial-services firm. As a mutual insurance company, owned by policyholders, Burns claimed that the bottom line didn't matter because the company could take the long-term view. Burns's plan called for Confed to launch its new strategy by buying a trust company, turning it into a bank, and then folding the bank back into the insurance company.

Douglas, who was actually the puppeteer pulling Burns's strings, declared that within five years Confed would be Canada's largest insurance company. For a while, that goal seemed within the company's grasp. From 1986 to 1989, Confed's annual growth rate of 25 per cent was the fastest of any life insurance company in Canada. But trouble began as interest rates rose.

Consumers demanded and got 12 per cent interest on guaranteed income certificates. As a result, Confed had to find assets that would earn at least 15 per cent in order to make any money on the spread between what it paid for deposits and what it could earn with the money. Interest rates on bonds weren't high enough and the stock market seemed too risky, so Confed began plowing money into commercial real estate where returns tend to be higher than in other areas of investment. Confed was already extended in that market. At the same time, financial services were evolving into a far more competitive sector than it had been for the previous one hundred years. In 1987 ownership of Canadian securities dealers and brokerage houses was opened up to anyone, including foreign firms and other Canadian financial institutions.

The banks were the biggest buyers. The Royal bought Dominion Securities, CIBC acquired Wood Gundy, Bank of Nova Scotia got McLeod, Young, Weir, and Bank of Montreal bought Nesbitt Thomson. The banks also began buying insurance companies but were restricted from competing with the remaining life insurance companies head-on: banks were not allowed to market life insurance directly through their branches – they could act only through subsidiaries.

Taking on Risks

With the change in the rules, Confed got into the expansion act too, buying slightly less than 10 per cent of the brokerage firm Midland, Walywn as well as 100 per cent of Halifax Trust, which was nothing more than a corporate shell, and renaming it Confederation Trust. By 1990, the previously tiny trust company had $1.5 billion in assets, much of that money pulled in from consumer deposits on which Confed paid higher interest rates than the competition. As for investing that money, 80 per cent was put into mortgages, most of them at lower rates than the competition – in order to attract business. As a result, compared to other firms, Confed's profit margins were razor-thin.

Trust company management planted other landmines that included tax-sheltered real estate investments where mortgages were issued for up to 95 per cent of the appraised value of a property, a policy that permitted no downturn in the real estate market. Rewards to those running Confederation Trust were large despite the high-risk nature of the volatile business they pursued. The top four trust company officers each earned more than $1 million a year in 1988, 1989, and 1990, twice what Burns was paid.

In the life insurance company, the dollar value of real estate investments kept getting bigger, the locations more far-flung. In 1985 Confed purchased a 50 per cent share in six office buildings in Calgary and Vancouver, and then expanded its interest to shopping malls and other commercial space across Canada. In Britain, Confed booked £400 million in mortgages in just four years. In 1989 it bought a 50 per cent interest in The Portals, a $650-millon office-hotel-retail complex in Washington, D.C.

As if the pace of change in those risky new areas weren't enough, Confederation Life began replacing staid and predictable whole life policies – the backbone of the company's business since it was founded – with innovative products such as annuities that were sensitive to rising interest rates. By 1989, almost 60 per cent of Confed's business with individuals in the United States was in the hot-money arena of annuities, to which customers were attracted by high rates and away from which they could be wooed by the competition just as easily.

Adding to the organizational complexity, in 1989 Confed acquired controlling interest in a small leasing company with assets of $101 million. By 1993, Confed had invested $700 million in the company, which had six offices across Canada and half a dozen subsidiaries, all in Barbados. The company purchased a six-bedroom mansion, Highlands House, on that Caribbean island's Sandy Lane, for $2 million. The intent was to provide visitors with a spiffy place to enjoy rest and relaxation when they came to check on business matters.

The increases in staff needed to handle the growing workload in turn required more office space. The company acquired new regional headquarters buildings in Atlanta, Georgia, and Stevenage, north of London. With assets up sevenfold and space at a premium in Toronto, Burns decided Confed also needed a new and much grander head office. Groundbreaking for the $90-million structure on Mount Pleasant Road, just behind the Bloor Street headquarters, took place on 4 December 1989. The edifice was huge, half a million square feet, its faux parliamentary architecture boasting a fitness centre, art deco stainless-steel door fixtures, and elevators lined with Swiss pearwood. Statuary by Michael Snow was commissioned. The exterior featured three kinds of granite. Marble was shipped from Italy for use inside and out.

The Regulators Begin to Raise Issues

Insurance, like all other aspects of financial services, is supposed to be a closely regulated business. Ottawa keeps an eye on solvency and the provinces monitor contracts. At the time of Confed's extraordinary expansion, the main federal watchdog was Michael Mackenzie, a former auditor with Clarkson, Gordon.[3] Mackenzie was appointed in 1987, around the same time that Ottawa combined the Department of Insurance and the inspector general of banks into a new entity, the Office of the Superintendent of Financial Institutions.[4]

Mackenzie was given a sweeping mandate. No one wanted any more surprise collapses of the sort that had occurred in 1985 when two banks, Canadian Commercial Bank and Northland Bank, had failed. But OSFI's oversight role was sprawling: it was responsible for 61 banks, 163 insurance companies and fraternal societies, 231 property and casualty insurance companies, and 1,100 pension plans. To supervise all those entities, OSFI had 400 employees, only 10 per cent of whom were on-site life insurance examiners.

Mackenzie was frank about OSFI's limitations and told corporate directors he was counting on them to be his eyes and ears when it came to spotting and reporting problems. Inspections were carried out every two years. In 1987 Confed passed muster. By 1989, the regulators were dismayed to find that Confederation Life's real estate exposure had reached 73.8 per cent of assets (including mortgage loans as well as ownership positions in commercial properties such as office towers and shopping malls). By comparison, the figures for Manulife were 28.5 per cent, Sun 32.1 per cent, Canada Life 35.9 per cent, and Great-West 42.2 per cent.

Burns dismissed Mackenzie's concerns. The Confed directors continued to support Burns and in 1990 rewarded him with the title of chairman of the board, the third jewel in the corporate crown, to go with his two other titles, president and CEO. Burns's sidekick, Bill Douglas, was promoted to senior vice-president, corporate development.

In a speech to the Canadian Club of Toronto in January 1990, mere weeks after Mackenzie's warning shot about real estate, Burns boasted: 'We simply are not who you think we are. We are not afraid of competition. We are ready to take on the world – which, by the way, includes the big banks.' As for Confederation Trust, the initial focus of Mackenzie's concern, it continued to expand. Growth in Britain was so strong that Burns described it as 'almost unheard of in terms of financial services in the U.K. And I'm proud of this.'[5]

Confed management was equally unperturbed when the Ontario Ministry of Financial Institutions raised concerns about the trust company in 1990. It took months for the regulators to convince Confed to stop lending money to itself. However, the regulators missed a more troubling sign. By 1991, more than half of Confederation Trust's $959-million commercial and residential loan portfolio was lodged with one borrower, Reemark Group. The law declares that no one company should account for more than 1 per cent of loans. Confed was way over the line but inspectors could not see the problem because numerous corporate names were used although ultimate ownership belonged to Reemark.

Still, when Michael Mackenzie met with the Confederation Life board in October 1991, he was worried enough to tell directors that Confed needed to raise additional capital, among other steps. No one appeared to be listening. Mackenzie sent a two-page follow-up letter to each director outlining his concerns and urged them to call for a full briefing. Only Adam Zimmerman, who had known Mackenzie since birth, phoned Mackenzie and he told his old friend that he had not made a convincing case. 'Mike,' said Zimmerman, 'you've got to realize this guy Burns is a crackerjack.' Mackenzie replied, 'Read the letter again.'

The Recession Arrives

When recessions occur, life insurance companies are among the first to feel the effects. Policy sales collapse, few new employee-benefit plans are purchased, existing business shrinks as companies cut back, and long-term disability claims increase as unemployment rises. As well, non-performing loans skyrocket as mortgage holders miss payments and walk away from properties, and competition for investment dollars means a decline in predictable margins and rental income as office-vacancy rates rise.

No one was immune from the downturn that arrived with a vengeance in the early 1990s. In 1992 the six largest banks in Canada made provision for $6.9 billion in bad loans, half of which were caused by commercial real estate. Foreign banks in Canada had net losses of $380 million, the first since they came to the country. Trust and loan companies lost $1.2 billion in the period from 1991 to 1993. In January 1992 Les Coopérants Mutual Life Insurance Society failed, the result of imprudent investments in U.S. real estate, leaving 160,000 policyholders in the lurch. Like Confed, Les Coopérants had 'head-office syndrome,' opening a new $125-million building on Montreal's Maisonneuve Boulevard that boasted a marble lobby, private dining rooms, and a museum.

With Confed directors unaware, some members of Confed management knew that the company was in trouble so they launched a creative way to make money. In 1991 the firm set up Confederation Treasury Services Ltd (CTSL) and within a year had $10.2 billion of derivatives on its books, a brand new area of financial vehicles about which Confed knew nothing. CTSL also piled into interest rate swaps, foreign currency exchange, and hedging services.

As if that weren't enough, Confed eyed the cash sitting in the trust account of the company's operations in Michigan. While each U.S. state oversees insurance in its own geographic area, Michigan acts as the licensee for 'alien' companies. Under the rules, each foreign company must keep sufficient assets in the Michigan-based trust account to cover any and all liabilities in the United States. If a company went bankrupt in its home country, Michigan wanted full and guaranteed protection for all American policyholders and investors.

Beginning in 1991, CTSL began daily taking cash from that Michigan trust account, moving the money to Canada, and issuing IOUs in place of the withdrawn funds. After a while, when cash wasn't coming into the trust account quickly enough to cover its growing needs, Confed began selling bonds held in the trust account and transferring those proceeds to Canada, again leaving promissory notes.

Between 1992 and 1994, CTSL issued more than 700 notes to the Michigan trust with face amounts totalling more than $54 billion. Of that amount, less than 2 per cent was ever paid off. The remainder were rolled over using new notes from CTSL.

Notarized forms, claiming that Confed's U.S. assets were greater than its U.S. liabilities, were signed annually and submitted to the Michigan authorities by Pat Burns and three other senior executives. The statements just didn't make clear that those assets were in another country, not in the United States, where they were supposed to be. 'Although I was required as president to sign the statement, I had no reason beyond my usual due-diligence practices to check behind the employees who performed those job functions,' said Burns.[6]

Burns Confesses to His Board

On 27 May 1992 Burns finally admitted to his board that he had problems. In addition to a capital shortfall, Confed faced a liquidity crisis because the company had invested in long-term assets while many of the matching liabilities were short term. As a result of this mismatch, Confed was about $1.5 billion short of being able to cover all potential demands with liquid assets.

Some members of the board wanted to replace Burns immediately, so they established a search committee to seek a successor. Others remained loyal to Burns and weren't ready to toss him overboard just yet. Meanwhile, Confed hired a new internal auditor to give the company better financial information and to try, belatedly, to put some controls in place.

Burns's pal, Bill Douglas, defended him but was nevertheless aware of his shortcomings. 'Pat Burns had a tremendous capacity, ability, and tremendous accomplishments, and he also had some weaknesses,' said Douglas. 'One of the biggest was absolute trust in people to get involved in the trust-company affair or the real-estate investments that Confed did without adequate controls. He had sufficient confidence in the people who were involved in these operations – and confidence in humanity in general – that was overplaced. That was his biggest weakness. It's very frequent that your biggest strength is also your biggest weakness.'[7]

Confed's balance sheet was strengthened through two Eurobond issues, one for $100 million and the other for £100 million. Orders were issued to stop selling guaranteed accumulation annuity plans because Confed had no place to invest the funds gathered at rates high enough to make any money. Confed also sold about $100 million in real estate as well as another $100 million acquired through foreclosures.

In September 1992, when independent rating agency TRAC Insurance Services warned that Confed had failed six out of eight solvency tests, Burns took TRAC on for one final fight. He claimed that TRAC had not taken into account a $200-million capital gain that had been deferred for tax reasons. At the same time, OSFI unveiled a new way to measure financial health called the minimum continuing capital and surplus requirements (MCCSR). Confed's MCCSR ratio was a sorry 125, barely above the 120 required by OSFI. The average for all Canadian companies was 159.

New Hope from a New Man

At last, Confed's board members roused themselves into action. In October 1992 the directors replaced Burns as president and CEO with Paul Cantor, who had just lost out in a succession battle at his previous employer, Canadian Imperial Bank of Commerce. But the Confed board couldn't bring itself to get rid of Burns completely. He was allowed to keep the title of chairman as a way to save face.

Cantor spent his first few months on the job touring offices and trying to develop a thorough understanding of the company. Many on staff were not welcoming; they saw him as a banker who knew nothing about insurance. He drew up a plan he called the three Cs: consolidating operations in the core businesses, concentrating resources on supporting those businesses, and committing to high levels of customer service.

Cantor brought in two lieutenants from the outside, Michael White, a chartered accountant who had been a senior credit officer at Bank of Montreal, and Chris Davis, former president of commercial real estate services at Royal LePage. Neither knew anything about the insurance business; the entire liability side of the balance sheet mystified both Cantor and White. 'It was only three or four months before [Cantor] was overwhelmed,' said Michael Mackenzie. 'The first year [Cantor] probably didn't realize what was going on. In the second, he couldn't figure out what to do about it,' said David Murray, of Deloitte and Touche, who served as the court-appointed monitor after Confed collapsed.[8] Cantor fired Bill Douglas and got rid of Mike Regester, Burns's protégé. Regester might have been able to help because he knew how the troubles arose but was too tied to the former regime. Cantor also replaced Burns as chairman of the board with director Adam Zimmerman.

Profit continued to fall – from $17 million in 1991 to $1.9 million in

1992. That year, some individual agents selling Confed products made more money than the company. In 1993 Confed lost $29 million. Cantor tried to raise capital and sell Confederation Trust. He soon discovered that no one was interested either in investing in Confederation Life or in taking the firm's beleaguered trust company off his hands.

After a year as CEO, Cantor could point to some improvements. First, he had cut annual expenses by $54 million, down 10 per cent from the previous year. Second, the percentage of assets in real estate was down from the 1989 peak of 73.8 per cent to 50 per cent, but that was still twice as high as it was in the 130 largest U.S. life insurance firms. Asset quality continued to deteriorate; non-performing assets totalled $807 million in bonds, mortgages, and foreclosed real estate.

At the same time, Cantor inexplicably turned down an offer of $115 million for the head office. The deal would have raised helpful cash and included a leaseback arrangement but Cantor concluded he didn't want to tie the company down to a twenty-five-year deal.[9] Cantor was able to sell the company's 9.8 per cent stake in brokerage firm Midland Walwyn as well as its controlling interest in Confederation Leasing.

Time Runs Out

But such deals were mere dribs and drabs. With almost one-quarter of Confed's mortgage portfolio in trouble, major rating agencies were beginning to downgrade Confed. Time was running out. The only solution was to find a buyer for the entire company. OSFI's Michael Mackenzie warned Cantor that he should try to sew up a private-sector deal because there would be no government support. When Sovereign Life failed in 1992, Standard Life had stepped in as a buyer. CompCorp, a life insurance fund paid for by the industry, covered losses at Les Coopérants. Mackenzie was looking for similar action by the industry to bail out Confed, if it came to that.

The government's track record was not very good when it did become involved in such matters. In 1985, when Canadian Commercial Bank and Northland were both on the brink, Ottawa convinced the other banks to invest $60 million and then pulled the plug on the two beleaguered institutions anyway.

Cantor began the search for a buyer with a sense of 'foreboding and loneliness. I became acutely aware that a lot of people and their futures were riding on how well I did at the bargaining table.'[10] He approached eighteen insurance companies, banks, conglomerates, and other financial institutions. Only five showed interest and just one, Great-West Life, was prepared to make an offer. Lengthy negotiations over a three-month period in early 1994 led to a tentative deal. On the one-page balance sheet that Confed and Great-West Life showed Michael Mackenzie for approval in March 1994 was a huge hole: intercompany loans worth US$620 million, the money taken from the Michigan trust account. Michigan authorities had begun making noise that any deal would require repayment of the IOUs. The understanding between Great-West and Confed had other difficulties: it did not include either the British division or Confederation Trust; those would have to be sold separately.

The Industry Gathers

Great-West did not want a particularly complicated and troublesome part of Confed's business, $1.1 billion in corporate-owned life insurance (COLI). In mid-June 1994 Confed's competitors were called in to help handle the COLI business. Tom Di Giacomo, fired from his position as Manulife CEO the previous year, was hired as a facilitator to find a solution among a consortium of CEOs from the five biggest life insurance companies: Manulife's Dominic D'Alessandro, Sun Life's John McNeil, Canada Life's David Nield, London Life's Gordon Cunningham, and Mutual Life's Bob Astley. Over the next month, the five came to an agreement that they would assume the COLI business and share $100 million of Confed's losses.

But the Great-West takeover of Confed, scheduled to close at the end of July, was running into other troubles. Great-West had concluded that Confed's financial condition was worse than had previously appeared. 'Every time they'd turn over a rock, they'd find a snake,' said Zimmerman. Matters were made worse at the end of June when Michael Mackenzie took his scheduled retirement after seven years as superintendent rather than helping to shepherd the deal through.

Great-West suggested that the five industry CEOs who had agreed to do something about COLI should offer more help. At a meeting on Saturday, 23 July 1994, Great-West told the five CEOs that Confed needed $300 million in capital. Great-West would invest $75 million if they would share $225 million. The group was upset to hear that a problem limited to one area of Confed's business had seemingly spilled elsewhere so quickly. Moreover, they were riled by Great-West's refusal to share any of the information gleaned from their due diligence, numbers that would prove the accuracy of the figures. Other suggestions were bandied about but the day passed with no progress.

As discussions continued over the next ten days, Great-West's assessment of how much capital was needed by Confed mushroomed to $450 million and then $600 million, twice the amount Great-West had said was required only days earlier. At one point, the industry seemed willing to invest up to $600 million, but only if the government gave the salvaging companies some tax relief and set up a fund for the life insurance industry like the Canada Deposit Insurance Corporation that backstopped the banks. The government refused; the consortium crumbled.

Agencies such as Standard and Poor's, Duff and Phelps, and A.M Best lowered their ratings. Confed could no longer issue commercial paper or draw on credit lines. 'What they did was sort of drop the ratings of Confederation Life down the elevator shaft,' said John McNeil, CEO of Sun Life.[11]

Attempts had been under way to bring in a group of American life insurance companies, but once those organizations heard that the Canadian CEOs had lost interest, so did they. Without support from either government or the industry, Cantor feared that Confed would face a liquidity crisis. Such a run on cash in hand would be caused by policyholders looking for surrender values, investors wanting to cash in guaranteed investment certificates, and institutions looking to dump commercial paper. The trouble with such perceptions is that, once liquidity appears to be a problem, those people who can get their money out quickly – such as institutional investors – can ask for and get money owed within twenty-four hours. Long-time policyholders who want to bail might wait three months for their money – by which time all available funds may be gone.

The Government Steps In

Rather than face a run on the institution, OSFI decided to take control of Confederation Life under the Winding-Up Act. On 11 August 1994 the federal government seized Confed; regulators, liquidators, and accountants replaced management. This was not a case of creative destruction. Confederation Life did not fail because of the arrival of an innovator, and, further, no new companies arrived to fill the void.

In fact, competition was reduced. Before the end of the month, three of Confed's major divisions had been sold to competitors. Great-West got U.S. group life and health insurance; Sun Life acquired the British arm. Manulife bought the biggest prize of all, the Canadian group life and health business, a division that generated about $1 billion in annual premium revenue from 800 clients, most of them large corporations, employing a total of 1.5 million Canadians. It was a popular purchase. When the news was announced to a gathering of some of the 900 Confed employees in that division, a spontaneous cheer erupted, followed by a standing ovation. They were relieved they hadn't fallen into the cheese-paring hands of Great-West, which had let them down.

As for the cause of the debacle, there was plenty of guilt to go around: members of management who took the company into risky businesses about which they knew nothing; directors who were asleep at the switch and did not ask tough questions; regulators who tried persuasion but did not exercise the strong-arm tactics available to them; auditors who looked at the past but failed to warn of future trouble; and insurance industry leaders who bickered, preferring to wait until Confed failed so they could snap up pieces of the prize.

Making matters worse was the fact that neither the company nor the industry had a champion in Ottawa. There was no politician who thought that either the firm or the industry's credibility was worth the fight. It would have been easy, for example, for one of Ottawa's powerful ministers to pick up the phone and make a call to prod Great-West into doing a deal, thereby saving everyone the cost of a clean-up. After all, Great-West was owned by Power Corp, which in turn was controlled by the Desmarais family, which had long-standing familial and business connections to both Prime Minister Jean Chrétien and Finance Minister Paul Martin. No such phone call was ever made. Indeed, fears of conflict of interest may have kept Chrétien and Martin too aloof from the situation, a stand-offish posture that kept their noses clean but caused an estimated 70 per cent of Confed employees, including those who transferred with their divisions to other firms, to lose their jobs.

Confederation Life could have been saved from such an ignominious end if any one of a series of individuals along the way had done their jobs. If there had been adequate management controls, if one director had stood up to the nonsense, if the regulator had been firmer, if the auditors had been more watchful, if the industry had made a more concerted effort, or if the CDIC had bailed out Confederation Trust in 1989 when the trouble became apparent, then the rest of the well would not have been poisoned.

OSFI claimed it did not have a mandate to prevent failure and could only influence events in order to minimize losses. 'Failure is a fact of life in the United States. In Canada, we have difficulty in coming to terms with it,' said John Palmer, who replaced Michael Mackenzie as superintendent. 'In Canada when people lose money, there is a need to search for a villain who is always by definition not the person who loses the money. We have to mature as a country and part of that maturity is to allow failure of financial-services companies.'[12]

Yet some circumstances evoked a more aggressive response than others. When Saddam Hussein invaded Kuwait in 1990, an executive at a Canadian bank phoned Michael Mackenzie to say that the bank had received a message, with all the appropriate authorization codes, to transfer $US10 billion in Kuwaiti funds out of an account in London. What should the bank do? Mackenzie looked into the matter and discovered he had no authority. He checked with U.S. and British regulators and discovered that they did. Emboldened by their powers, Mackenzie made up a phrase saying it would be 'unsafe and unsound' for the bank to release the money. The money stayed put. In the case of Confederation Life, a similar holding pattern could have been created to prevent any unfair distribution of funds while the company worked its way back to health. No such action was taken.

Lessons Learned

The failure of Confed is full of lessons for financial-services companies and other businesses:

- 25 per cent annual growth is not sustainable for three years running; that excessive rate alone should have been sufficient for someone inside the company to blow the whistle on Confed's expansionary strategy.
- Various groups – directors, officers, and agents – could have been more watchful and raised the alarm when they saw problems.
- The quick sale of three major divisions showed that competitors could have put a rescue package together if there had been any kind of polite pressure from Ottawa. Even Great-West, which had been notoriously slow at making an offer, was able to organize a one-inch-thick memorandum of agreement to buy the U.S. group business only five days after the seizure.

A full-blown inquiry into the collapse of Confederation Life might have provided more lessons, but no such scrutiny was ever carried out. Such inaction was unusual given Ottawa's usual penchant to flog dead horses. The 1985 demise of two much smaller institutions, Canadian Commercial Bank and Northland Bank, merited a full judicial inquiry under Mr Justice Willard Estey.

Derivatives, one of the many investment vehicles in Confed's arsenal, remain as little understood by regulators all these years later. The fact that no rules apply to derivatives, hedge funds, subprime mortgages, asset-backed paper, and a host of other investments was a major cause of the 2008 financial crisis.

Some elements of Confed's collapse turned out far better than initially feared. Sales by Canadian insurance companies of their products in the United States took a one-year dip but then returned to higher levels than before. Credibility was not an issue. The other surprise was that, in the years following the seizure, as real estate values returned to their previous heights, liquidators were able to sell assets and repay all creditors, even those bondholders in Europe who stood so far down the line of creditors that they believed they would never see their money.

Suggested Questions

1. Who was to blame for the debacle: management, directors, auditors, regulators, the industry, the government?
2. Which of the following alternatives would you have preferred:
   a) other large life insurance companies step in and conduct a rescue operation;
   b) permit the company to fail and have the debtors, creditors, and policyholders suffer the consequences;
   c) the government of Canada seize the company?

Suggested Readings

Dey, Peter. 'Where Were the Directors? Guidelines for Improved Corporate Governance in Canada.' Toronto Stock Exchange, December 1994. Insurance Executive Report, winter 1993/4.

McQueen, Rod. *Who Killed Confederation Life? The Inside Story*. Toronto: McClelland and Stewart 1996.

Mulcahy, Colleen. 'Confederation Life/Great-West Life Deal Breaks Down.' *National Underwriter*, 15 August 1994.

Rod McQueen Fonds. University of Western Ontario Archives.

NOTES

1 In those days, family ownership of large life insurance companies was commonplace. The Gooderham family, of Gooderham and Worts Distillery, owned the control block at Manufacturers Life. With the exception of a fourteen-year hiatus, George Gooderham and his two sons ran Manufacturers from its founding in 1887 until 1951.
2 Author interview.
3 Now Ernst and Young.
4 Although OSFI was created in the same year as the 'little bang' – legislation allowing financial institutions to own securities firms – there was no direct connection. The review leading to OSFI began in 1984.
5 Speech to the Canadian Club of Toronto, 22 Jan. 1990.
6 Burns affidavit, dated 5 Sept. 1995 and filed with the circuit court of Ingham County, Michigan.
7 Author interview.
8 Author interview.
9 In 1996 Rogers bought the former Confed head office for $33.5 million, about one-third of the construction cost of the building that had been officially opened four years earlier. Confed's art collection was thrown in for good measure.
10 Speech at the National Club, Toronto, 17 May 1994.
11 Senate hearings, 27 Sept. 1994.
12 Author interview.

CASE 12
RBC Yesterday, Today, and Tomorrow

KATHERINE MACKLEM, with guidance from JOE MARTIN

[This case study begins in December 2005, and the description of events at the 2006 annual general meeting of the Royal Bank of Canada (RBC) – discussed both at the opening of the study and in the Suggested Questions at the end – is fictional.]

In a few short months, Gordon Nixon, CEO and chair of RBC Financial Group, will be addressing the shareholders at the 2006 Annual General Meeting. Nixon's speech will be an opportunity to spell out to shareholders and other observers his strategy for the bank going forward. John Cleghorn, Nixon's predecessor, had negotiated a merger with Matthew Barrett, CEO and chair of BMO, only to see it shot down in 1998 by Paul Martin, the federal minister of finance. Nixon would like to see the merger debate resolved in favour of allowing banks to merge. If Canadian banks are going to compete globally, they will need to have size.

Internationally, the position of most of the Canadian banks has been slipping in regard to size by assets, and shareholders will be anticipating a plan of action from the CEO on moving ahead with a global vision. Within Canada, while RBC has held a fairly steady position, the global marketplace is increasingly competitive. Nixon has an interest in history and doesn't want to repeat the mistake of misjudging Ottawa's position on bank mergers and banking policy in general.

One of the significant, recurring factors in the history of Canada's banks is the interplay between the banks and the federal government, which has not always been a friend of the financial sector. On the other hand, at times Ottawa has been good to the industry, allowing banks to enter the brokerage business and then to own trust companies. The challenge now is to prepare a strategy for the future that will both reflect RBC's important stature inside the current business landscape in Canada and ensure that Ottawa is onside and the bank continues to thrive and grow.

Banking Sector in Canada

A spectacular force in the Canadian economy, the financial-services field is one of the largest, most influential industries in Canada. At the end of 2004, the assets of the six largest banks totalled $1.7 trillion. Of that pie, the portion belonging to RBC amounted to $429 billion or 25 per cent of the total. On these assets, the six banks made more than $13.3 billion in profit, making RBC one of the most profitable banks in the world.[1]

Four banks vie in terms of size with RBC. (See Table 1.) There is also National Bank, which is often included with the others, but, with assets of $82 billion (less than a quarter of RBC's), it is considerably smaller. There are a few even smaller banks, including Laurentian Bank of Canada and Canadian Western Bank, as well as credit unions, some of which are forces to contend with even though they are a fraction of the size of the major banks. Examples are the Caisses Desjardins, based in Quebec, and the Vancouver City Savings Credit Union, which has branches throughout British Columbia.

Part of the major Canadian banks' bulk was added during a period of rapid expansion in the late 1980s and early 1990s. In the late 1980s

Table 1
Total assets of Canadian banks
($ millions Canadian, 31 Oct. 2004)

Bank	Total Assets
RBC Financial Group	429,196
TD Financial Group	311,027
Scotiabank	279,212
CIBC	278,764
BMO Financial Group	265,194
National Bank of Canada	88,806
All Other Schedule I (domestic) Banks	30,362
Total Assets	1,682,561

Source: Schedule I Balance Sheet Items, Office of the Superintendent of Financial Institutions.

Canada experienced its own 'little bang'[2] when the 'four pillars' of commercial banking, investment banking, trust business, and life insurance were taken down. Canada's major commercial banks were quick to take advantage of these changes and experienced tremendous growth as they became large financial-service companies rather than simply commercial banks.

There are a surprising number of corporations that are not traditional banks but that nonetheless have a banking charter. Sears Canada is one; Canadian Tire is another. Some financial-services companies also have bank charters. Manulife Financial Group, the life insurance company that has become a global force under the leadership of the feisty Domenic D'Alessandro, has banking capabilities, and possibly major banking ambitions. And then there are the international banks.

In the 1980s Michael Wilson,[3] Canada's then finance minister, allowed American Express to set up shop in Canada – a move the Canadian banks, with the exception of RBC, fought vociferously. Amex was followed by other U.S. and global mega-institutions, some of which have challenged the different lines of business of Canada's banks. For instance, the credit-card operations of the Canadian banks have seen stiff competition from MBNA Canada, a subsidiary of MBNA Corporation, based in Wilmington, Delaware, which is the world's largest independent credit-card issuer. Other international competitors that had earlier carved out a presence in Canada include such institutions as Wells Fargo, Capital One Financial, Fidelity, ING, GE Capital, Hong Kong Bank (now HSBC), and Citibank.

The Canadian banking system, dominated by national banks with branches from one end of the country to the other, is dramatically different from the U.S. system. South of the border, there are thousands of small banks, many of which are one-branch only. Still, in the United States, as well as around the world, there has been massive consolidation in the banking business. In the space of a decade, through much of the 1990s, the number of financial institutions in the United States dropped from 14,000 to 9,000. As well, more than $1 trillion, or one-fifth, of banking and thrift assets was consolidated in the United States in the three years between 1994 and 1997, with each year's consolidation accelerating over the previous twelve months. In 1994 the value of mergers of financial institutions in the United States was US$15 billion; in 1997 it was US$95 billion.[4] Similar consolidation was going on in Japan, Switzerland, the Netherlands, and Germany.

In the first half of 1998, five merger proposals in the United States were double 1997's total: first off, NationsBank and BankAmerica struck a US$60-billion deal, followed quickly by Banc One and First Chicago, at US$30 billion; Norwest and Wells Fargo, at US$34 billion; and Sun Trust Banks and Crestar, at US$10 billion. The biggest deal ever, at that time, was the merger of Citigroup and Travelers Group in a marriage worth US$70 billion, bringing together one of the biggest banks and one of biggest insurance and brokerage companies. This deal contravened a U.S. law, passed in the Depression era, that kept separate banks, brokerages, and insurance companies. However, the merger momentum had so much force that U.S. lawmakers allowed the Citigroup-Travelers deal.

As mergers have occurred around the world, the international rankings of three of Canada's largest banks have slipped, with only two – Scotiabank and Toronto-Dominion Bank (TD) – maintaining or improving their ranking. RBC, which was the thirty-eighth-largest bank in the world in 1978, is now Number 50, measured by assets. (See Table 2.)[5]

RBC

Every year since 1999, the Royal Bank has made more money than it did the previous year, a record that none of the other major banks can claim. In addition, RBC has reported greater earnings than each of the other banks each year, going back to 1999, when its profit was $1.8 billion and TD Bank Financial Group made $3 billion.

Table 2
Ranking of Canadian banks by assets, 1978 and 2003

Bank	1978 Assets [$ US million]	World Ranking	2003 Assets [$ US million]	World Ranking
Royal Bank of Canada	33,517	38	300,894	50
Scotiabank	22,798	61	211,473	61
Canadian Imperial Bank of Commerce	31,551	44	206,114	62
Toronto-Dominion Bank	19,290	73	202,233	63
Bank of Montreal	26,264	55	190,106	66
All Banks	133,420	NA	1,110,820	NA

Source: The Banker, 1978–2003.

With 60,000 employees, the Royal Bank is a complex enterprise, offering personal and commercial banking, wealth-management services, insurance, corporate, and investment banking, and transaction-processing services on a global basis. On 1 November 2004, day one of the fiscal year, Royal restructured its business, realigning its five business segments into three (a fourth segment was created to hold operations and technology groups, corporate treasury, and other corporate functions). The bank's financial results, as reported in 2004, for the first time followed the new lines. The same structure remains in place today.

The first of the three segments is Canadian Personal and Business, which consists primarily of banking and investment businesses in Canada, as well as the bank's global insurance businesses. The financial products and services offered consist of deposit and investment accounts, debit and credit cards, mortgages and other loans, life and non-life insurance, and financial, investment, and transactional services. These businesses serve about eleven million individuals as well as small- and medium-sized business clients in Canada. Clients are dealt with through multiple channels, including the bank's branch network, business banking centres, financial planners, mobile sales representatives, automated banking machines, telephone and Internet channels, and independent insurance brokers.

The second segment is the U.S. and International Personal and Business Group, which consists of RBC's banking and retail brokerage businesses in the United States, banking in the Caribbean and Bahamas, and private banking internationally. In the United States, the Royal Bank offers investment, advisory, and asset-management services to individuals and clearing and execution services to small and mid-sized independent broker-dealers and institutions. Internationally, it offers private banking, trust and investment management, and investment advisory solutions to high-net-worth clients. Included in this segment are the following businesses: RBC Centura, RBC Mortgage, and Caribbean and Bahamas banking.

Also part of this second group is the wealth-management activities of RBC Dain Rauscher. Headquartered in Minneapolis and a wholly owned subsidiary of the Royal Bank, Dain Rauscher is a full-service securities firm serving individual investors and businesses across the United States.

Excluded from RBC Dain Rauscher is the fixed-income business, which is reported in the third business segment, Global Capital Markets, as part of its wholesale fixed-income business. Global Capital Markets provides financial products and services to corporations, governments, and institutional clients in North America and offers specialized products and services globally. Products include debt, equity, and investment banking, credit, money markets, foreign exchange, commodities, and alternative assets. Also offered are financial services including: advisory, origination, sales and distribution, structuring, analytics, research, trading and execution, custody and investment administration services, and correspondent banking. Global Capital Markets also undertakes proprietary investments and trading.

Before the restructuring, the bank's lines of business were banking, investments, insurance, capital markets, and global services – and the annual report for 2004 reported along these lines. Here's how each of the five divisions did in 2004, and how much each contributed to the bank's overall income:

- Banking earned $1.3 billion, or 44 per cent of the bank's total income.
- Investments earned $490 million, or 17 per cent of total income.
- Insurance earned $271 million, or 9 per cent of total income.
- Capital Markets earned $658 million, or 22 per cent of total income.
- Global Services earned $224 million, or 8 per cent of the total income.

The net income for the banking group was $1.3 billion – almost half of the bank's total $2.8 billion, or the segment that made the most profit by far. Still, net income from that segment was at 45 per cent of the total, down from the previous year's 51 per cent. The drop in the banking division's income was blamed on its U.S. operations, where a $183-million loss more than offset earnings growth in Canada.[6]

Taken as a whole, RBC is a highly sophisticated, world-class institution. The reach of its business, and that of its banking peers, is far broader than ever could have been imagined in the early decades of the twentieth century. As a measure of the Royal Bank of Canada's status as a powerhouse, it was the only Canadian company included in 2005 on the influential Forbes 100 list. Still, the sector has seen its influence diminish. It is arguable that the Royal Bank and the other existing large banks were even more powerful in Canada's early days than they are today. But even then, they didn't always get their way. Sometimes politics interfered.

The history of Canadian banking has been marked by one significant, ongoing factor: the relationship between the financial institutions and the government. Politics has always played a central role in banking, from the country's early days, when prominent politicians[7] sat on the boards of directors of the banks, to the present day, when government mandates a 10 per cent cap on ownership for any single entity. Over time, this relationship has had an impact on the strategy of the banking institutions, including the Royal. At other times, it has had an impact on the role the financial-services sector played in the Canadian economy.

In more modern times, the relationship between the government and financial services sector has been most prominently on display with respect to the opening up to banks of markets that are related to their core business. Banking, trust, investment banking, and insurance businesses had been kept separate and banks were prohibited from providing the other three services. But, one by one, with insurance still an exception to some degree, the walls between the pillars have come down.

Like many other government decisions, this was a political one. The driving force behind it was not an attempt to create optimum conditions for banks to grow, nor even to improve the Canadian economy. Instead, what was important to the politicians, and what drove the policy, was a need to balance national, political interests. This was pure political jockeying among regions of Canada and between levels of government – not an uncommon story in Canadian politics.

The principal rivals were the cities of Toronto and Montreal. By the mid-1980s, Toronto had long surpassed Montreal as the country's financial centre, but a rivalry still remained between the two cities. In an attempt to recoup some of its lost ground, Montreal lobbied to become a centre of offshore banking, where international banks could shelter from taxes. They called it 'New York North.' Ottawa allowed Montreal's plan to go through, but, in an attempt to balance the effect nationally, the federal politicians awarded the same advantages to Vancouver as well. Queen's Park, Ontario's provincial legislature, was not to be outdone. Ontario announced that banks would be allowed to hold a controlling stake in Ontario investment firms, an ambition both the banks and investment firms had been lobbying for. The plan, of course, would have given Ontario-based banks a clear advantage over their counterparts based in other provinces.

The move by Ontario left the federal government with little choice. Wanting to exert its power over the financial sector and desiring to maintain a level playing field across the provinces, Ottawa quickly stepped in and allowed all banks and other financial institutions to own a range of financial intermediary services.

But the biggest example in modern times of the interplay of politics and bank strategy is one that has not worked out in the banks' favour and that may not yet be over. In the late 1990s, two sets of mega-mergers among the largest banks in Canada were thwarted by the federal government, which refused to allow the mergers to go forward. The story of how the government turned down the banks' proposed mergers illustrates the intense relationship between banking strategy and public policy.

Failed Merger Attempts

Five days before Christmas, in 1997, John Cleghorn, then Royal Bank's chairman and CEO, walked alone from RBC's golden-glass tower up Bay St to First Canadian Place, the white-marbled headquarters of Bank of Montreal. He rode the elevator to the 68th floor, where Matthew Barrett,[8] BMO's chairman and CEO, was hosting a staff Christmas party. The two men disappeared for about twenty minutes and emerged with what was later called the eggnog agreement. They had privately agreed to work together to build a globally competitive, Canadian-based financial institution with a $400-billion merger of equals; but for now, that was still a secret. They would get down to business after the holidays.

As noted above, merger frenzy had gripped the financial-services business south of the border. Canadian bankers weren't immune – and they had already quietly discussed mergers among themselves. For instance, earlier that year Barrett had approached Al Flood, the chairman and CEO of CIBC, about the possibility of a merger. Flood had declined the offer because he felt that an RBC-CIBC merger would not be politically feasible.

Cleghorn and Barrett and their teams of lawyers, analysts, and consultants worked quickly. On 23 January 1998 the two CEOs announced their plan to merge, saying that the deal was a response to the sharply rising level of global competition in financial services. 'These international financial services giants threaten to marginalize much smaller Canadian banks in the international market, and gain a competitive advantage in Canada by applying their greater scale and investments in technology,' said Cleghorn.

The bankers promised that the new entity would invest more than $7 billion in developing state-of-the-art technology over the following five years. The new bank, which was never named, would rank in the top ten in North America and the top twenty-five worldwide. It was an exciting day to be a banker in Canada, especially one working with one of these two organizations.

Hours before their morning press conference, the BMO-Royal team gave a heads-up to Finance Minister Paul Martin. But, in the view of many, the bank leaders had misread the politician. When asked to comment, Martin appeared angry. In a press conference, he called the merger plan 'somewhat premature.' The banks' merger announcement, he said, had pre-empted an ongoing bank review that had been requested by Canadian bankers and that was already under way. Known as the MacKay task force after its chair, Harold MacKay,[9] its mandate was to report on the future of the financial-services industry. Martin said he feared the merger would derail the task force. Others thought the finance minister was put off because he had barely been forewarned about the deal. It was an ominous beginning for a process that took almost a year.

Still, Barrett and Cleghorn initially remained confident. 'Our attitude is, why wouldn't you want to approve the creation of an international financial player à la Alcan or the Bombardiers or the Nortels?' asked Barrett. 'Why wouldn't you want to have one of your banks in that league?'[10]

Not to be outdone, two of Canada's other large banks, Canadian Imperial Bank of Commerce and Toronto-Dominion Bank, tried to follow suit three months later. They announced that they too had a merger arrangement, a plan clearly triggered by the BMO-Royal deal. This new merger plan changed the landscape entirely for the first merger deal that had been announced. If both mergers went ahead, two super-banks would control 70 per cent of Canada's entire banking assets. The stakes were now even higher, and the onus on Paul Martin even greater. Still, many thought that Martin would allow the mergers. 'Any one who thinks Paul Martin is going to stand in the way of his banking buddies also believes in pink elephants,' said New Democratic Party house leader Nelson Riis. Yet Martin replied that the latest merger proposal was 'by no means a fait accompli.'

Among the Big Five, only Scotiabank was left out, without a marriage partner, and its CEO, Peter Godsoe, lobbied vociferously against the two mergers. His bank, he pointed out, had successfully penetrated markets in Central and South America without being a massive international player.

Through the summer months, public opinion grew steadily against the mergers. Canadians were suspicious of the bankers' underlying motives and unconvinced that international giants were a threat. They didn't like the multi-million-dollar pay packages for senior bankers.[11] The overriding sense was that the banks were already too big, too powerful, and too immune to the needs of average Canadians. Consumer groups, anti-poverty organizations, labour unions, economists, and provincial leaders lined up against the mergers. Some of the organizations opposed included the South Okanogan Labour Council, the Canadian Association of Retired Persons, the city of Yellowknife, and the Atlantic Canada Opportunities Agency. As opposition to the mergers mounted, the politicians in Ottawa listened, through their consultations, task forces, and committee hearings. At the same time, through the spring and summer months, Martin held his cards close to his chest. No one, and certainly not the bankers, knew what he would do.

Towards the end of September, the MacKay Report, at 258 pages, was released. It recommended scrapping the long-standing prohibition against mergers of major banks if the public interest was not jeopardized. 'There should be no absolute ban on mergers among large banks, insurance companies, or other financial institutions,' the report said. It called for strategies to enhance consumer protection and made suggestions for creating more competition, including the recommendation to allow life insurance and mutual fund companies, among others, to have access to the national system used by banks to process transactions. It also recommended allowing more activity from foreign-owned banks. MacKay told the federal government that Canada needed to adapt to the new world of commerce, and that this was urgent. 'No country is immune to change. The real issue is how well we manage it to our own benefit.' He repeated a comment from an unnamed software executive: the 'banks are road kill on the information highway.'[12] To reporters, MacKay suggested that the recommendations could be interpreted as neither a green nor a red light to the two proposed mergers. Rather, he said, they should be viewed as a 'flashing yellow light.'[13]

Next, in November 1998, came the much-anticipated report of a task force of Liberal MPs headed by Toronto MP Tony Ianno. By then, the debate had acquired the bitter tones of a high-stakes political fight. Ianno's group took the banks to task for their treatment of Canadians and said that they had failed utterly in making the case for mergers. The proposed mergers would result in large-scale job losses, reduce consumer choice, and concentrate too much political and economic power in the two new entities.

Coming from his own party, the Ianno Report made it very difficult for Martin – given his ambition to assume the Liberal Party's leadership – to support the merger plans. For bank executives, who months earlier had been confident of an approval, the Ianno Report was like the writing on the wall. Privately, they now began to say that their plans had little chance of success. Wrote Hugh Brown, a leading financial-institutions analyst: 'Essentially the Ianno Task Force appears to believe banks are social institutions or public utilities that should be used to subsidize perceived disadvantaged groups.'

One of the important reports still to come was from the Competition Bureau. However, even before it arrived, Martin met one-on-one with the chairmen of the merger partners, and signalled that he was unlikely to approve the deals.

On 14 December 1998, just days before the first anniversary of Cleghorn's eggnog agreement with Barrett, Martin announced that the mergers were a no-go and 'not in the best interests of Canadians.' He had three main points. First, the mergers were unacceptable because of the immensity of the institutions that would be created. Post-merger banks would be so big that, if one of them ran into financial trouble, the problem would be intractable. Secondly, the mergers would raise anti-trust issues and would lead to higher prices and lower levels of service. Thirdly, they would put the decision-making power on credit allocation in too few hands; in other words, the post-merger banks would be too powerful.

Scott Brison, then the Progressive Conservative finance critic and a merger supporter, accused Martin of making a 'politically expedient decision ... that obviously put politics ahead of public policy.' Quashing the merger plans made Canada look like a 'banana republic,' he said. Others thought that Prime Minister Jean Chrétien was behind the decision to quash the banks' merger ambitions. Early on in the debate, he had revealed his lukewarm sentiments about the merger proposals. 'It's very important that Canadian consumers have a choice between different financial institutions,' said Chrétien, who, from 1987 to 1990, had been a member of TD's board. 'If not, they will find themselves prisoners of one or two or three organizations.' It was known that Chrétien did not hold the banks in high esteem. Earlier, in his autobiography, *Straight from the Heart*, he had been blunt, calling the four financial

institutions 'a small clique of extremely powerful banks whose officers were more or less entrenched regardless of what they did or didn't
do.'[14]

Shortly after the bank mergers were halted, Cleghorn was asked
whether Canada was better off for having had the debate. Sure, he said,
'the debate is long overdue.' He added that, even though Martin had
blocked the mergers, discussions and policy-making decisions were
continuing. It would be reasonable, he continued, for the government
to bring in new legislation within a year or so. 'What would be frustrating is if we got into endless debate [and] nothing happened,' Cleghorn
said. 'We get into another election [and] it's all put off. Then you're
looking at ten years before really anything gets done.'[15]

Conclusion

Since the abortive merger plan of 1998, RBC has been casting about for
a clear strategy. The plan was in part a response to a changing global
marketplace for financial services, where banking institutions around
the world were merging and expanding exponentially. It was also a
response to the growing role of technology in the banking business –
and the growing cost of that part of its business. As a much larger
institution, a merged entity would have found considerable savings in
high-technology spending.

The failure of the merger illustrates the role government plays in
this all-important sector of the Canadian economy. What is in the best
interests of the banks is not necessarily in the best interests of politicians who are answerable to their constituencies. It could be argued
that most politicians are driven by what is in the best interests of their
own political careers and so are unlikely to support unpopular measures, such as bank mergers. And there is certainly no doubt that the
decision in 1998 to block the mergers was popular with the public. 'The
federal Department of Finance has ... surveyed Canadians on the bank
merger issue and found a majority opposed to bank mergers. Ipsos-
Reid surveyed 1,000 Canadians in August 2004 and found that 60% of
Canadians thought it would be in their best interest if Ottawa didn't
allow bank mergers. A majority (56%) doubted that bank mergers were
in the public interest generally.'[16]

For decades, the role of Canada's banks has been debated. Are they
in existence, like utilities, primarily to provide essential services to
the public? Or are they purely private-sector enterprises, with their

shareholders' best interests as their primary objective? This debate, which recurs on a regular basis, has never been resolved. This is in part because it is recognized that banks play both roles and this creates a tension that must be managed. Serving shareholders and the public interest requires negotiation and compromise between the banks and government bodies, as noted by Gordon Nixon in his 2003 testimony regarding bank mergers to the House of Commons Standing Committee on Finance. In advocating the need to allow mergers, Nixon suggested that the public-interest concerns could be addressed.

However, should Ottawa stand fast in opposition to mergers, two possible areas where RBC could set its expansion sights are: 1) the U.S. market; and 2) the domestic insurance business, by offering insurance advice and products through RBC's extensive branch network. Both options present significant challenges to RBC.

With a market dominated by mega-giant financial firms, the United States is costly to enter. According to Allan Taylor, RBC's chairman and CEO from 1986 to 1995, the risks of entry are high, akin to 'betting the farm.' Still, other banks have made inroads into the United States. Notable is Bank of Montreal, which bought Chicago-based Harris Bank in 1984 and quickly established it as its platform for state-side expansion. BMO has been subsequently criticized for not making much progress with that expansion. Also notable is the life insurance giant, Manulife, which was already aggressive in Asia. In 2004 Manulife's CEO, Dominic D'Alessandro, struck the largest ever cross-border deal, merging with John Hancock of Boston. This deal was arguably the most successful cross- border expansion by a Canadian financial-services firm.

Today, the insurance business is the one remaining pillar of the financial-services sector that is off-limits to banks – at least in terms of selling insurance products from a bank branch. Although banks are permitted to own insurance companies which sell their products to consumers, the insurance business must remain separate from the banking operation. Canada is the only developed country in the world that prohibits consumers and small business owners from buying insurance products, or even getting information about insurance, from their bank. Bankers complain that this is absurd. They point out that stores like Loblaw and Costco can provide this financial service, but banks (which are in the business of providing financial advice) cannot.

As well, similar restrictions on bank products do not apply to the insurance industry. For example, Manulife can sell mortgages and provide savings accounts to its clients. The network of insurance brokers that owns Alberta-based Bank of Western Canada can offer their clients a full range of financial products including insurance, investments, and banking. And credit unions in Quebec have been able to sell insurance since 1987.

Bankers argue that greater competition for insurance leads to better pricing and more availability. History shows, they say, that the size of a market actually increases when new competitors enter it. For example, when banks began selling mutual funds, access went up, fees went down, and the size of the market increased significantly. Bank entry into the mortgage market also led to greater availability of mortgages across the country as well as more competitive rates.[17]

But, for the time being, insurance at the bank branch level is not an option, and – given the recent history of friction between the banks and the federal government over mergers, and general public opposition to banks providing insurance[18] – perhaps this can of worms is not worth opening. Additionally, so far the federal government has signalled that it will not permit a merger between one of Canada's largest banks and one of the largest insurance companies. (The general policy is that big should not buy big.) Still, there's no doubt that a merger of RBC and Manulife, Canada's largest bank and largest insurance company respectively, would create a giant financial institution, not only nationally but also on a global scale. While this sort of merger may not be an option, it might be worthwhile for RBC to consider the possibility of acquiring a smaller insurance company or of being more active on the international scene.

Sequel

Since Paul Martin closed the book on the two mega-mergers, Royal Bank has reported ever-increasing returns. In 2001 TD Bank aimed at a target a little smaller than CIBC and took over Canada Trust, in a $7-billion deal that received federal blessing. Then, last spring, TD completed another merger, acquiring 51 per cent of Banknorth, a smallish bank (assets of $28.7 billion) based in Portland, Maine. Also, the Manulife takeover of John Hancock of Boston occurred. Other rumoured marriages between major Canadian financial institutions never saw the light of day – they were quashed by Ottawa before they were even announced. If rumours are correct, there was a deal in 2002 that would have put Scotiabank (with an apparent change of heart at the top) together with Bank of Montreal in a new merger.

Suggested Questions

At the 2006 annual general meeting of the Royal Bank, the chief executive officer presents a number of options to the shareholders. They are:

1. Stick to their knitting, i.e., stay focused on their core business and in particular on retail banking.
2. Expand into the United States – a strategy that RBC has pursued over recent years, with limited success (note: U.S. banking operations in 2004 carried a significant loss).
3. Expand elsewhere – à la Scotiabank.
4. Merge with another bank or another financial institution.
5. Merge with a non-Canadian financial institution.

Recommend one of the options for adoption and presentation to the annual general meeting, and give your reasons.

Suggested Readings

Canadian Bankers Association (CBA), http://www.cba.ca/en.
Martin, Joe. 'Going International.' *Business Quarterly*, 57, no. 4 (1993).
Whittington, Les. *The Banks: The Ongoing Battle for Control of Canada's Richest Business*. Toronto: Stoddart Publishing 1999.

NOTES

1 CBA, http://www.cba.ca/en/resource.asp, Bank Financial Results.
2 As distinct from the 'big bang' in London, U.K. which resulted in deregulation of financial services in 1986.
3 Michael Wilson later became CEO of UBS Canada, a subsidiary of the Zurich-headquartered global giant. In 2005 he was Canada's ambassador to the United States.
4 Whittington, *The Banks*, 69.
5 Note that the value of the Canadian dollar has fallen during this period.
6 For more RBC financial data, see RBC Quick Facts, http://www.rbc.com/investorrelations/index.html. Also, see Gord Nixon, 'Enhancing our Leading Position,' presentation to the NBF Financial Services Conference, 30 March 2005, http://www.rbc.com/investorrelations/invpres.html. Both websites accessed April 2005.

7 For example, R.B. Bennett sat on the Board of the Royal Bank before becoming prime minister in 1930.
8 Matthew Barrett was named chairman of Barclays Bank in 2004 and is based in London. He left BMO in 1999 to become Barclays' president.
9 Harold MacKay is a highly respected corporate lawyer based in Regina, Saskatchewan. A frequent consultant to government on public-policy issues, he was seconded to Ottawa to head the task force. MacKay has since been made an officer of the Order of Canada.
10 Whittington, *The Banks*, 147.
11 Ibid., 101.
12 Ibid., 41.
13 Ibid., 202.
14 Jean Chrétien, *Straight from the Heart*, rev. ed. (Toronto: Key Porter Books 1994), 93.
15 Whittingdon, *The Banks*, 236.
16 Suzan Lott, *Bank Mergers and the Public Interest* (Ottawa: Public Interest Advocacy Centre [PIAC] 2005), 10; see also Sandra Cordon, 'Bank Mergers Still Unpopular with Consumers,' Toronto *Star*, 26 Dec. 2004, H7.
17 When banks acquired the power to take chattel mortgages on automobiles, the rate of interest on new cars went down from about 20 per cent to 11 per cent.
18 'Canadians' Views of Banks and Life and Health Insurance,' Report prepared for Advocis by Pollara Inc., April 2005.

CASE 13
Canada: The Next Oil Superpower?

STEWART MELANSON and JOE MARTIN

[This case study ends in 2006. Murray Edwards was not interviewed; his musings come from the minds of the authors, not from his.]

Report on Business reporter Gordon Pitts has described Murray Edwards as 'the man who is surely the most important figure in the modern Alberta economy. What [former premier Peter] Lougheed was to the 1970s, Edwards is to the 2000s – the man who makes Alberta work.'[1] Edwards is the legendary 'butterfly of the oil patch' and a major activist shareholder in Canadian Natural Resources Limited (CNRL).

As 2006 draws to a conclusion, Edwards is pondering what to do. While no longer in an executive position at CNRL, Edwards is still vice-chairman of the board and an influential figure in corporate affairs. CNRL is not his only enterprise, but it is certainly one of his most successful. By 2006, the company is well on its way to becoming a $11-billion-plus corporation, one of Canada's largest non-financial enterprises, with operations in Canada and the United States as well as the North Sea and offshore West Africa. CNRL is also one of the major players in the Athabasca oil sands, its Horizon project drawing workers from St John's, Newfoundland, to Shanghai, China. But 2006 is presenting opportunities as well as new challenges, with the run-up of oil prices and increasing logistical bottlenecks in the development of the oil sands. The average selling price for gas has declined and resulted in the company shifting natural gas spending to heavy crude oil drilling. On the other hand, oil prices are continuing to rise, increasing from $10 per barrel in 1998 to the mid-$60s in 2006. However, since CNRL makes significant sales in the United States, the increasing strength of the Canadian dollar is becoming problematic.

There are two other issues that have to be addressed. While CNRL is among the largest non-financial corporations in Canada, like a number of other Alberta-based energy companies, it is a widely held company with just over one-half of the shares in foreign hands. What would Edwards do if someone made a hostile takeover bid, or if a sovereign wealth fund attempted to acquire the company? In the latter case, what would the government of Canada do? While Investment Canada was not as hostile to Foreign Direct Investment as the Trudeau-era Foreign Investment Review Agency, the government would be required take a position if a foreign purchaser was involved.[2]

As he ponders these questions, Edwards thinks of the many changes in the energy sector and in CNRL in particular since 1989.[3] He also thinks of the increased concerns for security since the 9/11 attacks on the World Trade Center and the beginning of the Iraq War, of the shift of oil company head offices within Canada from Toronto to Calgary, of the growth of Canadian independents helped by rising oil prices, and of the growing number of indications that the Chinese are interested in the oil sands.

From Net Importer to a 'World Energy Superpower'

By 2006, Canada was poised to become a major global energy player, with the Athabasca oil sands the crown jewel. At the 2005 annual meeting of Imperial Oil, Canada's oldest and largest energy company, Tim Hearn, chairman, president, and CEO, stated: 'We continue to believe that oil-sands of western Canada provide major opportunities for long term growth. The oil-sands are one of the world's largest deposits of crude oil. They will be needed to help meet rising demand, and they are the foundation on which Canada's future as an oil-producing country will be built.'[4]

The intensifying activities in developing the Athabasca oil sands coincided with a run-up in prices of crude oil as supply and demand became tight, with one of the lowest spare oil-production-capacity cushions in history.[5] Further, estimates of natural gas reserves in North America proved to be optimistic and natural gas production started to decline. Recent global developments relating to world supply of oil and gas in the face of mounting demand, particularly from rapidly industrializing China and India, plus unstable markets among some of the producing nations (not to mention hurricanes in the Gulf of Mexico), had led to interesting and sobering remarks from some of the oil majors:

Energy will be one of the defining issues of this century. One thing is clear: the era of easy oil is over. What we all do next will determine how well we meet the energy needs of the entire world in this century and beyond.[6]

The challenges of supplying the expanding energy needs on which rising living standards for billions of people depend – while still preserving our environment – are increasingly apparent. I believe they are among the greatest challenges ever faced by mankind.[7]

Canada's importance as a major reliable source for oil and gas has not always been recognized. The International Energy Agency (IEA) recognized the oil sands only in recent years and British Petroleum was even more reluctant to acknowledge them in its widely cited Statistical Review of global reserves of oil and gas. Part of the reason is that the oil sands are not conventional reserves, being very difficult and expensive to extract and refine. Only recently has the price of oil risen sufficiently to make oil-sands production economical.[8] Yet, though recognition of the oil sands' potential has been slow in coming, they are now credited with making Canada the runner-up only to Saudi Arabia in what is termed 'pinpointed and producible' reserves.[9]

Canada's current status has been evolving over the past six decades. In 1947 Imperial Oil's discovery of the Leduc No. 1 oil well in Alberta resulted in Canada quickly moving from being energy-starved, supplying less than 10 per cent of domestic needs, to becoming an important energy player and a net exporter of oil and gas. Twenty years after the Leduc discovery, Suncor, then known as Great Canadian Oil Sands, began commercial development of the Alberta oil sands. It would be more than a decade before Syncrude, a consortium, also began operation in the oil sands.

Development was brought to a virtual halt when the government of Pierre Elliott Trudeau introduced what was called the National Energy Program in 1980. The NEP, which purported to seek energy independence but appeared to investors to be confiscatory, resulted in a massive withdrawal of foreign direct investment and the province of Alberta's GDP growth rate dropped precipitously in one year from 8 per cent positive to 16 per cent negative.[10]

The Free-Trade Agreements

The National Energy Program was dismantled when a new government was elected in 1984, which, to the surprise of many, decided to negotiate a highly controversial Free Trade Agreement between Canada and the United States. While the debate about the FTA was often hyperbolic, there was little discussion about the energy sector, which seemed to skate under the radar of public scrutiny both before and after the signing of the agreement (in sharp contrast to softwood lumber).[11]

But, for Canadian energy producers, free trade in energy was an important objective. Lorne Larson, president and CEO of ProGas, a producer-owned Alberta natural gas marketing organization, concluded his remarks to the American Bar Association Annual General Meeting in August 1988 with these comments: 'Under the Free Trade Agreement, with respect to energy, the United States has agreed to become a reliable buyer without the threat of protectionist-driven tariffs or taxes and Canada has agreed to remain a reliable seller without discriminatory price or supply interference. If you believe secure energy is important to America, then let me urge you to support the Free Trade Agreement and so advise your congressman or senator.'[12]

That, in a nutshell, was what the energy section of the FTA spelled out in detail: a guaranteed customer for Canada and a guaranteed supply for the United States. The FTA committed the United States and Canada to letting market forces dictate the price of energy and the development of energy reserves. It also set North America on the path to energy deregulation and increasing integration of continental energy markets. In addition to achieving integration and deregulation, the controversial 'proportional access clause' (Article 904[a]) stipulated that Canada would maintain exports to the United States in the same proportion of supply even if it meant shortages in Canada (see Appendix C).

Five years after the signing of the FTA, Canada and the United States entered into a North American Free Trade Agreement with Mexico. Many of the energy provisions under the FTA remained intact under NAFTA. But, while the energy provisions of NAFTA were intended as a North American continental integration of energy resources, Mexico, unlike Canada, insisted on opting out of proportional-access provisions. The Mexican government viewed such provisions as an unacceptable intrusion into its sovereignty over its energy resources. Mexico also insisted on maintaining control over its national oil company PEMEX while Canada moved in the opposite direction by privatizing its crown corporation, Petro-Canada.

In the years after the signing of the agreement, Canada's exports to the United States boomed, more than tripling, with the United States buying 84 per cent of all of Canada's exports. The sale of oil and gas was a big part of the increase as oil and gas extraction exports jumped nearly sixfold to $66 billion in 2005. This represented nearly 20 per cent of all of Canada's sales to the United States, with much of the increase due to the increasing value of the product as distinct from an increase in volume. Canada, along with Saudi Arabia and Mexico, became a major source of American-imported oil and a supplier of nearly 90 per cent of U.S. imported gas (see Appendix A).

The FTA and NAFTA, supplemented by the Security and Prosperity Partnership (SSP) signed by Prime Minister Paul Martin at the trilateral summit held at Waco, Texas, in March 2005, deepened Canada's trade relations with the United States and increased economic integration between the two nations and with Mexico as well. The growing economic integration between the United States and Canada especially applies to the energy sector where Canada has become a major supplier to the United States of oil, gas, and electricity. The FTA and NAFTA have to be seen in this light. These agreements did more than foster Canadian oil, gas, and electricity exports; they created a common regional market for energy that was highly interdependent, allowing for energy to move freely across national boundaries in either direction as each participating country's needs warranted.[13]

As Canada and the United States continue to deepen their economic integration on a continental scale with the aim of continental energy self-sufficiency,[14] important questions arise about the future of Canada's energy sector within the context of continentalism. Although Canada is a net exporter of oil, the pipeline system is mostly oriented north-south to supply U.S. markets. Eastern Canada must import oil to meet domestic needs, and consequently, in the absence of a strategic petroleum reserve, it is vulnerable to disruption of imports.

'Days of Future Passed'[15]

Peter Foster writes in *Blue Eyed Sheiks*:

> Oil. The single most important factor shaping our lives today. Without it our cars and machines, our economy – our whole way of life – will grind to a halt. The entire industrialized world is threatened by shortages and embargoes and in the midst of this crisis, Canada finds itself in a paradoxical position – with enormous petroleum potential but inevitably vulnera-

ble to the disruptions of the world oil market ... There has been a dramatic shift in economic and political power from Ottawa and the industrialized provinces of the East to Alberta, the major oil and gas producing province; a shift which has the profoundest implications for Confederation ... Not since the great days of transcontinental railway building has this country known such economic excitement, and here, revealed with authority, is the fascinating and mind-boggling story of the realities of oil, money and power in Canada today.[16]

Anyone reading this could easily assume that it describes the situation in the oil and gas industry in the first decade of the twenty-first century. Most would be surprised to learn that it was written in 1979 – almost thirty years earlier – at the height of the energy crisis of the 1970s and only a few years before the crash in oil prices of the 1980s that impoverished many oil towns from Calgary to Houston. At the time, dire predictions about our energy future were common.

By 2006, such predictions were being heard again, with many voices gloomily forecasting an impending energy crisis and an irreversible decline in oil supply in the years to come. Oil supply was then struggling to meet growing global demand, and so the price of oil and gas was not only increasing but was also highly volatile. High prices enabled the oil majors to reap record profits in a time of painful prices at the gas pump – much to the shock of an outraged public. However, the intense media focus on the enormous profits of the oil and gas sector revealed a telling lapse of memory. The oil and gas industry is cyclical, with times of famine and times of plenty. History has shown that, whenever oil prices have risen, the plentiful times have been followed by a drop – or even a crash – in prices. As recently as 1998, oil declined to U.S.$10 a barrel (in 1980 oil was over U.S.$90 in 2007 – see Exhibit 1), a price that would render the Canadian oil sands uneconomical to develop.

Since 2002, oil prices have been moving in the direction of the all-time historical high set in 1980, and prices in 2006, even adjusted for inflation, were higher than the historical average world price. The question in 2006 was whether it was different this time, or would oil prices crash again? Or would they continue to climb, possibly even destabilizing the highly energy-dependent global economy? These were and are important questions, and not just to managers in the energy sector. Energy issues affect, and are important to, everyone in both the United States and Canada.

Exhibit 1
Crude oil prices, U.S. $ per barrel, 1980–2006

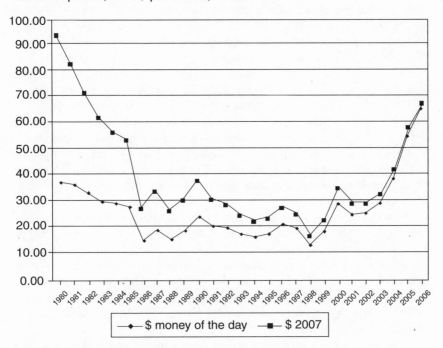

The Athabasca Oil Sands

The Athabasca oil sands, named after the river that flows through the vast deposits located northeast of Edmonton, were originally called the tar sands even though they contain no tar. Eighteenth-century fur traders such as Peter Pond and Alexander Mackenzie recorded their impressions of the deposits. Pond was the first European to see the sands and Mackenzie was the first to record his impressions in writing, referring to them as 'bituminous fountains.'[17]

By 2006, the rising price of oil had contributed to a growing sense of optimism about investments in the Athabasca oil sands. Yet the first commercial development did not begin until 1967, when Great Canadian Oil Sands began the extraction of the oil from the bitumen which, after processing, results in synthetic crude oil (SCO). Great Canadian was alone in the area until after the oil shocks of the 1970s when a consortium of companies, Syncrude, began operation. The consortium included more than a half-dozen companies including Imperial Oil and Petro Canada.

The next major investor was Dutch-owned Shell with its Muskeg River development. The fourth and largest was the Horizon Oil Sands Project – valued at $11 billion and backed by Calgary-based Canadian Natural Resources, one of the country's largest gas producers. In 2006 the Horizon Project was forecast to produce 110 thousand barrels of oil equivalent per day (mboe/d) by mid-2008 and 500 mboe/d by 2020.

The oil sands are viewed as the next greatest untapped reserves in oil which, if added to conventional reserves of oil, place Canada second after Saudi Arabia in total oil reserves. This is particularly important in light of a concern that sources of conventional oil will not keep up with demand, which is growing by about 2 per cent per year.[18] It also means that Canada has become an important player on the world energy stage – an 'energy superpower.'

With improving technology and higher oil prices, oil sands production is not only profitable, it represents, with an estimated 170 billion barrels of recoverable oil (by itself enough to supply all U.S. oil needs for twenty years at current consumption), one of the few large existing reserves in the world. However, development of the oil sands would have to be intensified if production is to make even a dent in the energy needs of the big players such as the United States and Japan, not to mention the future demand of China and India.[19] This involves important issues such as huge investments of capital and technology. For example, in the twenty-first century, annual capital spending on the oil sands increased from over $4 billion in 2000 to over $10 billion in 2005. By 2006, there were fifty projects representing over $90 billion.[20]

Environmental concerns are an issue as well.[21] As the popularity of oil sands grows in Canada, so do concerns over environmental damage from mining and processing the material. Enormous amounts of natural gas and water are used to extract and upgrade the crude, greenhouse gas emissions are high, and, in mining operations, environmentalists worry that the land – which companies are required to restore – may never quite bounce back. The process also transforms vast amounts of water into a mixture too toxic to return to bodies of water, forcing companies to create large lake-like impoundments. Dan Woynillowicz of the Calgary-based Pembina Institute, says: 'We're dealing with a form of oil extraction where the intensity of environmental impacts is at an order of magnitude greater than any other form of oil extraction we have seen on the planet.'[22]

The Canadian Energy Sector

By 2006, rising oil prices and the oil sands had not only transformed the energy sector in Canada, they had significantly altered the relationship between the provinces of Alberta and Ontario and the cities of Calgary and Toronto. It wasn't that long ago when there were four major oil companies in Canada – Imperial Oil; Gulf Canada, formerly British American Oil; Shell Oil of Canada; and Texaco Canada, formerly McColl Frontenac. All four were subsidiaries of foreign firms with their Canadian head offices in Toronto.

This had changed by 2006. There were then seven major energy companies ranked among Canada's largest non-financial corporations, where there had been four before. Only two of the seven – Imperial and Shell – were Canadian subsidiaries and all seven were based in Calgary, with Imperial, the largest, having recently moved its head office to be closer to the upstream activity. The five major Canadian independents included Petro Canada and Husky Energy, both integrated producers, as well as Encana, Suncor, and Canadian Natural Resources. The latter three companies were in the business of exploration for and production of natural gas, but they all had additional businesses.

Encana, created in 2002 with the merger of Alberta Energy Company, originally a 50/50 Alberta government/public company, and Pan Canadian Petroleum,[23] is a large producer of crude oil as well as natural gas. Suncor Energy is best known as the original investor in the oil sands, which is still its core business, but it is also an integrated oil and gas company with natural gas operations, energy marketing and refining in eastern Canada, and both refining and marketing in the United States. CNRL, the smallest of the group, entered into oil and gas through acquisitions in 1999. In 2006 its main focus was on exploration and production. The main areas of exploration were various North American locations, the North Sea, and West Africa. CNRL also has pipeline operations and is the key backer of the huge Horizon Oil Sands project.

Canadian Natural Resources Limited

This company's roots go back beyond 1989 to the early 1970s when AEX Minerals Corporation was listed on the Vancouver Stock Exchange. In 1975 the company's name was changed to Canadian Natural Resources. In the late 1970s the company was primarily involved 'in the exploration and development of oil, gas, and mineral prospects in Canada and the United States.'[24] When it ceased operating in the mid-1980s because of an inability to meet financing obligations, the company was continued under an Alberta statute. It continued to lose money and as recently as 1989 the stock could have been bought for less than twenty-five cents.

That year, the bankrupt company was acquired by a group of investors which included Murray Edwards and friends. Before embarking on an aggressive expansion program, CNRL sold U.S. assets as 'part of the company's planned disposition of minor, higher-cost properties' as well as discontinuing operations in Abu Dhabi.[25] Starting in 1989, when the company was acquired, it began to grow at an exponential rate. By the mid-1990s it posted assets in excess of $2 billion and operating revenue of well over $500 million. In 2000 CNRL reported assets close to $8 billion and operating revenue of over $2.7 billion. By 2006, assets had swelled to over $33 billion and revenue to over $11 billion.

Edwards describes himself as a consolidator who made strategic acquisitions: 'Scepter Resources in 1996, Ranger Oil in 2001, Rio Alto in 2002, the private acquisition of BP Amoco's Canadian oil assets in 1999 and Andarko Petroleum's Canadian assets in 2006.'[26] Originally, CNRL focused on exploration and development, and then production, of oil and natural gas in the Western Canadian Sedimentary Basin (WCB). By 2006, the company had operations in the North Sea and offshore West Africa, as well as in western Canada. And it was heavily invested in the oil sands, with its huge Horizon project employing a workforce of 10,000 people flown to and from the site from all over Canada.[27]

Implications of Oil Sands Development

'Second only to the Saudi Arabia reserves,[28] Alberta's oil sands deposits were described by *Time* magazine as "Canada's greatest buried energy treasure," and "could satisfy the world's demand for petroleum for the next century."'[29] This is a misconception. Despite the huge reserves locked up in the oil sands, logistical and other constraints will limit production. Logistics, technology, and environmental constraints limit the upper bounds of production capability. Even if the deposits were infinite, five million barrels per day (mmbd) by 2030 represents the likely upper bound of oil sands productive capability by 2030. While five mmbd is an impressive figure, this represents an increase of only four mmbd from the current production of approximately one mmbd and this to be achieved over a twenty-five year period. World oil demand is predicted to increase between 1 and 2 per cent per year into the foreseeable future. Hence, the increase in demand for oil alone will outstrip the production coming from the oil sands. Even if demand for oil does not increase, an average annual rate of decline in production of 4 per cent to 6 per cent occurs for mature producing fields.[30] Thus, it requires about four mmbd in new production every year just to keep supply the same. This is the 'Red Queen'[31] of oil supply.

The oil sands represent a significant reserve of oil for decades to come, but they are not by themselves a solution. The easiest oil to extract has largely been exploited and the remaining oil reserves are more expensive to exploit: 'John Hofmeister, president of Shell Oil Co., the U.S. subsidiary of Royal Dutch/Shell Group, said in Washington yesterday that the oil sands would be a "great boost" to the company and a "great supply source for the United States." Although many analysts have said that oil sands projects are only profitable if oil prices are more than $30 to $35 a barrel, relatively high by industry standards, Hofmeister said that "the easy oil is running out."'[32] The reason for this is that there are problems with managing and maintaining high output from an aging field as well as finding oil deposits in increasingly less hospitable environments, such as deep Arctic water.[33] Further, although high prices are good for the oil sands prospects, shortages of both labour and material are driving up costs. This means that oil prices may need to be even higher to justify the huge capital-intensive oil sands projects with their long lead times to production. However, high oil prices could cause a global recession and a collapse in oil prices.

Other Policy Issues with the Sands

The United States seeks raw bitumen to upgrade locally, and in Canada there is a debate over whether it is better to export bitumen or to upgrade it at home in order to capture a greater share of the energy value chain. This is a debate that is almost as old as Canada itself, dating back to the cries in nineteenth century to create a 'manufacturing condition' rather than simply selling the raw products from the forests and mines of Ontario. As one observer writes:

Canada seems utterly content to act as a storehouse of resources for the U.S. market. We pump (or dig) it out of the ground and export it as fast as we can, end of story. Exports alone utterly define the value proposition

... Canada could instead move up the value chain, and become a world-class upgrading and refining centre. It could create an entire industrial economy around the oil sands. Yet all the big recent business decisions are pushing the country in the opposite direction. EnCana recently signed an $11 billion pact with ConocoPhillips to expand EnCana's oil sands production, and send the bitumen to Conoco's refineries in Illinois and Texas, where it will be turned into gasoline. This is the equivalent of sending raw logs to the United States to be turned into finished products like flooring and furniture ...

Many MPs and Alberta MPPs were upset by EnCana's decision to ship unprocessed oil to U.S. refineries. But both levels of government are guilty of shortsightedness. The Alberta government created a traffic jam in the Athabasca oil sands. It licensed dozens of projects, than compounded the error by dropping royalty rates on new projects to practically nothing until after capital costs are recovered. The result was outrageous cost escalation, with some of the bigger developments running billions of dollars over their original budget estimates. There is no money left for refineries, and no spare workers to build them even if someone wanted to.

The fed's sin is the failure to promote an industrial policy that would move the Alberta oil industry up the value chain. Instead, Ottawa has provided the industry with billions of dollars in tax breaks, such as the accelerated capital cost allowance, to expand production at a reckless rate. Upgrading Alberta's bitumen is becoming the right and privilege of U.S. energy companies.[34]

Conclusion

All of these considerations are running through Murray Edwards's mind at the end of 2006. A competitive person, the owner/spokesperson for the Calgary Flames, he likes his hockey team to win. And he likes to win too. But Edwards, who is approaching fifty, is also beginning to look at lifestyle alternatives. His preferred organizational structure – flat with minimum levels of management – is putting more demands on his time than anticipated. Should he be prepared to let CNRL go in the event of a hostile takeover bid? And if he did let go, what would be the implications – particularly if the takeover bid came from China? (See Appendix B for more information on China.)

Suggested Questions

1. What should Murray Edwards do, if anything, to protect CNRL

from a hostile takeover bid, either from North American private investors or from a Chinese sovereign wealth fund?

2. If Edwards agrees to sell to foreign investors, what should the government of Canada do about it?

3. From an historical perspective, do you think oil prices in the future will be sufficient to justify continued investment in the oil sands and Canada's claim to oil superpower status?

Suggested Readings

Chastko, Paul. *Developing Alberta's Oil Sands: From Karl Clark to Kyoto.* Calgary: University of Calgary Press 2004

Duckert, Joseph M. 'North American Energy, 2000–2007: What a Difference Those Years Make!' *American Review of Canadian Studies,* 25, no. 6 (2007).

Hart, Michael. *A Trading Nation: Canadian Trade Policy from Colonialism to Globalization.* Vancouver: UBC Press 2002. Chapter 16 ('From a Trading Nation to a Nation of Traders').

Pitts, Gordon. *Stampede! The Rise of the West and Canada's New Power Elite.* Toronto: Key Porter Books 2008. Chapter 16 ('Hollow Men: The Gathering Storm over Foreign Investment').

Simmons, Matthew R. *Twilight in the Desert: The Coming Saudi Oil Shock and the World Economy.* Hoboken, N.J.: John Wiley and Sons 2005.

Appendix A: Continental Energy Markets, 2003[35]

Part I: Oil

- In 2003 Alberta exported more than 1 million barrels per day (bbl/d) of crude oil to the United States, supplying 11 per cent of U.S. crude oil imports, or 5 per cent of U.S. oil demand.
- The province's proven reserves of 176 billion barrels are second only to Saudi Arabia.
- Saudi Arabia, Mexico, Canada, and Venezuela supply the majority of U.S. crude oil imports, about 62 per cent combined.

In 2003 Alberta produced more than 1.6 million bbl/d of crude and equivalent, or about 66 per cent of Canada's 2.5-million bbl/d crude and equivalent production. Alberta then led the world in oil sands development, enabling Canada to increase oil production and exports. About CDN$30 billion was invested in the oil sands between 1994 and

Chart 1
U.S. Crude Oil Imports by Country of Origin, 2003
Total = 9,665,000 bbl/d

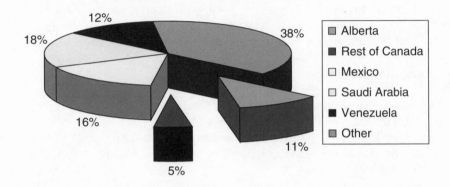

2003, and approximately $80 billion of further investments in oil sands projects were announced by industry for the period 2004–20. Alberta's oil sands' average daily production had already more than doubled from 398 thousand bbl/d in 1994 to 853 thousand bbl/d in 2003. The province's vision is to become a world-scale hub for oil and refined products, with production of marketable oil sands reaching 1.9 million barrels per day in 2010 and growing to 3 million barrels per day by 2020. Alberta and the U.S. market will require more refining capacity to absorb this increase in Alberta's heavy crude production.

U.S. Energy Import Ranking, 2003

Alberta is Canada's energy leader for oil and gas investment, production, and exports, supplying about 70 per cent of Canadian crude oil and gas exports to the United States. Canada was the third-largest supplier of crude oil to the United States in 2003, with exports of about 1.55 million bbl/d. Canada is the top U.S. supplier when refined petroleum products are included in exports. In 2003 Alberta delivered about 1.04 million bbl/d of its crude oil and petroleum products to the United States. The largest American market for Alberta oil is PADD (Petroleum Administration for Defense Districts) II, which includes the Chicago hub.

Part II: Natural Gas

• In 2003 Alberta exported more than 2.6 trillion cubic feet (Tcf) to the

Chart 2
U.S. natural gas imports by place of origin, 2003

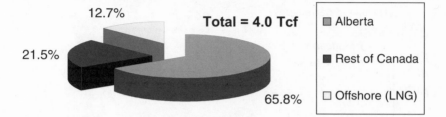

12.7%

21.5%

Total = 4.0 Tcf

☐ Alberta

■ Rest of Canada

☐ Offshore (LNG)

65.8%

United States, supplying 66 per cent of U.S. natural gas imports and meeting about 12 per cent of U.S. demand.
- The Alberta Gas Hub is key to delivering the potential of Arctic gas.
- U.S. imports of natural gas from Alberta would, if converted to electricity, light up over 25 million U.S. households.

Canada delivers 100 per cent of its natural gas exports to the United States and is that country's largest supplier of natural gas. In 2003 Canada supplied about 3.5 Tcf, or about 87 per cent of the natural gas imported into the United States. Alberta directly supplied over 2.6 Tcf of gas to the United States, equal to 66 per cent of total U.S. gas imports and about 12 per cent of U.S. demand. Improved interconnections to and within the United States have allowed more gas to be exported to growing U.S. markets. PADD II in the Midwest is the largest recipient of Alberta natural gas in the United States. Current supply projections show Canadian production holding steady through 2010, while new supplies (northern gas, offshore, natural gas in coal) are being developed.

Appendix B: China and Energy Issues

Oil demand is exploding in China. In 2006, for the third summer in a row, China rationed energy, limiting production in industrial areas. By then, China had changed from being a net exporter of oil into the world's second-largest importer. (See Exhibit 2.)

The Central Committee of the Communist Party is concerned about the future capabilities of China's domestic oil production,[36] which supplies about one-half of its crude oil needs. Chinese experts estimate that they will need eleven million barrels of oil per day by 2020, more than triple the expected Chinese domestic output; the rest will have to be imported.

Exhibit 2
Chinese oil production and consumption, 1986–2006

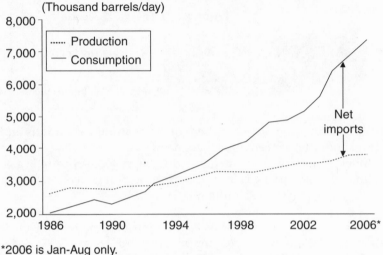

*2006 is Jan-Aug only.
Source: EIA International Petroleum Monthly.

China is making great efforts to achieve its national goal of energy security. However, for Chinese officials, the geopolitical situation has changed significantly in recent years, and not in China's favour. To meet China's growing thirst for imported oil, Beijing has long focused on the Middle East, which holds roughly two-thirds of the world's oil. According to Pan Rui, an international relations expert at Fudan University in Shanghai: 'The Middle East is China's largest source of oil. America is now pursuing a grand strategy, the pursuit of American hegemony in the Middle East. Saudi Arabia is the number one oil producer, and Iraq is number two [in terms of reserves]. Now, the United States has direct influence in both countries.'[37]

Since 2003, American military intervention in Iraq has added urgency to China's goal of lessening dependence on Middle Eastern supplies. 'Many people argue that oil interests are the driving force behind the Iraq war,' Zhu Feng, a security expert at Beijing University, has reported. 'For China, it has been a reminder and a warning about how geopolitical changes can affect our energy interests. So China has decided to focus much more intently to address its energy security.'[38]

The 11th Five-Year Development Guidelines presented to the National People's Congress in March 2006 confirmed the need for secure energy supplies.[39] If China fails to secure adequate supplies of oil to meet increasing demand, economic growth will be harmed, with implications for domestic stability and the global economy. Further, the United States should take into account the importance of China's economic development since China finances U.S. debt though its trade surpluses.

The biggest emphasis has been on securing new stocks abroad, particularly in neighbouring countries such as Kazakhstan and Russia, to limit dependence on shipping lanes subject to U.S. naval interdict capability. The Five-Year Plan calls for several pipelines that could carry energy from fields in Russia, Central Asia, and Burma, thereby avoiding shipping lanes. Further, China plans to develop, modelled on the U.S. Strategic Petroleum Reserve (SPR), a reserve of its own located in Zhejiang province. When fully operational it will allow China to operate without imports for as long as three months. China sees such a reserve as insurance against disruption of supply of oil imports. With U.S. military intervention on the rise, Chinese leaders attach high importance to the creation of the SPR.[40] However, for China to fill its SPR, it will require significantly greater imports of oil. This means securing oil supply from all over the globe and imports through shipping lanes cannot be avoided.

China's interest in Canada's oil sands is due to several factors. Oil security is a pressing concern. More than half of Chinese oil imports currently come from the volatile Middle East. Canada is a stable political and social environment, unlike some other countries in which China has petroleum investments, such as Iran,[41] Sudan,[42] and Burma.

Should China seek supply from Canada, it is unlikely the U.S. Navy would blockade Canadian exports of oil or bitumen to China; U.S. influence on Canada does not depend on military power. Canada has been deepening its energy integration with the United States under FTA, NAFTA, and, more recently, the Security and Prosperity Partnership. This integration is geared to the goal of continental energy self-sufficiency, where Canada's energy is considered as one with the United States to the extent that Alberta oil is not seen by the United States as 'foreign' oil.[43]

Canadian politicians at the federal level have been sending mixed signals to China since the election of the Stephen Harper government. These mixed signals have increased tensions in Sino-Canadian relations.[44] Chinese officials are sensitive to the signals coming from Ottawa and, given Chinese government involvement in the operations of their large state oil companies, Sino-Canada relations may have a material impact on the success or failure of any negotiations for energy exports to China from Canada.

Appendix C: Canada-U.S. Free Trade Agreement, Energy Clauses[45]

The Canada-U.S. Free Trade Agreement is a legal document of over 200 pages that includes provisions that govern energy trade between Canada and the United States. The energy provisions are covered in Chapter 9 of the agreement (pages 113 to 118). Article 904 is the most often cited part of the chapter owing to its proportionality clause; the full text of Article 904 is reproduced below:

Article 904: Other Export Measures

Either Party may maintain or introduce a restriction otherwise justified under the provisions of Articles XI:2(a) and XX(g), (i) and (j) of the GATT with respect to the export of an energy good of the Party to the territory of the other Party, only if:

a) the restriction does not reduce the proportion of the total export shipments of a specific energy good made available to the other Party relative to the total supply of that good of the Party maintaining the restriction as compared to the proportion prevailing in the most recent 36-month period for which data are available prior to the imposition of the measure, or in such other representative period on which the Parties may agree;

b) the Party does not impose a higher price for exports of an energy good to the other Party than the price charged for such energy good when consumed domestically, by means of any measure such as licences, fees, taxation and minimum price requirements. The foregoing provision does not apply to a higher price which may result from a measure taken pursuant to subparagraph that only restricts the volume of exports; and

c) the restriction does not require the disruption of normal channels of supply to the other Party or normal proportions among specific energy goods supplied to the other Party such as, for example, between crude oil and refined products and among different categories of crude oil and of refined products.

NOTES

1 Pitts, *Stampede!* 37.
2 FIRA was replaced in 1985 by Investment Canada under the Investment Canada Act.
3 At the macro level, that was the year that North America became one market for energy purposes after the signing of the FTA. At the corporate level, it was the year that Murray Edwards and some of his friends invested in Canadian Natural Resources in a successful effort to turn around the fortunes of CNRL.
4 Imperial Oil, 2005 General Annual Meeting, Address by Tim Hearn, chairman, president, and CEO. See www.imperialoil.ca/Canada-English/News/Speeches/N_S_Speech050421.asp for the full transcript.
5 The U.S. Energy Information Administration (EIA) has estimated spare capacity at no more than 1.5 million barrels per day. This is how much oil production recently went off line as a result of hurricanes Wilma and Katrina. These events resulted in the rare release of oil from the U.S. Strategic Petroleum Reserve. The EIA predicts that spare capacity will rise to 2 to 2.2 million barrels per day by 2010, which is still tight and assumes no unpleasant surprises – something that cannot be assumed in such an uncertain global industry as oil and gas. (Note: gas is more of a continental commodity owing to difficulties in its transport.)
6 www.chevron.com/about/real_issues.asp (accessed 25 Oct. 2005).
7 Malcolm Brinded, E.D. Exploration and Production, Royal Dutch Shell plc, 8 Sept. 2005, 'Investing in Uncertainty: The Challenge of Meeting Expanding Energy Demand,' 3, www.shell.com/static/media-en/downloads/speeches/mb_oxford_energy_seminar.pdf (accessed 7 Nov. 2006).
8 Proven reserves are booked only if they are economical to produce at current prices and only using current technological capabilities.
9 Duckert, 'North American Energy,' 61.
10 Irene K. Ip, *Big Spenders: A Survey of Provincial Government Finances in Canada* (Toronto: C.D. Howe Institute 1991), 219.
11 A review of Michael Hart's *A Trading Nation*, Derek Burney's memoirs (Burney was responsible for Canada's side of the negotiations), and Allan Gotlieb's diaries (Gotlieb was Canada's ambassador to the United States

at the time of the negotiation) reveals little mention of energy despite
the significant ramifications for Canada of the energy clauses in the FTA.
Derek H. Burney, *Getting It Done: A Memoir* (Montreal and Kingston:
McGill-Queen's University Press 2005); Allan Gotlieb, *Washington Diaries,
1981–1989* (Toronto: McClelland and Stewart 2006).

12 Lorne Larson (president and CEO of Pro Gas), 'Canada/U.S. Energy Trade
after the Free Trade Agreement.' Presentation to the American Bar Association Annual Meeting, Energy Program, 9 Aug. 1988.

13 Duckert, 'North American Energy.'

14 Sonia Shau, *Crude: The Story of Oil* (New York: Seven Stories Press 2004),
147–50.

15 Album title, *Moody Blues*, released 1967, Decca Record Company Ltd.

16 Peter Foster, *The Blue Eyed Sheiks: The Canadian Oil Establishment* (Toronto:
Collins 1979), inside leaf.

17 Chastko, *Developing Alberta's Oil Sands.*

18 Global demand for oil has exceeded 80 million barrels per day, so a 2 per
cent increase is 1.6 million barrels per day in additional supply!

19 See Peter S. Goodman, 'Big Shift in China's Oil Policy: With Iraq Deal Dis-
solved by War, Beijing Looks Elsewhere,' Washington Post Foreign Service,
13 July 2005, D01. See also David E. Sanger, 'China's Oil Needs Are High
on U.S. Agenda,' New York *Times*, Asia Pacific, electronic version, 19 April
2006.

20 www.alberta-canada.com/statpub/albertaConstructionProjects/mp0610.
cfm (accessed 5 Nov. 2006).

21 National Energy Board, 'Canada's Oil Sands: Opportunities and Challenges to 2015 (update): An Energy Market Assessment, June 2006,' 37–40, 43.

22 Cited in *Boston* Globe, 9 Oct. 2005, www.boston.com/business/
articles/2005/10/09/oil_sand_a_booming_commodity (accessed 17 Oct.
2005).

23 Pan Canadian Petroleum was created through the amalgamation of
Canadian Pacific Oil and Gas Company (a CP Enterprises company) and
Central-Del Rio Oils.

24 Financial Post Corporation Service, 6 March 1979, card on Canadian Natural Resources Limited.

25 *Financial Post*, 18 Oct. 2000.

26 Dianne Francis, *Who Owns Canada Now: Old Money, New Money and the
Future of Canadian Business* (Toronto: HarperCollins 2008), 75.

27 Pitts, *Stampede!* 38–40.

28 1.6 trillion barrels of oil are estimated to be oil sands reserves, and, of
those, 175 billion barrels are considered proven reserves that can be

extracted using current technology. Saudi Arabia claims 260 billion barrels in reserves, but many experts are wary of this estimate, with some thinking it is closer to 160 billion barrels.

29 http://www.energy.gov.ab.ca/89.asp. For background on the oil sands, see 'Canada's Oil Sands, Opportunities and Challenges to 2015,' Executive Summary.

30 Norman J. Hyne, *Nontechnical Guide to Petroleum, Geology, Exploration, Drilling and Production*, 2nd ed. (Tulsa, Okla.: Penn Well Books 2001). Note: some fields show decline rates significantly higher than 4–6 per cent.

31 Derived from the Red Queen in Lewis Carroll's *Alice in Wonderland*, who said: 'It takes all the running you can do, to keep in the same place.'

32 Steven Mufson, 'Oil Sands Are a Hot Commodity; Shell Seeks to Buy Canadian Unit, Tap Supply Source for U.S.,' Washington *Post*, 24 Oct. 2006, D05.

33 Joseph Pratt, Tyler Priest, and Christopher Castaneda, *Offshore Pioneers: Brown & Root and the History of Offshore Oil and Gas* (Houston: Gulf Publishing 1997).

34 Eric Reguly, 'A Superpower? Try Gas Jockey,' *Globe and Mail*, 14 Nov. 2006, B2.

35 Source: http://www.energy.gov.ab.ca/docs/oil/pdfs/continental.pdf. Although the data is for 2003, the fundamentals remained much the same in 2006.

36 Simmons, *Twilight in the Desert*, 290.

37 Cited in Goodman, 'Big Shift in China's Oil Policy.' See also Sanger, 'China's Oil Needs Are High on U.S. Agenda.'

38 Goodman, 'Big Shift in China's Oil Policy.'

39 See also http://www.china.org.cn/features/guideline/node_1156529.htm (accessed 10 Nov. 2006).

40 See also the China Institute at the University of Alberta (CIUA), www.uofaweb.ualberta.ca/chinainstitute/resources.cfm.

41 Sinopec (China's state-owned oil giant) signed a $70-billion deal with the Iranians in November 2004 to develop the Yadavaran oil field.

42 Sudan now supplies about 7 per cent of China's oil imports.

43 Eric Reguly, 'A Superpower?' For a short essay on nationalism versus continental integration, see 'CD replies to Paul Kellogg, Anonymous,' *Canadian Dimension*, vol. 37, no. 2 (2003): 34.

44 Mary Nersessian, 'China and Canada: A Year of Frosty Relations,' CTV.ca News, 30 April 2007.

45 Source: http://www.worldtradelaw.net/nafta/CUSFTA.pdf.

Conclusion

In the final chapter of *Creating Modern Capitalism*, Thomas K. McCraw compares four different capitalist economies over time. Such a comparative approach is useful in reminding the reader just how successful the Canadian economy has performed in this context. Table 1 compares the Canadian economy's performance with that of three other predominantly English-speaking economies. One hundred years ago, both Australia and the United Kingdom were much richer than Canada. Canada surpassed the United Kingdom in the mid-1940s and Australia in the early 1950s. It even made progress in relation to the United States over those 100 years.[1]

However, given the relentless nature of change in capitalistic economies, there is never room for complacency. A more finely granulated analysis shows that Canada's more recent economic performance has not been keeping pace either with other countries or with our own record since the recession of the early 1980s. The question must be asked: What has happened in more recent times and why hasn't the Canadian economy performed better in the past twenty-five years? From Table 2 it is clear that, in or about 1980, Canada reached a high point and has been slipping, relatively speaking, since.

This book attempts to give clues as to the reasons for Canada's economic success for most of the past century and for the more recent slowdown.

Laying the Foundations: 1850–1905

In the mid-nineteenth century, the Province of Canada was one of a collection of colonies making up British North America (BNA). By the

Table 1
Comparative GDP per capita (Canada = 100)

	1850	1900	1950	2000
Australia	148	138	102	97
United Kingdom	175	154	95	89
United States	136	141	131	127
Canada	100	100	100	100
Argentina	79	95	68	38

Source: Adapted from Angus Madison, *The World Economy: Historical Statistics* (Paris: Development Centre of the Organisation for Economic Co-operation and Development 2003).

Table 2
Comparative GDP per capita (Canada = 100)

	1980	2005
Australia	92	97
United Kingdom	89	93
United States	119	123
Canada	100	100

Source: Adapted from Organisation for Economic Co-operation and Development, *The World Economy: Historical Statistics*, and *OECD Factbook 2007: Economic, Environmental and Social Statistics* (Paris: OECD Publications 2007).

beginning of the twentieth century, the situation had changed dramatically. Canada was now a country spanning the continent, and, while its economy was still relatively small, it was prosperous enough to make Canada the tenth-richest nation in the world.

What had happened in the intervening half-century to propel such economic performance? Early on, under the guidance of Lord Elgin, Canada's governor general, a reciprocity agreement was negotiated with the United States in 'natural products,' an agreement that was in line with British policy. One of the unfortunate side effects of the election of Abraham Lincoln and the Republicans in 1860 was that the Republicans were highly protectionist and abrogated the treaty in 1866, the year before Canadian Confederation.

In 1867 the British Parliament passed the BNA Act and the colonies gained a measure of independence from 'the mother country.' The Parliament of Canada moved expeditiously to put in place policies that would benefit the country economically, including ensuring that the powers of currency and banking were vested in the national government (see Case 1). In addition, the BNA Act provided for the acquisition of Rupert's Land from the Hudson's Bay Company by the new country (see Case 2).

When the United States continued to pursue protectionist policies, Sir John A. Macdonald, Canada's pre-eminent politician, proposed a tripartite National Policy in the election campaign of 1878. The policy consisted of a transcontinental railway to the Pacific, the settlement of the prairies (made possible by the earlier acquisition of Rupert's Land), and a protective tariff (see Case 3). The National Policy became the foundation for Canada's economic development for decades. Throughout this period, the attitude of government towards business was generally positive.

Turning from public policy to the financial system, by the early twentieth century, Canada had a relatively sophisticated banking system with many more banks than at present. The oldest and largest was the Bank of Montreal and its major rival was the Toronto-based Canadian Bank of Commerce. Canada Life was the dominant life insurer alongside important mortgage companies (because banks were not allowed to lend money for mortgages).

There were many successful Canadian entrepreneurs and sometimes the lines were blurred between the entrepreneur and the enterprise, as was the case with Donald Smith, Lord Strathcona, an entrepreneur who headed up major corporations (HBC, Bank of Montreal), and William (later Sir William) Mackenzie, who invested in both railways and electrical public utilities.

Larger Canadian corporations were beginning to emerge and required professional managers. As in the rest of the world, the major non-financial corporations were the railways – the CPR, the Grand Trunk, and what was originally known as the Mackenzie and Mann system, later the Canadian Northern Railway. A whole host of investor-owned electrical public utilities spread across Canada and beyond, to Latin America.

The biggest extractive company was the Lake Superior Corporation in the Sault, a large conglomerate by North American standards. Coal mining corporations in Cape Breton and British Columbia fed the railroads with the fuel they need to create steam to drive their engines. Manufacturing equalled agriculture in terms of share of GDP early in the twentieth century and Massey-Harris emerged as the largest Canadian manufacturer. No national retail chains existed, although entrepreneur Timothy Eaton opened a store in Winnipeg, the heart of HBC territory, in 1905.

That is the broad background. The case studies dig deeper into specific situations.

Case 1 deals with the Bank Act of 1871. In Canada, unlike in the United States, the BNA Act provided that banking and currency were the responsibility of the federal authority. Absent in Canada, therefore, were the battles that occurred in the United States in regard to the power of the federal authority over banking. The major battle in Canada was between the Bank of Montreal and the other banks, primarily the Toronto-based ones. Case 1 traces the laying of the foundations of the Canadian financial system – early evidence of the interplay between public policy and an effective financial system, which resulted in the beginnings of a successful, growing economy in Canada.

Case 2 is about the Hudson's Bay Company. No Canadian business-history textbook would be complete without a study of the HBC, North America's oldest corporation. This case study deals with both public policy and corporate policy. The key public-policy decision was the new government of Canada's decision to acquire Rupert's Land, the vast tract of land granted to the HBC by royal charter in 1670. Once the transaction was completed in 1869, the HBC had to decide what business it should enter into with the cash and real estate at its disposal. It was clear that the fur trade was a mature business, moving into decline, and the company had important decisions to make regarding its future. The HBC was two hundreds years old and had professional management, but it was also presided over by a powerful entrepreneurial shareholder, Donald Smith, 1st Baron Strathcona and Mont Royal. This complicated the decision-making process.

Case 3 explores another aspect of public policy and private-sector reaction. In 1878 Sir John A. Macdonald, Canada's first prime minister, was campaigning to be re-elected after a defeat five years earlier. Macdonald proposed a National Policy that included a protective tariff. While many Canadian manufacturers liked the proposal, one prominent manufacturer did not. He was Hart Massey, an entrepreneur who was building the largest manufacturing company in the country and the largest agricultural manufacturer in the British Empire. Case 3 explores why Massey did not warm to a public policy which, on the face of it, should have been to the corporation's benefit.

Wars, Depressions, and Dynamic Growth: 1905–55

The first half of the twentieth century was one of the most difficult half-centuries in world history, with two world wars, two depressions, and a worldwide influenza epidemic. Early in the century, there was promise of free and open markets but this changed as protectionism reared its ugly head, particularly in the United States.

Fortunately, attitudes changed and this led to freer trade and, in 1947, to the General Agreement on Trade and Tariffs.

While the half-century was a difficult period for Canada in many ways, just as it was for the rest of the world, the country was also remarkably successful in economic terms during these years, especially from 1939 on. By mid-century, Canada was the tenth-largest economy in the world and the sixth-richest.

Canada's export markets shifted in the decade of the 1940s from the United Kingdom to the United States, the major source of Canadian imports since the nineteenth century. During this period, foreign investment also shifted from British debt to American equity as, in many ways, Canada became a branch-plant economy. Canada continued to require foreign investment as the economy was transformed from one based on agriculture to one based on manufacturing.

Over this period, public policy in Canada, as in most of the rest of the world, became more interventionist. Early in the century, provincial and municipal governments entered the public utility field, principally electrical utilities – but on the prairies telephone utilities. The Great War saw the introduction of a 'temporary' income tax as well as the creation of the first great federal crown corporation, the Canadian National Railways (see Case 4). With the Great Depression of the 1930s, free markets were discredited and government policy was perceived as a solution to most problems. This propelled the government to become involved in many spheres of economic activity through crown corporations, a policy given impetus by the demands of the Second World War.

Canada's financial system also evolved during this period. The most important development was the creation of the Bank of Canada, which would become responsible for monetary policy. In the immediate post-war years, the Central Mortgage and Housing Corporation was created and the chartered banks were allowed into the mortgage business. However, post-war reconstruction efforts did not include the creation of a national securities regulator.

Banks remained the major financial intermediaries in the country, although they lost some of their significance. This led to consolidation among the banks as the successful survivors pursued a strategy of both organic growth and growth by merger. The Royal Bank moved from Halifax to Montreal in 1907 and emerged as the largest bank in Canada, surpassing the Bank of Montreal.

In addition to banks, other financial institutions grew and prospered. Life insurance companies fared particularly well, as did trust companies and acceptance companies, which offered consumer credit. The largest of these companies were all Montreal-based.

As the banks and other financial intermediaries, including investment houses, grew, both entrepreneurs and large businesses had greater access to capital (apart from the Depression years). The major source of foreign capital switched from the United Kingdom to the United States in the 1920s, and from debt to equity capital.

Canada continued to produce its share of highly adventurous and successful entrepreneurs, although during this period some of the more successful, for example, Max Aitken, Lord Beaverbrook, and Garfield Weston, felt it necessary to emigrate to the United Kingdom. The early part of the period saw Sam McLaughlin and Gordon McGregor convert their carriage businesses into auto manufacturers. And later Sam Bronfman converted his distillery business into one of the largest and most successful Canadian-based international corporations in the world.

The non-financial big business sector was marked by the emergence of Big Auto, (see Case 5), Big Oil, and, to a lesser degree, Big Steel. General Motors of Canada, which had not existed a half-century earlier, was the largest of the non-financial corporations, and Imperial Oil was the third-largest. Both GM and Imperial Oil had originally put down roots as independent Canadian companies but early in their corporate lives they were taken over by American parents.

There were other large manufacturers in the distilling, brewing, and food subsectors as the manufacturing sector reached its zenith at mid-century. The second-largest Canadian corporation was Sam Bronfman's Seagrams, a distiller that had benefited from Prohibition in the United States and had moved quickly into the U.S. market once Prohibition was repealed.

In addition, the period was marked by the emergence of regional and national department stores and supermarkets. The largest department store chain was the T. Eaton Company, but there was a challenger on the horizon in Simpsons-Sears (see Case 6) and there were now regional supermarkets as well.

The half-century saw the destruction of certain industry sectors, or at least a reduction in their significance. The period was marked by massive government intervention in both the railway and electric utility industries and the resultant absorption of once great investor-owned corporations into the public sector. It also saw the eclipse of the once great coal mining companies, not only by Big Oil, but also by new mineral mining companies, specifically International Nickel and Alcan.

As in Part One, Part Two's case studies delve deeper into the bigger picture. Case 4, focusing on the creation of the CNR, demonstrates that irrational exuberance can exist in both the public and private sectors simultaneously. Canada, with a population of only eight million people, had three transcontinental railways prior to the First World War. The Laurier government which authorized the railways, the entrepreneurs William Mackenzie and Donald Mann who built the Canadian Northern Railway, even professional manager Charles Melville Hays of the Grand Trunk Railway – all were irrationally exuberant. From the flood tide of construction that came with new transcontinental railways in a country of Canada's limited population base there followed the inevitable penalty stage. Choices had to be made under unfortunate circumstances.

Case 5 deals with the new automobile industry and the role that trade policy played in its rise. The automotive and railway industries present a number of interesting contrasts. The railways linked the country east to west. The automotive industry resulted in strong north-south linkages, particularly between Ontario and Michigan. The railways were Canadian corporations financed with British debt. The automotive companies were primarily Canadian subsidiaries of American parents financed by equity – although the early years of the Ford Motor Company of Canada were a deviation from that pattern. The automotive sector was very much an Ontario-based industry while the railways tended to have their head offices in Montreal. This case study examines issues of trade – the 1911 defeat of the reciprocity agreement with the United States, the 1926 Robb budget, which introduced Canadian content requirements as well as lowering tariffs, and the cataclysmic events of the Great Depression which were compounded by major tariff barriers.

Case 6 traces the venerable T. Eaton Company from the Price Spreads Commission of the Great Depression to the post-war challenge from Simpsons-Sears. Eaton's was already a great Canadian success story by the time of the Great Depression. A family-owned and managed company, it dominated the Canadian retail market in the 1930s the way that Wal-Mart dominates the U.S. market today. During the Depression, in order to keep consumer prices low, Eaton's pushed suppliers to the wall, paid low wages, and eliminated smaller competitors. Government intervened with the Price Spreads Commission and a private company was exposed to public gaze. How Eaton's handled public exposure is compared with the situation that Sears Roebuck faced in the United States. Then the case study traces how the family dealt with, or failed to deal with, the boom period during the war and post-war period with the arrival of consumer credit, the shift to the suburbs, and the arrival of a new competitor in Simpsons-Sears.

The Buoyant Years: 1955–80

During this period, the world shifted into the third industrial revolution, one that was driven by computers rather than by steam power or by the internal combustion engine, one where the service sector became increasingly important and the manufacturing sector less so, at least in the First World.

It was a period when Canada experienced remarkable economic growth. By 1980, Canada was richer than any European nation, with the sole exception of Switzerland, and was 87 per cent as rich as the United States, an historic high. And it became even more of a trading nation, first with the benefit of GATT then, in the 1960s, with the Auto Pact agreement with the United States, which proved of immense benefit to Canada, particularly Ontario.

But storm clouds loomed. In the 1970s the country experienced inflation, high interest rates, and high oil prices. Investors and traders were challenged as Canada switched from a fixed exchange rate to a floating one and the dollar reached historic lows.

There were unfortunate public policy responses to many of these issues including wage and price controls, a 'national' energy policy, increased regulation of foreign investment, and higher levels of taxation as a percentage of GDP. Provincial governments became much more important and as interventionist as the federal government.

Canada's financial system saw a number of developments. The first of these was the government's decision to permit the mutualization of life insurance companies as a measure of ensuring Canadian ownership. A new governor, James Coyne, was appointed at the Bank of Canada, which caused many difficulties. His replacement, Louis

Rasminsky, smoothed over troubled waters and ensured a clear distinction between monetary and fiscal policy (see Case 7). The recommendations of the Porter Royal Commission on Banking led to increased competition in the banking sector and also to a removal of the 6 per cent ceiling on interest rates. A variety of financial crown corporations were created by Ottawa but there was still no move to create a single securities regulator.

On the surface, change was relatively modest within the financial sector. The Canadian Bank of Commerce and the Imperial Bank followed the example of the Toronto and Dominion banks and merged. A number of the large life insurance companies mutualized although Great West and London did not. The trust company scene was relatively quiet. And there was evidence of the shift of the financial centre of Canada from Montreal to Toronto.

Interest rate ceilings were lifted and the banks became active in the residential mortgage field. As Canadian nationalists decried foreign investment, Canada was gradually becoming more financially self-sufficient.

As always in Canadian history, entrepreneurs played an important role. The two most formidable ones took very different routes to amassing their wealth. Roy Thomson, later Lord Thomson of Fleet, followed an honoured Canadian tradition of emigrating to the United Kingdom where he significantly increased his fortune. K.C. Irving, on the other hand, made his fortune by focusing on opportunities in the province of New Brunswick.

Among the major non-financial corporations, Big Auto, Big Oil, and, to a lesser extent, Big Steel were the major players. Big Auto was beginning to show the vulnerability of U.S.-based companies to foreign competition, particularly from Japan; and Chrysler was close to bankruptcy. But, from a Canadian perspective, the major change was that Canada now exported more cars than it imported. Big Oil was dramatically different in this regard as well, ever since the Leduc discovery in 1947 (see Case 9). Canada had changed quickly from an oil-importing nation to an oil-exporting one.

While manufacturing was declining in importance, Massey Ferguson was still an important corporation. The 'new' large manufacturers were Moore Corporation and Northern Telecom, both of which had been around for decades. In the extractive sector, the major change was that Inco, losing its monopoly position, was surpassed by Alcan as Canada's major mining company (see Case 8).

Retail saw dramatic changes – the decline of Eaton's and the sale of Simpson's. On the creative side was the startling growth of Weston/Loblaw and also of Hudson's Bay. Interesting too was the development of large Quebec-based retailers – Provigo and Steinbergs.

But the largest corporation of all in 1980 was once again Canadian Pacific, not because of its rail business but because of its many non-railway-related acquisitions. This pattern of diversification into holding companies was not restricted to CP. Other conglomerates included International Thomson, which moved into oil and tour operations as well as media; Genstar, involved in a dozen enterprises; and Hiram Walker-Consumers' Home, a combination of distilling, gas distribution, and oil production.

The three case studies in Part Three deal with the interaction of public policy and the financial system; the challenges faced by professional managers when they lose a monopoly position; and the tensions generated when entrepreneurs and managers of Canadian subsidiaries encounter hostile public policy.

Case 7 – dealing with the 'Coyne Affair' at the Bank of Canada – is a good example. In Part One the Bank Act case study dealt with the establishment of the environment in which the Canadian chartered banking system has functioned since 1871. The major innovation in the Canadian financial system in the next sixty years was the creation of the Bank of Canada in the midst of the Great Depression of the mid-1930s. In spite of the initial opposition of most of the major banks to the creation of the central bank, the Bank of Canada soon became accepted as an important part of the Canadian financial system. However, in the late 1950s, problems began to emerge after the appointment of the second governor, James Coyne. Those problems became so severe that the government fired Coyne and chose Louis Rasminsky to succeed him. Rasminsky insisted on the signing of a protocol between the government and the bank before accepting the position. The protocol was later adopted as part of the Bank of Canada Act.

Case 8 deals with the mining sector, an area of historic economic strength in Canada. The Sudbury basin is the greatest nickel deposit in the world. Inco was an American corporation that legally moved to Canada in 1928, because of concern about action that might be taken against it by the U.S. Department of Justice. (That same year Inco became the only 'Canadian' company ever to be part of the Dow Jones 30.) With the boom in demand for nickel products during the Second World War and the post-war era, nickel prices increased and Inco controlled the world price. But Inco also lost its monopolistic control. As a consequence of these changes, Inco began to diversify into unrelated areas.

Case 9 covers the post-Second World War oil boom in Alberta, from 1947 until the enactment of the National Energy Program in 1980 following the oil shocks of the 1970s. At the end of the war, Canada was energy poor and could supply only about 10 per cent of domestic needs, prior to the big strike near Leduc, Alberta, in 1947. From 1947 until the 1960s, foreign oil majors poured expertise and capital into the Alberta oil and gas patch, leading to major gains in domestic production and construction of the largest oil and gas pipeline system in the world. But, whereas the governments of Alberta and Ottawa in this period were largely passive and allowed nearly unfettered development of western oil and gas, the 1970s ushered in an interventionist phase that saw the creation of the crown corporation Petro-Canada in 1975 and culminated in the National Energy Program in 1980. Case 9 examines foreign direct investment in Canada's energy sector.

The Challenging Years: 1980–2005

Among the most notable events globally in this period were the destruction of the Berlin Wall and the end of world communism. North America also saw rising economic challenges from Asia, first from Japan and then from China. In terms of trade there was a significant increase as GATT gave way to the World Trade Organization and numerous bilateral and multilateral trade agreements were signed. Contributing to increased globalization was the development of computer software and the Internet.

Canada's economic growth slowed noticeably in the period from 1980 to 2005. Contributing to the slowdown were the recessions of the early 1980s and 1990s, the most severe since the Great Depression. As a consequence, some of the smaller European nations were now richer than Canada, and the gap with the United States grew wider. Throughout this period, managers were challenged, initially by high interest rates and then by huge swings in the price of oil and in the value of the Canadian currency.

In public-policy terms, there was modest evidence of government retreat from the interventionist stance of the 1970s. At the federal level there were some important privatizations, although fewer at the provincial level. The provinces were more important, relatively speaking, than they had been in 1980, buoyed by revenue from both liquor boards and lottery winnings. But, on balance, there was less taxation, deficits were eliminated, and debt and regulation were reduced.

In terms of trade, the Auto Pact of the 1960s was followed by the Free Trade Agreement with the United States in the late 1980s (see Case 10) and the North American Free Trade Agreement, involving Canada, the United States, and Mexico, in the 1990s. These agreements led to a greater degree of integration of the Canadian and American economies. Both exports and imports boomed, but exports more than imports, and Canada had a healthy trade surplus for most of the quarter-century. An interesting development in the late 1990s was that Canadian investment abroad exceeded internal investment – an historic first, in spite of a low Canadian dollar.

There were many changes to the financial system. The 'little bang' of the late 1980s permitted the banks to own trust companies, investment dealers, and mutual fund companies and to sell insurance. The Bank of Canada began targeting the level of permissible inflation. The insurance companies were permitted to demutualize, less than a half-century after they had been encouraged to mutualize. Yet still no move had been made to introduce a national securities regulator.

As a consequence of the 'little bang,' Canadian banks became noticeably larger as they took over the trust companies and investment dealers and started their own mutual funds and insurance operations. To curb this growth, in the late 1990s, the minister of finance blocked attempts by Canadian banks to merge within Canada. In response, Canadian banks began to look more aggressively beyond Canadian borders (see Case 12).

Some life insurance companies demutualized and others disappeared as they were acquired or collapsed (see Case 11). Manulife emerged as the most powerful Canadian insurer, with a major presence in the United States and internationally. Credit unions became more important, as did family- or entrepreneurially owned diversified financial companies, the largest of which was Power Financial, owned by the Desmarais family. Meanwhile, the trust companies, the Canadian-owned acceptance companies, and the independent investment dealers largely disappeared.

While both entrepreneurs and large corporations made contributions to Canada's economic growth, it is interesting to note that in 2005 there were more large corporations with entrepreneur/founders still in charge than was the case in 1980. The names of the individuals are well known – Frank Stronach, Galen Weston, Gerry Schwartz, Laurent Beaudoin, the Sobey family, Jean Coutu, Ken Thomson, Alain Bouchard, Pierre Peladeau, Murray Edwards, Ted Rogers, and the McCain and Asper families. A new wrinkle has been added in that one of the richest Canadians, Jeff Skoll, unlike his earlier predecessors, decided to seek fame and fortune in the United States rather than in the United Kingdom.

In the non-financial sector, both Big Auto and Big Oil continued to be important but they had changed dramatically. And Big Steel had been replaced by Big Automotive Parts. Big Auto had changed from an American big three to an American, German, Japanese big four or five. Another change was that Canadian production and exports had continued to escalate and Ontario had surpassed Michigan, at least temporarily, in level of automobile production.

Big Oil had changed as well. In 1980 there were the Big Four major integrated producers, all subsidiaries of foreign parents, all with head offices in Toronto. In 2005 only two of the four were still in existence and they were based in Calgary; in addition, there were a number of major Canadian independents, many with large investments in the oil sands (see Case 13).

Retail, too, was transformed. Gone were the large department store chains and supermarkets headquartered in Toronto, with the sole exception of Weston's, owners of Loblaw. In their place were Arkansas-based Wal-Mart, Nova Scotia-based Empire, owners of Sobeys, and two Quebec-based companies – Jean Coutu and Alimentation Couche-Tard, whose main market was the United States.

The conglomerates of 1980 no longer existed as that form of holding company increasingly lost favour. The Thomson Corporation was very much still around but as a provider of electronic information. Only BCE remained as a constant, a reminder of over a century of continuity. But it too was being challenged in the new century by vigorous competition and the possibility of less protection from foreign ownership.

There are four case studies in Part Four. Two deal with free trade: Case 10, involving the wine industry leading up to the FTA; and Case 13, involving the energy sector post-FTA. Cases 11 and 12 deal with financial services, the first with the collapse of Confederation Life, one of Canada's oldest insurers, and the second with the issues faced by the Royal Bank of Canada in the late twentieth and early twenty-first centuries.

Case 10 is the third of four dealing with trade. It describes the lead-up to the Free Trade Agreement and the generally accepted wisdom that the one industry in Canada that would not survive was the wine industry. This case study describes some of the entrepreneurs who faced the challenge of extinction from a change in public policy and what they and governments did in order to ensure that their fears were not a self-fulfilling prophecy. Like the Massey case study in Part One, this is an example at the industry or corporate level where there is a significant difference between what big-picture policy makers predicted and what entrepreneurs on the ground actually found to be the case.

Case 11 is one of four studies dealing with the financial system, specifically the collapse of Confederation Life, one of Canada's oldest and largest life insurance companies. It examines the challenges faced by the industry, particularly after rules were changed to permit the chartered banks to become financial-services companies with the ability to sell life insurance, although not through their branch network. Management in this case study adopted a very aggressive posture, focusing on top line rather than bottom line. The company ran into trouble in the 1990s. Since an insurance company is subject to financial regulation by the government of Canada, this inevitably led to government involvement in the affairs of 'Confed.' The roles of the government, the life insurance industry as a whole, and company management are all examined in order to discover what actions by the corporate, industry, and government decision makers could have made a difference.

Case 12 focuses on the Royal Bank of Canada and the issues it faces 135 years after the passage of the first Bank Act and seven decades after the creation of Canada's central bank, the Bank of Canada. Throughout all of this time, certain verities have remained. On the one hand, RBC has experienced both the benefits and the difficulties of being a centrally regulated industry within the Canadian economy. The 'benefits' include protection from foreign competition; the difficulties include governmental restrictions in terms of mergers and acquisitions. This became even more important after the 'little bang' of the late 1980s as the banks moved into different lines of business.

Case 13 deals with the energy sector in a post-FTA environment which includes escalating oil prices and the development of the oil sands. While much public attention has been devoted to softwood-lumber disputes, the fact remains that there have few, if any, disputes between Canada and the United States in the energy sector. Canada has obtained assured markets and the United States has acquired assured supplies. This case study also looks at the changing dynamics within Canada and beyond. Economic power is shifting within Canada from

Toronto and Ontario to Calgary and Alberta just as it had earlier shifted from Montreal and Quebec to Toronto and Ontario. And, just as the United States supplanted the United Kingdom as Canada's major export market, there are now major export opportunities in Asia, particularly China.

This marks the end point of the book, but not of the change and growth of capitalism in Canada because, as Schumpeter wrote, 'capitalism is a continuous evolutionary process without an end point.'[2] Looking back at the beginning of that evolutionary process, it is clear that Canada enjoyed a remarkable twentieth century. It is equally clear that the period since 1980 has not been as good for Canada economically as it has been for other developed nations; nor has it measured up to Canada's own historic performance. But, again, 2005 is not an end point; it is only one point in Schumpeter's 'continuous evolutionary process.'

It is important to pay attention to the whys and wherefores of Canada's long-term economic success. The Ontario Institute of Prosperity and Competitiveness has been doing a remarkable job in recent years of analysing just this issue, but a national body is required and action needs to be taken on the findings. The challenge ahead, to restore Canada's growth rate to previous levels, is a shared responsibility. But too often the Pavlovian cry in Canada is: What is the government doing? From this book it is clear that appropriate public policies are a necessary prerequisite but not sufficient as a guarantor of future prosperity. Appropriate vision and action are required from the financial system, from Canada's entrepreneurs, and from the professional managers of large corporations.

Canada has had a sound if cautious financial system. The banks have been protected but there is increasing evidence that they are rising to meet the challenge of international competition by moving into key markets, starting in the United States. The life insurance companies have been operating in competitive international markets for over a century and would appear to be better placed than the banks to deal with a global marketplace.

One thing is clear: over the years Canada's entrepreneurs have been highly successful operating both at home within the Canadian market and abroad – in the United Kingdom and more recently in the United States. But the drive to expand and excel in foreign markets is less impressive on the part of Canada's largest corporations. Part of the reason is that many are foreign-owned and their Canadian subsidiaries play only a minor role in their total global enterprises. This is true of Big

Auto and Big Oil and retail. For Canadian corporations to be successful in a globalizing world, they have to possess a global mindset.

A quarter-century ago, Kenichi Ohmae, the McKinsey managing partner in Tokyo, wrote *Triad Power: The Coming Shape of Global Competition*. Ohmae's prescription for business success was being strong in one's 'home market' before going global. For Canadian business, even before the FTA, a North American 'home market' of nearly 300 million people was, therefore, a necessary prerequisite for success, not a population base of fewer than 30 million with interprovincial trading barriers.

Ohmae's prescription for success is still vital today. For Canadian capitalism to be successful, it must have the economies of scale of a large market, the sales, marketing, and distribution network to reach that large market, and a sophisticated management team able 'to plan for the future, to adjust to changing market conditions, and to invest in new, large projects.'[3] This must be the focus of the interaction among key players – public-policy makers, the financial system, entrepreneurs, and professional managers of the large corporations – if Canada's economic growth is to achieve the robust levels of the past and the even more robust levels attained by the current competition.

One final dimension is required and that is education. And it has to begin earlier than business school. Although Canadian business schools must do a better job of preparing their graduates for international competition, business education must begin in public schools. Junior Achievement of Canada has already done yeomen work in this area, but a huge gap exists between what may be learned in high school and in an MBA program. Missing almost entirely from a basic college education are courses devoted to the historical importance and benefits of business within Canada.

While it is necessary, obviously, to produce teachers, civil servants, doctors, engineers, scientists, and politicians, it is also necessary that the country encourage entrepreneurs and business executives – young Canadian men and women who possess an international vision and historical perspective, who can compete and thrive in a global economy, and who will ensure that Canadians continue to enjoy one of the highest standards of living in the world.

Suggested Readings

Madison, Angus. *The World Economy: Historical Statistics*. Paris: Development Centre of the Organisation for Economic Co-operation and Development 2003.

McCraw, Thomas K. *Creating Modern Capitalism*. Cambridge, Mass.: Harvard University Press 1997.

Ohmae, Kenichi. *Triad Power: The Coming Shape of Global Competition*. New York: Free Press 1985.

Organisation for Economic Co-operation and Development. *OECD Factbook 2007: Economic, Environmental and Social Statistics*. Paris: OECD Publications 2007.

NOTES

1 Argentina is included in the Table because of the comparability of the two economies a century ago and as an object lesson in what not to do in terms of public policies.
2 Thomas K. McCraw, *Prophet of Innovation: Joseph Schumpeter and Creative Destruction* (Cambridge, Mass.: Belknap Press of Harvard University Press 2007), 433.
3 George D. Smith, Richard Sylla, and Robert E. Wright, 'The Diamond of Sustainable Growth,' *STERN business*, spring/summer 2007, 28.

General Bibliography

Principal Secondary Sources

Amatori, Franco, and Geoffrey Jones, eds. *Business History around the World*. Cambridge: Cambridge University Press 2003.

Berns, Rima. 'The Real Story behind Free Trade (A History of the Canadian Tariff).' School for Advanced International Studies (SAIS), Johns Hopkins University, MA thesis, 1988.

Bliss, Michael. *Northern Enterprise: Five Centuries of Canadian Business*. Toronto: McClelland and Stewart 1987.

Bloomfield, Patrick. *The First 75 Years*. Toronto: Ticker Club 2004.

Bothwell, Robert. *The Penguin History of Canada*. Toronto: Penguin Canada 2006.

Bothwell, Robert, and J.L. Granatstein. *Our Century: The Canadian Journey*. Toronto: McArthur 2000.

Boyce, Gordon, and Simon Ville. *The Development of Modern Business*. Houndmills, U.K., New York: Palgrave 2002.

Brown, Craig, *The Illustrated History of Canada*. Toronto: Key Porter Books 2002.

Chandler, Alfred D., Jr, and Stewart W. James. *A Nation Transformed by Information*. Oxford, New York: Oxford University Press 2000.

deSoto, Hernando. *The Mystery of Capital: Why Capitalism Triumphs in the West and Fails Elsewhere*. New York: Basic Books 2000.

Hart, Michael. *A Trading Nation: Canadian Trade Policy from Colonialism to Globalization*. Vancouver: UBC Press 2002.

Jennings, Peter, and Todd Brewster. *The Century*. New York: Doubleday 1998.

Johnson, Paul. *A History of the American People*. London: Weidenfeld and Nicholson 1997.

MacIntosh, Robert. *Different Drummers: Banking and Politics in Canada*. Toronto: Macmillan Canada 1991.

Madison, Angus. *The World Economy: Historical Statistics*. Paris: Development Centre of the Organisation for Economic Co-operation and Development 2003.

McCloskey, Deidre N. *The Bourgeois Virtues: Ethics for the Age of Commerce*. Chicago: University of Chicago Press 2006.

McCraw, Thomas K. *Creating Modern Capitalism: How Entrepreneurs, Companies and Countries Triumphed in Three Industrial Revolutions*. Cambridge, Mass.: Harvard University Press 1997.

– *The Essential Alfred Chander: Essays Toward a Historical Theory of Big Business*. Boston: Harvard Business School Press 1988.

McDowall, Duncan. *Quick to the Frontier: Canada's Royal Bank*. Toronto: McClelland and Stewart 1993.

Merrett, David Tolmie. 'Australia in the Twentieth Century.' *Insights: Melbourne Economics and Commerce*, 3 (April 2008): 9–13.

Mussio, Lawrence. *Becoming Bell: The Remarkable Story of a Canadian Enterprise*. Bell Canada 2005.

Neufeld, E.P. *The Financial System of Canada*. Toronto: Macmillan of Canada 1972.

Norrie, Kenneth, and Doug Owram. *A History of the Canadian Economy*. Toronto: Harcourt and Jovanovich Canada 1991.

Powell, James. *A History of the Canadian Dollar*. Ottawa: Bank of Canada 2005.

Rea, K.J. *A Guide to Canadian Economic History*. Toronto: Canadian Scholars' Press 1991.

Schumpeter, Joseph A. *Capitalism, Socialism and Democracy*. New York: Harper and Row 1950.

Tanzi, Vito, and Ludger Schuknecht. *Public Spending in the 20th Century*. Cambridge, New York: University of Cambridge 2000.

Taylor, Graham, and Peter Baskerville. *A Concise History of Business in Canada*. Toronto: Oxford University Press 1994.

Urquhart, M.C. *Canadian Economic Growth, 1870–1980*. Kingston, Ont.: Queen's University, Institute for Economic Research, 1988.

Vance, Jonathan F. *Building Canada: People and Projects That Shaped the Nation*. Toronto: Penguin Canada 2006.

Wonnacott, Paul. 'U.S. and Canadian Auto Policies in a Changing World Environment.' Toronto, Ont., Washington, D.C.: Canadian-American Committee, 1987.

Other Sources: Archives, Journals, Online Resources

Archives.gov.on.ca

Au Courant, Economic Council of Canada, 1 (2007)

Bank of Canada
BCE.ca
Canadian Business
Canadian Encyclopaedia
Canadian Nuclear Society, Cns-snc.ca
Canadian Register of Commerce and Industry
Chronicle of the 20th Century, editor-in-chief Derrik Mercer
Civilization.ca
Department of Finance, Canadian Financial Services Sector, 2005; Fiscal Refer-
    ence Tables, 2007
Dictionary of Canadian Biography
The Economist, 1 July 2006
Financial Post Corporation Service; FP Corporation Service cards[1]
Financial Post FP 500
F.P.infomart.ca: FP Historical reports
Historical Atlas of Canada
History in Quotations: Reflecting 5000 Years of World History. M.J. Cohen and
    John Major, comps. London: Cassell 2006
Industry Canada
International Journal, 'Canada/USA: The Troubled Relationship,' 60, no. 2
    (2005)
Karlgaard, Rich. 'Digital Rules,' *Forbes Magazine*
Maclean's
Monetary Times
National Geographic, *Concise History of the World: An Illustrated Time Line*, ed.
    Neil Kagan
OECD Outlook, 81 (June 2007)
Report on Business, Globe and Mail
Saturday Night
Statistics Canada, CANSIM database; Historical Statistics of Canada
University of Western Ontario: Lib.uwo.ca/business
Veterans Affairs Canada: Vac-acc.gc.ca

NOTES

1 The Financial Post cards are now held in the Rotman School of Management
  Business Information Centre (BIC).

Index